D0999646

MY TWENTY-FIVE YEARS
IN CHINA

THE MACMILLAN COMPANY
NEW YORK · BOSTON · CHICAGO
DALLAS · ATLANTA · SAN FRANCISCO

MACMILLAN AND CO., LIMITED
LONDON · BOMBAY · CALCUTTA
MADRAS · MELBOURNE

THE MACMILLAN COMPANY
OF CANADA, LIMITED
TORONTO

MY
TWENTY-FIVE YEARS
IN CHINA

BY JOHN B. POWELL

NEW YORK

THE MACMILLAN COMPANY

1945

PRINTED IN THE UNITED STATES OF AMERICA

To all those who were instrumental in effecting my release from the Japanese, and to the many others whose active help and sympathy, since my return, have materially aided my recovery: this book is dedicated.

Contents

MY TWENTY-FIVE YEARS
IN CHINA

I

Eastward Ho!

THE SMALL CARGO BOAT upon which I was a passenger edged slowly up to a jetty in the Hongkew section of Shanghai, and I walked ashore carrying my suitcase. It was early in February, 1917. A baggage coolie followed, carrying on his shoulder my old-fashioned tin-covered trunk. It was raining, and the narrow streets between the shipping godowns, or warehouses, which lined the Whangpoo River were running with sloppy mud. Two ricksha coolies dashed up, and while there was sufficient room in the man-drawn vehicles for both passenger and baggage, I chose to walk to the hotel, the Astor House. I had seen rickshas in Japan, had ridden in one in Yokohama, but I was still too new to the Orient to feel at ease in a vehicle drawn by a human being.

My trip to the Orient, destined to develop into active newspaper work for a quarter of a century in one of the most politically turbulent areas on earth, had been inspired by a cable from Thomas Franklin Fairfax Millard, an alumnus of the University of Missouri, who had become widely known as a correspondent in the Far East.

Millard's cable, which was dated at Shanghai and addressed to Dean Walter Williams of the School of Journalism of the university, stated that he wished to employ a graduate of the school to assist him in starting a paper in Shanghai. Dean Williams handed me the cable, the first transoceanic telegram I had ever seen.

For some time I had been trying to make up my mind regarding two offers, one from the publisher of a trade journal in Des Moines, Iowa, and the other from the publisher of a newspaper in Atlanta, Georgia, who required an assistant. The idea of a trip to the Orient was too much of a temptation, however, and after talking the offer over with my wife and my colleagues, I began to wind up my work at the university.

Unlike the hero in an Upton Sinclair novel, who was "born to the realm of international society and diplomatic intrigue," I was born on a northeast Missouri farm, attended and later taught in a country school, and earned my way through high school and business college in Quincy, Illinois, by carrying two newspaper routes, morning and evening. Later I worked as a cub reporter on the old *Quincy Whig* in order to obtain funds to pay my fare to the University of Missouri, where I enrolled in the new School of Journalism. Four years later, after graduation, I returned to northeast Missouri to work on the *Courier-Post* in Hannibal, a town immortalized as the boyhood residence of Mark Twain. After four years as a circulation solicitor, advertising manager, and city editor, I returned to the university as instructor in journalism.

Like other American youths of the period and locality, my total knowledge of such distant strange lands as China and Japan had been acquired from a few chapters and some misleading maps in the school geographies and history textbooks. Even in the university I remembered only one or two history lecture periods in which the professor in "ancient, mediaeval and modern" history referred to China; and these references were not complimentary to that country.

To be sure, I had known students from both China and Japan who had enrolled in journalism courses at the university. One, a Chinese named Hin Wong, from Honolulu and Canton, cooperated with me in organizing a Cosmopolitan Club which included all of the foreign students in the university. The idea of forming such a club had developed from an article I had written for the college paper about foreign students in the university. Another Chinese who had enrolled in one of my classes was Hollington K. Tong, from Shanghai. Both Wong and Tong were destined later to become prominent in journalism in their homeland, but on opposite sides of the political fence. Another student from the Orient, a Japanese named Toda, was the shortest in stature, but the best drilled cadet in my company in the student military corps. I didn't know then that he had already served three years as a conscript in the Japanese Army before coming to the United States.

The fact that I was actually going to Shanghai to help start a newspaper caused me to be regarded with much curiosity and some envy on the part of my associates at the university. The fact that I had no advance knowledge whatever regarding the type of paper that was to be started naturally did not help my peace of mind. I was the object of much humorous questioning; could I read "chicken tracks," one friend inquired, and added to my confusion by producing a receipt from the local Chinese laundry and asking me to decipher it. The college barber asked whether I wanted a "queue" haircut.

My apprehension regarding the job in China increased as the scheduled date of my departure neared. I had once written an outline and description of an office system for a small-town newspaper plant, which had been published by a trade journal and had been widely adopted. Would this be of any use in my new job? What kind of paper would the new Shanghai journal be? Would I write editorials, solicit ads and subscribers and do everything else, as in a typical country newspaper office? I was accustomed to this type of journalism, as I had done everything in a small-town daily office except set type. I wondered if the Chinese had printers' unions. Also, I wondered whether Chinese papers had linotype machines capable of setting 5,000 characters or ideographs, which I was told often appeared in a single issue of a Chinese newspaper.

Feeling the need of more information about the lands I was to visit, I went to the university library, where I found only two descriptive books. They were "Chinese Characteristics" and "Village Life in China," both by the same author, Dr. Arthur H. Smith, a veteran of the Gospel, who had spent more than a half century as a missionary in China. He was widely known for his humorous lectures, and his humor was to some extent evident in his descriptions of China and its people. Chinese students in American universities disliked the books because of the author's bizarre impressions of Chinese life. Once, shortly after my arrival in Shanghai, I heard Dr. Smith deliver a lecture dealing with political conditions in Peking, where the Republican Government had just weathered a crisis in which reactionary interests had plotted to restore the Manchu Dynasty. Dr. Smith was then on his way to the United States to retire. The feelings of everyone, particularly newcomers in the audience, were at a low ebb as Dr. Smith concluded his talk by saying, "China is standing on the brink of a precipice." But the tension was relieved when the speaker, with a humorous twinkle in his eyes, added, as an afterthought, "In fact the country has been on the brink of a precipice ever since I arrived in it a half century ago."

I finally sailed from San Francisco, in January, 1917, on the ancient Japanese passenger steamer *Nippon Maru*. At that time I did not think the United States would be drawn into the war, then in its third year. But there was an ominous happening when our boat reached Nagasaki, last stop in Japan before sailing for China. I went ashore with the other passengers and was exploring the shops of that ancient Nipponese city, the first place in Japan to have contact with Europeans, when a messenger from the ship came running with a note from the captain stating that it was necessary for all passengers scheduled for Shanghai to return to the ship at once and get their baggage. The captain had received instructions from the head office of the steamship company, the old Toyo Kisen Kaisha line in Yokohama, to drop all Shanghai passengers at Nagasaki and proceed directly to Manila. Two or three other passengers and I, who had tickets for Shanghai, thus found ourselves marooned in the strange little Japanese port of Nagasaki.

Inquiry at the Nagasaki steamship offices disclosed that no steamer carrying passengers was scheduled to sail for Shanghai for three weeks. As my funds were running low, I decided to investigate the possibility of obtaining passage on a cargo boat, several of which were loading in the harbor. After paddling about the harbor in a sampan for some time I finally found a captain who was willing to provide a cabin in exchange for the unused portion of my trans-Pacific ticket, plus $10 in American money and on condition that I provide my own food. The boat was sailing in a few hours, hence I had time only to get my baggage and purchase a few articles of food for the run across the China Sea. The captain of the cargo boat spoke little English and evinced little interest in his American passenger.

The weather was cold and cloudy, but after the ship had cleared the western cape of Kyushu the sun came out and it became quite warm. I began to notice a disagreeable odor about the ship, which rapidly became nauseating as the weather moderated. I appealed to the captain as to the cause of the odor. The captain pointed to large bales of merchandise wrapped in straw matting which were exposed on the deck and in the open hatches, and said, "Rotten fish—only Chinaman eat." It took me several weeks to get the smell of that cargo out of my clothes, and the memory of it remained with me through the years.

It was fortunate I had embarked on this ship, however, because another ship, the *Poltava*, of Russian Vladivostok registry, upon which some of the passengers sailed about a week later, was caught in a typhoon in the China Sea and driven ashore on the coast south of Shanghai. The passengers were saved with great difficulty.

I had not known until I reached San Francisco on my way to the Orient that the only passenger or cargo ships engaged in trans-Pacific trade at that time were of Japanese registry. Captain Robert Dollar, who later became an extensive operator of steamship lines on the Pacific, had been forced to transfer his cargo ships to Canadian registry, and the Pacific Mail, the only American passenger line, had withdrawn its ships to the South American and Panama Canal routes. The situation which had driven the few American ships from the Pacific at such a crucial time, when America was on the verge of war, had resulted from the passage by Congress of the original La Follette Act—designed by the liberal Wisconsin Senator to help American seamen. One provision in the act forbade American ship owners to employ Oriental seamen. Since American ships with highly paid American crews had to compete with Japanese and British ships, both of which employed full crews of low-salaried Oriental seamen, it was impossible for the American lines to continue operating. They therefore either withdrew from the field or switched to British registry, which always permitted the employment of Chinese merchant seamen, long considered as efficient and trustworthy as the seamen of any nationality. Since most British-registered ships had been withdrawn to the Atlantic because of the war, the result was that the Japanese were left in complete control of the Pacific. After the war American shipping under Federal assistance, in the form of government-built ships with fantastic mail contracts, returned to the Pacific; but the fact remains that for a considerable period during America's participation in World War I the United States possessed on the broad Pacific no important ships of any kind except a few naval vessels.

II

So This Is Shanghai!

THE ASTOR HOUSE HOTEL, then Shanghai's leading hostelry, had grown from a boarding house established originally by the skipper of some early American clipper, who left his ship at Shanghai. He christened his establishment in honor of the then most famous hotel in the United States, the Astor House in New York; however, he was compelled to add the designation "hotel," as the fame of the New York hostelry had not yet reached the China coast. Aside from the name, the two establishments had little in common, as the Astor House in Shanghai consisted of old three- and four-story brick residences extending around the four sides of a city block and linked together by long corridors. In the center of the compound was a courtyard where an orchestra played in the evenings. Practically everyone dressed for dinner, which never was served before eight o'clock. At one time or another one saw most of the leading residents of the port at dinner parties or in the lobby of the Astor House. An old resident of Shanghai once told me, "If you will sit in the lobby of the Astor House and keep your eyes open you will see all of the crooks who hang out on the China coast."

At the hotel I asked the clerk where I might find my boss-to-be, Mr. Millard, and was relieved to learn that he lived there and would come down to the lobby shortly. What would he be like? Soon a Chinese boy called my attention to a man coming down the stairs. He was a short, slender man weighing perhaps 125 pounds and dressed so perfectly that I wondered how he would be able to sit down without wrinkling his immaculate suit.

7

I soon learned that my boss, who had served the old *New York Herald* many years, first as dramatic critic and later as international political correspondent, had taken on many of the eccentricities of his employer, the late James Gordon Bennett.

I naturally was anxious to obtain answers to a hundred questions concerning my new job, but Millard appeared in no hurry to enlighten me. In fact we were soon the center of an interesting group of local residents who strolled in for afternoon tea, but the "tea" they consumed consisted chiefly of cocktails and whisky-sodas.

The profusion of drinks aroused my curiosity, because I had grown up in dry local-option territory in the Middle West, and America was within a few years of the "great experiment" of 1920 when I sailed from San Francisco.

The circle about our table expanded and the Chinese boy added a new table to hold the accumulating bottles and glasses. As the newcomers came up and were introduced they usually ordered a new round of drinks, which meant that each finally had several drinks standing on the table. After the boy had brought the drinks he would present the one who placed the order with a little piece of paper called a "chit," which no one ever looked at before signing.

While waiting in the lobby for Mr. Millard, I had seen on a bulletin board a Reuter dispatch from one of the local English newspapers carrying the momentous news that the United States had broken off diplomatic relations with Germany. It was February 3, 1917. But the conversation about the table did not concern America's entrance into the war; on the contrary it was confined to the subject of possible prohibition in the United States and the increasing cost of drinks in Shanghai due to the shortage of shipping from England. Agreement was unanimous that Shanghai would never go dry, and that the British were more intelligent, on the liquor question at least, than were the Americans.

Suddenly the conversation became hushed as a gray-haired man of medium height entered the lobby and approached our table. I was introduced to him, Thomas Sammons, American Consul-General, a likable official, who was constantly obsessed by the fear that something would happen in the community which might involve him in complications with the State Department.

America's entrance into the war later added tremendously to the Consul-General's responsibilities and anxieties, due to the character of the government of the International Settlement. Since China was still neutral, German and Austrian consuls and their nationals went about their affairs practically without restraint, although all Britons and most Americans had ceased speaking to them or doing business with them.

When the group finally broke up, Mr. Millard suggested that I take a room at the Astor House and introduced me to the manager, Captain Harry Morton. Since most of the managers of the Astor House had been sea captains, the hotel had taken on many of the characteristics of a ship. The corridors were painted to resemble the passageways leading to the staterooms of a passenger liner. I was therefore not surprised when the manager told me that he could give me a room in the "steerage" for $125 a month, including meals and afternoon tea. That figured out at about $60 in United States currency.

It was not until the next day in his apartment that I had opportunity to discuss my new job with Mr. Millard, and to get some of the background of his own experience in China.

Millard first went to China as a foreign correspondent for the *New York Herald* to cover the Boxer Rebellion in 1900. At this time, and during his later coverage of the Russo-Japanese War in 1905 and 1906, he became acquainted with the Chinese political leaders, including Yuan Shih-kai, Tong Shao-yi, Wu Ting-fang, F. C. Tong, organizer of the first modern bank in Shanghai, and the Kuomintang leader, Dr. Sun Yat-sen. China at that time was still an empire, but there was plenty of evidence indicating that a revolution was brewing. In 1911 Millard founded the first American newspaper in China, the *China Press* at Shanghai. In this enterprise he was assisted by B. W. Fleisher, who later became publisher of the *Japan Advertiser*, in Tokyo. Most of the money for the purchase of type and mechanical equipment for the *China Press* was supplied by Charles R. Crane, a Chicago manufacturer, who became a stockholder and director in the enterprise. Crane had diplomatic ambitions. In 1909 he was appointed Minister to China, but resigned before assuming his official duties; later he accepted the post after World War I.

A number of well known Chinese in Shanghai, including Tong Shao-yi, and some bankers had also agreed to purchase stock in the new paper, but when Millard arrived in Shanghai with his machinery, he discovered that some of the leading Chinese who had agreed to cooperate with him had developed cold feet. Investigation disclosed that the opposition paper, the long-established British organ, the *North China Daily News*, had been responsible. That paper, known as the N.C.D.N., was the leading British organ outside of Hong Kong, and the proprietors naturally desired no American competition, particularly of the type of the *China Press*, which always had a number of Chinese stockholders and editorially supported Chinese Nationalism and American-Chinese cooperation. The American population of Shanghai, although small, was growing and there was a general feeling that it should have an American paper.

The *North China Daily News* had further reason for opposing the establishment of an American newspaper when the *China Press* by its enterprising methods, comics and other features soon passed the British paper in circulation. But the *China Press* could not exist on circulation revenues alone, and soon was in financial difficulties. Millard was forced to resign the editorship, and the principal interest in the paper was taken over by a local American real estate and insurance concern, which promptly sold a controlling interest, at a handsome profit, to a local Briton.

This was the newspaper set-up when I arrived in Shanghai, in 1917, to help Mr. Millard establish another paper, this time a weekly, which he had decided to call *Millard's Review of the Far East*. Aside from the purchase of type and a supply of paper, nothing had been done to get the publication started, so that it devolved upon me to officiate at the birth of the new American journal.

Office space adjacent to the printing plant was rented, and we set to work. More questions: "Would we do our own printing or make a contract with a commercial printing house?" "How much circulation did Mr. Millard think we would have?" "Where would we obtain our advertising?" "Would the Chinese read our paper?" Finally I asked one question which brought a quick and unexpected response. The question was, "What will we print in the paper?" Straightening up stiffly in his chair, Millard snapped, "Anything we damn please."

When I repeated this declaration of editorial policy to potential subscribers and advertisers as I made my rounds among the foreign and Chinese merchants, I always got a laugh—for, as I learned later, it was Millard's insistence on printing "anything he damn pleased" which had caused his resignation from the editorship of the *China Press*. Millard never modified his principles on the fundamentals of the Far Eastern situation as so many of his colleagues did—for a quick profit.

Busy days followed. An office was rented and a contract signed with an ancient printing establishment owned by French Jesuit priests, who were happy to have our new American type in their plant. But I was dismayed to learn that neither the Chinese foreman nor any member of the numerous Chinese typesetting staff knew a single word of the English language. When I explained this predicament to the manager of the printing plant, Mr. Cowan, an American printer-manager who had gone to China originally as foreman of a plant owned by Protestant missionaries, he laughed and said it was better for the native printers not to understand what they were setting up in type, for if they did understand English they would constantly be trying to improve on the reporter's and editor's copy—with disastrous results. I later discovered, however, to my sorrow, that a Chinese printer's inability to understand what he was setting up in type also had its dangers. A reporter sent the office boy with a note to a nearby bar inquiring, "What in 'ell has happened to the beer I ordered?" In some mysterious manner this note got into the personals, and it caused considerable questioning on the part of our missionary subscribers. On another occasion the proprietress of a resort in the "Kiangsi Road" (red light) district sent out an engraved invitation to a selected list of the town's bachelors announcing a reception to meet some new recruits who had recently arrived from San Francisco. The notice fell into the hands of a Chinese reporter, who put it in the society column, causing a commotion among the town's housewives. But this was only part of the education of a new editor.

While getting out sample columns illustrating our different fonts of type for heads, text, and advertisements, I made a survey of our field and tried to pick out a typical reader—obviously a difficult task in Shanghai, where the Anglo-American community at that time numbered probably no more than 8,000 or 10,000 individuals and was about equally divided between business people and missionaries. I soon found that our possible readers were not confined to the American and British communities. There were several thousand other foreign residents in Shanghai—Scandinavians, Frenchmen, Germans, Russians, Portuguese, Dutchmen, and a large population of Oriental Jews, most of them from Iraq, who had come to Shanghai many years previously by way of India. Several were fabulously rich. Many of the foreigners could read English and were anxious to see a paper containing American news and editorial comment. I discovered, however, that the largest English-reading group of all was the younger generation of Chinese, the intellectuals, graduates and undergraduates of mission and municipal schools, who were just beginning to take an interest in outside world affairs. They were tremendously concerned by the World War, and, like everybody else, were deeply anxious to find out what America was going to do about the war and a number of other things. For the first time I began to realize the importance of America's position in world affairs. All these people were studying the English language, and I soon discovered that hundreds of students were using the *Review* as a textbook. We constantly received letters inquiring about the meaning of words, particularly when we had given them an American twist.

These bright young Chinese college and middle-school graduates, including many young women, were employed in the offices of the large foreign and Chinese trading houses, factories, banks, newspaper offices, on the faculties and staffs of colleges and universities, and in the professions and in government offices. Old-time officials and executives were helpless without these young modern educated assistants.

I always credited myself with being the first foreign editor in China to discover the young English-reading Chinese subscriber. I promoted the organization of study clubs and classes in current events in the colleges and universities, the members of which subscribed for our paper in dozen or even in hundred lots. I taught a course in journalism in one of the colleges myself.

I also discovered another class of reader, most important for any paper in the Far East. He was the "out-port" subscriber who lived in some out-of-the-way place and might be a missionary, a buyer of native products for some coastal import and export house, or a salesman in some interior town for a foreign cigarette house or oil company. Again he might be a British, American, Scandinavian, or what-not customs officer stationed at some frontier point, or he might even be a lighthouse tender "gone native" on some lonely island off the coast. These people were hungry for "something to read," and they lived out of the advertising pages. One not-to-be-forgotten subscriber was an Englishman who was captain of a tramp steamer that touched at

Shanghai only once in six months. He would visit the office and take his half-year's supply of papers in a bundle to the ship. Then he would place them carefully in a pile in his stateroom and have his cabin boy bring one copy, the oldest, every morning as he ate his breakfast. Nothing could induce him to change the routine, not even news of a major engagement on the western front.

But the typical subscriber! Never was an editor more sorely tried in attempting to picture in his mind a typical subscriber— a combination American, Briton, Continental European, Chinese intellectual, businessman, missionary, what not. I gave it up and decided to print the kind of paper that anyone could pick up with assurance of finding a fairly complete story of what had happened in our local, national, and international Far Eastern world. In deciding on the relative importance of happenings in the international field I always kept in mind the fact that since Shanghai was one of the world's largest ports there were as many people interested in business, financial, and economic news as there were interested in politics or religion. This was in 1917, before there was a *Newsweek*, *Reader's Digest*, or *Time* to serve as a model. But we did have the *Literary Digest*, the *New Republic* of Walter Lippmann and Herbert Croly, and later the *Nation* of Oswald Garrison Villard. We had permission to follow the general form of the *New Republic*, then regarded as the most attractive paper, typographically, in America. However, we differed from the *New Republic* as to content, as we printed more 8-point matter, consisting of news reports and contributed articles dealing with political, commercial, and financial subjects more along the line of the English economic reviews.

An advance notice mailed to prospective subscribers brought in more than a thousand subscription orders, most of them accompanied by checks. It seemed that we had a field!

Work started in earnest on the first number, which we decided to publish on June 2, 1917. Several days prior to the date for which issuance of Vol. 1, No. 1 was scheduled, I happened to meet one of the officials of the United States Court for China, the presiding judge at that time being Charles S. Lobingier, from Nebraska. The court official told me confidentially that the judge was working on an important decision, and we might be able to obtain a scoop for our first edition if we would hold off publication for a week. I investigated, and decided the delay was justified—which explained why the first issue of *Millard's Review of the Far East* happened to be dated June 9, the second Saturday of the month, instead of June 2, the first Saturday, as originally intended.

Judge Lobingier's decision was a momentous one and caused unexpected repercussions, one being the undying hatred of an influential group of local promoters headed by an American named Frank J. Raven. This hatred was directed not only at the judge of the court but at our paper, which had published the exclusive report of the decision. The case involved the refusal of the court to permit Raven and his associates to incorporate the American-Oriental Banking Corporation, a private bank, under the regulations of the court. Aside from the legal elements involved, the judge's decision referred to the necessity of preventing "loose and reckless incorporation" by Americans in their commercial activities in China.

Dating back to the American occupation of the Philippines, Shanghai had served as headquarters for American get-rich-quick operators and adventurers. Most of this gentry had gone to the Philippines following the occupation, but had been forced to get out by the first Civil Governor, William Howard Taft. Being unable to operate in the British Colony of Hong Kong, most of them came to Shanghai, where there were no restrictions. As a result Shanghai became the base of operation for salesmen of fake jewelry, worthless stocks, patent medicines, dangerous drugs, etc. One group had promoted an insurance company with the object of unloading the stock on rich Chinese in Malaya, and were astonished when Chinese business flowed in and the company unexpectedly became prosperous and respectable.

Raven had come to China from California and obtained a position in the Public Works Department of the municipal government of the International Settlement. He worked in the department long enough to obtain information regarding new road extensions, then resigned and organized a real estate company. Using his inside knowledge of the location of new roads and streets, the company successfully promoted a new subdivision which it called "Columbia Circle." With this start the company branched into various promotional activities, including the organization of the American-Oriental Banking Corporation, Raven Trust Company, American Finance Company, and various other enterprises, retail and industrial, all of a speculative character. Shares in the various enterprises were widely sold to Chinese and foreigners, and the banks launched an intensive drive for deposits in the missionary community and among foreign residents of the Settlement.

Although distrusted by responsible businessmen and bankers, Raven promoted his "Wallingford" enterprises by clever advertising and came to exercise considerable influence in local affairs, on occasion even dominating official policies of the American Consul and Minister. His enterprises finally collapsed like the proverbial house of cards, resulting in widespread losses in the foreign and Chinese communities. Some of the mission boards lost large sums which they had invested in Raven's securities, and thousands of depositors in the American-Oriental Bank, trust company and finance company lost their nest eggs. Most serious were losses suffered in the Russian and other non-American communities which were led by Raven's high-powered publicity to believe that the American flag with which he so copiously decorated his literature guaranteed security for the capital and high rate of interest he paid on deposits. Raven's activities had much to do in discrediting the system of extraterritoriality, as he had taken advantage of its provisions to build up his house of cards.

The last chapter in Raven's activities was written in 1935, in the form of a heavy sentence for the promoter and two or three of his associates in the United States Court for China at Shanghai. The judge who convicted Raven was Milton J. Helmick of New Mexico, and the special prosecutor who unraveled the tangled web of Raven's promotional activities was George Sellett of Illinois, who went to China as a professor in the Shanghai Law College, which was established by American missionaries.

III

An International City

I HAD NOT REALIZED, as I went ashore at Shanghai that February day in 1917, that the jetties and godowns which lined both banks of the Whangpoo River for many miles had once resounded to the shouts of American sailors as they loaded and unloaded cargoes from sailing ships which had made the long voyage around the Horn, up the west coast of both Americas to Vancouver Island and the Aleutians for cargoes of furs, and then across the Pacific, perhaps by way of Hawaii, to the coast of Asia.

There was a long period in the first half of the nineteenth century when the trade of Canton, Manila, and Shanghai, as well as shipping along the China coast and on the Yangtze River, was dominated by a famous Yankee firm, Russell and Company. The old godowns of this company, resembling blockhouses because of their solid construction, still extended along the Shanghai Bund, or river-bank street, fronting the French Concession and the native Nantao area for several blocks. Founded about 1818 by Samuel Russell of Middletown, Connecticut, this firm, with its head office in Boston, did more business in China than any other American house and contributed materially, with its trade and profits, to the economic well-being of the infant American Republic, which was having hard going following the disruption of its political and economic ties with Great Britain.

Russell and Company began to decline in the middle of the century, and as a consequence of serious financial reverses suffered as a result of the American Civil War and the Taiping Rebellion in China (1848–1865) it was forced to sell its various properties and retire from business in 1877. Its large fleet in

China waters and its extensive property holdings in all Chinese ports were taken over by the Chinese Government and incorporated into the China Merchants Steam Navigation Company. This company continued in operation up to the outbreak of the China-Japan war in 1937, when most of the ships and much of the property were taken over by William P. Hunt and Company, an American concern, in order to prevent seizure by the Japanese. However, all of the valuable properties of the company passed into Japanese hands following Pearl Harbor.

Shanghai, more than any other Oriental port, showed the results of early American influence. Shanghai owed its curious form of international municipal administration to an early American merchant consul named Cunningham, who in 1852 put up the American flag in the British Concession and claimed equal rights despite the protests of the indignant British Consul. The Chinese, embarrassed by the row among the foreigners, sought to settle it by offering the Americans a concession of equal size north of Soochow Creek on the northern border of the British Concession. Local Americans accepted the Chinese gift, and our mission boards established their offices and residences in the area, which was known as Hongkew. But Washington refused to ratify the deal, declaring it was contrary to our policy to assume jurisdiction over Chinese territory. When the Americans at Shanghai learned that their government had turned them down, they induced the Chinese to permit the amalgamation of Hongkew with the British area south of Soochow Creek, and thus the "International" Settlement came into being. Later another area known as Yangtzepoo was added, and in time the section "north of the creek," originally regarded as slums, became the richest industrial area in China. The British and later the Japanese established their cotton mills in that section, as it was adjacent to canal and river transportation, but, of more importance, it was even closer to vast pools of cheap, skillful, industrious, and generally docile Chinese labor. Most of the modern industrial development which the Americans brought to Shanghai, including a modern power plant, also went into the Hongkew area.

Chinese industrial establishments, which exceeded in number and importance those of the foreigners at Shanghai in the past decade, were located chiefly in the Chapei section adjoining Hongkew. Here too was located the famous Commercial Press, rated as one of the largest and most complete printing establishments in the world, and the most advanced industrial enterprise in the Orient in the treatment of its thousands of laborers.

Shanghai in 1917, from the standpoint of modern development, reminded one of an American country town, despite the fact it was one of the world's leading seaports. Shanghai was listed among the first half dozen ports of the world in ocean-borne merchandise which crossed its wharves, but the major part of the tonnage was not carried by sea-going craft; it was carried on native Chinese junks which plied the eastern seas from Vladivostok to Singapore. Shanghai, early in 1917, had more than a million and a half people but did not have a single paved street. It had a small electric light plant, which belonged to the municipality, and a primitive telephone system, owned by the subscribers. The telephone system was operated with cumbersome instruments made in Sweden, which required persistent cranking in order to get the operator. Once there were international complications when an exasperated American businessman, whose conversation was repeatedly interrupted, tore his telephone off the wall and threw it out of the window into the street. The manager of the telephone company, who was British, refused to install a new phone in the American's office. The American then appealed to the American Consul and charged discrimination and violation of treaty rights under the Open Door doctrine. Friends finally intervened, and the American's phone was restored without the matter being referred to the State Department and the British Foreign Office.

Both the telephone company and the power plant were later

purchased by Americans and modernized, but when I made my
first visit to the office of the electricity department in the
municipal building, to have lights installed at my office, I had
my first glimpse of a "punkah" fan. The punkah was said to
have been invented in India; it consisted of a large oblong bam-
boo frame, covered with cheesecloth fringed at the bottom and
suspended from the ceiling by cords. Another cord attached
to the frame extended through a hole in the wall to a courtyard,
where a native servant kept the punkah in motion by pulling
the cord back and forth. Frequently the coolie would fall asleep
at his task. It did not seem incongruous to local residents or to
members of the electricity department that the offices were
cooled by punkahs. I was told that electric fans were unhealthy
and caused pneumonia and stomach trouble. Almost everyone
wore a "stomacher" or wide woolen band about his middle next
to his skin, even in warmest weather, in order to ward off
stomach ailments supposedly caused by breezes chilling one's
internals.

The picture of Shanghai in 1917 would not be complete without an account of the local fire department, which was a
"volunteer" organization. Firemen, aside from a few native
assistants, were all members of the European community and
served without pay. The equipment had been imported from
England in earlier years, and resembled museum pieces. But the
department made up in picturesqueness for what it lacked in
modernity. I had not been in Shanghai very long before I was
awakened one night by a fire alarm in one of the densely populated sections near the hotel. I dressed and ran to the fire, along
with the rest of the native and foreign population, and was
astonished to find that most of the firemen were attired in full
evening dress and were running about carrying hoses, with their
black coat-tails flapping in the breeze and their white shirt fronts
and ties besmeared with soot. As the native assistants wore
regulation firemen's uniforms, including brass helmets which
would have been the envy of a Latin American policeman, I was
puzzled by the formal dress of the young Britishers who made

up most of the fire-fighting crew. I learned that the fire had occurred on the eve of an English national holiday, when most of the members of the community were attending a formal dinner and dance at the Shanghai Club. Since there was no time to change, all of the members of the department hurried to the fire in their evening clothes. I was assured that the municipality assumed responsibility for cleaning, pressing, laundry, and repair bills which resulted from fighting a fire in formal attire. The department's slogan carved in enduring stone over the front door of the central building was, "We Fight the Flames."

The fire department was the butt of numerous jokes in the foreign community. It was charged that the firemen often showed partiality when the property happened to be owned by someone who was not popular in the community. Allegedly they would take their time in fighting such fires, and usually there was little left of the property when they got through with it. In later years, after the American insurance companies discovered Shanghai, there was agitation for a modern fire department which resulted in a hot fight, as the old department was a social institution with membership strictly confined to "taipans" (managers) or juniors in the large British firms. However, progress triumphed, particularly as insurance premiums were exorbitant—largely because of the primitive conditions of the fire-fighting apparatus.

For protection against internal and external foes Shanghai depended upon a Volunteer Corps of local militia which was made up of companies representing the various national groups, including the Chinese, who resided in the International Settlement. Thus there were companies of American, British, Scottish, Japanese, Chinese, and Portuguese national groups, and other contingents including the Scandinavians, and other smaller European groups. The Shanghai Volunteer Corps probably was the first "international" police force. Since the British community was the largest, its companies, including the Scottish contingent in native kilts, were the most numerous. The Americans had three companies—infantry, mounted, and machine gun—and there was a company of Filipinos who served under American officers. These units, which totaled probably twelve or fifteen hundred men, were made up chiefly of employees of the large foreign firms in Shanghai. In later years, after conditions became disturbed, Shanghai became a "garrison town," and large bodies of foreign troops were stationed there for protective purposes, but the fact that the Settlement could be protected by an international volunteer regiment of only 1,500 men was indicative of the generally peaceful conditions which prevailed in the lower Yangtze Valley region at that time. The Volunteer Corps, like the fire department, also took the complexion of a social organization, and the annual dinners of the various units were gala events.

The United States, Britain, Japan, France, and occasionally Spain, Italy, and Portugal, kept destroyers stationed in the Whangpoo, estuary of the Yangtze which served Shanghai as a harbor, but the sailors were seldom landed and always were withdrawn to the gunboats after the particular trouble had subsided.

In the weeks following my arrival I learned of many amusing beliefs and customs of the European community, which had lived in comparative isolation for decades. One was that window screens, along with electric fans, were regarded as "unhealthy." Shanghai at that time was crisscrossed by numerous canals which at low tide had the consistency of spinach soup and served as breeding places for clouds of mosquitoes. Beds had to be enclosed in mosquito nets suspended from the ceiling. The swarms of mosquitoes were reduced somewhat by the generous use of burning punk, made from wood, finely ground, scented, and pressed into sticks or coils. Another method was for a servant to walk about, spraying the ankles of the family and guests with a solution of kerosene. A missionary of an inventive frame of mind supplied his family and guests with oblong bags of muslin which were drawn on over the feet and tied securely above the knees. The use of "mosquito bags" became general and they

were sold in the local English stores. An American friend who
once spent the night at my home woke up in the morning with
the soles of his feet so irritated that he could hardly walk. A
servant explained the mystery: "Master very tall man and feet
stick against net." Later the mosquito menace was considerably
reduced by filling the canals and ponds, and still later the
municipality caused all open drains to be sprayed with an oil
solution, which practically eliminated the insects. However,
there still remained the flies, which feasted on the piles of garbage that accumulated in the alleys and back yards.

As these conditions prevailed in the "foreign" sections, the
situation was worse in the surrounding Chinese areas, particularly in the congested areas occupied by the poorer classes.
Typhoid, cholera, dysentery, and other germ diseases were so
prevalent that one wondered what prevented the entire population from being swept away by epidemics. The universal Chinese habit of drinking hot tea or boiled water was credited by
the doctors with chief responsibility for preventing the spread
of epidemics. However, among both foreigners and Chinese the
number of deaths from intestinal ailments was startling. A missionary organization undertook a campaign to teach sanitation,
emphasizing the dangers of the house-fly in the spread of disease. The promoters of the campaign prepared a set of charts
and illustrations showing the facts of life in the fly family. Large
lithographic posters in colors were put up about the lecture halls
where talks on sanitation were given, and on billboards about
the city showing flies enlarged to huge proportions in the pictures in order to give emphasis, walking about garbage cans and
then strolling with their dirty feet over food intended for human
consumption. One day after the campaign had been in progress
for some time one of the missionary doctors saw a group of
country women talking excitedly while pointing at one of the
illustrated posters. The woman was saying, "No wonder the
Americans are afraid of flies, if they grow so big in their
country; fortunately our flies are small and are not dangerous."

Today Shanghai is one of the few large cities outside the

United States which contain American-style skyscraper hotels, office and apartment buildings, but three decades ago the tallest buildings in the Settlement did not exceed five or six stories, and only one or two had elevators or "lifts." All were located on the Bund. Between these buildings and the river was a parkway where most of the foreign population took its recreational walks on summer evenings. The municipal orchestra gave concerts in the park on Saturday evenings, which were attended by practically the entire foreign community. At that time no Chinese was admitted to any municipal park in the foreign area. However, the foreigner's exclusive enjoyment of his parks was not entirely without hazard, for in addition to the mosquitoes the trees were filled with flocks of raucous crows which competed with the orchestra for attention. The crows were no respecters of dignity, and I often suspected them of "anti-foreignism," as they seemed to select for desecration the best-dressed women and the whitest linen suits of the men. The Municipal Council finally offered a bounty for the heads of the crows, which enabled a small army of Chinese boys to earn handsome fees by trapping them wholesale. The Council, however, had to abolish the bounty when it was discovered that crows were being secretly raised by would-be collectors.

One park, known as the Bund Garden, became a serious political issue in Sino-foreign politics due to a sign erected over the gateway containing the regulations for the use of the garden. Among the regulations warning against picking flowers or destroying the property were two special items, one of which stated that dogs could not be taken into the park and another, further down the list, reading "No Chinese, excepting work coolies, are admitted." Later when trouble between the foreigners and Chinese developed, student agitators made effective use of the slogan, "Dogs and Chinese Not Admitted."

Shanghai consisted of three distinct political units: International Settlement, French Concession, and Chinese City. The International Settlement had three important subdivisions—

Hongkew, Yangtzepoo, and Western District where most of the foreigners lived. The French Concession consisted of a narrow strip squeezed in between the International Settlement and the ancient Chinese City. When the International Settlement Administration was created the French refused to participate, and established their own municipality. The so-called Western Residential District, which in 1937, following Japanese occupation, became one of the most notorious gambling and night-club "hot spots" in the world, was, in 1917, largely open country containing a few isolated Chinese villages.

The only tax which resident foreigners as well as Chinese in the Settlement had to pay was a "land tax" based on rental value. If the property was rented, one paid from 10 per cent to 15 per cent of the rental value in taxes. Thus if one paid rent amounting to $100 a month, taxes amounted to $10 a month or $120 a year. Property which was not improved paid practically no taxes. The system under which the renters of houses were forced to pay the bulk of the taxes was imported from England when the Settlement was established, and although later changed in England, was never changed in Shanghai. The taxation system which placed the burden of the taxes upon the renter rather than the property owner also became a serious political issue between the Chinese and foreigners.

Shanghai streets were paved with a mixture of broken stones and clay. Chinese street laborers kept the streets in order by first tamping in the broken stone and then filling the crevices with a sloppy solution of clay of the consistency of rich cream. The section would then be fenced off until the mud dried sufficiently for a coolie-propelled roller to smooth the surface. It made a fairly good pavement until the next rain, when all the clay would be washed out and the job had to be done over again. But labor was cheap, and fresh mud was plentiful; besides, some contractor made a good thing out of it.

The International Settlement possessed no sewage disposal system or modern plumbing, except in one or two new buildings located on the Bund. Modern flush toilets were regarded, along with screens and electric fans, as "unhealthy." Bathrooms were equipped with round earthenware tubs in which one sat upright to take a bath, and with sanitary devices known as "commodes" which consisted of a square wooden box with a hole in the top and an earthenware chamber pot. The house boys collected the pots in the mornings and derived a considerable income by selling the contents to the farmers for use as fertilizer. The International Settlement Administration also collected ordure and sold it to contractors, who in turn sold it to the farmers and gardeners of the surrounding countryside. Complaints often were made that the sale of such fertilizer was detrimental to public health, but the council refused to listen to the complaints because it received an annual revenue of about $100,000 (US$50,000) from the sale. The farmers spread this on their crops with long-handled ladles, the process being called "feeding" the plants. The custom was not restricted to China, but prevailed also in Japan and in some European countries. The larger earthenware pots which Chinese farmers used as containers for the fertilizer probably were responsible for the phrase "stink-pots of Asia" which appeared in Marco Polo's description of his travels in Cathay more than six centuries ago.

IV

Sun Yat-sen and Yuan Shih-kai

AT THE TIME OF MY ARRIVAL in Shanghai, Dr. Sun Yat-sen, the founder and leader of the Kuomintang, was residing in the French Concession, in a modest little house on Rue Molière which served the double purpose of a home for himself and Madame Sun (Ching-Ling Soong), and an office from which he directed his far-flung political activities.

Today one hears serious criticism of the one-party Kuomintang dictatorship at Chungking, but a study of the early struggles of the Kuomintang shows that this leading Chinese party is justified in its claim for consideration as one of the world's great political parties. It originated in a secret society founded by Dr. Sun Yat-sen in the little Portuguese settlement of Macao near Hong Kong, where he had gone to practice medicine, after his graduation in 1892 from the newly formed medical school in Hong Kong. He was soon forced by the Portuguese Government to leave Macao, and when he returned home to Canton he attempted to form a branch of the society there, but the authorities became suspicious and he was again forced to leave. Some of his associates were captured and executed, but he himself was able to escape to Hong Kong and from there abroad.

Being a courageous and persistent youth, he continued his activities among Chinese natives outside of China. Chinese residents abroad contributed to the revolutionary cause considerable sums which Sun Yat-sen used to good effect among disaffected elements, even in circles close to the Imperial Court in Peking. While in London in 1896 he was kidnaped by officials of the Chinese Legation and confined in a secret room by his captors, who planned to send him back to China, where a reward of $250,000 had been offered for his apprehension. Sun was able to smuggle out a note to his friend, Dr. James Cantlie, head of Hong Kong University, who happened to be in London at the time. Dr. Cantlie, who sympathized with the earnest young revolutionist, informed the British authorities and the London newspapers of the high-handed action of the legation officials, and as a result pressure was brought to obtain his release. Since it was now impossible for him to return to China or even to the British Colony of Hong Kong, he continued his revolutionary activities against the Manchu Government in other countries.

While in Japan in 1905 he succeeded in uniting the various factions of the anti-dynastic movement into a formidable revolutionary society which he named the Tung Meng Hui (China Brotherhood Society). By this time his revolutionary program had gone beyond the mere overthrow of the corrupt Manchu Government, and was concentrating on definite plans for a new China. These plans and the principles on which they were based provided the theoretical foundation for the present-day Kuomintang Party and the "Constitution of the Five Powers" which formed the basis of the National Government organized two decades later at Nanking. In 1905 he was already working toward the concept of a Chinese nation based on nationalistic and democratic principles, and the newly organized society came out boldly for a Chinese republic and an equitable distribution of land.

Although revolutionary propaganda spread by Dr. Sun and his followers had exercised great influence, there were other forces at work which hastened the collapse of the Ching (or Manchu) Empire. These elements were official corruption and inefficiency, wretched conditions of the people, internal unrest, and foreign pressure. Sensing too late the drift of affairs, the Manchu Court had hastily attempted to institute reforms, but the reforms were unpopular and had already precipitated the Boxer Rebellion of 1900, which was originally directed against the throne but which Tsu Hsi, the Empress Dowager, had cleverly turned against the foreigners.

The revolutionary movement was gathering strength throughout China, supported by funds which Sun Yat-sen was busily engaged in raising throughout the world. Numerous uprisings in various parts of the country were promptly put down by the imperial forces. On March 29, 1910, Dr. Sun Yat-sen made a further attempt to organize a revolt in Canton, but again failed. On this occasion there was a major tragedy, for seventy-two of his followers were caught and executed at Yellow Flower Hill. The names of these martyrs today have an exalted place in the annals of the revolution. The leaven was beginning to work; unrest was growing all over the country.

Leaving an associate, General Huang Hsing, in charge, Dr. Sun Yat-sen hurried to the United States to raise more funds for the cause. While he was in San Francisco a delegation of small Cantonese merchants called on him and offered to close their businesses and return to China to fight in the revolution. Dr. Sun asked one how much he earned. The man, operator of a small laundry, said he had an income of $18 a week. Dr. Sun asked him if he could live on $12 a week. The man replied in the affirmative. Dr. Sun then said, "We have plenty of man-power, but we need money. You remain here and continue your business, but contribute $6 a week to the revolution."

Dr. Sun Yat-sen was in Denver, Colorado, in October, 1911, when he received a cable from General Huang Hsing telling him that the government troops in Wuchang, important city on the Yangtze (now part of the Wu-Han, or Wuchang-Hankow-Hanyang municipality), were ready to revolt. As Dr. Sun was on the other side of the world, there was considerable confusion, and several revolutionary leaders were executed. But this only spurred the rebels to greater effort and as a result the troops, which had been bought over, rebelled against the Viceroy and he was forced to flee to a foreign concession.

The Viceroy tried to induce the foreign consular authorities to use their Yangtze gunboats to suppress the revolt, but Dr.

Sun's propaganda abroad had borne fruit. The French and Russian Consuls supported the republicans at a meeting of the consular body which had been invoked by the Manchu Viceroy.

When Dr. Sun was advised by cable regarding the situation, he hurried to Washington where he conferred with officials and then sailed for London where he urged the British authorities to follow a three-point policy toward China: (1) No loans were to be advanced by British banks to the Manchu Government; (2) an order against Dr. Sun's residence in Hong Kong, Singapore, Penang, or other British colonies in the Far East was to be canceled; (3) Britain would cooperate with the United States in preventing Japan from interfering in the revolution.

Dr. Sun Yat-sen returned to China on January 5, 1912. He called his faithful followers together at Shanghai and proceeded to Nanking, where he took the oath of office as provisional President of the new republic at the request of the National Convention in Nanking.

Prior to the collapse of the Empire the Manchu Court had called to its assistance a promising military politician, named Yuan Shih-kai, who helped reorganize the army. He had been dismissed shortly after the deaths of the Emperor Kuang Hsu and the Empress Dowager in 1908 and the accession of the infant Hsuan T'ung to the throne, but as the outstanding military leader he was frantically recalled when the revolution broke out. But his heart was not in the imperial cause, for after a successful show of authority at Hankow, which was retaken and burned, he began negotiations with the revolutionary forces. On February 12, 1912, the Manchus abdicated, having been convinced by Yuan Shih-kai that their cause was hopeless; and negotiations between Dr. Sun Yat-sen and Yuan Shih-kai continued. A few days later Dr. Sun Yat-sen yielded to the superior military force which Yuan Shih-kai controlled, and resigned the presidency in favor of Yuan Shih-kai.

A provisional constitution was adopted by the Republican Government at Nanking in March, 1912, placing the President under the control of Parliament, which when assembled proved to be dominated by members of the Kuomintang. Dr. Sun Yat-sen and his followers retired to Shanghai, and Yuan Shih-kai moved the capital back to the ancient city of the Manchus at Peking, where the atmosphere was anything but favorable for a democratic form of government.

In 1913 Dr. Sun Yat-sen and his followers led the opposition against President Yuan Shih-kai, who was negotiating loans with English, French, German and Russian bankers and which the republican group felt would be used to augment Yuan's personal military power, while placing him under further obligation to foreign nations. When active rebellion broke out in the south due to changes in military command which Yuan Shih-kai had inaugurated to increase his personal power, it was ruthlessly put down by the government forces, and Dr. Sun Yat-sen, who had supported the movement, was forced to flee to Japan. He took with him, among others, Charles Jones Soong, a printer of Christian missionary tracts and Chinese revolutionary literature, and Soong's daughter, Chingling, who had been acting since his return to China as his confidential secretary. While still in Japan in 1915, Dr. Sun Yat-sen divorced his wife and married Chingling, thus bringing about a union of the famous Sun-Soong, and later, Kung families.

In November of 1913 Yuan Shih-kai had unseated the Kuomintang members of the Parliament, and two months later he dissolved it entirely. Yuan, who had been motivated throughout by a growing personal ambition, attempted in 1915 to restore the monarchy with himself as Emperor. China was not yet ready for the republicanism of Dr. Sun Yat-sen, but neither would it countenance a return of an imperial form of government. Yuan Shih-kai, who had not yet had himself formally enthroned, rescinded the imperial referendum, and died of disease and chagrin on June 6, 1916. The presidency was assumed by Li Yuan-hung, who had held the office of Vice President since the beginning of the republican regime, and who had actively opposed Yuan's attempt to restore the monarchy. Parliament was recalled, Tuan Chi-jui continuing as Premier, since he was liked by the military forces which Yuan Shih-kai had built up in support of the Government.

After the death of Yuan Shih-kai, Dr. Sun Yat-sen and his wife had returned to Shanghai, and soon after my arrival I arranged an interview with him. I was met at the door by a colorful character named Maurice Cohen who had come to the Far East by way of New York, Chicago, and Canada and who served as Dr. Sun's personal bodyguard. Cohen always sat on a bench in the front hall and carried a large revolver in his hip pocket, which caused the seat of his trousers to sag grotesquely. His title of "General," which was later conferred on him by a grateful Canton Government, was the subject of frequent puns in the local English newspapers, but Cohen was a faithful watchdog and was credited with saving Dr. Sun, on several occasions, from assassination. He ushered me into an adjoining room overlooking the garden, where I was introduced to China's revolutionary leader.

Dr. Sun, then 51 years old, with thinning front hair and graying mustache, was wearing traditional native costume, a long gown of light material, which gave him an impressive appearance as he stood in meditative mood looking out of the window toward the garden.

After an exchange of greetings, Dr. Sun inquired about my trip to China. He was interested in my description of Honolulu, where he had attended school and where he later resided as a political refugee. The conversation shifted to Japan, when I told him of my experiences at Nagasaki, and this led to a spirited discussion of current Japanese activities, as Japan was then in occupation of the Chinese port of Tsingtao, from which she had evicted the little German garrison after the outbreak of the war in Europe. But the Japanese had not stopped with the occupation of the formerly German-controlled port. Taking advantage of the preoccupation of Great Britain and America in the war, the Japanese were busily extending their influence throughout Manchuria and North China.

Turning to me, Dr. Sun exclaimed, in an accusing tone, *"The United States should have put Japan out of Korea."*

Noticing the puzzled look on my face, Dr. Sun explained rather sadly that the United States had a treaty with Korea in which we had promised to protect the Hermit Kingdom in the event it was attacked by a foreign country. But we had not lived up to our commitment when Korea was attacked and later annexed by Japan. He said, "Had America acted promptly and energetically, Japan would have been prevented from obtaining her first foothold on the continent." Korea, which Japan had originally described as a spear pointed at her heart from the continent, now served, following her occupation of the peninsula, as a convenient bridge to the continent, stated Dr. Sun. He held President Theodore Roosevelt largely responsible for America's failure to act in Korea's behalf, and said that President Roosevelt was overanxious to bring about peace between Russia and Japan, and had sacrificed Korea in order to accomplish that objective.

As I knew practically nothing about the circumstances surrounding the Korean incident, I did not discuss the question further, but I later had occasion to speculate upon Dr. Sun's statement that the United States should have "put Japan out of Korea." Japan was weak then, and a determined protest might have changed the course of history.

Later I interviewed Dr. Sun again on the subject of China's participation in the war in Europe (World War I), to which he was strongly opposed. President Li Yuan-hung, a friend of Dr. Sun, also opposed China's participation in the war. Dr. Sun insisted there was no point in China's declaring war on Germany merely to take sides in a struggle in which China had no direct interest. He declared that China's participation in a war to which the Kuomintang was opposed would precipitate serious domestic dissension. He made the significant statement: "The Chinese people may not be able to distinguish between foreigners of different nationalities and if the simple and honest people are taught to kill Teutons, they might be led to slaughter all white foreigners in the country."

V

Shadows of Civil War

THUS WHEN OUR FIRST ISSUE of *Millard's Review of the Far East* appeared, on June 9, 1917, affairs in Peking were rapidly approaching a crisis. There were two fairly well defined political groups in the Government, one known as the Military or "Tuchuns'" Party, and the other the Liberal Party—which was the Kuomintang. The Military Party was largely made up of so-called Tuchuns, or military commanders of the various provinces and districts, chiefly in North China. With few exceptions the Tuchuns had previously served as officers in the army of the late Yuan Shih-kai in the latter days of the Empire and the early days of the Republic. Generally they were men of abysmal ignorance and selfishness, whose power was based entirely upon the number of regiments they commanded or claimed to command. The Liberal Party had a majority in the Parliament, but, because of military weakness, had never been able to obtain control of the Government. President Li Yuan-hung, a Liberal, who had succeeded President Yuan Shih-kai, lacked actual power for the same reason. This had been the chief handicap of the Kuomintang leaders from the early days of the Republic, when Sun Yat-sen yielded his office to Yuan Shih-kai.

The political struggle in Peking had been triangular in that it involved the President, Li Yuan-hung; the Premier, General Tuan Chi-jui, who derived his power from the military or Tuchuns' group; and Parliament itself. The *Review* explained in an editorial on the political situation that there was little in the contest between the Peking Parliament and the executive

35

branches of the Government to distinguish it in principle
from similar contests in other countries, as the struggle was
as old as democratic government anywhere. The struggles involved the usual disputes over rights, precedents, powers, and
privileges, questions which have not been settled today, even in
the most advanced democracies. These struggles were more
complicated in China because the Government did not enjoy
complete sovereignty. Furthermore it was functioning under
a temporary constitution, of disputed legality. Frequently the
more progressive Chinese officials in desperation would go to
their foreign friends in Peking for advice, but the advice they
received usually was flavored by the selfish interest of the
adviser and his associates.

The principal issue at stake was that of China's entry into
the World War. Tuan Chi-jui, the Premier, who favored
China's participation in the war, and the Liberal or Kuomintang block in Parliament were at a deadlock. To resolve this
situation President Li Yuan-hung had dismissed Premier Tuan
on May 23, and Tuan immediately went to Tientsin, where he
got in touch with reactionary military leaders and was stirring
up revolt against the Peking Government. The departure of
Tuan from Peking did little to relieve the political struggle
and on June 13, 1917, four days after our first issue appeared,
President Li Yuan-hung dismissed Parliament, on the advice
of General Chang Hsun, to whom he had turned for support
after the dismissal of Tuan Chi-jui.

Early in the spring of 1917 the Military Party had called
a conference in Peking, and since no one trusted his neighbor,
each Tuchun took along with him a sizable bodyguard. General Chang Hsun, who previously had been stationed at a small
town on the Yangtze River opposite Nanking, was one of the
military leaders who attended the conference. One of the stories
told of him was that he once called a dozen military commanders to a conference at his headquarters. The conference passed
off smoothly, and was followed by the usual elaborate dinner
given by the host. Suddenly and without warning the lights

went out all over the compound, and there was deadly silence in the banquet room. When the lights were suddenly switched on, much to the embarrassment of those present, each held his revolver in his hand.

Chang Hsun took a sizable force with him when he went to the military conference in Peking, and immediately after his arrival in the capital he distributed his troops in strategic positions about the city, apparently without consulting his associates, and since the uniforms were similar his action attracted little attention.

The Japanese were still sitting on China's doorstep, hoping to force the Chinese to accept Group 5 of the Twenty-one Demands presented in 1915, and the Germans were also active in protecting their vested interests and concessions, and were striving strenuously, but quietly, to prevent China from declaring war.

This had been the scene at Peking in the spring of 1917, when the United States became worried over the prospect of civil war in China. In order to head off such an eventuality the State Department decided to send China a note deploring the danger of civil strife and pointing out that peace among China's political factions was of extreme importance to the world at that particular time. It was suggested that the maintenance of peace in China was even more important than the matter of an immediate declaration of war on Germany, toward which China was being pressed by Great Britain and France. America's friendly advice to the Chinese urging them to maintain domestic peace stirred up a tremendous commotion, particularly among the Japanese, who argued that it amounted to interference in the domestic affairs of the Chinese and should not have been undertaken without prior consultation with Japan.

The Chinese themselves displayed no indignation at the receipt of the American note. The United States was just beginning, at that time, to expand commercially into the Far Eastern markets, and several bankers and engineers had arrived in

Peking to discuss a railway and canal construction enterprise. The Japanese did not approve of these schemes either, unless they were undertaken in partnership with the Japanese.

The Germans, while working strenuously to hold China out of the war, kept their activities well under cover. The first evidence of German activities became public unexpectedly in mid-June, 1917, when the American authorities arrested at Peking and deported to Manila a well known American missionary, Dr. Gilbert Reid, on the ground that he was involved in German propaganda. It developed that Reid had sponsored a Chinese-language newspaper in Peking which later was used as an organ of German policy in China. The United States Government, however, took no action further than to deport Dr. Reid to Manila, where he was given his freedom. He immediately proceeded to write a book denouncing President Wilson and the United States Government and questioning the expediency and wisdom, as well as morality, of trying to force China into the war against Germany.

Chang Hsun had continued to increase, secretly, the forces which he had distributed in strategic locations about the city. Some of the Chinese papers contained reports that Chang Hsun was spending a great deal of time in the company of members of the deposed Manchu Dynasty. But aside from the parliamentary issue the chief subject of discussion in the press in the Far East continued to be the American note advising the Chinese to compose their domestic troubles peacefully because of the complicated international political situation.

Chang Hsun was now ready for a trial of strength. Early on July 1, the "Boy Emperor," a prisoner of the Republican Government, was removed from his residence in the Forbidden City and placed on the dragon throne in ancient ceremonial manner. The entire *coup d'état* had been managed by Chang Hsun, using the troops he had secretly stationed about the city. It was not until many months afterward that disclosures were made indicating that the Germans had had a hand in the "restoration," their object, of course, being to embarrass the

Republican Government, which they felt would ultimately succumb to allied pressure and declare war on them. The Germans probably had paid the foxy Tuchun a considerable sum, as he had no regular source of revenue.

Chang Hsun quickly discovered, however, that to restore the monarchy in China was one thing, but to keep it restored was another. Rival political elements ridiculed Chang Hsun's action, but it had a sobering effect upon the various liberal factions which had been squabbling among themselves over control of the machinery of government. There was no available evidence that the Japanese were supporting the monarchial restoration.

Henry Pu-yi, last Emperor of the Ching or Manchu Dynasty, had ruled in Peking from 1908 to 1912, under the reign title of Hsuan T'uang. When Dr. Sun Yat-sen created the Republic at Nanking in 1911 he made the serious mistake of agreeing to permit the remnants of the Manchu Dynasty, including Henry Pu-yi, to remain within their quarters in the Imperial City as hostages of the Republic. That the arrangement was a serious error was proved in the Chang Hsun incident.

The restoration aroused widespread attention in foreign circles, but, much to everyone's surprise, it caused no great excitement among Chinese political leaders. Most of them realized that Chang Hsun, even though he had German financial support, possessed neither the funds nor the intelligence necessary to put through a restoration program. As a result, Premier Tuan, with the assistance of troops supplied by the military faction, moved against Chang Hsun and overthrew the Boy Emperor, who had actually been on the throne about two weeks. As for the "king-maker" Chang Hsun, he fled to the Diplomatic Quarter for protection, first by the Dutch Minister and later by the German Legation.

Even though the restoration scheme failed, the resulting situation left Chinese politics in a worse muddle than it was before the coup. The *Review* carried the following paragraph:

The monarchy is gone—and a good job too—but it requires a political necromancer to figure out what exists in its place, except that it is a republic in name. By trying to follow a constitutional and legal reasoning, we get the following: The only basis for government in China is the provisional constitution adopted by Sun Yat-sen in Nanking in 1912. Under that constitution Li Yuan-hung is President; Feng Kuo-chang is Vice-President, and there is a Parliament, which recently was dissolved at Peking and a majority of whose members are now in Shanghai or other places outside the recognized seat of government. Also there is, or was, a Ministry or Cabinet. The Ministry is nominated by the President and is supposed to be ratified by the Parliament. There is the framework—now what, or who, are the Government of China?

The Peking Cabinet, in order to curry favor with the Allies, issued a declaration of war against the Central Powers, on August 14, 1917. While China's participation in the war did not take the form of a dispatch of troops, China did perform a vital service in the military effort by dispatching thousands of laborers to the western front, where they built roads and harbor works, repaired railroads, and even dug trenches for the allied armies. In addition China supplied many of her vital raw materials to the war effort in both the United States and Great Britain.

China also discovered, contrary to Dr. Sun's belief, that the country did have an issue against Germany and Austria, and proceeded to cancel the extraterritorial rights of the two countries and seize their concessions at Tientsin. This action against Germany and Austria, plus Soviet Russia's later voluntary relinquishment of her special treaty position, proved to be of extraordinary importance, as it gave China a vantage point in her struggle against her "unequal" treaty status with respect to the other Powers, including her allies in the war, America and Great Britain.

Evidence of important events to come was provided by a short item in the *Peking Daily News* in mid-July, 1917, stating that Dr. Sun Yat-sen, "who had been studying the parliamentary deadlock in Peking, had proceeded to the South, in connection with a movement to organize a provisional government with the cooperation of political elements in Yunnan, Kwangsi and Kwangtung."

This brief but significant item received further confirmation on July 28, when the *Review* published an editorial stating that Dr. Sun had definitely decided to proceed to Canton with the object of establishing a new Republic of China with himself as President. The editorial stated that liberal leaders, including members of the former Peking Parliament, had already begun to assemble at Canton for the purpose. Dr. Sun was accompanied by two associates, who had become known as wheelhorses of the party. They were Wu Ting-fang and Tong Shao-yi, who were members of the first class of Chinese students sent to this country. Wu became well known as Chinese Minister to the United States. Tong had served as diplomatic representative of the old Peking Government to Korea.

The Chinese navy, which was largely controlled by officials from the southern coastal province of Fukien, sided with Dr. Sun, and also withdrew to Canton. The upshot of the extended conference at Canton, which was participated in by the officers of the fleet, was the formation of a "constitutional government," of which Dr. Sun was elected "generalissimo." A call was issued for a meeting of parliamentarians who had been ousted from Peking and who were sympathetic toward Dr. Sun's cause.

Members of the Parliament who belonged to the Kuomintang Party had difficulty in getting out of Peking, as the Government attempted to hold them. Dr. C. T. Wang (later Ambassador to the United States) who was president of the Senate in the Peking Parliament, had to slip out of the capital dressed as a student, and upon his arrival at Shanghai was compelled to reside with an American missionary friend, to escape assassination.

The establishment of a republican government at Canton by Dr. Sun Yat-sen amounted to an ultimatum to the northern military faction which controlled the Peking "Republican" Government. Since the Peking regime had the advantage of diplomatic recognition by the Powers, the political situation in China became so complicated as to defy description. It marked the beginning of a civil war situation resulting in bids for power by one war lord after another, extending over a decade. Seldom had the people been subjected to such oppression and exploitation as occurred in this period, which came to be known as the "Era of the War Lords."

VI

The Lansing-Ishii "Incident"

I WAS IN PEKING, on my first trip to the northern Chinese capital, when the Japanese made another attempt to force China to accept "Group V" of the Twenty-one Demands. The American Minister at Peking was Dr. Paul S. Reinsch, formerly professor of political science at the University of Wisconsin. Although of German extraction, Dr. Reinsch was a patriotic American and a more loyal citizen than many of his detractors in the American colony in Peking, who had been constantly alluding to his German background and disparaging his attempts to prevent China from succumbing to Japanese and German pressure.

Late one night there was a knock on my door at the old Wagons-Lits Hotel, where I was staying, and on opening the door I recognized a Chinese young man who had been a student in one of my classes when I was an instructor at the University of Missouri. It was Hollington K. Tong, who following his return to China had been appointed editor of the *Peking Daily News*, a small English-language paper in the capital. I noticed that he was agitated, and asked him to come in and tell me what was the matter. He began by reviewing Japanese activities in China from the beginning of the war in 1914, when Japan seized the port of Tsingtao from the Germans, afterward extending her control throughout Shantung Province. The following year, Tong explained, Japan had presented the notorious Twenty-one Demands to President Yuan Shih-kai. The presentation of the Demands was accompanied by an ultimatum that unless they were accepted Japan would send an expeditionary force to conquer the entire country. The

Japanese Minister, Count Kato, explained to President Yuan Shih-kai that since the Demands concerned Japan and China exclusively, the matter should be kept secret and under no conditions should any foreign country, particularly the United States and Great Britain, be informed. Pounding on the table with his walking stick, Count Kato threatened the Chinese President with imprisonment by the Japanese army in case the matter was permitted to leak out and Japan was "forced to intervene."

Despite the threats the facts did leak out, and as a result the American and British Governments lodged energetic protests with the Japanese Government. Despite repeated denials the Japanese were forced to withdraw "Group V," the most drastic of the Demands, which were designed to establish Japanese hegemony over North China and Manchuria. It was to be done under the guise of "preparing China for participation in the World War."

Tong, or "Holly" as everyone knew him, said that while Japan seemingly had receded from the position she had taken when the Demands were presented in 1915 and again in 1916, the Chinese knew that Japan was only biding her time and that when the situation was propitious Japan would make another attempt to force the Chinese to agree to Group V. Japan now considered the time ripe for action, as she wanted to have China securely "nailed down" before the United States became strong enough to interfere in China's behalf.

Tong became more and more excited as his account of Japanese aggression progressed—to that very day, when Count Kato had visited China's Foreign Minister, Dr. Lou Tseng-hsiang, in the late afternoon and told him that unless Group V of the Demands was accepted immediately, Japan would take military action. There had been more table-pounding by the Japanese Minister, who warned the Chinese Foreign Minister to keep the matter quiet or else—

As soon as Count Kato had left the Foreign Office a secretary telephoned Mr. Tong, who was still in his editorial office, and told him what had happened. The secretary urged Tong to notify the correspondents of the American and British papers, in order that the report could be cabled abroad. I typed out a note of what had happened, and made an appointment for Tong to meet me at the American Legation early the next morning. After we had explained the situation to Dr. Paul S. Reinsch, the American Minister, he agreed with us that China's best defense was publicity, otherwise the Japanese would repeat their previous action and deny that any ultimatum had been presented. Dr. Reinsch recalled his own experience in 1915, when he had been reprimanded by the Secretary of State for sending the original report of the presentation of the Twenty-one Demands—which the Japanese Ambassador in Washington had denied, on the authority of the Tokyo Foreign Office. Dr. Reinsch told us that the correspondent for the Associated Press in Peking had also been reprimanded by his home office for sending "unfounded reports." As a result the A.P. correspondent cabled his resignation, and only then did the A.P. office in New York issue the story to the American press.

Immediately following my interview with the American Minister, I wired the story to my paper in Shanghai, with instructions that a copy be turned over to Carl Crow, who was the representative in Shanghai of "Compub," otherwise the American Committee on Public Information, which had just been established. Crow cabled the report to Washington, and within a short time all correspondents in Shanghai and Peking received instructions to investigate the report of the Japanese ultimatum. This time, unlike the situation in 1915, the official report to the State Department regarding the Japanese ultimatum had the support of dispatches from a half dozen correspondents at Peking and Shanghai. I also received from a Chicago paper a cable requesting a story concerning the incident, and was able to wire a more complete report than most of the correspondents, due to the information I had received from Mr. Tong. The following day the story developed new angles when the Japanese actually conducted military demonstrations at Tientsin, Mukden, and Tsinanfu, the last-named city being capital of Shantung Province, where the Japanese had established themselves in 1914 at the beginning of World War I by defeating the small German garrison stationed at the port of Tsingtao.

When the correspondents called in a body on Count Kato that afternoon the Japanese Minister denied the whole story, and charged the Chinese with creating it from whole cloth.

The incident resulted in a tragic ending of the diplomatic career of the elderly Chinese Foreign Minister, Dr. Lou Tseng-hsiang, who was charged with weakness and indecision and forced out of office. As a result of the unmerited criticism the venerable Foreign Minister resigned and a few months later went to Belgium, and entered a Catholic monastery where he remained for many years.

Dr. Reinsch, the American Minister, was indirectly responsible for the creation of the Chinese Student Movement which became an important adjunct of the Nationalist Revolution. The movement started when students in the Peking National University began collecting money on the streets of the capital to finance telegrams to the Chinese Minister and delegates in Paris, urging them to protest to the "Big Four" against Japanese aggression. Soon the students, both boys and girls, in all the Peping schools were parading with banners, and the movement spread throughout the country, resulting in demonstrations against the Japanese everywhere.

No small part of his success in explaining America's objectives in the war to the Chinese people was due to his reputation as an outstanding political scientist. This enabled him to appeal with authority to the young generation of Chinese intellectuals, the returned students and graduates of mission schools who were beginning to feel the stirrings of nationalism. Through them he was able to influence public opinion as well as governmental policy on the subject of the war. It was largely due to his efforts that China joined in the war on the side of the Allies, despite the strong German pressure and propaganda, and it also was largely due to Dr. Reinsch's efforts that China was encouraged to withstand Japanese pressure, which was even heavier than German pressure. It was felt that if China had succumbed to Japanese pressure and accepted Japanese military and political control, Japan might have felt strong enough to defy the United States and desert the Allies for the German side.

But the promises of diplomatic support which Dr. Reinsch made to the Chinese, with the knowledge and approval of the State Department and the President, were never carried out and eventually led to disastrous consequences in the relations of the two countries as well as tragedy in the life of the American Emissary. Dr. Reinsch's job was made doubly difficult, if not impossible, by the failure of the Administration to support policies which were announced during the course of the war, particularly President Wilson's fourteen points, which the Chinese thought were designed especially to assist them in regaining their independence from international domination.

Dr. Reinsch's first serious rebuff came in November, 1917, when the news services carried a report from Washington stating that Secretary of State Robert Lansing had signed an agreement with Baron Ishii, special Japanese Ambassador, in which the United States had agreed to Japan's "special position" in both Manchuria and Shantung. The report created the opinion that the United States had given up its traditional policy of the Open Door and had decided to abandon China to the tender mercies of the Japanese military clique. Dr. Reinsch had not been advised that such an agreement with Japan was even under discussion, hence he was unable to supply any information when the Chinese demanded the meaning and purpose of the "Lansing-Ishii pact." The Japanese Minister thus had a free hand, and he proceeded to fill the Chinese papers with the Japanese version of the agreement. Translations of the Japanese reports supplied to the Chinese papers conveyed the impression that America had jettisoned its traditional policy of preserving China's territorial and administrative integrity and had consented to Japan's policy of grab.'

The story behind the signing of the Lansing-Ishii agreement, as later disclosed in Robert Lansing's book, following his resignation as Secretary of State, was startling in its revelations concerning the methods and motives of diplomacy as practiced by the Allied nations during the war, but particularly before America's entrance into the struggle.

In the first place Britain, France, Belgium, Russia, and Italy had signed secret agreements with Japan whereby they consented to Japan's permanent control of China's Shantung Province and the former German islands of the Pacific, which Japan had seized at the beginning of the war. These arrangements, which obviously had been signed in order to prevent Japan from deserting the Allied side, were kept secret from President Wilson, as the Allied diplomats realized that a knowledge of the secret treaties would have an adverse effect on American public opinion and conceivably might prevent the United States from entering the war. Lord Grey, chief British diplomatic emissary, stated later that he had informed President Wilson of the existence of the agreements, but if he did, President Wilson had not realized the actual import of the understandings. But even though the Japanese had "held up" the European Allies on the question of Japan's permanent possession of Shantung and the Pacific islands, the Japanese leaders nevertheless felt uneasy regarding possible American reactions when the agreements became public, as they certainly must, at the peace conference following the war.

According to Secretary Lansing's disclosures, he was astonished when a Japanese "ambassador of good will" named Baron Ishii arrived in Washington in November, 1917, with a proposal that America should recognize Japan's "special position" in China and the Western Pacific. Lansing said that he spurned the proposal as contrary to long-established American policy. But Baron Ishii had another string to his diplomatic bow. He went straight to New York and got in touch with a certain powerful financial leader who exercised potent influence with the Administration due to his financing of the war effort. Ishii succeeded in convincing this representative of American finance that it was necessary for the United States to recognize Japan's position, otherwise dire things might happen in the Orient. The clever Japanese diplomat then gravely shook his head, leaving the rest unsaid. Had Baron Ishii been in Peking he probably would have pounded on the table.

That night President Wilson received a confidential telephone call from New York over the private White House wire, and the next day Secretary Lansing received instructions from the President to sign the agreement with Ishii. Lansing claimed that he did so against his convictions, and sought to weaken the force of the agreement by inserting a qualifying phrase in the text to the effect that the agreement applied only where Chinese and Japanese territories were "propinquitous"—a new term in the already ambiguous language of diplomacy.

Secretary Lansing argued that the insertion of the word actually restricted the application of the agreement to South Manchuria, which bordered on the Japanese territory of Korea. However, the Secretary of State also was not aware of the secret agreements which Japan had already signed with the European Allies, copies of which Baron Ishii probably had in his pocket when he signed the pact with Lansing. Taken together, it meant that America had been tricked into signing an agreement diametrically opposed to American traditional policy in the Far East.

The secret treaties were disclosed by the Soviet authorities following their overthrow of the Czarist regime in 1917, and cast a blight over the heretofore friendly relations of the United States and China and also exercised potent influence in causing the United States Senate to refuse to ratify the Versailles Treaty and the League of Nations Covenant.

As a result of the rebuff to his policies and the developing complications in the relations of America and China, Dr. Reinsch resigned in 1919 and accepted a position as an adviser of the Chinese Government, in which capacity he attempted to rectify the damage by encouraging American businessmen and bankers to invest in China. However, the strain resulting from his disappointment was too great and while on a visit to General Wu Pei-fu, the Northern Chinese leader in Honan Province, he suffered a heat stroke. Dr. Reinsch was brought to Shanghai and died in a hospital there in January, 1924, without recovering his mental equilibrium.

The last chapter of the Lansing-Ishii incident, however, was written by the United States Senate following the Washington Arms Conference, when that august body voted unanimously to abrogate the agreement. The members of the Senate felt particularly exasperated over the Ishii incident as they had invited the Japanese "ambassador of good will" to address them on the subject of democracy in Japan when he was in Washington negotiating the agreement with the Secretary of State.

VII

Russians in Shanghai

IN THE FALL OF 1917 I had decided that it was time for my wife and young daughter to join me, so I cabled Mrs. Powell to come out and bring along my sister Margaret, who was a student in the School of Journalism at the University of Missouri. In the meantime I stayed on at the Astor House in Shanghai, in the "steerage" section, which consisted of single rooms and small suites at the back of the hotel. The section resembled an American club, because practically all of the rooms and suites were occupied by young Americans who had come out to join the consulate, commercial attaché's office, or business firms whose activities were undergoing rapid expansion.

Sanitary arrangements left much to be desired. There was no modern plumbing. The bathtub consisted of a large earthenware pot about four feet high and four feet in diameter. It was called a "soochow tub," due to its place of manufacture in a native pottery in the town of Soochow, about fifty miles from Shanghai. The Chinese servant assigned to me would carry in a seemingly endless number of buckets of hot water to fill the tub in the morning.

One of the consular clerks who lived in that section of the hotel cautioned me about keeping my room locked. He said, "Be sure to lock your door and leave the key with the boy, otherwise you are likely to have a visitor." Some days later I realized what he meant when I returned to my room late in the evening and found a young lady, wearing a Japanese kimono, asleep in my bed. I immediately called the boy and asked him what he meant by permitting her to enter my room. By this time the girl was awake and asked me, in pidgin English, if I was "Mr. Smith" who had sent for her. I assured her that I was not Mr. Smith, and the boy ushered her down the corridor. I spoke to Captain Morton, the manager, the next morning and he assured me that it would not happen again. The incident aroused considerable amusement among my friends, who called me "Mr. Smith" for several days thereafter.

My family arrived in mid-winter of 1917-18. I discovered too late that the influx of Americans had made it practically impossible to find a residence or an apartment except in some old English-style houses without modern conveniences. A friend told us of a new residential district known as the "Model Village," which some promoter had built to meet the influx of Americans. The village consisted of several rows of residences constructed of cheap mud bricks in a style the promoter thought was "American."

Although they were quite new, we had to exercise considerable care because the buildings were so flimsily constructed that we were frequently having embarrassing experiences. Once my wife was using the telephone, a heavy, cumbersome instrument attached to the wall which separated our house from the adjoining one. Suddenly there was a crash and the telephone, together with a large section of the partition, fell to the floor. Our neighboring housewife had also been using her telephone, which was attached to the other side of the wall, at the same time. The two ladies greeted each other through the opening. It was not unusual for the flimsy boards in the floor to give way while we were sitting at the dining-room table.

Life under these conditions, while trying, was not altogether unpleasant because the compound was filled with young American couples who were also pioneering. Housewives who had always done their own work and looked after their own children at home suddenly found themselves surrounded by servants. In our home we had two female servants or amahs, a cook, houseboy, and coolie. They all lived somewhere in the rear, which we never visited. Once, during a political crisis, my houseboy brought sixty-five of his relatives from the countryside to live in my garage until the storm blew over. I was informed that each paid him a small fee for the service. The Chinese, accustomed to adjusting themselves to meeting crises of this kind, were always practical. Once, when the situation in the Settlement was disturbed, many of the Chinese sent their wives and families to the country to live with their relatives. I asked my office boy (he was forty years old) if he had sent his wife to the country. He replied in characteristic English, "No send missie to country—if send missie to country, must pay money, but no can use."

Food was plentiful, and most of the housewives were accustomed to visiting the Hongkew Market conducted by the municipality. Many housewives experimented with native vegetables, and discovered that they were superior to familiar American items. The market was quite sanitary and provided every possible item of foreign and domestic food. I was told that the market greatly resembled the Fulton Market in New York City, except for the difference in food items. A visit to the market was almost a social event, because women would meet their friends there and compare notes as they visited the various stalls. The food was unbelievably cheap and generally of good quality. However, all green vegetables and fruits had to be dipped in a chemical solution to kill germs.

The American population, which had numbered only a few hundred when I arrived, grew rapidly as a result of the opening up of numerous business establishments. This led to the development of community activities in which I participated. During that first winter there were organized two American clubs, one a downtown businessmen's club and the other a country club on the outskirts of the city. The American School was organized, the most ambitious project of all, and was located in the French Concession. The school quickly became popular in the international community and was almost overwhelmed by applications from parents of other nationalities who wished to provide their children with an American education. A certain percentage of such children were admitted. American children had the opportunity of associating with children of other nationalities, including a considerable number of Chinese, and a few of mixed blood. Other nationalities were proud of the opportunity they had in sending their children to the American School, where they could receive American instruction and associate with American children.

The Americans also organized a Community Church, which was conducted on non-sectarian lines and soon became as popular in the community as the school. The pastors were carefully selected in the United States, and usually spent three years in Shanghai. Membership in the church also was not restricted to Americans.

The church had been in operation only a short time when a Japanese and his wife appeared on the scene and requested membership on the ground that they were Christians. The Japanese said that he had resided in the United States and could speak English. They seemed to be quite sincere, and it was not long before the man and his wife, who was of Japanese blood but born in America, were taking active part in the affairs of the church. The members were enthusiastic about Mr. Watanabe, who entered into the activities of the church with such enthusiasm. All proceeded happily until there was a Sino-Japanese crisis. A group of Americans visited the Japanese consulate, and were astonished to see Mr. Watanabe wearing a military uniform. Investigation disclosed that he was an intelligence officer in the army, and apparently had been assigned to the job of checking up on the religious and social activities of the American community. The next Sunday the familiar faces of the Japanese espionage officer and his wife were missing. They never attended church again. The incident attracted wide attention when it became known that Japanese army intelligence had used this method elsewhere in checking up on American missionary activities.

When I first arrived in Shanghai I was surprised to find that the Germans still went about the city in complete freedom and safety, despite the fact that they were involved in war with both the British and French, who occupied a dominating position in the city.

Two of the city's three leading clubs, the British Shanghai Club and the German Club, were located on the Bund, only about three blocks apart. The French Club, most popular in the international community, was located in the French Concession, several blocks distant. It was interesting, at noontime, to see the British and German businessmen passing each other on the Bund without a nod of recognition, each headed for his club for luncheon, where the chief subject of discussion was the war. Each club had a large mounted map of the western front, but the thumb tacks were on opposite sides of the line.

The situation changed, however, after China broke off relations with Germany in March, 1917. China's declaration of war on Germany automatically canceled the extraterritorial privileges which the Germans had enjoyed, and thus made them subject to Chinese law. The French immediately started an agitation for the deportation of the Germans from the International Settlement, and ultimately were able to exert sufficient pressure on the Chinese to cause Peking to adopt a deportation order applicable to all Germans and Austrians.

Things usually move slowly in China, however, and the matter of deporting the Germans was no exception to the general rule. Many Germans took advantage of the delay to move their possessions into Chinese territory, where they resided in boarding houses and received protection from local Chinese officials who paid no attention to the Peking Government's orders. As a matter of fact, public sentiment in Shanghai, particularly among the Chinese, deeply opposed the deportation of the Germans, so they were not deported until a considerable time after the Armistice. The Germans were greatly embittered by being driven out after the war was over, and their feelings were voiced in their publications in Shanghai as well as in the home press in Germany. Several books, including a novel, were widely circulated in Germany which were based on the alleged inhumanities involved in the Shanghai deportation. German bitterness over this incident undoubtedly was reflected in the later action of the Nazis in Shanghai as allies of the Japanese.

The Chinese Government, although it had been reluctant to declare war on Germany, soon discovered that the abolition of German extraterritorial rights enabled the Chinese to confiscate German possessions which included several banks, business houses, and community properties which long had served as social centers for the Germans. The German Club on the Bund was taken over by the Chinese Government and handed over to the Bank of China, while the German bank, also located on the Bund, was handed over to the Chinese Bank of Communications. Another large property which the Germans had purchased for the construction of a country club, located in the French Concession, was seized by the French and ultimately taken over by the French Club. The leading German drugstore, located on Nanking Road, was converted into an American company through the medium of a Delaware corporation, and from that time on flew the American flag, although the German personnel was not changed, and all of the German drug lines were retained. A clever American lawyer was responsible for the transformation.

But the most colorful phase of the international situation in Shanghai had to do not with the Germans, but with one of our former allies. One day during the winter of 1918-19 there was a report of a number of mysterious ships arriving at the mouth of the Yangtze River, several miles below Shanghai. As soon as I heard the report I hired a Chinese launch and made a trip to the mouth of the Yangtze. It was indeed a mysterious fleet. There must have been between thirty and forty ships of every possible description, most of them painted a dirty black. The "fleet" ranged all the way from small warcraft to harbor tugs, and there were even two large and powerful ice-breakers.

I directed the captain of my launch to approach one of the

larger warships. I finally attracted the attention of an officer, who came to the rail and spoke to me in Russian, which I could not understand. I indicated, however, that I wanted to come aboard. We finally came alongside, and with the assistance of sailors on the ship I managed to get on the gangplank and climbed the ladder to the deck. Incidentally, the Yangtze River at that point was quite wide and very rough.

When I reached the deck of the ship I was faced with a spectacle even stranger than the "fleet" itself. The deck of the ship was literally jammed with household equipment, ranging all the way from pots and pans to baby cribs. I noticed, not without amusement, that one Russian mother had hung out her babies' wash on one of the five-inch guns. I also noticed one almost new American automobile, a relic of the ill-fated American Siberian expedition.

After considerable delay the Russian commander of the boat found someone who could speak a little English. I was informed that the "fleet" was under the command of Admiral Stark, who had commanded Russian naval forces in the Far East during the war. The commander of the ship interrupted my questioning to tell me that they were greatly in need of food, as the supplies they had brought from Vladivostok were exhausted. He said they had evacuated Vladivostok on the eve of the Bolshevik occupation of that port. I asked him about the large number of women and children on board. He said many of them were the families of Russian navy men. In addition there were large numbers of other Russians, including women and children of civilians, who had gone aboard to escape the wrath of the Bolsheviks. The admiral wanted to land a large number of the civilians, but the Shanghai authorities had objected. Later most of them managed to leave the ships at night and come to Shanghai.

After remaining in the Yangtze River for several days, obtaining much-needed supplies which were donated by Shanghai charitable organizations, Admiral Stark sailed southward with his "fleet," finally ending up in Manila where most of the Rus-

sian evacuees became residents and where the "fleet" was broken
up and the ships sold. The Soviet Government later tried to
recover possession of these ships, but Admiral Stark had sold
them, and since the United States did not recognize Soviet
Russia, Moscow never succeeded in regaining possession. The
Bolsheviks were particularly anxious to recover the two ice-
breakers which were a vital necessity in Vladivostok Harbor
in the late fall and winter months, as the harbor freezes over
and it is necessary to use ice-breakers to keep it open for cargo
and fishing fleets.

The Russian emigrees who reached Shanghai by means of
Admiral Stark's "fleet" were the vanguard of an influx of Russians from Siberia and other parts of Russia as far west as
Moscow and Leningrad, which continued for several years. As
Shanghai was an open city where passport visas were not required, there was no way of restricting the flood of Russians
who came in by every train and ship from the north, most of
them in a destitute condition. The refugees included groups
from every possible class in Russia, ranging all the way from
indigent gypsy beggars to members of the nobility. Some of the
wealthier Russians managed to bring out with them considerable property in the form of jewelry. These people put up at
the best hotels and lived in luxury as long as the jewelry lasted.
Shanghai pawnshops were filled with these baubles, enabling
collectors to pick up many rare pieces for a fraction of their
original value. Some of these pieces of jewelry were of native
manufacture, containing rare precious and semi-precious stones
from the famous mines in the Urals.

The number of Russian emigrees who arrived in Shanghai
was never known accurately, but was estimated at from 25,000
to 50,000. Since the great majority were destitute, it was necessary for Shanghai to open soup kitchens in several parts of the
city, the funds being provided by local charitable organizations.

Among the refugees were a large number of soldiers, mainly
Cossacks who had served in the armies of the Czar and remained

loyal to him. They had escaped chiefly through Mongolia into Manchuria, and were accompanied by their families. A majority of the refugees came from small towns and villages all over Russia, but occasionally one met refugees in destitute condition who had previously been large landowners and prosperous businessmen in European Russia. Rich or poor, illiterate or educated, they had one thing in common, namely, hatred of the Bolsheviks who had dispossessed them and forced them to flee from their native land and to depend on foreigners. Prior to the influx of Russian emigrees, Shanghai had only had a half dozen Russian families, chiefly rich managers of tea companies or persons who had been connected with the large Russo-Asiatic Bank, the main branch of which in the Far East was located in Shanghai, with a palatial building on the Shanghai Bund.

Much to the surprise of everyone the Russian emigrees did not long constitute a problem from the standpoint of support. They quickly gained a foothold in the city. The former Cossack soldiers became bodyguards for rich Chinese merchants, who were in constant fear of blackmail or assassination, or they obtained jobs as night watchmen at banks and business houses throughout the city. Finally the International Settlement organized a so-called Russian Volunteer Corps as a part of the International Volunteer Corps which protected the city.

Hundreds of Russian women were assisted in opening fashionable dress shops, millinery shops, and beauty parlors. In addition other Russians, many of whom were Jews, opened a host of notion shops, selling everything from needles to baby carriages. Of course there were the ubiquitous Russian restaurants, one or two in almost every block, particularly in the French Concession where the majority of the Russians resided. Shanghai thus received its first introduction to Russian food, which immediately became popular in the foreign and Chinese communities. The Russians filled an important niche in the city, occupying a position between the normal white-collared Occidental population and the Chinese who did all the work.

Since Shanghai had always been a man's city in which a majority of the normal foreign population were bachelors, numerous friendships inevitably developed, culminating in large numbers of international marriages. These included many members of the United States Marine Corps stationed in Shanghai. Once I asked the chaplain of the Marine Corps whether these marriages were successful. He replied—in rather cynical vein, I thought—"As successful as any other kind." It became popular to speak Russian, and it was a poor bank clerk indeed who could not afford an attractive Russian teacher. The Russians even came to exercise considerable political influence in the affairs of the city. When I arrived in Shanghai there was not a single Russian church in the city. Ten years later, after the White Russian influx, there were more than a dozen Russian Orthodox churches, some of them large and richly decorated. The support of so many churches attested to the deeply religious nature of the White Russians. I do not think I ever visited a Russian home without seeing at least one sacred ikon, and often there would be one in every room and usually with a small incense burner and oil lamp attached which was kept burning. Almost the entire foreign community turned out to observe the colorful Russian services at Christmas and Easter.

VIII

Editor As Lobbyist

SINCE THE *Review* was now on its feet, I decided in the autumn of 1920 to make a trip to the United States in order to establish advertising contacts for the paper.

A few days prior to my sailing, J. Harold Dollar, Far Eastern representative of the Dollar Steamship interests, who was chairman of the American Chamber of Commerce, invited me to a farewell luncheon at the American Club. I was surprised at the turnout of prominent residents, and wondered what was up.

At the close of the luncheon Carl Seitz, a well known lumber merchant, got up and after the usual pleasantries, turned to me and said: "J. B., we want you to go to Washington and put through a China Trade Act, providing Federal incorporation for American concerns doing business in the Far East."

He then explained that the Chamber of Commerce would defray my hotel expenses if I would go to Washington and see what could be done about inducing Congress to pass our incorporation act. He was sure it would require "only a few weeks" to convince Congress of the necessity of this greatly desired measure.

I agreed to undertake the mission. I had never been in Washington, and was anxious to see what made the wheels go 'round in our national capital.

In traveling from the West Coast to New York I stopped over in Chicago and paid a visit to the famous Colonel Robert R. McCormick. I had covered two or three special assignments for the *Chicago Tribune*, and the Colonel asked me to stop over and see him. While I was talking with him I mentioned the matter of the incorporation bill which our commercial interests in the Far East desired to get through Congress, and told him that the Chamber of Commerce had commissioned me to make a trip to Washington and see what could be done about the matter. This gave the Colonel an idea. He said: "You catch the midnight train, and that will put you in Marion, Ohio, at 6 o'clock tomorrow morning. I will telegraph Phil Kinsley, our political correspondent, to meet you and introduce you to President-elect Harding."

This surpassed my fondest expectations—an opportunity to meet the President-elect of the United States and solicit his support for our incorporation bill.

I was at the famous little frame house with the front porch in Marion by 6:30 the next morning, and a few minutes later had found Phil Kinsley and explained my business. Kinsley said, "Let's go over and catch Harding before the nut brigade starts in."

I asked him what he meant by the nut brigade and he said, the visionaries with schemes for post-war Europe and world peace. He took me to the reception room, which was empty at that early hour, so I sat there and examined the scenery from the not-too-clean windows leading out on the famous front porch. As I sat there a rather portly individual arrived. His face appeared familiar, but I couldn't place him. Shortly afterward the attendant came out and calling my name, said Mr. Harding was waiting, but before I could get to the door, the portly gentleman who had come in later pushed me aside, stating he wanted to go in first because he had to catch a train back to New York. He also explained to me that he had a very important matter concerning world peace which he wished to discuss with the President-elect. Without further comment he pushed past me and went in. I waited fully an hour before he came out. Mr. Harding said, as he smilingly handed me a cigarette, "That was Nicholas Murray Butler."

He looked at my card and said, "I see you come from China."

I told him I had just arrived, and explained to him as briefly as I could the purpose of my visit to Marion. He listened with unexpected interest and told me he had always been curious about China because he had an aunt who had been a missionary in that country. I found out afterward his aunt had been a missionary in India, but I had become accustomed to having Americans confuse India with China, and even with Africa, when it came to the matter of missionaries.

I gave Mr. Harding a small booklet I had written about our proposed Federal incorporation act, and told him about the growing importance of American commerce in the Far East, how the new law would facilitate the development of American trade and would in time restore American business prestige which had been damaged, due to exploitation by adventurers and fly-by-night promoters. He said: "I can't do anything for you until I get to Washington, but if you will come to see me at the White House, I will do everything I can to help you get your bill through Congress."

As President, Mr. Harding lived up to that promise, and we became well acquainted in the months to come. I soon discovered, however, that the matter of getting a bill through Congress, unless it concerned some large national interest, cannot be accomplished in a few weeks—it usually requires months, and often years, and is a heart-breaking process. But whenever I got into a jam, I could always obtain help by writing a letter to President Harding about it.

Since I had had no experience whatever as a lobbyist, I consulted some of my newspaper friends about what to do to get a bill through Congress. This usually drew a laugh, particularly at the Press Club. Some of the veterans explained to me that Washington was crowded with people who had come to the Capitol "to get a bill through Congress" in the expectation that it would take a few weeks. They had stayed on and on, and in many cases the lobbying job became their sole source of support. I soon found out that my newness was an advantage, because I did not fall into the routine of the professionals. Also I worked like the very dickens interviewing Congressmen and others who could help.

I finally found a Congressman, Leonidas C. Dyer of St. Louis, who agreed to foster my bill. Dyer was a Republican, and was looking for some measure that would help him get his name in the newspapers. The incorporation bill which I was interested in served that purpose because it was concerned with foreign trade, a subject that was becoming prominent through the demand for our goods, resulting from the war. Congressman Dyer was a member of the House Judiciary Committee. I suggested to him that some other committee, possibly the House Committee on Foreign Affairs, might be more suitable, but he objected to that and I quickly discovered that tremendous jealousies exist between members of different committees.

While I was a student in the University of Missouri I had taken several courses concerning the general subject of government, but nothing I had ever studied in the university was of any value to me in this matter of getting a bill through Congress.

Congressman Dyer said the first thing we should do was to hold a "hearing," at which witnesses could be brought in to testify to the merits of the bill which we wanted to get through. We fixed a day, about a week in the future, and I got busy on witnesses. I induced several import and export houses in New York to send their foreign trade representatives to Washington, and on the day of the hearing I surprised everybody by bringing in the Secretary of Commerce, Herbert Hoover, to attend our hearing. Hoover had once been a mining engineer in China.

Everything went off in good order, except that two Senators got up and walked out in indignation when Secretary Hoover came in. I was astonished to learn that these gentlemen were not on speaking terms with the Secretary of Commerce, and one Senator told me that Hoover's support of our bill was likely to do more harm than good. However, we had our hearings printed in a special edition of the *Congressional Record*. I then arranged for copies to be mailed out to chambers of commerce, whose interest in the matter I was soliciting.

After a conference with Congressman Dyer we decided to call our proposed law "The China Trade Act," thus taking advantage of the growing interest in Far Eastern trade all over the country. It soon became apparent to me that the matter of getting a bill through Congress was a leg-breaking job, because it was necessary to see so many people. Once I nearly precipitated a small civil war between the State Department and the Department of Commerce. At first I was not able to arouse any interest in my project in either of those departments (aside from Secretary Hoover), but after I got the thing started and the chambers of commerce became interested in it, members of both departments began to prick up their ears. If Congress was going to pass our bill, then each department wanted to have a hand in the eventual administration of the law. Since our bill was concerned with trade, it naturally seemed to me that it should be under the administration of the Commerce Department, but the solicitor of the State Department did not agree with me, and we had a wordy battle about it at one of the hearings.

I found that one of the chief difficulties in getting a bill through Congress is that you can never get it through both houses in the same session. On two or three occasions we got the bill through the House, or the Senate, but the session would end before we could get them together for a conference to pass the final measure. Once we got it through the Senate and were all set for action in the House when Speaker Gillett (Massachusetts) told us they had many more important matters on and there was no time to bring up our precious bill.

I decided to try a little strategy. I went to Boston and got in touch with a banker who had been in the Far East and was interested in promoting trade with China. He gave me a luncheon at the Bankers Club, and invited the foreign trade representatives of the leading companies in the Boston district to attend. While I was explaining the purpose of the measure, there was an interruption at the door and our chairman, Mr. Weed, looked up and said:

"Why, there's the Mayor! Come in, Mayor, I want you to meet a man from China."

Mayor "Andy" Peters came in and sat down next to me. Turning to me, he said:

"But you aren't a Chinese, what are you doing in China?"

I started to explain the object of my trip, but I could see that his mind was a hundred miles away on some other subject. While I was talking to him I was toying with a Chinese silver dollar which I had brought along with me as a pocket piece. The Mayor happened to notice it and was tremendously interested, as it was the first Chinese coin he had ever seen. Turning to me he said:

"I'd give almost anything for two of those."

I said, "Well, Mayor, that isn't necessary. I have two of them, and here they are."

He said, "I want to take these dollars home and give them to my boys; both are coin collectors, and they will be supremely happy to get these Chinese dollars," and then turning to me he said:

"Now tell me what you want."

I then explained to him again the main features of the China Trade Act and told him how we thought it would improve the prestige and efficiency of American commercial activities in China. Sending for a bunch of telegraph blanks, Mayor Peters sent telegrams to all members of the Massachusetts delegation in Congress, urging them to bring our bill up for a vote and give it their full support.

When I returned to Washington a few days later I went around with Congressman Dyer to call on Speaker Gillett. We found Gillett quite friendly and he agreed to put our bill on the schedule, saying "I find there is a lot of interest in Boston in this measure."

I was almost tempted to remark, "Yes, it cost me two Chinese dollars," but refrained.

A few days later the House passed our bill, and it went to conference and ultimately emerged as the first Federal act ever passed for the incorporation of commercial companies directly under the government. At the final conference a clause was inserted specifying that the act was to be administered by the Department of Commerce, which cost me a complete snub the next time I met the solicitor of the State Department.

The China Trade Act, which was of great assistance to small business enterprises, unexpectedly fitted in nicely with Mr. Hoover's plans for the expansion of American business in China following the war. Previously, the Department of Commerce had maintained only one representative in China, Mr. Julean Arnold, long stationed at Peiping. After the passage of the China Trade Act the department sent a large number of experts, each experienced in his line, who made a thorough investigation of economic conditions in China. Much of America's trade expansion in China, leading finally to our leadership in that market, resulted from the foundation laid at that time.

I don't know how many millions of dollars of American capital were represented in corporations which had received corporate charters under the China Trade Act, but they ran into big figures. While it was impossible for Congress to interfere with that well known institution the "Delaware company," it was not long before China Trade Act companies began to enjoy greater prestige in the Orient, and in recent years practically all important American firms doing business in the Far East have been incorporated under the regulations of the China Trade Act.

I should have mentioned the fact that one of the advantages provided by the China Trade Act was a tax provision which put American firms on an equal basis with British firms which were incorporated under the regulations of the British Crown Colony of Hong Kong.

In this connection, I had an interesting and significant session with Senator La Follette, the elder. While I was promoting the

China Trade Act among members of Congress, I was astonished one day to see an interview in one of the papers in which Senator La Follette expressed strong opposition to the proposed China Trade Act. He alleged that it was a scheme for helping the big corporations, such as Standard Oil and United States Steel, to exploit China. I immediately sensed that some interested party had been supplying Mr. La Follette with misinformation. As a matter of fact, we had never been able to interest any of the Standard Oil companies in the China Trade Act, because they were already incorporated under State laws and, of course, were not interested in making any changes, and the same was true for other big companies. The concerns which the China Trade Act was designed to assist were smaller companies, particularly new ones which were engaging in business in the Far East for the first time and needed the prestige and security which such an act could give them. The big concerns which were already established did not need the prestige, hence were not interested in our measure. But this did not satisfy Senator La Follette, who had found a new stick with which to belabor the big corporations, his favorite exercise.

I consulted with my friends about it, and suggested that I go and see La Follette, but immediately there was a chorus of objections.

"Don't go to see him; he will use your arguments against you, and you can't trust him."

As a boy I had lived in the Chautauqua belt and heard many of La Follette's speeches, particularly those directed against the big corporations. I did not agree with those who contended that he was just another politician. I decided to go and see him. Luckily I had obtained, before I left Shanghai, a copy of the incorporation laws which had been adopted in the Crown Colony of Hong Kong. These laws entitled British companies to incorporate under the regulations of the Crown Colony of Hong Kong, in which manner they were able to escape the heavy war taxes to which companies incorporated in England were subject. It was this advantage of British companies in their competition with American concerns in the Far East that we wished to overcome. I took along with me, when I called on Senator La Follette, a copy of the Hong Kong ordinances.

When the eminent Wisconsin Senator saw those books about Hong Kong he was fascinated with them, and I thought I would never get them back. It was the first information he had ever received that Hong Kong was a British colony. He apparently had been under the impression all along that Hong Kong was merely an island dependency. He was not aware of the fact that the British had developed a government in Hong Kong which included a legislature, and that all property-owning citizens, regardless of sex, color, or race, could vote. La Follette was so fascinated by this information that he invited me to call on him again and ultimately gave us some of his time in the Senate, so that we got our bill through. I have often thought that our shipping people might have avoided much grief if they had also gone to La Follette at the time he was fostering the original Seamen's Acts, because La Follette came from an interior State and had little conception of shipping or maritime problems from the standpoint of international competition. He therefore believed everything the maritime union leaders told him. As for the union leaders, they did not seem to realize that if American ships could not compete with the British or Japanese, there obviously could be no jobs for American seamen.

One day the floor clerk at the Washington Hotel, where I resided while conducting my lobbying activities, brought me a calling card bearing the name "Mary Elizabeth Wood." I went down to the lobby and stood transfixed. Mary Elizabeth Wood was about sixty years old, was dressed entirely in black with a skirt that swept the floor, and a high stiff collar which came up to her ears. She explained to me that she had been engaged in missionary work for some forty years in China. She said that she had heard there was a prospect that Congress would vote to return to China for educational purposes several millions of dollars which we had taken from China to cover our losses in the Boxer Rebellion. If Congress did take this action Miss Wood wanted to get some of the money for developing modern libraries in China. She wanted to know what to do.

I thought a minute, and noticing a copy of the *Congressional Record* on my table, I had an idea. Taking up the book, I pointed out the list of members of the House and Senate and said:

"If you will take that book and call on every man whose name appears there and explain your proposition, perhaps you can put it over."

I had no idea she would take me seriously, but she did, and all through the fall and winter I used to see Miss Wood's familiar figure in the corridors as she called on the various members, taking them in alphabetical order.

Months after, when the House passed the bill returning the Boxer indemnity, there were a dozen members on their feet yelling, "What about Mary Elizabeth Wood's libraries?"

She got her libraries, of course.

IX

Shantung and Washington

OWING TO CONTINUOUS DELAYS, my stay in Washington was extended until late in 1921, when it was announced that President Harding had decided to call a conference for the purpose of limiting naval armament and settling Far Eastern problems. I decided to remain in Washington for the conference.

A few days later I happened to meet William J. H. Cochran, of Missouri, who had been publicity director of the Democratic National Committee during the Wilson incumbency. I asked Cochran what he thought of Harding's action in calling the Arms Limitation Conference. His reply was characteristic of the prevailing sentiment among the hard-boiled Washington correspondents.

Cochran said, "The Republicans are under strong obligations to do something to help China, because Harding owes his election to the Shantung Question, more than any other single issue." I asked him what he meant by the statement. He replied, "Of all the issues in the campaign, the best vote-getter the Republicans had was the Shantung Question. Harding himself frequently used the term 'rape of Shantung,' in his pre-election addresses." We verified this by referring to the *New York Times* index covering speeches delivered by the various candidates during the campaign. Every candidate on the Republican side from Harding down had repeatedly mentioned the Shantung case and the "rape of China," in endeavoring to discredit the Versailles Treaty and the League of Nations Covenant.

The public, during the campaign, also heard a great deal about the secret treaties Japan had exacted from the other Allies in which they had agreed to support Japan's demands at the

71

peace conference. These treaties not only confirmed Japan's possession of Shantung, but of more serious import to the United States the Allies also had agreed to Japan's control of the Marshall, Caroline, and Marianas Islands. Our naval people realized the danger, but they were helpless in arousing the public to an understanding of the menace of Japan, whose strategic position had been greatly strengthened in the war.

What was the Shantung Question?

About 1898, when it appeared that China was on the point of dissolution, Kaiser Wilhelm, not to be outdone by Britain and the other Powers, seized Kiaochow Bay, the best harbor on the East China coast. His justification for seizing this port was the murder of two German Catholic missionaries by Chinese bandits in Shantung Province. When the Kaiser seized Kiaochow Bay, he also took over a small Chinese fishing village known as Tsingtao. In order to outdo the British and Russians, the Kaiser sent some of his best city planners to Tsingtao, and they cleared off the dirty Chinese town and laid out the most attractive port on the China coast. It was like a little bit of Germany, had clean paved streets, attractive stores and residences, and quickly became the most popular seaside resort on the coast. The Germans also obtained a concession from the Chinese to build a railroad extending inland for a distance of about 250 miles, and connecting with the trunk-line Tientsin-Nanking R.R. at Tsinan, capital of the province. This was about the extent of German "aggression" in China before World War I.

The Japanese, of course, did not like the German development on the China coast any more than they had liked Russian development at Dairen, or British naval development at the port of Wei-hai-wei a few miles to the north of Tsingtao. Therefore when World War I broke out the Japanese wasted no time in launching an attack on Tsingtao. The Germans kept only a small garrison at Tsingtao, but the German forts were so well constructed, with modern revolving turrets, that the Japs never did succeed in getting inside the harbor with their fleet. They finally captured Tsingtao, but they had to do it by invading Chinese territory and attacking from the land side. When the Germans saw there was no chance of relief, they capitulated and were interned for the duration of the war. It was said that the great Japanese beer industry dated from this period, because the interned Germans taught the Japanese the art of making beer.

I once asked Dr. Sao-ke Alfred Sze, the Chinese Ambassador, why the Chinese raised such strong objection to Japan in Shantung, when they made no objection to the Germans. Dr. Sze replied, "The Germans were constructive, while the Japanese were destructive." The Germans adhered to the original treaty, but the Japs went beyond the treaty and overran the entire province. Also the Japs introduced the "dope" trade into the province and were actively demoralizing the Chinese by means of morphine and heroin, which the Japanese manufactured from opium in enormous quantities in their concession at Tientsin. Morphine and heroin, though chemical derivatives of opium, are far more harmful than the original opium, with which the Chinese were already familiar.

Americans were deeply stirred by the Japanese occupation of Shantung because it constituted a violation of the Open Door policy which had been traditional with us since the days of Secretary of State John Hay, but behind the Shantung issue was the more important matter of Japan's control of the Mandated Islands—the Marshalls, Carolines, and Marianas, which Japan had also seized from Germany at the beginning of the war. These islands constituted an impenetrable barrier between us and the Philippines, and the continent of Asia, despite the fact that the Japs had agreed not to fortify the islands.

As Cochran explained to me, the Republicans were under heavy obligations to do something about the so-called Far Eastern Question "because they owed their election largely to this issue." Cochran, of course, admitted that behind this incentive was a desire on the part of some members of the new Administration to uphold traditional American policies in the Far East, particularly the Open Door in China. Turning to me he said, "You have lived in China, what about the Open Door?"

I explained that along about 1898–1900 it appeared that China was on the point of being divided among the Powers. Russia had taken advantage of the Boxer incident to overrun Manchuria, Great Britain had established herself in the Yangtze Valley, and had taken steps to develop a naval base at the port of Wei-hai-wei. Germany had seized Kiaochow Bay, and was building a naval base at Tsingtao. The Japanese, who were late at the banquet, were preparing to fight the Russians for a share of Manchuria. The French had Indo-China, and a concession on the South China coast at Kwangchowan.

The Americans were definitely left out with no concessions, or spheres of influence, on the continent of Asia. It was at this point that Secretary of State John Hay made his proposal for an "Open Door" doctrine in Asia. Since Hay had been Minister to Great Britain, it was suspected that Great Britain was behind the program. And such was the case, as British commercial interests realized that the trade of a unified China was worth more than the exclusive trade of a section of the country.

The British also did not want to face the consequences of carving up a nation of 400,000,000 souls. They feared repercussions in European politics. A mission to the Far East, headed by Admiral Lord Beresford, had advised against the dismemberment of the Chinese Empire. Beresford had returned by way of Washington and consulted with the Americans.

Hence the Open Door, proposed in a series of notes to the other Powers by John Hay. It amounted to a repudiation of the "sphere of influence" policies of the other nations. The Open Door in the Far East took its place with the Monroe Doctrine as an American foreign policy.

We had heeded Washington's advice about keeping free of

Europe's quarrels (up to World War I), but never hesitated to involve ourselves in Asiatic politics, seemingly without objection on the part of the American public.

And now to return to the subject of the Conference:

After considerable thought the State Department finally decided to invite the Chinese to send a delegation. It was the first time China had ever sat in an international conference as a "free and independent Power." This element aroused so much enthusiasm in China that the Government sent a delegation of about three hundred persons, including secretaries, stenographers, and assistants; so many in fact that Dr. Sze, the Minister, had difficulty in feeding and housing them.

Since the State Department's invitation was sent to the Peking Government, the Kuomintang regime at Canton immediately raised a tremendous howl and sent a rival delegation which sniped at the Peking delegates throughout the meeting. There was even an attempt to assassinate Dr. Sun at Canton during the conference.

The Japanese were not enthusiastic about the Washington Conference, and approached the meeting somewhat in the mood of a naughty child called to the teacher's desk for a reprimand. They were suspicious of the conference because they knew it was designed primarily to obstruct their schemes for China. But with their potential ally, Germany, out of the running and with Russia involved in a communist revolution at her very back door, the Japanese felt it would be better to attend than stay out. Japan's acceptance of the invitation was actually not received until two weeks after all the other official acceptances were in; and it was widely reported that Japan's decision to attend the conference resulted from assurances from British sources that Japan "would not be treated badly" at the meeting. However, any assurances from British circles could hardly have carried much weight, in view of the fact that one of the chief objectives of the conference, though not stated in the formal invitation, was to abrogate the Anglo-Japanese alliance.

Although strong opposition to the continuance of the Anglo-Japanese alliance had developed in the United States during the war, it was the opposition of the Dominion of Canada that forced Great Britain to give serious consideration to the matter of discontinuing the pact. The Canadians felt, as did Americans, that the belligerent clauses in the alliance imposed dangerous obligations on Great Britain in the event of an outbreak of war between Japan and the United States. The Canadians, due to the geographical situation of the two countries, also had experienced complications with Japan over immigration questions. Immigration complications which the United States had experienced with Japan in California in 1908 were paralleled in Canada. Thus, when American-Japanese relations became acute in 1921, the Dominion of Canada was more affected by the so-called "North American" point of view as opposed to the London "imperial" viewpoint. In consequence there developed in Canada a national demand for termination of the alliance.

Arthur Meighen, the Canadian Premier, urged the substitution of a four-Power conference on Pacific affairs, to be participated in by the United States, Britain, China, and Japan. But at the Imperial Conference in London Meighen's efforts met strong opposition not only from Lloyd George, but from Curzon, Balfour, and Lee, all of whom feared the menace of an antagonized Japan toward India and Britain's other territorial and economic stakes in Eastern Asia and the Pacific. In the hot debate which ensued the delegates from Australia, New Zealand and India sided with Britain, while South Africa favored revision rather than abrogation. But Meighen stood his ground, and ultimately brought the imperial conference around to his point of view. It was this discussion in the Imperial Conference, plus England's desire to reach an understanding with the United States on the limitation of naval construction, that paved the way for the calling of the Washington Conference.

Aside from France and Italy, which possessed naval armament of considerable strength, and also held concessions in China, the other European Powers invited to the conference—

Netherlands, Belgium, and Portugal—held either concessions in China or colonial territories in the region of the Pacific.

The conference in many ways was of unusual significance: it was America's initial attempt to invoke an international conference for the purpose of reaching a peaceful settlement of questions which had long threatened war in the Pacific. Attendance was entirely voluntary in the sense that the conference was not made up of delegates representing victorious and vanquished nations, as had been the case at Versailles. The British delegation was made up of representatives not only of Great Britain but of Canada, Australia, New Zealand, and India.

European and Japanese delegates were astonished when Charles E. Hughes, chairman of the American delegation, announced at the opening session that the United States was prepared to stop its naval building program and, more, was prepared to scrap a number of warships which were in an advanced stage of construction. The American proposal was so contrary to professional diplomatic practice that the delegates stared at each other in wonderment, but it was a proposal which the British could hardly afford to contest, since the British Admiralty was already concerned by the American naval construction program.

It was finally agreed that the Anglo-Japanese alliance would be abandoned, and Japan was persuaded to accept a 5:5:3 naval ratio with the United States and Great Britain. A compensation for Japan was the agreement that the United States would not increase or continue its construction of fortifications on naval and military positions west of the 180th meridian. American naval experts did their best in private to prevent the limiting of our fortifications on naval positions in the Western Pacific, and also to prevent the curtailment of the United States naval building program, but they fought a losing fight.

All of the agreements, resolutions, and proposals at the conference were more or less linked together around the central document, which was the Nine-Power Treaty with China, upon which all commitments depended, including the major issue of limitation of naval armament and curtailment of construction on naval bases in the Pacific area. The Nine-Power Treaty came to be known as the "Chinese Charter of Liberty," because it put an end to the old sphere-of-influence doctrine which had obsessed Europe and Japan, and for more than a quarter of a century had threatened dismemberment of China. Aside from the Nine-Power Treaty, the Washington Conference also adopted other measures concerned with the future development of China as a unified state. The Japanese were forced to withdraw their troops from Shantung Province and restore the former German interests at Tsingtao, including control of the port and railway running into the interior of the province, to Chinese control. The conference also approved a resolution to send a delegation to China to investigate the relinquishment of extraterritoriality, which had hampered the development of modern Chinese courts and had infringed upon the sovereignty of the country. It also was recommended that steps be taken to assist China in modernizing her currency and her fiscal system, and finally the Powers agreed to withdraw their postal agencies from China and consented to the calling of a conference to revise the Chinese tariff, leading in the direction of tariff autonomy. Also of importance from the standpoint of Russian interests in the Far East, the Japanese were forced to withdraw their troops from Siberia, where they had been stationed since World War I.

I attended the various plenary sessions and sat in the press section, from which point it was possible to observe the workings of the conference. There were several amusing incidents which were not on the agenda. One occurred when the gallery shouted for Aristide Briand, head of the French Legation. William Jennings Bryan, ex-Secretary of State, and outstanding pacifist, sat in the front row of the visitors' gallery facing the press. Bryan's benign countenance had become familiar at receptions. He was quite happy over the arms-scrapping phases of the conference, and insisted that this was a direct result of his efforts on behalf of world peace. When the crowd yelled for Briand, Bryan thought they were calling for him and was on his feet before a friend seized his coat-tail and pulled him down.

The French displayed little enthusiasm for the conference and, while they agreed to restore to China the French-leased territory at Kwangchowan, southwest of Canton, they did so with poor grace and actually never carried out the terms of their agreement.

Another amusing incident at the first plenary session also concerned the French. The various delegations were grouped about the large rectangular table in alphabetical order, America first, then Britain, China, and so on. The heads of the various delegations at the opening session used the English language, until they reached the French, who insisted on speaking in French. It was the first important international conference in which French was not the official language. The French insistence on use of their own language necessitated a considerable delay while Briand's remarks were translated into English. The next day one of the Washington columnists referred to the French as "the only foreigners at the conference." This statement, plus a cartoon in one of the Baltimore papers showing La Belle France in the act of trying on the old German military helmet, caused the French to lodge an official protest with the State Department regarding the anti-French attitude of the Washington press.

Secretary of State Charles E. Hughes was the outstanding figure at the conference, but he resembled more the religious crusader than the statesman. There were two occasions during the conference when Hughes pounded on the table to enforce his point; the first concerned the scrapping of naval vessels, and the second occurred when he reminded the Japanese of their promise to evacuate Siberia. He accused them of violating an understanding with the United States and Britain when the decision was made to intervene in Siberia in the latter months of the World War. Each nation had agreed to send one division of troops for use in policing the railways to the east of Lake

Baikal. The United States sent 7,000 troops; the Japanese sent 70,000 and occupied the entire coast from Sakhalin Island down. Since the American troops had been evacuated from Siberia, Secretary Hughes asked the Japanese flatly what they intended to do. The question brought forth from the Japanese a mumbled reply that they were already making a plan for evacuation. The United States had turned down the application of the Russian Soviets to send a delegation to the conference, but the action of Secretary Hughes was of very great service to the Russians, who at that time lacked military power to force the Japanese evacuation of their Far Eastern territory.

The Japanese delegation retained counsel during the conference. Their legal advisers were the well-known firm of Cadwalader, Wickersham and Taft. The Taft was Henry, brother of President Taft, while Mr. Wickersham had served as Attorney-General.

Dr. Alfred Sze, chairman of the Chinese delegation, was responsible for another amusing story which was repeated about Washington during the conference. After the Japanese had finally yielded to pressure and announced their intention of withdrawing their troops from Shantung, Secretary Hughes issued instructions for the Chinese and Japanese delegates to confer at once in order to arrange the details of the Japanese evacuation. Secretary Hughes remarked, "I am an old man and I want to see the Shantung Question settled before I die." He authorized the American and the British delegations to appoint observers to sit in on the Shantung conversation, to see that the terms were carried out. The British representative was Sir John Jordan, former British Minister, an expert on China. The American observer was John Van Antwerp MacMurray, former American chargé d'affaires at Peking and later Chief of the Far Eastern Division of the State Department. At one of the sessions, when the Chinese and Japanese delegates were discussing the disposition of German properties, the Japanese, for some reason, insisted on keeping control of the municipal laundry in Tsingtao, an institution which had been established by the Germans. After squabbling over the control of this municipal property for several hours, Dr. Sze whispered to MacMurray, "Let the Japs have the laundry—the Chinese have always had the reputation of being the world's laundrymen. We are now glad to permit the Japs to share some of that reputation."

Why did the Washington Conference fail? A cynical newspaper friend recently declared: "It had to fail because the Republican Administration lacked sincerity—they never intended to put the provisions of the conference into effect. They were only interested in one thing, reduction of taxes; and they accomplished that objective by scuttling the American fleet. The adoption of the so-called 5:5:3 naval program which gave us equality with Great Britain was only a subterfuge, as there was no intention to maintain our end of the bargain. Neither the Coolidge nor the Hoover Administration constructed a single new warship. Coolidge was too stingy to spend any money, and Hoover, the Quaker, was opposed to any kind of a navy on principle. As for Harding, he never had any ideas on the subject aside from those of the Republican bosses, who wanted to save money and reduce taxes. Our fleet paid the penalty."

But this cynical view obviously did not tell the whole story. Another friend elaborated: "We were all responsible for the failure of the Washington Conference because we were a disillusioned people. The let-down and disillusionment which followed the war were so complete that we permitted the pacifists and internationalists and paid propagandists representing foreign interests to dominate our national policy. The Japs were quick to take advantage of this situation, ready-made for their purposes. It was estimated that the Japs expended no less than $10,000,000 annually in the United States on their various propaganda schemes."

A Chinese friend, too independent-minded to be in office, also explained the predicament of China resulting from the Washington Conference: "They gave us a charter of liberty, but failed to provide the means for making our new independence effective. Take the case of extraterritoriality—many months elapsed before the United States appointed its delegates to the international conference authorized to make an investigation. Silas H. Strawn, of Chicago, head of the American delegation, finally denounced the State Department for its dilatoriness. Worst of all, America continued to grant diplomatic recognition to the most reactionary elements in China, the military factions which supported the Peking Government, while ignoring Dr. Sun Yat-sen and his Kuomintang associates who were developing a more modern nationalist form of government. Finally, it was largely the fault of the United States and Great Britain that the new Nationalist Government at Canton was permitted to come under Russian influence."

X

Wars in the North

THE WASHINGTON ARMS CONFERENCE concluded its work on February 6, 1922, and since the China Trade Act had passed both houses of Congress and was in the hands of the conference committee, I decided to return to Shanghai immediately. At that time I felt very optimistic over the developments in Washington. I had succeeded in accomplishing what had been regarded as almost impossible in inducing Congress to enact a Federal incorporation law for firms engaged in foreign trade in the Orient.

In addition to this the Washington Conference had laid the foundation for a new deal in American policy in the Far East. Its chief accomplishment, it seemed to me, was the enhancement of American prestige in China. The United States at last had assumed a position of leadership, and through peaceful means had induced the other nations to agree to the fundamentals of American policy, particularly the Open Door and the establishment of a guarantee of China's political and territorial integrity as an independent nation.

Conditions in China, however, were far from encouraging when I arrived in Shanghai on the S.S. *Silver State* on May 4, 1922. The first of a series of "wars" between Marshal Chang Tso-lin, War Lord of Manchuria, who was supposed to have Japanese support, and General Wu Pei-fu, leading militarist of North China, had just broken out. Due to the interest in China aroused by the Washington Conference, the conflict received big headlines in the American papers.

I made a trip to Peking to survey the situation, and was interested to see that there was little disturbance of business or

83

even of railway travel. The only evidence of the war was the
frequent stops of our train to permit military specials to pass.
Chinese farmers along the way were working in their fields as
usual. I found that the northern provinces which made a pre-
tense of loyalty to the central government at Peking were controlled by politicians and militarists interested only in increasing
their own power. General Wu Pei-fu, with headquarters at
Loyang, was in process of defeating Chang Tso-lin with the
help of General Feng Yu-hsiang, the Christian General. I was
somewhat nonplussed to learn that Dr. Sun Yat-sen in Canton
was allegedly in alliance with Marshal Chang Tso-lin against
Wu Pei-fu. However, the alliance came to nothing, because
Wu Pei-fu succeeded in driving Chang Tso-lin back to Manchuria before Dr. Sun got started.

General Wu Pei-fu, who came nearer to unifying the country than any other leader during the difficult phase of the
"period of the War Lords," from 1922 to the advent of Generalissimo Chiang Kai-shek in 1928, was in many ways an able
and colorful figure. He always startled foreigners who interviewed him, because his appearance differed considerably from
the average Chinese of the northern provinces. Wu had a red
mustache, his head was longer, his forehead higher, and his nose
more prominent than the average. Also he was better educated
than other military men of the period, being a licensed graduate
of the old literary civil service examinations.

Wu had another characteristic which was unusual among
Chinese; he was a heavy drinker, not only of the native shaoshing
or samshu wine but of imported brandy as well. On one occasion when Wu's generals were giving him an elaborate birthday party a present arrived from Wu's then chief ally, the
Christian General, Feng Yu-hsiang. The present was bulky and
required two servants to carry it into the banquet room. When
unpacked the parcel was found to contain a large porcelain vase
of rare type. The servants removed the covering from the top
of the vase and placed it on the table in front of the guest of
honor. General Wu arose and poured himself a liberal tumbler

from the vase and raised it to his lips as he offered a toast to the donor. But he stopped short and spat out the mouthful—of water, which was what the vase contained. In view of Wu's well known drinking habits the suggestion implied in the Christian General's gift was not lost on the military men present.

My last interview with General Wu, and probably his last interview with any foreign newspaperman, was in the winter of 1926–27, after he had been appointed commander-in-chief of the Allied Anti-Red Army and had established his headquarters at Hankow in Central China. Despite his high-sounding title, Wu's position was pathetic, as it constituted the last stand of the reactionary northern militarists against the advancing Nationalist revolutionary forces from the south. I met Wu at breakfast in the garden of an old Chinese home where he had his headquarters. He had been drinking more heavily than usual, and was depressed because of the collapse of his forces in Hunan; they had been completely demoralized by the Russian-trained propaganda corps which preceded the advance of the Nationalist troops. The Communists exerted their best efforts in Hunan and executed their "fifth columnist" work so well that Wu's troops fell back without fighting, and while they put up a strong fight at Wuchang, last remaining stronghold in central China, they ultimately withdrew.

Wu was carrying an old and frayed Chinese book in his hand, and frequently glanced at it during our breakfast interview. I asked him what the title of the book was. He smiled and said, "Military Campaigns of the Kingdom of Wu," and then added, "They didn't have any machine guns or airplanes then."

Wu retired after his defeat. He always refused political office, and never profited personally, although for a considerable period he had been the most powerful military man in the country. He always insisted he was a military man and knew nothing about politics—which probably explained his failure, as warfare in China had become more political than military, as the all-conquering Nationalists proved.

General Feng Yu-hsiang, who in 1922 was supporting General Wu, was another unusual character. Feng's army, which marched to the tune "Onward, Christian Soldiers," was the predecessor of the Communist Eighth Route Army in the Chinese northwest. Like the commanders of the present-day Chinese Red Army, Feng Yu-hsiang also received special training in Russia and his soldiers carried Russian rifles, some of them being American-made, sold or given to the Czarist Government in World War I.

Karl Radek, former Soviet publicist and disciple of Trotsky, who was imprisoned in return for his confession, in Stalin's purge, used to entertain his friends with stories about Feng Yu-hsiang, who was in one of Radek's classes in revolutionary technique. He said that Feng, who came from northern Chinese peasant stock, sat stolidly through most of the lectures without evincing any outward interest in the subjects under discussion. One day, however, Feng suddenly pricked up his ears and began asking questions. The particular lecture which had aroused Feng's interest dealt with army finance and the financing of occupied territory, subjects of deep concern to Chinese generals, many of whom managed in one way or another to amass comfortable fortunes out of funds which passed through their hands.

Feng came up through the ranks and learned the art of war the hard way. Somewhere along the line he fell under the influence of an American missionary and was converted to Christianity. While Governor of Honan he once ordered an entire division baptized in the Christian faith by total immersion in the Yellow River. While he was stationed in Peking in 1924 he married the secretary of the Peking Y.W.C.A. Politically Feng was an undependable ally; in 1924, when Marshal Wu Pei-fu was engaged in a life-and-death struggle with Chang Tso-lin, Feng, who was holding the Peking district, rebelled and seized the capital. He made the then President Tsao Kun a prisoner and chased the Manchu Boy Emperor from the Forbidden City, where he had resided as a government ward since the revolution in 1911.

Once, in company with a number of other correspondents, I interviewed Feng. One of the newspapermen, I think it was the *New York Times* man, said in the course of his introduction, "General, you are a very big man." Feng, who was over six feet and large in proportion, replied, "Yes, if you would cut off my head and put it on top of yours, we would then be equal." The correspondent puzzled over that remark for several days.

While Feng was in command of northwest troops at Kalgan on the border of Inner Mongolia at the famous Nankow Pass in the Great Wall, he engaged a number of American missionaries and college professors to lecture to him on international politics. As it was necessary for the lecturers to stay in his yamen as guests for two or three days, Feng inquired of a friend as to what food foreigners preferred to eat. The friend, not realizing the purport of the inquiry, replied, "ice cream." As a result Feng fed his foreign professors on ice cream and little else during their entire stay in the Mongolian border town.

After his return from Russia, Feng joined forces with the Nationalists and helped oust the northern militarists, but later he rebelled against Generalissimo Chiang Kai-shek and joined other rebels, including Wang Ching-wei, in establishing a so-called "Coalition Government" in Peking. When the coalition was ousted from Peking, Feng went into retirement, but he rejoined the National Government when the Japanese invaded Manchuria in 1931.

I well remember an interview I had with Marshal Chang Tso-lin in the spring of 1923. I was on a trip through China with a group of American Congressmen who made a tour through the Orient following the Washington Conference.

Chang Tso-lin, military dictator of Manchuria, was popularly known among the Chinese as the Manchurian Hungutzu, which translated literally, meant "Red-Bearded Bandit." The term originated among the Chinese of North Manchuria, who applied it to the Russian buccaneers who first entered that country from Siberia several centuries ago. In consequence the term has since been applied to all outlaws of any nationality who operated in the wilds of Manchuria. Another term applied to Chang Tso-lin by foreigners was "Manchurian Tiger," indicating fearlessness and ruthlessness. I had frequently heard both terms and was prepared to meet a fierce, bearded outlaw with a gun on each hip. I was, therefore, astonished when Marshal Chang Tso-lin, small, mild, beardless, entered the room where I had been told to wait for him. However, the "tiger" designation returned to my mind when he escorted me to an adjoining room and asked me to sit on a sofa facing him. Directly back of the sofa, so near that their whiskers brushed the back of my head, were two stuffed Manchurian tigers which looked to be at least ten feet long. They were facing each other with their jaws open in a fierce snarl, and their heads were not more than six inches apart, directly behind my head.

I interviewed the Marshal regarding domestic Chinese politics, and he assured me that his intentions were entirely pacific; that he was only interested in unifying China—by force, if necessary. He denied that the Japanese had anything to do with his decision.

During my interview I repeated the reports about his relations with Japan. He told me that he had served on the Japanese side during the Russo-Japanese war as a guerrilla leader, harassing the communication lines of the Russians, and probably had a great deal to do with the defeat of the Russians in their war with Japan in 1905. No one was in a better position for this work than Chang Tso-lin, for he was a product of the Manchurian mountains and forests.

Little was known of his parents, but, according to popular report, his father was also a Hungutzu. I laughingly asked him where he obtained his education and, with a twinkle in his eye, he replied, through his interpreter, "I was educated in the School of Forestry," which answer indicated that he also possessed a sense of humor.

Following his defeat by Wu Pei-fu in 1922, Chang Tso-lin maintained an independent position in Manchuria, refusing to permit the Government in Peking to interfere in the administration of the Manchurian provinces, although the Chinese maritime customs, telegraph administration, and other organs continued to function in his territory.

Late in 1926 he again returned to Peking, this time to assist the northern Tuchuns, or military governors, in opposing Generalissimo Chiang Kai-shek and the Nationalist forces, which had just come into power in the Yangtze Valley and created the new Nationalist Government at Nanking.

It was widely believed that Marshal Chang Tso-lin was being pressed by the Japanese Kwantung or Manchurian military faction which wanted to prevent Chiang Kai-shek and the Nationalists from assuming control over North China. The element of Japanese support, however, was denied by Chang, who insisted that he was independent of the Japanese, which denial he reiterated in another interview which I had with him at Peking, prior to Chiang Kai-shek's advances into the northern provinces. I remembered that the Manchurian War Lord had once been in alliance with Dr. Sun Yat-sen, the Cantonese leader.

When Chiang Kai-shek's army reached Shantung Province, Chang Tso-lin, for reasons of his own, suddenly withdrew from Peking and returned to Mukden. As his train was passing through a viaduct, under the Japanese South Manchurian Railway, there was a tremendous explosion and Chang Tso-lin's private car was blown to smithereens, and with it Chang and several of his military subordinates and associates in the Manchurian Government. Since the explosion occurred at a closely guarded section of the Japanese railway, it was obvious that the Japanese army in Manchuria was responsible for the action, apparently as punishment for Chang's refusal to remain in Peking and oppose the Nationalist army. The incident caused a serious crisis in Tokyo, resulting in the resignation of the Premier, who stated in his official announcement that he was forced to relinquish office "because of an incident in another country."

Chang Tso-lin was succeeded as ruler of Manchuria by his

son, Chang Hsueh-liang, who immediately declared himself in favor of Chiang Kai-shek and the Kuomintang, and hoisted the Nationalist flag over all government buildings throughout Manchuria.

Although under the heel of the Japanese militarists and often forced to do their bidding, Chang Tso-lin was a patriotic Chinese for all that. He contributed much of his fortune to education, and while himself without the benefit of book learning, he had a good knowledge of the game of international politics played by the Russians and Japanese in northeastern Asia. He played his cards wisely, and managed to keep his territory intact.

During the year which followed my return from the Washington Conference, important developments were taking place at my office. Mr. Millard, who had been actively engaged in its management for only a short time after it was founded, decided to withdraw entirely from the *Review*. When he had left Shanghai for a trip to New York in 1917, I had no idea that he would not return, but his stay was extended from month to month, and year to year. In 1922 he decided to accept an advisory position with the Chinese Government, and I took over his stock interest in the *Review*, thus becoming financially and editorially responsible for the paper. The financial outlook was complicated by the fact that the support which Millard had received from Mr. Crane was not continued following his withdrawal. I was therefore left in the position of lifting myself by my own bootstraps. Had it not been for the advertising contracts I had obtained with Chinese concerns, we would have had difficulty in continuing publication. I decided at this time to change the name of the *Review*, the full title of which was *Millard's Review of the Far East*. I had in any case always regarded the original title as too restrictive and personal. We experimented with various names, the first being *The Weekly Review of the Far East*, and ultimately the title which we adopted in June, 1923, was *The China Weekly Review*.

While considering the matter of a new name for the paper,

I made an interesting discovery. I found the old saying "What's in a name" had a peculiar application in China, because a name once established could never be changed. This applies not only to the name itself, but also to the manner in which it is written. Foreign firms trading in China guard their names and the names of their products most jealously, because the slightest change often creates in the minds of the customers suspicions which may have disastrous results. This refers particularly to the name as written in the Chinese language, although the manner of writing or printing the English name is also important; Chinese naturally look at the Chinese characters first, even though they are familiar with the English language. We therefore continued the title as written in Chinese characters as it had appeared originally (*Millard's Review of the Far East*).

XI

Incident of the Blue Express

1—A Chinese Hold-Up

ON THE EVENING OF MAY 5, 1923, I was traveling between
Nanking and Peking, together with a few other newspapermen.
Our destination was a recently completed reclamation project
which the American Red Cross had financed in connection with
a famine-relief project on the Yellow River. Our train, consisting of first-, second-, and third-class coaches, was China's
crack "Blue Express," the first train of all-steel coaches ever
seen in the Orient, which had been purchased by the Chinese
Railway Administration in the United States only a few months
before. The first-class coaches were made up entirely of compartments and all were filled by passengers of a half dozen or
more nationalities, some on trips around the world, others businessmen on local trips.

Among the passengers were Americans, Britons, French-
men, Italians, Mexicans, one Rumanian, and numerous Chinese.
There were many women and children, including Miss Lucy
Aldrich, sister-in-law of John D. Rockefeller, Jr., and daughter
of the late Senator Nelson Aldrich of Rhode Island. Miss
Aldrich was traveling with a companion, a Miss McFadden, and
a French maid, Mademoiselle Schonberg. There were two
United States Army officers on board, Major Allen and Major
Pinger, with their wives and children, and several French and
American businessmen. The Mexicans were Mr. and Mrs.
Ancera Verea of Guadalajara, who were on a honeymoon trip
through the Orient. Mr. Verea was a well known industrialist.
Another passenger was "Commendatore" G. D. Musso, an ex-
ceedingly wealthy Italian lawyer who had amassed a fortune

in mysterious ways in the Shanghai International Settlement. For many years he was attorney for the Shanghai Opium Combine. Musso became one of the early backers of Mussolini and half owner of one of the leading newspapers in Rome. He was accompanied by his attractive secretary, Signorina Pirelli. I later learned that a number of Japanese, who had boarded the train at Shanghai with through tickets to Peking, had mysteriously debarked during the evening when the train reached the town of Hsuchowfu.

My compartment-mate was a Frenchman named Berube, an employee of the Chinese Customs Administration, who was returning to his work in China after extended service in the French army on the Western Front. I had not known him previously, but the recent war in Europe and the disturbed political situation in the Far East provided subjects for conversation that kept us up until 2 A.M. It was early spring and a bright moon was shining, making the barren rocky Shantung Mountains quite visible in the distance. We had raised the window so as to enjoy the warm breeze, and just before retiring I looked out the window and remarked to Berube that we were passing through "bandit territory," as the mountainous area including parts of three provinces, Kiangsu, Anhwei, and Shantung, had long been notorious as a haunt for roving bands of ex-soldiers who had served in the provincial armies and, being unable to find jobs, had taken up banditry. Some of the bandit leaders had a Robin Hood reputation, but most of them were engaged in plain outlawry, looting towns and villages and kidnaping their inhabitants.

The train had just crossed the divide from Kiangsu into Shantung Province and was proceeding slowly, when there was a sudden grinding of brakes and the cars came to an abrupt halt—so abrupt that many passengers were tumbled out of their berths. There was a great deal of shouting and firing outside, and I stuck my head out of the window to see what was going on. I quickly withdrew it, however, when a bandit fired his rifle in the air within a couple of feet of my head, but I had time to see what looked like a small army of men swarming down the embankment, yelling and firing their rifles as they came. They climbed into the cars through the windows, ran along the corridors and began routing the passengers out of their berths while they ransacked the baggage. One man, a Rumanian, objected to being pushed around and threw a teapot at his captor. The bandit raised his rifle and fired, killing the man instantly. There was no further resistance. I had in my bag a small .25-caliber automatic I had purchased in Washington. My French compartment-mate also had his service revolver, but we quickly decided that our armament was outclassed by the weapons in the hands of the highwaymen, and handed over our revolvers without protest. The bandits in our compartment were so elated by getting our guns that they permitted us to put on our clothes and shoes, a lucky break for us as most of the passengers, women as well as men, were attired only in their nightgowns and pajamas as the bandits lined us up along the embankment.

Placing a guard over us, the bandits completed the looting of the train, including the baggage and mail car. Even the mattresses and rugs were torn out, and I noticed one bandit who had filled his pockets with electric light bulbs. The job completed, the chief, a young man whom we later came to know as Sven Mao-yao, gave the order to march and we started out single file up a dry rocky ravine into the mountains. Each captive was accompanied by two bandits, one on each side. There were about two hundred passengers on the train, but the bandits numbered fully a thousand.

The Frenchman and I shook hands and made a mutual vow that we would stick together and help each other to the end, regardless of the outcome. As we stumbled up the ravine we heard a woman crying, and hurrying along we came on Mademoiselle Schonberg, the French maid, who was limping and holding her side as though she had been wounded. As we helped her over the rocks she told us, in a mixture of French and English, that she was Miss Aldrich's maid and was carrying, concealed inside her nightgown, a purse containing her mistress's jewelry. She had managed to conceal the purse from the prying eyes of the bandits by holding it inside her nightgown and pretending she was injured. She asked us what to do with the jewelry, as she feared the purse would be detected after daylight. Neither Berube nor I wished to take the responsibility of protecting the Aldrich diamonds, and I advised Mademoiselle to throw the purse into the field and trust that an honest farmer would find it. Mademoiselle decided, however, to keep the purse, even though it might cost her her life. We finally induced the bandits to permit her and the small son of one of the American army officers to ride one of the donkeys that the bandits had caught in a field through which we passed.

Daybreak revealed one of the strangest sights that these ancient hills had ever witnessed. The train passengers, each still accompanied by two individual captors, were strung out for a half mile up the side of the mountain, while to the rear there was another straggling line of bandits almost as long, sweating under the loot they had taken from the train, including our suitcases and even the precious mattresses from the sleeping berths. As the sun came up and it grew warmer and the climb more precipitous, the bandits would dump the mattresses on the ground and sit or lie on them.

All of the bandits had trinkets they had taken from the compartments, including tooth brushes and paste, safety razors and shaving cream, cameras and rolls of films, fountain pens, rings of keys, pocket knives, tins of talcum powder, and women's beauty accessories. One bandit had found a lady's brassière which he had tied about his waist; he was using the compartments to carry his valuables. Since most of the passengers were without shoes, the going was slow and hazardous and painful, as there was only a narrow rocky path leading to the summit of the mountain. Since Berube and I had our shoes we walked faster and soon were at the head of the long line. There I noticed a woman riding a donkey bareback and having considerable difficulty in staying on and keeping her silk nightgown from blowing away entirely in the gale. I searched my mind to think of something I could do to help her. Noticing a bandit carrying a lady's broad-brimmed straw hat which he had taken from the train, I asked him for it and pointed toward the woman on the donkey. He laughed and handed me the hat. I caught up with the donkey-rider, who was Miss Aldrich, and handed her the hat, but she soon threw it away, as it was impossible to keep it on and remain on the donkey at the same time. She needed other articles of attire more than the hat.

Our slow pace up the mountainside was suddenly accelerated by rifle shots fired from a considerable distance in the rear which zimmed over our heads and ricocheted off the rocks above us. The shots were fired by a contingent of militia which had been dispatched from a nearby town by the railway authorities. Our captors immediately returned the fire, while we dodged for protection behind the nearest rocks, but there was little actual danger, as both sides were firing wild.

At about 10 o'clock in the morning we reached the top of the mountain, on which was a crude fort with walls and rifle rests all about. We climbed through an opening and fell in a heap, completely exhausted and nearly famished. After resting a few minutes we went through the available baggage brought up by the bandits, and managed to find a few needed articles of clothing. Someone would yell, "Hey, there, give me my pants," and there would be an exchange, much to the amusement of the bandits. Several of the men sacrificed their pajama shirts for use as bandages for the bleeding feet and sprained ankles of the women.

But the strangest scene of all was enacted when Mademoiselle Schonberg caught up with her mistress and joyously restored to her the family jewels. With great presence of mind Miss Aldrich carefully inspected the surrounding terrain and when the bandits looked the other way, she concealed the purse under a large flat stone. Later she borrowed a pencil from a bandit chief and made a rough sketch of the place where she had concealed the purse. Carefully folding the little piece of paper, she placed it in the toe of her shoe. Weeks later, after the bandit affair had been liquidated, a Chinese clerk in the Socony office in Tsinanfu went to the district, found the purse and returned it intact to the owner.

While we were doctoring our scratches and bruises and trying to make the women captives comfortable, the bandit chiefs went to one side for a conference. These conferences, which became increasingly frequent, led to the impression that while the original wrecking of the train may have been carefully planned, they were not so sure about their next move. They were constantly sending men out to reconnoiter, and when they returned there were further conferences. It was late afternoon, and since we had had neither food nor drink since dinner the preceding day, we were wondering about the next meal. Just before dark there was a commotion at the gate, and some men arrived bearing a basket and several earthenware jugs. The basket was filled with fresh eggs which the bandits passed out, one to each captive. Someone demonstrated how to eat a raw egg by chipping a small hole in each end and then by holding back the head it was possible to suck out the contents without the loss of a precious drop. There was sufficient water in the jugs for a good swallow around.

During the afternoon the firing had been resumed from the direction of the railway, the bullets glancing off the rocks with an angry zing. About 5 P.M. one of the chiefs arrived and asked us to write a message to Generals Wo and Wu, commanders of the district, warning them that all foreigners would be immediately killed unless the firing ceased. We made a condition— that we would write only under a pledge that the women and children be released. Since I was the only foreign newspaperman in this particular group, the passengers unanimously chose me to write the letter. Larry Lehrbas, then a reporter on the *China Press*, later well known foreign correspondent for the Associated Press and still later a colonel on the staff of General MacArthur, had been on the train but had hid under a seat and managed to escape in the confusion. The chief at first insisted that one of the foreigners carry the message down the mountainside but later changed his mind and handed the note to one of his own followers, who tied a white rag to a pole which he held over his shoulder and cautiously advanced through the gate. After waving it a few minutes to attract attention, he descended the hill. The firing soon stopped.

As darkness came on the bandits began packing their belongings for a move and motioned for us to get ready. At this point one of the women captives approached me rather hesitatingly and said she wished to speak to me privately. She led me to one side and pointing to one of the women captives who was partly concealed behind two other women, asked me whether I would request the bandits to make a search through the baggage to find a dress. I then saw that the woman, or rather girl, as she wasn't over eighteen, was attired only in a thin cotton shirt and black tight-fitting sateen bloomers which came about half way down to her knees. The girl was Signorina Pirelli, private secretary to the Italian lawyer Musso. We then checked up on our personnel and discovered that Musso had not arrived. Since he was quite corpulent, weighing over 300 pounds, we decided he had experienced difficulty climbing the mountains. His secretary's lack of suitable mountain-climbing attire also presented a problem. However, the embarrassing situation was saved when someone found a thin silk dressing gown in one of the bundles of looted clothes carried by one of the bandits. Signorina Pirelli expressed her gratitude in voluble Italian which no one understood, but the import of which was taken for granted.

As night came on it suddenly grew cloudy and soon there were blinding flashes of lightning followed by thunder which reverberated through the mountains like heavy artillery. The chief gave the order to march as the rain began to descend in waves, a real mountain deluge that often made breathing difficult. Between flashes we stumbled down a precipitous path on the opposite side of the mountain from that by which we had ascended. We finally reached the valley and were led along a stream which was swollen out of its banks by the flood. After stumbling through the water and mud for several hours, we approached the environs of a village. We could see the dark walls and could hear what seemed like a dozen dogs barking at once. Finally we were marched into a dark rectangular compound with a low mud wall surrounding the four sides and some low buildings along one end. We were led to the open doors of the buildings and told to go inside. The buildings were stables, but the floors were dry and covered by kaoliang, a species of sorghum carrying grain in the tassel at the top which provides food for man and beast, and which takes the place of rice in the northern provinces. The peasant farmers in North China make flour of the kaoliang seeds, which they mix with water and salt and bake in large thin cakes. They then roll these cakes about a mixture of chopped meat and vegetables seasoned with hot peppers, somewhat in the fashion of a Mexican tamale. But there were none of these cakes available for us that night, although each captive was provided with a bowl of hot weak tea. Despite our wet clothes we dropped on the floor and went to sleep immediately from complete exhaustion, not waking until late afternoon.

The awakening was abrupt, and it was apparent the bandits were in a hurry. As we got ready to start there was a commotion in front of one of the buildings and we recognized our Italian fellow-passenger, Signor Musso. He had fallen over an embankment on the way up the mountains and had injured his spine, making it necessary for the bandits to carry him on an improvised litter made of poles and covered with straw.

As we were assembling we realized that all the women had vanished, and a hurried search of the compound failed to locate them. Inquiry of the bandits only brought the laconic reply, with a shrug of the shoulder, "Mei-yao," meaning literally "no have got." We were suddenly surprised to hear a feminine voice emanating from what appeared to be a well dressed youth. It was the bride of Ancera Verea, the Mexican businessman from

Guadalajara. Mrs. Verea said that the bandits who were looking after the women had led them away the night before and had tried to induce her to join them. She had refused to leave her husband, and had been fortunate in finding a suit of men's clothing in one of the bundles of loot taken from the train. The bandits had finally allowed her to remain with her husband. We hoped that the women had been returned to the railroad in accordance with the pledge the chief had given, but it was some time later that we were reassured on this score. Our party of captives was now reduced to about twenty.

2—A Sit-Down Strike

The next ten days were a nightmare of forced marches, always at night, doubling and redoubling on narrow rocky trails through the mountains, often only a few jumps ahead of pursuing soldiers. We crossed railway tracks twice, which puzzled us for several days until we learned that the bandits had taken us into an isolated area served by a branch line which ran to a coal mine. The nearest station was known as Tsaochwang, but we never saw it until we were released several weeks later.

The distance we walked in the first few days, usually at a rapid pace, could only be guessed at, but we were sure it exceeded a hundred miles. Since we were constantly passing donkeys grazing in the fields, we begged the bandits to permit us to ride, but to no avail. One day after a particularly exhausting stretch I suggested to the other captives that we refuse to move unless they provided us with donkeys. Since the bandit chiefs were aware that I was the ringleader in the "sit-down" strike, one of them approached me and drawing his revolver threatened me with it. Knowing that we were valuable only as live, not dead "guests," I laughed at the bandit and pulled my shirt open in a gesture of bravado. The bandit did not shoot, but he seized a heavy pole and struck me over the shoulders, causing bruises which I carried for many days. But it was worth it, as the bandits realized we were in earnest and provided donkeys and ponies. Most of the donkeys had such sharp backs that many of us decided that walking was preferable after all.

Signor Musso, the Italian, presented our chief problem, as he had to be carried and required constant attention. The soles of his feet were a mass of blisters resulting from stumbling barefoot over stones on our first night's march up the dry ravine. One day I saw a bandit with a safety razor in his parcel of loot. I borrowed the blade and opened the blisters on Musso's feet, thereby creating the impression among the outlaws that I was a doctor. After we were established several days later in the bandit lair the men constantly brought members of the gang to me for treatment. Fortunately by that time we had received some medical supplies, which had been sent in by the American Red Cross, and I was able to comply with the request for medical attention. Once when I was applying iodine to a curious-looking sore on a man's back, one of our interpreters, who was a medical student, came up and after examining the man, pronounced him a sufferer from leprosy. The crowd that had been standing around watching me, cleared out in short order. I also was alarmed until the student assured me it was not very contagious.

Lack of food was our chief problem on the long march. When we appealed to our captors, they would pat their own empty stomachs and complain that they "didn't have anything to eat either." One day they brought us some fresh meat which they said was "young cow." Two of us stayed up and boiled it all day and only by nightfall were we able to pull some of the meat from the bones. However, the soup was tasteful and everybody had a bowlful. Later, we were informed that our veal stew was Shantung dog, a particularly tough type of mangy cur. A missionary friend told me there was a superstition among the peasants that anyone who ate Shantung dog became possessed of the spirits which that particular dog had harbored, for a period of seven years.

On another occasion our captors produced a supply of the familiar Shantung "tamales," but these seemed to have a different kind of filling. I fished out a piece and asked one of our captors what it was. He walked to the side of the path, turned over a large flat stone and catching one of the scampering insects in his fingers carefully held it up for inspection. We recognized it as a scorpion. The man explained that it was customary for the peasants to cut off the stingers and then boil the bodies in salt water, after which the shells were removed and a palatable morsel left which somewhat resembled shrimps. Since I had once been stung by a scorpion I decided to pass up tamales until we reached a district where other forms of meat were more plentiful.

We began to realize that the bandits were nearing their destination. We passed over a high rocky divide and entered a fertile valley about thirty miles long and about fifteen miles wide. The valley gradually narrowed at the upper end to a gorge with precipitous sides along which ran a narrow path. At the head of the gorge was a "sugar-loaf" type of mountain, five or six thousand feet high and flat at the top. About half way up the mountain the incline was gradual, but the upper portion was a solid rock with precipitous sides apparently impossible to scale. There was a small village at the foot of the mountain, built on both sides of a mountain torrent that was fed by a spring which gushed from the rocks higher up the ravine.

We were guided up the narrow road for several hundred feet. In many places it consisted of narrow stair-steps cut in the solid rock. At last we came to a wooded glen and there we found an ancient temple abandoned and in ruins. Only one or two rooms were habitable, and apparently they had provided shelter for the bandit gang. Back of the temple we discovered several chambers of caves which had been hewn into the side of the mountain, and apparently had served as storage places for grain and other food and also, possibly, for loot. However, the caves were empty when we arrived at the temple. It was easy to see that the stronghold to which the bandits had brought us was impregnable against attack. The only entrance was up the narrow gorge or canyon, while the valley below was easily defended, as it was entirely surrounded by mountains. One day in rummaging about the place we found an ancient tablet containing carved inscriptions apparently written by Buddhist priests. One of our student captives translated the characters. They told a story of banditry and interference with the work of the priests for a period of several centuries, resulting in a final decision to abandon the temple to the outlaws.

As the bandits marched us through the villages the entire population turned out to see the spectacle of the captive foreigners, something never previously seen in China, with the possible exception of the disturbed period of the Boxer Uprising in North China in 1900. As we paraded through one village I saw an attractive Chinese girl dressed in silks and wearing so much jewelry that she had the appearance of a jewelry shop window display figure. As the girl waved at us, I recognized her as a former passenger on the ill-fated Blue Express. She had become hysterical on the night of the attack and her screams could be heard above the shouts and shots of the bandits. We had wondered what had become of her.

After we had been in the camp for several days and were allowed some freedom, I went down to the village with one of our student interpreters and two escorts supplied by the chief and made inquiry about the mystery of the Chinese girl—she was about sixteen years old. It developed that she was a "sing-song" girl, or entertainer, who was being sent to the camp of a well known northern general as a "present" from General Hu Feng-lin, who was then military governor of the Shanghai district. But she never reached her destination. One of our chiefs took a fancy to her and annexed her to his own private entourage. She seemed to be quite happy in her new surroundings and anxious to display the jewelry the chief had given her, most of which had been looted from the foreign passengers on the train. I looked in vain, during the interview, for my class ring.

3—*Word from the Outside World*

The bandit lair to which we had been taken was called Mount Pao-tzu-ku. It was somewhat separated from the regular Shantung Mountains and was about forty miles from the railway station and coal mine of Tsaochwang, from which it was visible on clear days.

Since we had been on the move continuously for practically two weeks, we had no knowledge whatever of the tremendous commotion which the kidnaping had stirred up in the outside world. Our first news came to us in a most unusual but welcome manner. It was a copy of the *China Press,* published at Shanghai, and it was the wrapping of a parcel which contained something even more welcome than the paper, namely, a well cured ham from one of the half-wild pigs which roamed the wildest parts of the Shantung countryside.

On the margin of the paper was a note stating that the parcel was sent to us by an American missionary, the Rev. Carroll H. Yerkes, who conducted a school under the jurisdiction of the Presbyterian Mission in a district known as Yihsien, which was a considerable distance from the place where we were held. Later Mr. Yerkes informed us that he had learned of our whereabouts from a Chinese petty officer who had been sent with a small contingent of soldiers to Yihsien by the governor of the province to protect the mission property and inmates from the bandits. After he had notified the American consular authorities, Mr. Yerkes induced a Chinese convert to carry the parcel through the bandit lines to our camp on Mount Pao-tzu-ku. Several days later the same messenger arrived with another parcel, containing another ham, some coffee and a number of books. I unwrapped the books and passed them out, one each, to all of the captives. The books were copies of the New Testament.

Some days later, Leon Friedman, the motor car dealer from Shanghai, looked up from perusal of his copy of the Holy Scriptures and exclaimed, "What is a Jew supposed to do in these circumstances? First we starve, and a missionary sends us a ham; then when we want something to read he sends us the New Testament!"

Before long, we had our first visitor from the outside world, an elderly German Catholic missionary, the Rev. Father Lenfers, one of the few survivors of a band of missionaries sent to Shantung from imperial Germany in the last quarter of the preceding century. Several of these priests were killed by bandits, possibly predecessors of our captors, which provided Kaiser Wilhelm with his excuse for seizing the port of Kiachow Bay on the Shantung coast and demanding the right to build a railway into the interior of the province. But the Kaiser's policy had not helped missionary work; only a few of the German priests remained. They wore Chinese clothes, spoke Chinese, and had almost forgotten their native tongue. Our little band of captives, foreigners and Chinese, Jews and Gentiles, Catholics and Protestants, welcomed Father Lenfers with open arms, for he not only brought us news from the outside world, and valuable information about the strength of the bandit gang, he also brought us several bottles of excellent wine which he had made himself.

According to the news brought us by Father Lenfers and the newspapers sent us by Mr. Yerkes, the foreign Powers, led by the United States and Great Britain, had made a strong demand on the Peking Government that steps be taken immediately to effect the rescue of the foreign captives. Only Japan held off and remained cold to all proposals to bring pressure to bear on the Chinese authorities. Tokyo officialdom shrugged its collective shoulder and called attention to the fact that no Japanese were held captive by the bandit gang. When as a result of dilly-dallying on the part of provincial and central government authorities, it was suggested that the United States, Great Britain, France, and Italy stage a naval demonstration at Tsingtao and Pukow, the nearest Chinese ports to the scene of the bandit escapade, Tokyo spokesmen called attention to the "unseemly attitude of the Powers in view of their recent action at the Washington Arms Limitation Conference in forcing Japan to evacuate the province." The Japanese also let it be known that the bandit incident might never have occurred had Japan been permitted to remain in the province "to maintain order."

Of greatest personal interest to myself, I learned from the copies of the *China Press* which we received that two accounts of the wrecking of the train and the highlights of our ensuing captivity, which I had secretly written on scraps of waste paper during our long trek through the mountains, had finally reached the outside world and had been printed in my paper, the *China Weekly Review*, at Shanghai, and had also been cabled abroad. After writing the accounts, I wrote the name and address of the American Consul at Tsinanfu, the provincial capital, on the back of the folded sheaf of pages and one day when the bandits were not watching I handed the papers to a villager as we were being marched through a town. The manuscript was delivered to the Consul and my account, "written from the inside," got out without undue delay. It was so miraculous that many people wouldn't believe it and insisted that the story was faked. Even some of my friends did not believe the story was genuine until I was released and confirmed the details of what I had written.

The American Minister to China at this time was Dr. Jacob Gould Schurman, former president of Cornell University, probably the most intelligent and effective diplomatic representative sent to China by the United States in the disturbed period of a quarter of a century following the close of World War I. As soon as he received word of the bandit affair, Dr. Schurman called the attention of the Peking authorities to the seriousness of the incident, and warned them to take all possible steps to assure the safety of the captives and obtain their early release. Dr. Schurman then went to Paoting, where he conferred directly with the militarist General Tsao Kun, following which he repeated his warnings to the Chinese officials at Tsinan, Nanking and Shanghai.

But of more importance, from the standpoint of the actual

safety and welfare of the captives, Dr. Schurman arranged with the American Red Cross to send a mission to Tsaochwang with supplies of food and clothing. In addition, he arranged with the diplomatic representatives of Great Britain, France, and Italy to send consular representatives to establish direct contact with the Shantung provincial authorities and even with the bandit chiefs, if possible, so as to facilitate negotiations for the release of the captives. The American consular representative was John K. Davis, stationed at Nanking, while the representative of the American Red Cross was Carl Crow, well known journalist and former managing editor of the *China Press* of Shanghai.

Another well known American who participated in the parlous negotiations was Roy Anderson, son of missionary parents, who was born in China and probably had a better knowledge of the Chinese language and a wider acquaintance with China's officialdom than any other foreigner in China at the time. Anderson was assisted by S. T. Wen, the Chinese Commissioner of Foreign Affairs at Nanking. Both entered the bandit lines at great personal risk and initiated negotiations which led to the bandits granting permission for food to be sent to the foreign prisoners.

4—Red Cross to the Rescue

One day we saw in the distance across the valley a long caravan of carrier coolies approaching our stronghold. After a wait of what seemed to be hours the head of the caravan appeared at the gate of the temple courtyard. The sweating coolies were carrying several large boxes, each bearing the insignia of the Red Cross. We tore into the boxes in short order. They were filled with food—bread, cans of bully-beef, vegetables and fruit, and even several boxes of California raisins.

The leader had a letter explaining that the American Red Cross had negotiated a deal with the bandit leaders whereby they agreed to permit food to be sent through their lines to the captives, provided the Red Cross would at the same time send along a large supply of rice and flour for the bandits. Carl Crow, director of the Red Cross expedition, asked us to check up on the supplies to see that the bandits had observed the agreement. We found nothing missing, although the coolies had carried the cases for practically forty miles through the outlaws' country.

That night we staged a never-to-be-forgotten banquet, with an invocation by Major Pinger, one of the captive American army officers, and speeches by everybody present. Sounds of festivity also reached us from the adjoining courtyard, where our captors and the Chinese prisoners were celebrating the arrival of the first real food they had eaten in about three weeks. Everybody wrote letters to be taken back by the caravan the following morning.

A later caravan brought us folding camp cots and mosquito nets, contributed by the United States Fifteenth Infantry Regiment then stationed at Tientsin. Our sojourn as guests of the bandits began to take on the character of an outing in the mountains—except for the presence of our ragamuffin "hosts." The arrival of food greatly improved our relations, at least with those of our captors who were in our immediate vicinity. We learned that the reports of the success of the bandits in obtaining supplies of food had spread through the mountains and in consequence the bandit gang had swelled from the original thousand to more than three thousand, most of the new arrivals being deserters from nearby provincial armies. We also learned that the force the Government had sent against the bandits numbered about eight thousand, but they were more or less powerless due to the constant threat of the bandit leaders to execute the captives in case they were pressed too hard.

One minor chief, an ill-natured rascal, known as "Bo-bo" Liu, who had had trouble with the Germans at Tsingtao, constantly argued in favor of killing one or two of the captives in order to speed up the negotiations. These reports and other gossip constantly seeped in to us through our student interpreters, who hobnobbed with the bandits and passed the information on to us.

Father Lenfers, the German Catholic priest, returned to our camp one day and motioning me to one side told me a story that made my flesh creep. He said that he had been told by a member of the gentry who lived in one of the railway towns that a particular group among the bandits concerned itself with the kidnaping of children, and that the gang was holding a number of children for ransom in a hut on top of the mountain, the precipitous sides of which towered over our temple. Father Lenfers suggested that we investigate.

Early the next morning I asked one of the chiefs to provide me and Father Lenfers with an escort, as we wished to take a walk around the side of the mountain. No one was permitted to leave the temple compound without two guards. The Catholic priest, more familiar with the habits of soldiers and bandits, told me to fill an army canteen with some of the brandy he had brought us. I followed his advice, and after climbing briskly for about an hour we reached the base of the cliff, which rose almost perpendicularly to the summit, a distance of perhaps five hundred feet.

Hot and out of breath from the climb, we sat down on a flat rock in the sun to rest. With a wink at Father Lenfers, I handed our captor-guides the canteen containing a full quart of home-brewed brandy. The two worthies gulped it down like so much milk, and within a few minutes both were stretched out on the rock sound asleep. Father Lenfers and I then set out along the narrow path that led around the base of the cliff. Our search was soon rewarded: we came to a crevice or gigantic split in the face of the cliff, as though a thin slice had been cut off an enormous cake, which the upper part of Mount Pao-tzu-ku resembled. There we discovered the way to the top—a crude ladder made of hand-holds chiseled in the granite. There were small platforms or landings at intervals of about fifty feet up to a point where the ascent became more gradual and a steep stairway, also cut in the rock, led to the top.

Glancing back toward our guards, who were still sprawled on the rock, with their mouths open, snoring loudly, we decided to attempt the ascent. I led the way, with the venerable Father following a few rungs behind with his robe tucked up under his belt to give him freedom of movement. After we had reached the second landing, about one hundred feet up, Father Lenfers put his hand to his heart and sat down. He could go no further.

I told him to return to the base and watch the guards, while I climbed on up to the top. Knowing that I did not have much time, I hurried, and finally reached the top. Like the mountain top where we had first been taken, this also had been converted into a fort, but more effort had gone into the work here. There were several huts covered with thatch, well weighted down with rocks. There were several large wells or tanks cut in the stone to catch the rain-water, while other tanks were filled with grain and fuel. The bandits could hold out here almost indefinitely. I remembered the inscription on the tablet at the temple —a bandit stronghold for six centuries!

While exploring the mountain top, which was three or four acres in extent and nearly flat, I heard voices coming from one of the shacks. Pulling the straw-matting curtain aside, I realized with a shock that the story which had been told to Father Lenfers was correct. The room was filled with children, little boys ranging in age from eight to fifteen years. As they crowded about me I saw them glance apprehensively over their shoulders toward a door at the other end of the room. Almost immediately there emerged a bandit carrying a rifle, which he immediately swung off his shoulder as he saw me. Since I was unarmed, all I could do was smile and greet him with a friendly gesture. He understood the gesture, for I was holding out toward him a package of cigarettes. After hesitating a moment he also smiled, and reached for the cigarettes. I rapidly counted the children; there were twenty-three, and most of them were in rags, remnants of silken costumes indicating they had been kidnaped from better-class homes.

After making a mental note of the situation, I indicated my intention of departing, and handed the bandit another package of cigarettes. He made no attempt to hinder my departure, and I hurriedly descended the steep stairway and ladder and rejoined Father Lenfers, who was sitting on the rock watching the still sleeping bandits. I told him of my discovery, and after awakening our captors we hurried back to the temple. I kept quiet about my discovery, but wrote a description of what I had seen which I gave the priest to take out and send to my office in Shanghai. Its publication created a tremendous sensation throughout China, and when the bandit incident was finally settled the children were taken down the mountain and to the town of Yihsien, where they were temporarily placed under the care of Reverend Yerkes's mission. Later they were turned over to the civil governor, who managed to restore some of them to their parents. In many cases, however, it was impossible to find the parents, probably due to the fact that the children had been abducted in places far distant from the bandit hideout. Those whose parents could not be found were placed in an orphanage managed by one of the missions. We were told afterward that it was customary in cases where parents of abducted children were unable to raise sufficient money to redeem them for the bandit chiefs to adopt the boys as their own sons and bring them up in the ways of their foster fathers.

The disclosures concerning the kidnaping phase of the bandit industry served further to discredit the whole situation of military politics and anarchy which had prevailed in North China for so many years, and paved the way for the ultimate overthrow of the provincial Tuchuns and the establishment of more orderly government.

5—A Mission of Peace

Time dragged slowly in the bandit camp, and our impatience mounted at the apparent inactivity of our would-be rescuers at the railway station. We could not understand why four powerful governments couldn't outsmart a gang of Shantung bandits. However, we knew in our hearts that our bravado was assumed, for we were well aware that the real reason for the delay in our release was fear on the part of our friends as well as the Chinese officials that they would provoke the bandits to retaliation against us.

Some days later, when another consignment of food arrived, I was digging into a parcel of raisins marked with my name when I found a note written on thin paper, carefully folded and secreted in the center of the box. The note came from an American army officer, stationed at the United States Legation at Peking, who had been sent to Tsaochwang to investigate the matter of speeding up our release. The officer's note said that negotiations between the bandit chiefs and the provincial authorities were deadlocked because of the unreasonable demands which the bandits had made. The bandits practically insisted on the abdication of the top provincial officials and the substitution of themselves as rulers of the province and controllers of the main trunk-line railway which ran through Shantung. I remembered the demands of the Shantung bandits at a later date when the Chinese Communist faction made its demands for the abdication of high government officials in World War II.

In view of mounting indignation at the delay in releasing the captives, the officer asked me to sound out the other captives regarding a daring rescue scheme which had been proposed. According to the plan which he unfolded, the rescue party at the coal mine would secretly bring to the nearest railway station a contingent of about fifty United States soldiers and marines. They would be brought from Peking and Tientsin in small groups, attired in plain clothes so as not to attract attention.

But first the carrier coolies who brought in our food would smuggle in to us, concealed in boxes of raisins, a number of revolvers and a supply of ammunition. When all was in readiness on a designated day, of which we would be notified in advance, we would proceed to one of the caves in the cliff back of our temple, barricade the entrance, and prepare to stand off the bandits until our rescuers could make the forty-mile raid through the mountains and effect our release.

That night, after our guards had gone away, I called the captives together and put the proposition to them. I voiced my approval of the scheme, and was supported by the two American army officers, Major Robert Allen and Major Roland Pinger, and also by two of the British prisoners. The Mexican Verea and his wife also approved, but most of the others objected, particularly the Italian lawyer Musso, who was unable to walk. Some doubted the ability of such a small force of American servicemen to penetrate the bandit lines and fight their way through if the bandits put up resistance. We all realized what would happen to us if the scheme failed.

I shall never forget the looks on the faces of our little band when I disclosed the daring plan of the American army officer. Extreme danger and the hardships through which we had passed caused a bond of fellowship to develop among the captives which broke down racial, religious, and nationalistic barriers. This was evident that night in the little temple on the side of Mount Pao-tzu-ku as we huddled in the dim candle-light and discussed a plan which meant life or death to every man present. The unexpected element in the situation was that the Chinese students who had been with us from the beginning, serving as interpreters and in innumerable other ways, were also willing to go the whole way if the rescue scheme were attempted. I wrote a guarded report on the reactions of our party to the proposal, and it was smuggled back to the rescue party, but we heard nothing further regarding the scheme.

However, our discussion that night developed an idea which

ultimately resulted in our release. Someone suggested that we call
the chiefs together and try to discover what they really wanted.
The next morning we acted on the suggestion, and a committee
was appointed to visit the village where the chieftains had
their headquarters and invite them to come to our temple that
night. Six of them showed up, all but the No. 1 leader, Sven
Mao-yao, but he sent his representative. In the meantime the
captives held a preliminary meeting and elected officers. I was
given the job of secretary and possessed myself of a blank book,
apparently somebody's address book which a bandit had picked
up on the train. The possession of this book in which I frequently made notes gave me considerable prestige with our
bandit "hosts."

When the chiefs arrived that night, each with a bodyguard,
we invited them into our quarters and served them tea from
our stock of provisions. We then told the leaders that we understood their situation and wanted to help them settle the incident
so we could get back to our families. "But we can't do anything to help you until we know your terms," we explained.
The serious faces of the bandit chiefs and the equally serious
bearded faces of the captives, in the dim flickering candle-light
of the temple chamber, made another unforgettable picture.

"Just what did the bandits want?" I made copious notes in
my book and turned to the first chief. After some hesitation he
began to talk, and I wrote down his statement as the interpreter
translated. Turning to the next chief I repeated the question,
and so on until my book was nearly filled. I kept that little book
for several years, because it constituted an invaluable sidelight
on the political chaos which had prevailed so long in the
northern provinces, particularly in Shantung.

After I had taken down the last demand of the last chief it
was suggested that each side, that is, the captives and the chiefs,
should appoint a representative to proceed to the railway station
where the rescue party and the provincial officials were stationed. The chiefs agreed, and said they would have their man
and two horses at our temple early the next morning.

The party broke up about midnight and everybody felt
relieved, believing that something would come of our attempt
to negotiate ourselves out of our captivity, which was now
in its fourth week. The captives selected me to accompany
the bandit representative on the fateful trip. I slept little that
night; and I think my experience must have been general, for
everybody was up at sunrise. The news had spread through the
whole camp and our courtyard was filled with captives and
captors waiting for the arrival of the bandit emissary with the
horses. As our equerry entered the compound, I noticed that
our "horses" had turned out to be Shantung mules, whose back-
bones were even more razorlike than those of the donkeys we
had ridden previously.

Traditional ceremony was observed. The No. 1 Chief lined
up all the captives in a row. Then he ordered his followers to
form a guard of honor leading from the door of the temple
to the gate of the compound. Approaching me, the chief presented me with a sealed envelope containing an address in
Chinese. The name was that of the chief representative of the
provincial governor, known as the "Pang-ban." After he had
given me the letter he drew his revolver, and walking down
the long row of foreign captives, he pressed the muzzle of the
gun against each man's chest. In this manner he indicated that
one or possibly all of the captives would be killed if I failed to
carry out the mission or possibly should attempt to double-
cross the bandits by causing their emissary to be held by the
provincial officials. As I mounted my mule and we started out
on the forty-mile ride, the chief broke the tension by clap-
ping his hands and cheering. Everybody followed suit so
enthusiastically that our mules bolted down the hill at a
gallop.

When we reached the village at the foot of the mountain
the entire population was waiting, and we were again cheered
on our way. As we reached the outskirts of the village I heard
someone galloping after us. It was a Chinese youth about fifteen
years old, riding a pony. He was well dressed and indicated

he wanted to accompany us. The bandit emissary smiled and gave his assent, and we were off on the fateful journey.

6—Formal Negotiations

We rode all day, only stopping a few minutes in the little mountain villages for a drink of tea. We finally reached the outer edge of the bandit zone, waved good-bye to the last bandit sentry, and entered "no-man's-land"—a stretch about a mile wide between the outposts of the opposing sides. Anything could happen here, but nothing did, and we reached the government outpost without incident. After examining our letters, the officer in charge permitted us to proceed. We were still a considerable way from our destination when darkness fell. Noticing that my companions were inclined to hang back as we neared our destination, I insisted they ride ahead of me as we approached the walled compound wherein was located the coal mine pit head, with power plant and quarters for the engineers and staff. The railway station and yards were also within the walled compound. The wall was of thick stone construction, with towers at intervals, and in each tower was a sentry with a machine gun. There was one of these towers on each side of the heavy sheet-steel gate. The stoutly fortified mine compound gave an indication of the disturbed situation of the countryside.

When we were still a considerable distance from the gate a sentry shouted an order, and suddenly the roadway facing us was illuminated as light as day. I recognized the rays as coming from a powerful searchlight mounted on one of the towers, but not so my precious companions, who suddenly turned their mounts off the road and dashed across the field. Realizing the predicament my fellow captives and I would be in if I lost them, I spurred my mule to a gallop and dashed after them. The gateman helped me by keeping them spotted with his searchlight. After exhausting my limited supply of

Chinese expletives, I succeeded in overtaking the bandits and finally got them headed back toward the gate.

When at last I heard the heavy steel gate clang shut with my bandit emissaries inside, I heaved a sigh of relief and nearly fell off my mule from sheer weakness. I felt that the most serious obstacle to our release had been overcome.

A soldier took us to the railway coach where John K. Davis, the American Consul, and the British, French, and Italian Consuls and military representatives had their temporary offices and sleeping compartments. There was great excitement when we arrived, and enormous curiosity regarding the two bandits I had brought with me. Soon Roy Anderson and Carl Crow greeted me, and also another personal friend and former classmate at Missouri University, Roy Bennett. Bennett had been passing through Shanghai on his way to Manila to accept a position on the *Manila Bulletin* when the bandit incident occurred. He immediately wired Carson Taylor, publisher of the *Bulletin*, for permission to remain over, and went to work on my paper, *The China Weekly Review*, in Shanghai in my absence.

I wish I could have been of equal assistance to Bennett when he was confined by the Japanese in an old Spanish prison at Manila for almost three years because of his refusal to collaborate with the invaders following Pearl Harbor.

I explained to the American and British Consuls my sudden and strange appearance and introduced my bandit companions, who were now my guests. It was decided to take them at once to the Pang-ban or Governor's representative, whose headquarters was in another car. We were taken to him by Mr. Davis and formally introduced. The Pang-ban received the bandit emissary with all the formality of a high government dignitary, and they were shortly in deep conversation. I soon slipped away and joined my friends in the official car, where I was served my first real meal in more than a month. There was so much to talk about that it was past midnight before we noticed the passage of time. Before retiring I was taken to the mine manager's house where I took a bath, also the first in a month, and changed into a complete outfit of clean clothes which Bennett had thoughtfully brought with him from Shanghai.

When I was shown my sleeping compartment in the official car, I was surprised to find Wang, the chief's son, waiting for me. He had been provided with a sumptuous supper and had eaten so much cake and candy that he appeared on the point of exploding. He spurned a sleeping berth and insisted on sleeping on the floor of the corridor next to my compartment.

The next morning there was a conference participated in by Mr. Davis, the Pang-ban, Roy Anderson and myself. The Pang-ban explained that he was ready to negotiate with the bandit leaders, and suggested a village midway between the two camps. He suggested that each side be represented by an equal number of principals and guards, and recommended that Roy Anderson and I also attend as witnesses in order to guarantee the good faith of both sides. After the Pang-ban had written out his proposals he carefully folded the paper, sealed it in an envelope and handed the original to the bandit emissary and a copy to me.

I went back to the mine manager's house to change back into my old clothes, and was astonished to find my friend Bennett preparing to accompany me, as I thought, back to the bandit roost. I was mistaken; Roy had decided to return in my place, and insisted that I agree. He said that he had talked the matter over with my family, and all had agreed that he should enter the bandit camp as my substitute. It required considerable argument to convince Bennett that despite the anxiety it would cause my family it was necessary for me to return, otherwise the bandit chiefs would regard it as a breach of faith. Bennett finally was convinced that I was determined to return to the bandit stronghold, but he was sure that I would never get out again alive. There were tears in his eyes as I and my two bandit companions rode out through the iron gate on our long trip back into the mountains.

We rode steadily, only stopping briefly in the villages to drink tea and eat the sandwiches we had brought with us. After we had passed through no-man's-land and were back in bandit territory the bandit youth rode up alongside me and laughingly pulling up his jacket he showed me a large army revolver in a holster strapped to his body under his shirt. I was startled at the discovery and was never able to unravel the mystery. Was he provided with the gun by his father in order to kill me in the event I double-crossed him and the bandit emissary? Or had a secret friend of the bandit chief in the Governor's camp provided the boy with a revolver as a present to his father? I puzzled over the circumstance for several days, and was never able to find an answer.

It was nearly midnight before we reached the bandit headquarters at Mount Pao-tzu-ku. There was great rejoicing at my report of developments and all now felt sure of our early release. The next day the bandit leaders visited our camp and congratulated me on the success of my trip. They said they had agreed to the Pang-ban's suggestion for a conference, and as soon as arrangements could be made they wanted me to take their answer back to Tsaochwang. I rubbed the bruised part of my anatomy which had come in contact with the donkey's razorlike back and thought of that forty-mile ride back to the station. Luckily (from the standpoint of my bruises) the bandits waited a couple of days before they gave the word for my return.

My return to the station, again accompanied by a representative of the outlaws, was uneventful, but my ride back to the bandit camp this time was an event long to be remembered. This time I was accompanied by Roy Anderson, the official "go-between," and what appeared to be a considerable portion of the Chinese army, including several heavily laden carts, each pulled by a half dozen ponies and mules. I learned that these carts contained a large quantity of silver for the bandit leaders and several thousand army uniforms for the rank and file of the bandit gang, which was being taken into the Shantung provincial army. This had been the chief demand, concurred in by all of the leaders, which I had noted in my little book during the conference at the temple. I wondered how many of the other demands the provincial governor had been compelled to agree to as a result of pressure by the central government as well as the Powers, in order to get us out of the clutches of the outlaws.

7—Release and Reparations

The full extent and significance of the bandits' demands were not fully realized until the "peace conference" between the outlaws and the Government's representatives got under way. Never was a stranger or more dramatic conference held. In the little temple on the side of the mountain, visible from the village where the conference was held, sat the little band of captives whose lives hung in the balance as the talks seemed to sway from one side to the other. Most disconcerting to Anderson and me were the frequent "off-side" sessions of little groups, usually held in secret behind the rambling one-story building where the meeting was held. We never could tell whether they were walking out entirely, and we always heaved a sigh of relief when they returned. Each chieftain wanted a large sum of money "in real silver," some of the demands running as high as a million dollars. But this was not to be regarded as sordid ransom; it was "back pay" for the rank and file, practically all of whom at one time or another had been connected with some provincial army. Each chief naturally demanded that all of his followers be taken into the army and provided with new uniforms. Also there were demands for enormous quantities of rice and flour, the amounts being specified in tens of thousands of piculs, the Chinese unit, equivalent to 133 pounds avoirdupois.

The most significant demand, constituting evidence of political and possibly foreign intrigue, was that the so-called bandit area, embracing a section of several hundred square miles and including portions of the three provinces, Kiangsu, Shantung, and Anhwei, be "neutralized" under some form of international guarantee by the foreign Powers. The area which the bandit leaders specified included the important railway junction point of Hsuchowfu where the north-south Tientsin-Nanking line crossed the east-west Lung-Hai line. The bandits insisted that their force, now expanded to possibly a division, be stationed inside the "neutralized" area. The demands included specific conditions regarding collection and apportionment of taxation, exploitation of coal mines and other minerals, and development of communications. It seemed to me that the bandits must have had outside assistance in working out the plan which appeared to be beyond the capacity of a band of mountain outlaws.

The inspiration behind this particular demand, aside from the element of self-preservation, still remains a secret. Some thought it was Japan's method of retaliation for the action of the Powers at the Washington Arms Conference in forcing Japan to restore Shantung to Chinese sovereignty. Others thought the bandits were instigated by southern political interests antagonistic to the Peking Government and hoped in this manner to discredit their political enemies. Dr. Jacob Gould Schurman, American Minister, told me several months afterward that he had never been able to get to the bottom of the incident, and was surprised when the central government suddenly offered to refund the losses suffered by the passengers and agreed to pay the captives an indemnity figured out on a per diem basis for the time they were held in captivity.

There had been a time in the not too distant past when a foreign Power or group of Powers might have taken advantage of the bandit incident to establish control over Chinese territory. Germany had seized the port of Tsingtao on the Shantung coast twenty-three years earlier, in retaliation for the killing of three

German missionaries; Russia had seized Port Arthur on the Gulf
of Chihli (Po Hai); and Britain had established a training station
at Wei-hai-wei on the north side of the Shantung Peninsula. But
imperial Germany and imperial Russia were temporarily out of
the running, and the other Powers with interests in the Pacific
had adopted a new program, in their relations with each other
and with China, which had gone into effect at the Washington
Conference. All of the Powers, including Japan, had agreed to
abandon their old spheres of influence and concessions, and had
signed a treaty guaranteeing China against just such interference
in her domestic affairs as the bandits were inviting. It was certain that the bandits had not originated the foreign-concession
idea themselves; there must have been instigation from some
outside quarter, possibly for the purpose of testing out the
Powers as to their sincerity concerning the Nine-Power Treaty.

After eliminating the ridiculous, the conference finally settled down to the familiar old-fashioned game of bluff and compromise so dear to the hearts of all true Sons of Han. The bandits'
demands for the release of the foreign captives finally narrowed
down to two points: Was the Government willing to take the entire gang into the army and to hand over to the chieftain a sufficient sum to pay the salaries of the "new army" for six months in
advance? The Government, under pressure by the Powers, was
willing, but it wanted the amount of money involved and the
number of bandits taken into the army held down to reasonable
proportions. The exact amount paid over and the number of
soldiers decided upon was never announced, but the debate was
long and acrimonious. The conference had a dramatic conclusion when Sven Mao-yao, the youthful leader, held up his hand
and after proclaiming his loyalty to the Government, signed
the agreement. The other chiefs then walked up and signed,
following which the Government officials affixed their signatures or seals to the document, which was then pushed across
the table for Anderson and me to sign as witnesses and guaran-
tors of the good faith of both participants.

One day six months later Anderson telephoned me and

stated in great indignation that he had just received word that the Governor of Shantung had violated the agreement and through some subterfuge had enticed the bandits away from their guns and had massacred some six hundred of them with machine guns. Sven Mao-yao, the youthful chief, was also executed. Most foreigners approved the action of the Shantung Governor, but Roy Anderson, better versed in current Chinese "checker-board" politics, predicted that the action of the Shantung Governor would have tragic results in case other foreigners were kidnaped by bandits or rebel troops in future—a forecast which was borne out by later developments when many foreigners, chiefly missionaries, lost their lives when ransoms were not immediately forthcoming. The missionaries were the chief sufferers, because they generally refused to pay ransoms, on the ground that such payments only incited further kidnaping of mission workers.

As the foreign captives were aware of the negotiations proceeding in the village in the valley, they spent many anxious hours awaiting the conclusion. As the day drew to a close they had practically given up hope when a messenger arrived with a slip of paper ordering the release of the captives. "Thank God," was the involuntary utterance, but there was still further delay; the bandit leaders insisted on providing sedan chairs for all members of the party so that they could depart in a manner befitting foreign guests. We didn't actually get away until after nightfall, and in consequence didn't reach the rescue party at the coal mine until long after midnight. When we woke up the next morning our train was moving; the government railways had provided us with a special running straight through to Shanghai. When the train arrived the next day Shanghai's entire foreign population, which had been demanding strong punitive measures in reprisal for the bandit outrage, turned out in such a crowd that they blocked the streets leading to the railway station.

Just twenty years later—following Pearl Harbor, when

the Japanese seized the Shanghai International Settlement—an American and a Briton, who had been prisoners of the Shantung bandits, found themselves confined in the same cell in the notorious Japanese Bridge House concentration camp at Shanghai. As the two ex-prisoners of the Shantung bandits recognized each other they involuntarily stuck out their hands in a hearty clasp and exclaimed in unison, "I prefer Chinese bandits to these Jap scoundrels."

I was the American.

XII

Affairs in South China

ALL DURING THE EARLY 1920's I was following with particular interest the situation which was developing in Southern China. After various difficulties with reactionary military officials in the southern province, Dr. Sun Yat-sen finally succeeded in establishing himself as the legal and constitutional President of China, having been elected by the reconstituted Parliament in Canton on April 27, 1921. He formally assumed office on May 5 of that year.

The first foreign diplomatic contact by Dr. Sun Yat-sen's new constitutional Government at Canton was with the Russian Soviets. China's contact with the Union of Socialist Soviet Republics, however, began somewhat earlier, in Peking, when the Russians, in 1919, offered to relinquish their extraterritorial rights in China, including control of the Chinese Eastern Railway in Manchuria. The Peking Government was suspicious of the unexpected Russian generosity and did not respond to Moscow's invitation to open negotiations. Acceptance of the invitation would have implied recognition of the new Soviet regime.

In 1922 Moscow sent its official representative, M. Joffe, to Shanghai to confer with Dr. Sun Yat-sen. I covered the conference, which was held in the Palace Hotel at Shanghai, with Eugene Chen, a Trinidad-born Chinese, acting as Dr. Sun's secretary and press representative. Joffe and Dr. Sun issued a joint statement of friendship and pledge of mutual assistance between the two countries, and also made preliminary arrangements for Soviet assistance to the new Chinese Administration at Canton in the form of a loan and the dispatch of Soviet representatives to serve as advisers to the Canton Government.

China agreed to send a delegation of students to Moscow for training in Bolshevist revolutionary tactics.

The Sino-Soviet agreement contained an interesting provision whereby the Soviet Union agreed to help the Chinese establish a national oil monopoly which would make it possible for China to become independent of the Anglo-American oil trusts, represented by the Standard Oil Company, the Vacuum Oil Company, Texas Company, and Asiatic Petroleum, a British subsidiary of Royal Dutch Shell. The Chinese built large oil-storage facilities at Shanghai and elsewhere for the handling of imports of Soviet oil. It later developed that Moscow's real objective was to bring pressure on Anglo-American oil interests in connection with dealings in Europe and the Near East. After the Russians had made a satisfactory deal with Standard Oil they grew cold to the China project, and ultimately abandoned it and withdrew their staff from the Far East. The large oil-storage depot which the Russians helped the Chinese construct on the banks of the Whangpoo River at Shanghai passed ultimately into the hands of the foreign oil companies.

Dr. Sun Yat-sen's action in establishing contact with the Russian Soviets in 1922 was followed by outright recognition of the USSR by the Peking Government the following year. The negotiations at Peking were conducted by Dr. C. T. Wang and Dr. V. K. Wellington Koo, two Chinese diplomats who were just coming into prominence. The Soviet representative was L. M. Karakhan, an Armenian. The negotiations began in 1923, and a preliminary agreement was initialed by Dr. C. T. Wang, but it aroused so much opposition that Dr. Wang was forced to withdraw. The final agreement, whereby China granted full diplomatic recognition to the USSR, was signed by Dr. V. K. Wellington Koo, acting Premier of the Peking Government in March, 1924.

But there was a notable difference in the texts of the Peking and Canton agreements. Whereas the Peking Government's recognition agreement contained a definite commitment on

Russia's part not to propagate communistic doctrines in China, the situation at Canton was the exact opposite in that the propagation of communism was a chief Russian objective.

Among the considerable number of radical advisers who joined the Canton Government were two outstanding Soviet personages, Michael Borodin and General Galens (or Blücher). M. Joffe, who negotiated the original alliance with Dr. Sun, did not remain in China but returned to Moscow. It was generally known in China that the motivating influence in Moscow behind the China adventure was Leon Trotsky, proponent of world revolution. China was regarded as the most fertile field for the initial experiment. These are generally known facts, but it is not so widely known, particularly in the United States, that Americans and Britons professing leftist or communist faith, who flocked to China, exercised perhaps even greater influence upon the course of events in China than did the Russians.

In the first place, only two of the Russians, Borodin and Karakhan, could speak English, the only common language between the Russians and Chinese. While Borodin has been listed as a Russian, he had lived in the United States for most of his life and probably was an American citizen. His wife was an American and their two sons, who attended the American School in Shanghai, registered under the name of Grusenberg, were born in Chicago. Borodin had emigrated to the United States when a youth and attended Valparaiso University, following which he taught school in Chicago and for several years operated a Russian-language school in that city. He returned to Russia after the 1917 revolution and was associated with Trotsky, who sent him to China as the Soviet's chief political emissary. From the inception of the Nationalist Government at Canton, Borodin probably exercised more influence in China than any other foreigner. He was in constant conference with Dr. Sun and other Nationalist leaders, and directed the propaganda activities of a horde of Chinese students, some of whom had been trained in Moscow under

Karl Radek, or in China under Chinese communist teachers, who in turn had received their training in Russia.

The new socialist Government functioned with considerable efficiency and harmony as long as Dr. Sun remained at the helm. The only discordant elements were Wang Ching-wei and Hu Han-ming, whose squabbles and intrigues for power were usually settled by Dr. Sun or by General Chiang Kai-shek.

Chiang Kai-shek, whose activities were destined to affect vitally China's future and the destiny of the entire Far East, was a native of the central seaboard province of Chekiang. His father, Chiang Soh-an, was a wine merchant in the small village of Fenghua, about 150 miles southwest of the great port and metropolis of Shanghai. The father died when Chiang was only eight years old, but his mother, though of modest means, managed to raise sufficient money to enable him to accompany a class of some forty other Chekiang youths to the military academy at Paotingfu, near Peking. Here young Chiang showed such promise as a student of infantry tactics that the Manchu Government sent him in 1907 to the Tokyo Military Academy for advanced training. Although Chinese students were not granted the facilities extended to native Japanese students, Chiang made excellent progress not only in military science but in Japanese language, history, and affairs.

Of greater significance, however, greater even than his academic accomplishments, was his contact with Dr. Sun Yat-sen, then a political refugee in Japan. Chiang was only eighteen years old when he entered the Tokyo academy, hence was able not only to absorb ideas about Japan at this critical time in the transformation of that country following its emergence from feudalism, but also to absorb revolutionary ideas about his own country. He was obviously impressed by the fact that Japan had been able to humble giant Russia, whereas his own country had been the victim of aggression by Russia and other European Powers as well as by Japan.

Chiang remained in Japan for four years, and returned to

his homeland just in time to participate in the first revolution, in 1911. He recruited a brigade of troops and assisted Dr. Sun Yat-sen and the local controller of the Lower Yangtze area, Chen Chi-mei, in holding Shanghai against the Manchu forces. Two years later he assisted Dr. Sun in the conflict with Yuan Shih-kai, and when Dr. Sun was forced to retire to Nanking, Chiang gave up military activities and became a broker in the International Settlement at Shanghai. As a result of participation in a stock-exchange boom he reputedly acquired a considerable fortune, much of which he contributed to Dr. Sun's war chest at Canton. In 1923 Chiang accepted an invitation to become principal of the new Whampoa Military Academy, which Dr. Sun had organized, with Russian assistance, for the purpose of training officers to serve in the revolutionary army then being recruited and organized.

Chiang won his first military spurs when he rallied the cadets from the Whampoa Academy and suppressed a revolt against Dr. Sun which had been instigated by the Canton Volunteers, a sort of militia, which had been organized by Canton merchants. Chiang also participated as commander of government troops in fights against other military factions in the Canton area which were opposed to Dr. Sun Yat-sen. Most of these revolts were secretly organized by General Chen Chiung-ming, who, although a professed member of the Kuomintang, was, nevertheless, strongly opposed to Dr. Sun. When General Chen engineered a coup against Dr. Sun and forced the Cantonese leader to flee to Hong Kong, Chiang rallied revolutionary forces which were friendly to the Government at Foochow, and marched on Canton. Chen's forces were defeated on January 15, 1925, and he was forced to withdraw to Wuchow, a strongly fortified city located several miles from Canton.

With his reputation as a military commander established, General Chiang became the outstanding leader of government troops and in two years eliminated all military opposition to the new government in the southern provinces of Kwangtung, Kiangsi, South Hunan, and part of Kweichow.

Dr. Sun Yat-sen, father of the revolution, who had devoted forty years of his life to the cause of China's reconstruction, was not destined to see the fruition of plans for a unified and modernized China. He became seriously ill and fainted while addressing a political gathering at Canton, and was taken to Peking for treatment at the Rockefeller Institute. His ailment was diagnosed as cancer, and he died on March 12, 1925. His body was taken to a temple in the Western Hills near Peking, where it remained under guard until it could be removed to the new national capital at Nanking for official burial in a specially constructed mausoleum on the slope of Purple Mountain.

There was an undignified squabble between the Soviet Russian advisers, members of Dr. Sun's immediate family, and Kuomintang leaders over the type of coffin in which Dr. Sun's body was to be encased as well as the type of funeral and the mausoleum in which the body was to rest permanently. The Soviet advisers strongly urged the use of a glass coffin in which the body could be kept on permanent exhibition, as had been done with Lenin's body in Red Square, Moscow. They even had a glass-and-copper casket sent to Peking from Moscow, but it was found to be defective, so the body was finally placed in a bronze coffin imported from the United States. The funeral, which was held at Nanking, the new capital, followed with few modifications traditional Chinese lines. The Government constructed a new road, known as the "Chung-shan" Highway, which extended from the banks of the Yangtze to the new mausoleum constructed at great expense on Purple Mountain. Although designed by a modern educated Chinese architect, the mausoleum for China's great republican leader does not differ fundamentally from the concept of the ancient Ming tomb in the same vicinity.

Fierce struggles for power among his followers began even before his death on March 12, 1925, first between the Wang Ching-wei and Hu Han-ming factions. Even more serious were the later complications which developed between the right-wing Kuomintangists and the left-wing radical socialists and the communists. Dr. Sun's last will and testament, which implied close cooperation between China and Soviet Russia, was supposedly written by Wang Ching-wei while Dr. Sun was on his deathbed. There were allegations that the will was a forgery perpetrated by Wang Ching-wei and the Russian adviser Michael Borodin, although the document contained Dr. Sun's signature. Despite its detractors, however, the document stands above the laws of the land among members of the party. It is recited every morning by all Chinese students throughout the length and breadth of the country, and is repeated in unison at the weekly meetings of the chief government committee.

The full text of the will is as follows:

I have devoted myself to the revolutionary cause for about forty years, with the sole object of securing liberty and equality for China. From my personal experience gained during the last forty years, I fully understand that if we are to attain our object we must arouse the masses and also ask for the cooperation of such nations as have been willing to treat us as their equals. At present the revolution is still incomplete. All our comrades must act in accordance with my declarations known as "Outline of Reconstruction," the "Reconstruction Plan," the "Three People's Principles," and also the declaration of the "First National Conference of Kuomintang Delegates." They must continue the fight for realization of our latest principles. Again the call of the People's Conference and the abrogation of all unequal treaties must be accomplished in the immediate future.

The Three People's Principles were (1) the Principle of Nationalism, (2) the Principle of People's Rights, and (3) the Principle of People's Livelihood. Under the first, Dr. Sun held that nationality had developed through natural forces—the state, through force of arms; and that Western supremacy in world affairs sprang not from a superior political philosophy but from advancement in material civilization. Under the second Principle he presented his ideals of applied democracy, and under the third, industrial organization within the state and the elevation of living standards of the people.

XIII

Factional Troubles of the 1920's

THE CHINESE COMMUNISTS, who were admitted to membership in the Kuomintang on an equal basis as a result of a conference of delegates in Canton on January 20, 1924, had from the first endeavored to exert pressure on the party. The first indication of serious trouble between the Kuomintang and Communist factions was given early in 1926.

Four young military officers, all graduates of the Whampoa Academy, organized an anti-communist movement. The four men, all destined to become prominent in the next few months in the military drive to the Yangtze Valley, were Li Tsung-jen, Li Chi-sheng, Chu Peh-teh and Ho Ying-chin. General Chiang Kai-shek, head of the Central Military Academy, steered clear of the Kuomintang-Communist controversy, but his trip to Russia in 1924 caused him to be suspected of pro-Red leanings. A record of his activities in Russia, however, indicated that he had been cold to Soviet blandishments. As a result of pressure by the four young military officers, General Chiang, on March 24, 1926, issued a statement that he would follow the teachings of Dr. Sun's Three Principles (see preceding chapter), and would discontinue all connections with the Communist wing.

General Chiang Kai-shek's disinclination to side with the Communists was due to two factors: First, his birth and environment in industrialized, conservative Chekiang Province and his association with the banking and commercial elements from that province which dominated Shanghai business; second, the advice of a fellow provincial, Chang Ching-kiang, an almost mythical character who had become immensely wealthy in the

silk and curio trade between China and France in the latter
years of the Ching Dynasty. (Many of the rare Chinese works
of art purchased by American millionaires came to this country by way of France.) Chang Ching-kiang, the curio dealer,
espoused the revolutionary cause and contributed large sums
to Dr. Sun's war chest. He participated in the conferences
preliminary to the formation of the Nanking Provisional
Government, but refused to accept office. Two years later he
again helped Dr. Sun in opposing Yuan Shih-kai's monarchist
plot, and as a result was proscribed, along with many others,
by the Yuan regime. Chang Ching-kiang fled to Paris, where
he opened a profitable curio and art store and also a popular
restaurant where Chinese foods, particularly soya-bean products, were sold. After the passing of Yuan Shih-kai, Chang
returned to Shanghai, where he further increased his fortune
in the stock and gold-bar exchanges. It was here that he became acquainted with Chiang Kai-shek, and assisted him financially. In 1925 he went to Canton and became a member of the
Constitutional Government. He accompanied General Chiang
Kai-shek on the military advance to the Yangtze, and after
the split between the Kuomintang and Communist factions he
joined the Nanking Government. In his later years his health
failed, and it became necessary for him to travel about in a
wheel chair. But there was no impairment of his opposition to
the Communists.

Hu Han-ming, civilian leader of the right-wing Kuomintang
group, also opposed the Communists, but Wang Ching-wei, the
other civilian contender for the position held by the late leader
of the party, Dr. Sun Yat-sen, sided with the Reds and in company with a number of the Russian and American advisers of
the Canton Government departed for Hankow.

By the summer of 1926 the Nationalist army, under the
command of Chiang Kai-shek, started its northward advance
from Canton. As a result of the anti-imperialist propaganda
inspired by the Communist faction of the Kuomintang, foreigners, particularly missionaries residing in the interior of the

country, were seriously affected by the Nationalist Revolution which was sweeping northward. Mission schools, churches and residences were looted and thousands of missionaries were forced to flee to Shanghai.

But the most dramatic developments of the revolution took place at Hankow, Nanking and Shanghai, where the smouldering hatred and intrigue for power between the Kuomintang and the Communists broke out in furious internecine conflict. General Chiang Kai-shek's charge that the Communists had sent secret emissaries into the cities for the purpose of seizing control prior to the arrival of his troops, was borne out by developments at both Hankow and Shanghai. In both cities Communist activity originally was directed at the control of student and labor organizations.

Students of the Chinese Nationalist Revolution whose sympathies have been on the side of the radical or communist factions have purposely ignored the developments at Hankow which tell the most significant story of the failure of Chinese Communists, and their foreign advisers, to accomplish their ambitious plan of seizing control of the Nationalist movement and establishing communistic government in China. They blame "foreign capitalist-imperialist influence," "new militarism" and native "banker-landlord influence" for their lack of success, but while these elements did contribute, there were other and more fundamental causes.

Of the many causes for the failure of the Red regime at Hankow not the least was the action of the leaders in preaching class warfare and catering to radical student-labor groups in a society which was predominantly agricultural and where there had never been any classes, except the old educated or "literati" group which was, theoretically at least, open to all youths of ability who could pass the official examinations. After the capture of the Wu-Han cities, which had been accomplished largely by the military strategy of General Chiang Kai-shek, the leftist Chinese leaders and their foreign advisers staged a veritable "Roman holiday" in celebration of their victory over "capitalistic imperialism." There was a trial of two "war prisoners" staged in the Russian manner, the culprits being two northern generals who were captured at Wuchang. Thousands of laborers employed in the mines, factories, and processing plants (Hankow is popularly known as the Pittsburgh of China) ceased work, and led by radical elements spent the days and nights in speechmaking, parades, and demonstrations. Streets were filled with marching students and laborers carrying banners inscribed with slogans, "Down with Capitalists and Imperialists," "Support the World Revolution," "Workers of the World, Unite," and similar sentiments. Thousands of young peasants from Hunan Province, where an intense Red propaganda had been conducted for a considerable period, flocked into Hankow to join the festivities.

The industries of the Wu-Han area were forced to close down: press-packing plants where native products were prepared for foreign markets; manufacturing industries, including cotton spinning and weaving mills; vegetable-oil pressing plants, hundreds of small native-owned industries, the great Han Yeh Ping coal and iron interests (controlled by Japan), large cigarette factories owned by Britons and Americans, the shipping industry operating large sea-going steamers on the lower Yangtze and smaller but more powerful steamers capable of negotiating the rapids of the Upper Yangtze, and an enormous junk trade operated by the Chinese on the great canal system and lakes of central China. Thousands of workers, who had been spending their days celebrating the revolution by holding parades and demonstrations, suddenly found themselves without meal tickets.

Since the Government had catered to the radical elements and encouraged the strikes, the student-labor groups naturally turned to it for support. The Government thus found itself in a vicious circle of its own making, and had to adopt the suici-

dal method of issuing floods of paper money in order to purchase rice for the hungry multitudes. Prices for food, particularly rice, shot up to prohibitive heights.

In order to save the Government itself from retaliation by
the hungry crowds, propagandists attempted to turn the
revolutionary sentiment against the foreigners. More parades
were organized, with banners denouncing foreign imperialism,
and the British Concession was over-run. No attempt was made
to invade the Japanese Concession, which was bristling with
machine guns. The British Concession was guarded only by a
small naval contingent and a local volunteer corps and police
force. Unable to cope with the excited demonstrators who
stormed the borders of their Concession, and fearing a debacle,
the British Consul-General, an Irishman named O'Malley, ordered the British population to withdraw to British ships in
the harbor—which was accomplished without incident. Possessed of more political sagacity than most of his compatriots,
Consul-General O'Malley immediately entered into negotiations
with the radical Foreign Minister, Eugene Chen, and the outcome was the sensational Chen-O'Malley Agreement whereby
Great Britain agreed to return the British Concession at Hankow to China. The official release from the Foreign Office in
London stated that the action "accorded with Britain's long-
existing intention to return her Concessions to Chinese control."

When the Chinese found themselves in possession of the
British Concession calmer counsels prevailed, the excitement
died down, and the paraders returned to their quarters.

Another element which had a calming effect on the situation
at Hankow was the receipt of alarming reports from Nanking,
some four hundred miles down the Yangtze, stating that American gunboats had been forced to fire on a mob of demonstrators, including troops, which were attacking the American
community, with officials of the American Consulate and their
families. Suddenly realizing the seriousness of the complications

in which they had become involved, Foreign Minister Eugene Chen sent a wire to the State Department disavowing responsibility for the Nanking outrages but offering remuneration for damages suffered by foreigners at the hands of Chinese radical elements.

The Chen-O'Malley Agreement providing for the return of the British Concession at Hankow to Chinese control, and the official telegram from the radical Chinese regime at Hankow to the State Department, marked the high point in the strange career of Eugene Chen, who had figured prominently in Chinese politics for a decade. Born in Trinidad, British West Indies, of a Chinese father and a Trinidad woman, Chen was educated as a British barrister in England and had been admitted to practice in Inner Temple, London. But the pull of his Chinese blood was too strong, and he returned to China, along with thousands of his compatriots from the Seven Seas, to participate in the revolution. Having a fair classical education in English (he could neither read nor speak Chinese), Chen naturally gravitated into newspaper work and on occasion stirred the sluggish English communities in the Far East to white heat with his editorials, filled with classical quotations from English literature. He edited radical papers in Shanghai and Peking, and once when the Chinese authorities in Peking arrested him and threatened him with execution, he remembered his British nationality, through birth in Trinidad, and appealed to the British Minister to save his life. Sir John Jordan, the aged, kindly, and influential British Minister, asked the Chinese authorities to release Chen—who, upon obtaining his liberty, fled to the sanctuary of the International Settlement at Shanghai. Later, Chen went to Canton and joined Dr. Sun Yat-sen's revolutionary Government and participated in the northern advance as a member of the radical faction, becoming Foreign Minister of the Hankow Government.

There was an illuminating incident in connection with the British evacuation at Hankow which was prophetic of later developments in British Far Eastern diplomacy. When the British were evacuating their nationals from the Concession to their ships in the harbor, the British Indian community, consisting largely of Sikhs, was overlooked. After the white Britons were safely aboard the ships someone thought about the Sikhs, most of whom had been employed as policemen or guards and watchmen by the various foreign and Chinese business houses and manufacturing establishments. Some had become wealthy as money lenders. One of the consular officials went ashore to rescue the missing Sikhs, who had disappeared completely. While returning to his ship the British consular official stopped to observe a parade which had been organized by the students to celebrate the taking over of the Concession. At the end of the procession, also carrying banners denouncing foreign imperialists, were the missing Sikhs. They had "gone over" to the Chinese and Communist revolutionists.

The action of the little group of British Indians in joining the Chinese revolutionists was prophetic of events to come: events in 1941-42, when British Indian troops at Hong Kong, in Malaya, and in Burma, and the Congress Party in India, either refused to support Great Britain or adopted an attitude of non-cooperation with respect to the war with Japan in the Far East.

The acquisition of the British Concession at Hankow enhanced considerably the prestige of the radical branch of the Kuomintang, but this could not be exchanged for the wherewithal to feed the hordes of unemployed laborers who had been encouraged to strike and agitate against the imperialists and capitalists. With adversity came treachery within the ranks of the radical factions. Wang Ching-wei, who already had a reputation for treachery, grew cold toward the radical Chinese and Russian elements.

Mao Tse-tung, spokesman of the radical faction, attributed the failure of the Red regime at Hankow to the weakness or treachery of another Chinese leader, Chen Tu-hsiu, who allegedly compromised on fundamental policies concerning land redistribution. Mao was quoted in Edgar Snow's "Red Star Over China" as charging the Russian adviser Borodin and a British Indian radical named Roy, a delegate of the Comintern, with joint responsibility with Chen Tu-hsiu, the party dictator, for the collapse. According to Mao, Borodin, the official representative of the Moscow Comintern, had ceased being an "adviser" and had become a dictator of the Kuomintang Party. Chen Tu-hsiu had concealed the real situation from the party leaders, but Borodin's activities allegedly were exposed by the Indian delegate Roy. This is said to have caused the defection of Wang Ching-wei and the split in the Hankow Left Wing Government which facilitated the victory of Chiang Kai-shek and the Nanking faction over the Radical-Communist branch.

Another unexpected element in the situation was that the collapse of the radical Hankow Government had serious repercussions in Moscow and contributed considerably to the collapse of Trotsky and advocates of world revolution. Stalin and his group seized upon the failure of the China adventure, which had cost the Soviets large sums of money and great effort, to discredit Trotsky and the whole group of advocates of "permanent world revolution." Borodin returned by a tortuous overland trip to Moscow in disgrace and became editor of the four-page English-language *Moscow Daily News*.

Sun Fo, son of Dr. Sun Yat-sen, who participated in the Hankow Government, but later withdrew, also confirmed Mao's statements, particularly the reference to the "dictatorial attitude of the Russians." Chen Kung-po, an American returned student and graduate of Columbia University, New York, who had specialized in economics and had served as secretary to Wang Ching-wei, wrote a series of articles (published in the *China Weekly Review* shortly after the collapse of the Hankow Government) in which he analyzed the causes of the collapse of the Hankow Red regime. He concluded by advocating a system of state capitalism and state ownership of industries as a means of surmounting the complications which develop when privately owned industrial establishments suspend operations and throw laborers back on the Government for support. Chen argued that only through the development of state capitalism could the Chinese Government hope to cope with powerful foreign interests established in the country, which in times of crisis usually are able to marshal the support of the large native Chinese industrial and banking interests in opposition to socialistic experiments. Chen Kung-po, formerly a political associate of Wang Ching-wei, later became head of the Japanese puppet Government at Nanking, following the death of Wang Ching-wei in Tokyo in 1944. Chen Kung-po was the only Chinese student, educated in the United States, who voluntarily joined the Nanking puppet. No Chinese student of any American university, to the writer's knowledge, ever joined the Chinese Communist faction. Thousands of American returned students are members of the Kuomintang.

XIV

Fighting in Shanghai

I—*Imperialism, Nationalism, Communism*

I HAD RECEIVED numerous intimations long before the Nationalist armies reached the Yangtze that all was not going well with
the Kuomintang-Communist partnership. The information I
had received was in the form of two confidential pamphlets
addressed by General Chiang Kai-shek to the party leaders,
in which he charged that the Communists were secretly plot-
ting to oust the Kuomintang and seize control of the party
organization and ultimately of the Government. But I was not
prepared for the tragic developments which followed the
Nationalist-Communist occupation of Hankow, Nanking, and
Shanghai.

American and other Occidental missionaries whose stations
were in the path of the advancing armies were the first to feel
the effect of the Communist hook-up. Every boat and train
brought hundreds of refugee mission workers, men, women
and children to Shanghai. In most cases they were forced to flee
from their homes, which were looted by the disorderly soldiers.
Mission churches and religious schools were particular objectives of the Reds and were subjected to wholesale desecration.
The missionaries were attacked on two grounds—imperialism
and the Christian religion.

I remember attending a press conference called by missionary leaders, at which one man after another got up and told of
atrocities committed in his district by the political branch of
the army. I asked one of the speakers how he accounted for
the fact that the communist students and soldiers were able by
the use of intensive propaganda to counteract the accomplish-

ments of Christian missionaries extending over a long period of years. He replied, "It is always easier to destroy than to build," explaining that the widespread anti-imperialist and anti-religious propaganda directed at the missionaries was so closely linked with the question of nationalism and political reform that the majority of Christian converts were unable to come to the assistance of their foreign friends and benefactors. Any Chinese who helped a foreign friend was labeled a "running-dog of the imperialists."

Foreigners were aware of Soviet influence behind the Chinese Communists, but few realized that the struggle taking place in China was part of a similar life-and-death struggle which was going on within Russia between Joseph Stalin and Leon Trotsky, the two rival leaders in the Russian Communist Party following the death of Lenin. The struggle involved the fundamental objectives of the communist movement.

Lenin had declared, "China is seething—it is our duty to keep the pot boiling." But the attempt to communize China was the work of the Leon Trotsky faction, which advocated world revolution. Following failures in Germany, Austria, Hungary, and England, the directors of the Third International decided to attempt the communization of China and the millions of Asia. Also behind the ideologies lurked the desire on the part of the Russian Red leaders to even scores with the American, British, and other European capitalist-imperialists by attacking their loosely held colonial dependencies in the Far East.

They argued that if they were successful in China it would mean another communist state and a triumph for the Third International, which had lost prestige as a result of the rebuffs it had suffered in Europe. Also, there was the prospect that such success would put a crimp in the rising political prestige of Joseph Stalin, who was bitterly opposed to the world revolutionary program of Comrade Trotsky. Stalin believed in concentrating power in Russia itself. Finally there was the prospect of blocking or suppressing thousands of Russian emigrees who had fled from Russia into Chinese territory after the Red Revolution in 1917. All emigrees were anti-Red.

Reds from all points of the compass—French, German, American, British, Hindu, Turkish—flocked to China to help put over the revolution and, incidentally, participate in the expenditure of the considerable sums which the Third International had collected from the Russian peasants and the world's working classes. Propagandists and political manipulators who had walked to work or had ridden on street cars in their home countries quickly discovered that new American motor cars were a "necessary adjunct" to their activities in China. Shanghai dealers in American cars did a thriving business while the Red boom lasted. But when Earl Browder, head of the American Communist Party, arrived at Shanghai he quickly put a stop to the reckless spending. At an elaborate banquet given in his honor in Shanghai, Browder refused to eat anything but black-bread and water, which he said was the fare of the starving Russian peasants who had put up the money for the Chinese revolution. But Browder arrived on the scene too late; the autocratic and dictatorial actions of certain of the Russian advisers had already alienated the support of many of the Kuomintang leaders.

I interviewed Browder on the subject of the communist situation in China, and heard him denounce in emphatic terms the political agents "who rode around in limousines and went to banquets when the peasants and workers of Russia and China were starving."

The intimate connection between the failure of the Russian communist experiment in China and the ultimate downfall of Commissar Trotsky is revealed in a passage in Trotsky's memoirs (Charles Scribner's Sons) wherein he charged that the Chinese Communist Party had been "forced to join the bourgeois Kuomintang and had been forbidden to create soviets, compelled to hold the agrarian revolution in check and also to abstain from organizing the workers." Trotsky alleged that Stalin supported the Kuomintang-Communist hook-up and had defended General Chiang Kai-shek against attack. After the bloody suppression of the Chinese Communists at Shanghai, Trotsky said he had advised forbearance in the expectation that the action would attract more supporters to the Red banner. However, it did not work out in accordance with Trotsky's expectations and, to quote his words, "After the defeat of the German revolution, and the breakdown of the British general strike, the new disaster in China only intensified the disappointment of the masses in the international revolution, and it was this disappointment which served as the chief psychological source of Stalin's policy of national reformism."

It was natural that developments at Nanking and Hankow should arouse deep apprehension on the part of both Chinese and foreigners at Shanghai, China's largest and most Europeanized city. It is one of the world's largest ports, and more industries are concentrated in the Shanghai district than in any other area of equal size on the continent of East Asia. The city then had a population of approximately 3,000,000, of which some 75,000 or 80,000 were foreigners of almost every nationality and race. It was the Far Eastern headquarters for most of the Protestant and Catholic mission establishments concerned with the propagation of Christianity among the Chinese people. As a result there was a larger investment of American capital in the Shanghai district than anywhere else in Asia, with the exception of the Philippines. British investments at Shanghai were larger than the American investments, and were exceeded only by British investments at Hong Kong.

Alarmist reports of events at Hankow which appeared in the foreign press, particularly the leading British paper, the *North China Daily News*, created a situation of near panic among residents of the International Settlement and the French Concession. A well known British journalist at Peking named Putnam Weale made a trip to Hankow and wrote a series of articles regarding the situation there which he entitled "Red Wave on the Yangtse."

I attended a press conference called by the manager of a leading British brokerage firm where it was explained that the foreign chambers of commerce and other organizations had decided to raise a large fund and initiate widespread counter-propaganda against the Communists. The chairman of the meeting asked the cooperation of the local press and suggested that each of the papers publish a special supplement exposing the communist menace. When he asked for comment on the anti-communist program, I expressed the view that any attempt to label the entire Nationalist movement as "Red" would probably defeat the object of the promoters of the campaign because it would antagonize all Chinese and tend to throw the entire Nationalist movement into the arms of the Reds. I said that the Nationalist movement in China long predated the advent of the Russian Communists, and since the objectives of the two movements were antagonistic, the hook-up was not likely to last overlong unless the Powers adopted a policy of outright opposition.

I also expressed the belief that neither America nor Britain would approve of any program which opposed the Nationalist movement, or any attempt to discredit it by labeling it communistic. I therefore refused to cooperate in the campaign, and left the meeting. The *North China Daily News*, senior British paper in China, usually followed an austere, and on occasion supercilious, course with regard to Chinese politics; but on this occasion the editor forgot his dignity and went all out editorially against the entire Nationalist movement. With the assistance of two American journalists who were employed for the purpose, the paper issued a supplement on the Red question which still stands as a journalistic curiosity, due to the exaggerated and hysterical articles it contained. One article which aroused considerable amusement instructed readers on "How to Spot Communists at Moving Picture Shows and Other Public Gatherings." Later, after the excitement died down, the directors of the paper dropped the American propagandists, employed another editor, and brought the policy of the paper into accord with the changed conditions in China.

As a result of the self-administered propaganda, both foreign areas at Shanghai immediately went on a war basis, and thousands of coolies were employed day and night constructing trenches, barbed-wire barricades, and concrete blockhouses. The panic among the foreigners at Shanghai spread to foreign capitals, and was aggravated by further alarmist reports dispatched abroad by the foreign consulates and legations. Within a few weeks some 40,000 foreign troops were dispatched to the city, including American marines and soldiers, British soldiers, Japanese soldiers, Italian marines, and French Annamite troops from Indo-China.

The American forces were commanded by General Smedley Butler, a veteran of the Boxer campaign of 1900. Butler, a Quaker, constantly exasperated the other commanders by issuing pacifist declarations to the press.

At the height of the excitement I asked Butler, at a press conference, how many troops would be required for a general armed invasion in China sufficiently strong to suppress the Nationalist movement. Without hesitation he replied, "I would not dream of starting an armed invasion in China without a half million troops, and it probably would require a million more before the end of the first year." General Butler's statement was confirmed a few years later when the Japanese were unable to conquer China with more than two million troops and after years of warfare.

On another occasion General Butler disclosed that his orders from Washington were "not to fire on any organized body of Chinese troops." He declared that his sole purpose was to protect the American community against mob violence. Later, after General Butler had returned to the United States, he declared that his forces had not fired a single hostile shot while they were stationed in China. Following his retirement he delivered speeches advocating the withdrawal of all American and other foreign forces from China.

Another American official who preserved his balance and opposed an interventionist policy was Admiral Mark L. Bristol, commander of the United States fleet in Asiatic waters. Admiral Bristol had served as United States High Commissioner to Turkey after World War I, and had observed the futility of an interventionist movement on the part of the Allied Powers with regard to that country.

The first British commander in China, Lord Gort, returned to England in disgust when he discovered that the British Government also had no intention of embarking on a grandiose military adventure in China. Elaborate plans for an invasion of the Yangtze Valley and the creation of a "sanitary zone" fifty miles wide on each side of the Yangtze River between Shanghai and Hankow, a distance of six hundred miles, which had been in the files of the International Settlement for many years, were put back in the pigeonholes to gather more dust. The plans had been prepared by old-guard dyed-in-the-wool imperialists in Shanghai, who thought China could be frightened into submission by a show of foreign force.

The new British commander sent out to replace Lord Gort held a press conference shortly after his arrival. Exhibiting a new map on the wall of his office, he said, "I want you to see that I have changed the color of the thumb tacks indicating the location of the Chinese Nationalist troops; previously we used red tacks, now they are yellow." He declared that the British Government realized that the Chinese Nationalist movement was a genuine revolutionary effort designed to bring about a new day in China, and was not a "Red Wave on the Yangtze" designed for the purpose of driving Americans and Europeans out of the country, as had been pictured in the excited propaganda and exaggerated news reports circulated by Shanghai's die-hard imperialists.

Conservative Chinese commercial and financial interests at

Shanghai generally supported the Nationalist movement, which they hoped would bring an end to the political unrest which had prevailed in the country for a decade. They thought it would bring order to a sorely harassed nation and its impoverished people, but the bankers and businessmen at the same time realized there would be no permanent relief or reconstruction under the program proposed by the Communist wing of the Kuomintang Party. Delegations of businessmen and bankers sent from Shanghai to Hankow, and to Kiangsi and Hunan Provinces, for the purpose of investigating conditions under the Red regime, were seized and paraded through the villages in their shirt-tails by radical students bearing placards denouncing Chinese businessmen as "Running-Dogs of the Imperialists." When the delegates returned to Shanghai with their reports of the reign of terror which prevailed in Hankow and surrounding areas, they immediately took steps to prevent a recurrence of such developments in the Shanghai area.

The complete story of the Shanghai war between the right-wing Kuomintangists and the left-wing radicals and Communists never was told because those who were responsible for the suppression of the radical elements obviously did not wish to reveal their methods, while those who were suppressed did not survive to tell the story. The fact that the Communists had armed and trained thousands of laborers in Shanghai mills was known to the municipal authorities, who naturally took steps to meet the situation; they were spurred to action by the Communists' seizure of strategic points in the native areas.

Generalissimo Chiang Kai-shek was at his headquarters at Nanchang in Kiangsi Province, hence did not take part in the suppression of the Red elements at Shanghai; and the same applied to three of the four outstanding leaders of the conservative wing of the party, General Li Chi-sheng, General Li Tsung-jen, and General Ho Ying-chin, as they also were in command of Nationalist armies still hundreds of miles from Shanghai.

But the same could not be said of another Nationalist commander, who also had been associated with General Chiang in the advance from Canton. The commander was Chang Chien, who did not participate in the drive on Shanghai, but diverted his troops to the west and moved directly on Nanking. When General Chang Chien's troops entered Nanking they systematically looted the city, including the foreign consulates, mission stations, and residences and business properties of both foreigners and Chinese. Acting in accordance with an apparently prearranged plan, they staged a reign of terror, and numerous outrages were committed against foreigners. Evidence pointed to the fact that the Nanking incident had been staged by leftist elements for the purpose of discrediting General Chiang Kai-shek.

Opposed to the advancing Nationalists was the able Northern general, Sun Chuan-fang, who controlled the seaboard provinces of Fukien, Chekiang, and Kiangsu from his capital at Hangchow, about one hundred miles southwest of Shanghai.

Before the situation became critical, I had accompanied a group of correspondents to Hangchow to interview General Sun regarding his plans for the defense of the Shanghai district against the Nationalists. The Shanghai or Yangtze delta region embraced a triangular area, the three sides of which were 100, 200, and 250 miles in length respectively. Shanghai was at the eastern apex, Nanking at the north, and Hangchow at the south. Within this triangular area was the richest section of China, embracing fertile agricultural land devoted largely to the production of cotton, silk, wheat, and rice. There also were a number of prosperous industrial cities, chief of which was Wusih, center of cotton, silk and flour manufacturing within this section.

General Sun was one of the more enlightened of the Northern military commanders and had a good record as an administrator. He held a review of his troops, reputedly the best equipped in the country, and declared his ability to hold

Shanghai against the "Reds." One of the correspondents who represented a New York paper sent a story that Shanghai was "impregnable" and in no danger of occupation by the Nationalists. He was not aware of the fact that the morale of General Sun's well equipped forces had been completely undermined by propaganda of the Communists.

Since the foreign-administered International Settlement and French Concession were garrisoned by foreign troops and were heavily insulated from contact with the surrounding countryside by a string of fortifications and countless strands of barbed-wire barricades, the population inside had little knowledge of what was going on outside. For many days preceding the arrival of the Nationalist forces there was continuous gunfire in the densely populated areas of Pootung, Chapei, and Nantao, where most of the native-owned industries were located and where most of the laboring population resided.

Shanghai was in such a nervous state that the wildest rumors were constantly in circulation, and most of them were believed. One day there was a report that the authorities of the French Concession had decided not to offer resistance to the advancing Nationalist armies, and would permit the soldiers to enter the Concession without their arms. Since the two foreign areas were separated only by a street, this still further increased the prevailing panic in the International Settlement. That night the Settlement authorities put their army of laborers to work building a new barbed-wire barricade, this time between the International Settlement and the French Concession. I interviewed the French Consul-General about the new turn of events, but he only shrugged his shoulders. I suspected he knew more than he was willing to admit, which we soon found to be a fact, for the French already had established contact with the Nationalist (Kuomintang) officers. When the American correspondents learned that two Nationalist officers had arrived on the border of the French Concession, it was the French municipal police who opened the gates in the barricade and permitted us to pass through for an interview. The Nationalist officers were General Li Tsung-jen and General Ho Ying-chin. Both assured us that they had no intention of attacking the foreigners and that they had taken steps to restore order in the native areas about Shanghai. They informed us that the Northern commander at Shanghai had already fled, and that his troops had been disarmed.

Bearing in mind the fact that Shanghai is China's "key" city, which any political group seeking to govern the country must control, it was obvious that both groups in the Kuomintang had made preparations to seize control of the Chinese-administered sections of the city. Propaganda squads attached to the radical branch of the party were first on the scene and had completely undermined the morale of the Northern troops which controlled the lower Yangtze district, in which Shanghai is located. The demoralization of the erstwhile defenders of the city was so complete that their commanders did not wait for the advancing Nationalist armies to get within shooting distance; they evacuated before the Southerners were within a hundred miles of the city. The result was that the Shanghai district experienced an interregnum between the evacuation of the Northerners and the arrival of the Southern armies, which were forced to travel afoot as the Northerners had seized all of the railway rolling stock and available shipping along the coast and on the Yangtze River.

The Communists thus had an opportunity to make their preparations. There was no questioning the fact that prevailing sentiment among the student and labor groups favored the leftists and their program of social reform. Preparations had been made for seizure of control of Shanghai in the manner of Hankow, and, as at Hankow, there were parades, mass meetings, speeches, and distribution of literature. The walls of buildings were plastered with posters denouncing foreign imperialists. Any Chinese who helped a foreigner was designated in word and cartoon as a "running-dog" of the foreign imperialists. Chinese compradores, or native agents of the large foreign firms, who constituted a powerful group that controlled the native guilds and chambers of commerce, were singled out for special abuse by radical propagandists. The compradores were held up to public ridicule and no terms of opprobrium in a language which is rich in such expressions were overlooked in the poster campaign.

It appeared that Shanghai was on the point of experiencing a repetition of the incidents at Nanking and Hankow, particularly when it became known that thousands of rifles had been distributed to the factory workers by the radical leaders.

2—Benevolent Gangster

Out of the confusion then prevailing in Shanghai there emerged a figure, previously unknown, who took on the composite character of an earlier-decade American gangster and political boss. The character was Dou Yu-seng, now listed in the respectable China "Who's Who" as a "banker, philanthropist, and welfare worker." Dou's early life is not well known, as he was born of peasants in a little fishing village near the seacoast about twenty-five miles from metropolitan Shanghai. (The little town, renamed "Dou's Village" and inhabited by a few hundred people—boatmen, fishermen and farmers—was galvanized into sudden prominence in 1934, when Dou celebrated his fiftieth birthday by dedicating a family shrine in the village and staging a two-mile-long parade through the countryside which cost him well over a million dollars. Banners were carried in the parade containing messages of felicitation from leaders throughout the country.)

Dou Yu-seng started his career in the Shanghai French Concession as a youthful fruit peddler. He soon discovered the places where opium was sold illicitly, and familiarized himself with the racketeering, hijacking, and other practices which prevailed in Shanghai somewhat as they were practiced in the bootleg industry in the United States during prohibition days. Methods used by Dou Yu-seng in gaining control of the underworld situation followed traditional lines, and Dou shortly emerged from the sidewalks and malodorous gutters of the French Concession and the adjoining native district of Nantao as controller of opium, gambling, and the amusement industries. In his rise to power Dou solved a local political problem which previously had defied solution: he amalgamated two powerful secret political organizations whose activities extended far back into the era of the Manchu Dynasty. The organizations, known as the Blue Society and the Green Society, originally were engaged in intrigue against the Manchus, but after the creation of the republic they degenerated into gangsterism. The two groups were violently antagonistic, and their rivalries frequently broke out in gun battles similar to early tong wars in the Chinese communities in the United States. But Dou Yu-seng accomplished the seemingly impossible by amalgamating the rival groups, and became head of the rejuvenated organization known as the Blue-Green Society, which performed functions, according to Chinese lights, probably not greatly different from those performed by political groups which dominate the large cities of the United States.

Dou Yu-seng had two trusted lieutenants, one of whom controlled the amusement industry and the other the native chambers of commerce and guilds. They previously had been active in the rival Blue and Green societies respectively.

Political conditions in the French Concession facilitated Dou's rise to power. The Shanghai French Concession, although regarded as a "little piece of La Belle France," was governed not directly from Paris, but second-hand through Hanoi, capital of the French Colony of Indo-China. The inefficiency and corruption which prevailed in the French Colony were repeated in the French Concession at Shanghai. French officials, particularly chiefs of police, appointed to Shanghai quickly amassed fortunes from underworld activities which prevailed in the Concession. These conditions were exposed to the world when the French Administration at Hanoi surrendered abjectly to the Japanese.

Dou Yu-seng and his associates took advantage of this situation and became the real controllers of the French Concession.
Dou ruled his empire from his home in the Concession, which
resembled an arsenal. But he was a liberal contributor to chari-
ties and he came to hold more chairmanships on directorates
of Chinese banks and business houses than any other man in
the city. His orders were enforced by hundreds of armed
guards, popularly known as "Dou's plain-clothes men."

When conditions became chaotic after the withdrawal of
the Northern troops, Dou Yu-seng stepped into the breach and
notified the local foreign authorities that he would assume
responsibility for the maintenance of law and order, pending
the arrival of the Nationalist troops. It was at this point that
the shooting began; it continued without intermission for many
days. Preparations which the radicals and Communists had made
for seizing the city back-fired, and the reign of terror which
the Reds had planned was turned against them.

No accurate count was made of bodies which littered the
streets of the native areas, but Edgar Snow, who was then on
the staff of the *China Weekly Review*, estimated that more
than 5,000 leftists were killed. According to Snow's account,
Chou En-lai, the Communist leader, had organized 600,000
workers who staged a general strike, completely tying up the
industries of the city. Order among the strikers was maintained
by some 50,000 trained pickets. Police stations and the local
arsenal and garrison headquarters were seized by some 5,000
armed workers, of whom about 2,000 had been specially trained.
A so-called "citizens' government" was proclaimed, stated
Snow's account.

But the Communist coup was short-lived. It could not stand
up against the experienced gunmen of Dou Yu-seng. When the
Nationalist troops under General Li Tsung-jen, General Pai
Chung-hsi, and General Ho Ying-chin arrived at Shanghai they
found the job already completed; the city was handed over to
them by Dou Yu-seng and his lieutenants. Chou En-lai, the

Communist leader, was imprisoned and other radical leaders, who were not captured and executed, fled to Hankow. Shortly afterward, when General Chiang Kai-shek arrived and assumed control of the situation, he issued an edict expelling the Communists from the Kuomintang and ordering the deportation from China of all Russian Soviet advisers. The enforcement of the expulsion and deportation order at Canton was accompanied by serious rioting and the massacre of many members of the leftist group, including several Russians. The lives of a number of the Russian advisers were saved by American Consul Houston, who permitted them to seek refuge in the American consulate at Canton.

After the collapse of the "Canton Commune" the Reds attempted to set up a regime at Swatow on the coast of Kwantung Province, north of Canton, but it could not stand against the Kuomintang troops led by General Chiang Kai-shek. Finally the defeated Red forces which were scattered over Central and South China combined with those driven from Hankow, and formed a "Soviet Government of China" in the mountainous areas on the border between Kiangsi and Fukien Provinces, where they held out for several months, but ultimately were ejected by Chiang Kai-shek's air-bombers and forced to flee to the Northwest, where they established another communistic government at Yenan, Shensi—which is still in existence.

The last episode staged by the Red wing faction in the Kuomintang was at Nanking when Communists within the Nationalist army staged the attack on foreign residents. Several Americans and Britons were killed and wounded, and it became necessary for American gunboats on the Yangtze at Nanking to fire on a mob of soldiers attacking members of the American consulate and local American residents, including several women, who were marooned on a hill overlooking the city wall. The soldiers were frightened away by the gunboat barrage, and the Americans were evacuated over the wall to the gunboats on the river. After General Chiang Kai-shek's loyal commanders succeeded in restoring order, the leaders of the Communist coup, which was designed to discredit the Kuomintang with the foreign Powers, were tried and several of them were executed.

On the evening of the day following the Nanking incident, the correspondents were summoned to a press conference at the American consulate. I was accompanied to the meeting by Prof. Manley O. Hudson of the Department of International Law at Harvard, and we were introduced to an American missionary who had been in Nanking at the time of the "reign of terror." He told us of the murder of Dr. Williams, President Emeritus of Nanking University, and that of an American woman secretary in one of the mission offices because she refused to hand over the keys to the safe; and also of the shooting and wounding of the British Consul.

These incidents had already been reported, but the intense interest of the correspondents was aroused when the speaker, who was in a highly excited state as a result of his experiences, declared that there had been several instances where foreign women had been raped by the crazed Red soldiers. Copies of the missionary's statement, which had just been typed by one of the consular staff, were passed out to the correspondents. Before the conference broke up, Dr. Hudson suggested to me that I ask the spokesman whether he had personal knowledge of any of the rape cases. He replied with considerable heat that he did not have first-hand information, but had been told of the incidents by persons whom he trusted. This immediately aroused a serious controversy, in the course of which Dr. Hudson explained that he had served on a commission which had investigated World War I atrocities, and that few alleged rape cases had stood up under investigation.

The upshot of the matter was that most of the correspondents who cabled the rape story qualified it as not based on first-hand information. It should be stated that so-called "rape" stories had been freely circulated about the city and had appeared in some of the papers. These stories were exploited by reactionary interests with the object of provoking armed intervention on the part of the foreign Powers.

Several weeks after the above happenings I received a letter from an American woman physician who was in Nanking at the time of the incident and had made a first-hand investigation of the rape allegations. She said that there had been only one case, and that it was "attempted" rape. Her account stated that three soldiers had entered a house and, finding an American woman alone, had dragged her to an upstairs room. However, they became frightened and ran away without accomplishing their purpose. This was the only case of the kind which came to my attention in more than a quarter of a century of newspaper work in China.

Dou Yu-seng was hailed as the deliverer of Shanghai from the Red menace. Shortly afterward the home French Government became exasperated over the corruption and gangsterism which had prevailed for so many years in the French Concession, sent an admiral and a naval force to Shanghai, and effected a complete clean-up of gangsterism. After that Dou Yu-seng became a respectable businessman and philanthropist and was decorated by the Government. However, he kept an anchor to windward by retaining control of his Blue-Green Society and his small army of plain-clothes men.

When the Japanese intervened at Shanghai early in 1932 in order to suppress anti-Japanese activities which flared up following Japan's seizure of Manchuria, Dou Yu-seng's "army" again went into action in the Hongkew section of Shanghai, which the Japanese had occupied. Firing from concealed positions in upper stories and on roofs of buildings, they wreaked havoc among Japan's naval forces as well as civilians. Dou's plain-clothes men aided materially in the defense of the city and made the intervention so costly to the Japanese that they were glad to accept mediation and withdraw their naval forces. When the Japanese launched their war in China proper in 1937, Dou Yu-seng and his followers, after defending the

city to the last ditch, withdrew with the Nationalist forces to
West China, where they have stayed.

Many months after the suppression of the Communists at
Shanghai, Stirling Fessenden, American chairman of the International Settlement and popularly known as the "Lord Mayor
of Shanghai," told me the following story of the "saving" of
Shanghai from the Chinese Reds and their Soviet advisers. So
far as I know the full story has never appeared in print, as it
was "off the record" until Fessenden's death in Shanghai following the Japanese occupation.

Fessenden said that the authorities of the French Concession were chiefly responsible for bringing Dou Yu-seng into
the Shanghai "war" between the Kuomintang and the Russian-
supported Chinese Communists. Dou had "grown up" in the
French Concession, hence it was natural for the French to turn
to him for assistance, as all governmental authority had collapsed in the Chinese areas surrounding the foreign districts.
Fessenden said:

"The French chief of police phoned me one day and asked
me to meet him for a confidential talk about the local situation.
I went to the address he gave me and was surprised to find it
was a Chinese residence surrounded by a high wall, with armed
guards at the front gate. I was admitted and immediately
ushered into a waiting room. I could not help but notice that
the large entrance hall was lined on both sides with stacks of
rifles and sub-machine guns. Soon I heard voices, and the
French official entered with two Chinese. One was Dou Yu-seng
and the other was an interpreter. We got down to business
immediately, the French chief of police explaining that he had
been discussing with Dou the matter of defending the foreign
settlement against the Communists, as the local Chinese Government, which was composed of Northerners, had collapsed
following the evacuation of the Northern defense commander
and his troops. Dou went to the point in a businesslike manner. He was willing to move against the Reds, but he had two

conditions: first, he wanted the French authorities to supply him with at least 5,000 rifles and ample ammunition. Then turning to me," said Fessenden, "he demanded permission to move his military trucks through the International Settlement, something which the Settlement authorities had never granted to any Chinese force. Dou said this was necessary in order to move arms and munitions from one section of the native city to the other."

Fessenden told Dou he would agree subject to the approval of the Municipal Council. Continuing, Fessenden said:

"I realized we were taking a desperate chance in dealing with a man of Dou's reputation, but the situation was critical, as an attempt by the Communists to seize the Settlement and the French Concession was certain to result in widespread disorder and bloodshed, involving the lives of thousands of Americans, Britons, and other foreign residents as well as tens of thousands of Chinese who resided in the foreign-administered sections of the city. Since the Communists had plotted to seize the foreign areas and defend themselves against the Kuomintang troops, it would mean that the foreigners would be sandwiched between the contending forces. The result would have been international complications far more serious than anything which had occurred since the establishment of the Settlement nearly a century ago. It took Dou about three weeks to complete his job, and by that time sufficient foreign troops had arrived to preserve order within the foreign sections; and also by that time General Chiang Kai-shek had arrived and assumed control in the native area. He immediately announced that the Kuomintang troops had no intention of attacking the foreigners, as had occurred at Nanking. He also announced that the perpetrators of the Nanking outrages would be punished."

Many American professional defenders of the Chinese Communists have written tearful paragraphs about the "massacre" of Chinese workers and students by the Chinese "fascists and capitalists" at Shanghai, Canton and elsewhere. They either gloss over or omit entirely the all-important point that the so-called workers and students had been trained in revolutionary methods and terrorism either in Moscow or by Russian agents in China, and that these same workers and students were provided with arms by agents of the Third International operating in China. So long as the Communists maintain the principle of "force" as a means of accomplishing their political designs, they can have no cause for complaint when their enemies use similar methods in opposing them.

XV

Diplomatic Juggling on Intervention

AN INTERESTING ASPECT of the situation in Shanghai in 1927 has recently been brought to light by the publication of dispatches exchanged between the State Department and the American Consul-General at Shanghai.

Two particular dispatches referring to the *China Weekly Review* were exchanged between Clarence E. Gauss, Consul-General at Shanghai (1926-27), and Frank B. Kellogg, Secretary of State, at the time of the advance of the Chinese Nationalist forces from Canton into the Yangtze Valley.

Mr. Gauss (who retired as Ambassador to the Chungking Government in 1944) wired the State Department late in March, 1927, questioning the authenticity of a dispatch from Washington by the *China Weekly Review's* correspondent, J. J. Underwood, which indicated that the Coolidge Administration did not intend to intervene in China in company with other countries under a "unified command," which was being demanded by die-hard interests in Shanghai. Owing to the stirring developments which followed publication of the dispatch in the *China Weekly Review* and other Shanghai papers, the dispatch is quoted here in full as a significant and, as later developments showed, an accurate statement of American policy toward the Chinese Nationalist military and political movement. The dispatch read as follows:

WASHINGTON, March 30 [1927].—It was explained at the White House today that the President is convinced of the fact that the situation of China is more promising. It is intimated in official circles that there is no purpose in joining in any unified demand of punishment of those guilty in connection with the Nanking incident.

Although the Shanghai situation demands cooperation, it was intimated in administration circles that the United States Government did not as yet feel that the China situation demanded the necessity of creating the unified command. Furthermore, it is felt that there is no necessity for additional troops, that is in addition to those now in China and en route. It was emphasized again at the Department of State that the American forces in China are merely acting in a police capacity and that this does not mean intervention. In reference to the Nanking incident it was stated that it has not been determined the Cantonese were responsible.

At the time of the publication of this dispatch none of the Shanghai newspapers received dispatches directly from the United States through any American news service, and in consequence the papers depended entirely upon the British Reuter's service, which then reported happenings in the United States by the roundabout route of London-Calcutta-Singapore-Hong Kong. Shanghai was therefore not in direct touch with official or public opinion in the United States as it had developed on the question of armed intervention in China.

Shanghai for weeks had been panicky over the advance of the Nationalist armies from the South, and the chambers of commerce, municipal government and foreign consuls, as well as the legations at Peking, had been frantically cabling for more troops to protect the city, which had already been barricaded by a hastily constructed system of trenches, concrete block-houses, and innumerable strands of barbed wire. The intense propaganda against the Nationalist movement, variously described as "controlled and directed by Moscow" and as a "Red Wave on the Yangtze," had created a psychological situation among the foreign population closely akin to mass hysteria. The French authorities, possibly due to their close relationship with the Catholic missionaries scattered over the country, were not alarmed at the advance of the Nationalists and, as I have said, had established contact with the Nationalist leaders long before they reached the environs of the city. However, the

French had also barricaded the borders of their Concession which fronted on native territory.

The United States, Great Britain, France, Italy, and Japan had already responded to the appeals for troops, but as indicated in the telegram to the *Review* from its correspondent in Washington, there apparently was no intention on the part of the Administration, or at least of President Coolidge, to intervene in China under a so-called "unified command," as Shanghai's old-guard reactionaries had been demanding for many years.

I was never able to find anyone who had seen this grandiose plan of strategy designed to block the Nationalist movement at the Yangtze and prevent it from extending into North China, but most residents believed such a plan was in existence and that the Powers were now prepared to put it into effect. It was common talk around the clubs and hotel lobbies that the upstart Nationalists, who had declared their intention of abrogating long-established foreign treaties, were to be put in their proper place and soundly spanked in the bargain. Old ideas regarding Chinese armies, that they were a ragamuffin outfit which would run away at the first shot from a rifle in the hands of a foreign soldier, still prevailed.

Old-guard merchants and residents with vested interests in the Settlement who dominated the port and controlled most of the newspapers, believed, under the hypnotism of their own self-made propaganda, that the long-awaited day of deliverance had arrived. Plans for the creation of a vast "free city" area at the mouth of the Yangtze were pulled out of pigeonholes, dusted off, and revised for immediate use.

Therefore the publication of the Washington dispatch in the *China Weekly Review*, intimating that there would be no intervention, no unified command, no fantastic creation of a neutral zone on the Yangtze, and that the troops being sent to Shanghai were for police purposes only, created a feeling of exasperation and frustration difficult of description except in technical terms of mass psychopathy. The *China Weekly Review*, which had published the dispatch, was regarded somewhat in the light of the traditional bearer of bad tidings. Diehard reactionaries argued, "Surely the dispatch cannot be true; obviously the Powers cannot let us down at this crucial stage; the dispatch must have been inspired by the Bolsheviks; the United States Government could not be guilty of such a 'pusillanimous' policy."

Indignation mounted to feverish proportions. The fact that the *Review* had long argued editorially that it was necessary for the foreigners to meet the rising tide of Chinese Nationalism with concessions, otherwise they would lose everything, caused the old guard to blame me, as editor of the paper, for the failure of their well-laid plans.

As a result of the agitation Consul-General Gauss cabled the State Department to the following effect:

> This message not only is disconcerting to Americans here who, whatever their previous opinions, now are awakened to the necessity for strong action of the Powers on the Nanking incident in order to check the dominant control of the Nationalist movement by the radical communist element, but is distinctly encouraging to that radical element now rapidly gaining control of the situation. I trust the report in the *China Weekly Review* is incorrect and that I may be instructed to repudiate it. The situation here remains unchanged, with the radical and lawless elements holding a large measure of control and Chiang Kai-shek with limited forces taking no drastic measures to suppress them.

The State Department sent a reply to Mr. Gauss's telegram which should be preserved in the museum of diplomatic curiosities, if such an institution exists, for it confirmed in typical diplomatic circumlocutory terms every statement which appeared in Jack Underwood's dispatch to the *China Weekly Review*—but ended with an allegation that the dispatch "had no basis of truth" and, if Mr. Gauss "considered it wise," he was authorized to repudiate it. The reply:

WASHINGTON, March 31 [1927].—Apparently the press report you quoted is based on the White House press conference March 29, during which in replying to questions the President stated that he had nothing to add to his statement the other day concerning the movement of American forces to China, at which time he had said he saw no necessity for increasing American forces in China. However, he wanted to say that he had hardly made that statement when a telegram was received from Admiral Williams requesting 1,500 additional marines, and these were of course being sent by the Navy Department. The President said he expected that these forces would suffice, that it might be possible that there might be no need for them, but that China was a long distance away in any case, and to get a force assembled ready to send takes time. We have to anticipate what events might arise and we are depending upon the Admiral's request for more forces. The Admiral, up to the time when the first statement was made, had not thought the sending of any larger force than he had in China was necessary. For a considerable length of time three cruisers were held at Honolulu awaiting his call, and some days ago they were dispatched. The purpose of our forces there is to protect our people and their property. Our forces are not an expeditionary force. They are in the nature of a police force to give our people protection in so far as they can. They are not allowed to make war on anyone. There is no organized military attack on our people, but sometimes disorganized attacks are made by soldiers who are not acting, we presume, under authority from anyone attempting to function as a government, but who rather are acting as a mob. The liability of something like that breaking out at any time is the reason we are increasing our forces. There will not be a change in the command of our forces in China. Our forces will of course be commanded by our own officers and it is not intended so far as I know to have any unified command. As is necessary, of course, we are cooperating there with other nations. I do not understand that the location of the foreign settlements is such that our people are altogether separated from the people of other nations. There is no separation of the French Settlement from the settlement of other nationals or the International Settlement, so that we all should act together in order to prevent a mob from forcing its way through at any time and to give protection to our own people. The above report is for your confidential and private information. You will understand that the statement published in the *China Weekly Review* has no basis of truth and if you consider it wise to repudiate the statement you are authorized to do so.   KELLOGG

The contents of this dispatch were soon known and whis-· pered about Shanghai. Two days later the American Chamber of Commerce in Shanghai passed a strong resolution demanding armed intervention in China by the Powers. The Chamber's resolution expressed the view that the American people at home "are easily cajoled into tearful sympathy for any cause, righteous or otherwise, and have been duped in regard to the Chinese situation by Soviet propaganda."

Shortly after the passage of this resolution the board of directors called a special meeting of the chamber and formally requested the resignation of the editor of the *China Weekly Review* because of the paper's editorial policy. Although an active member of the chamber almost from the date of its organization in 1917, I was not notified of the special meeting and only through accident learned of it in time to reach the meeting place before the vote on the resolution was taken. I had that morning received another telegram from the *Review's* Washington correspondent, Mr. Underwood, confirming further the opposition of President Coolidge and Secretary of State Kellogg to any armed interventionist program, and had a copy of it in my pocket when I went to the meeting. The meeting was attended by only a small percentage of the membership, and as I looked over the gathering I had a feeling that it was a "packed" meeting. My surmise was borne out when the members present, one after another, got up and condemned the *China Weekly Review* for its editorial attitude as being contrary to the interests of American business in Shanghai and of foreigners generally in China.

Before a vote was taken I stated that I realized fully the seriousness of the crisis in China, but was convinced that armed action by the Powers would only have the effect of strengthening the radical elements and their Soviet supporters who were trying to overthrow the moderate Kuomintang faction, led by General Chiang Kai-shek. I also explained that the views I had expressed editorially in the *Review* coincided with the traditional views of the United States Government, and particularly with the views of the Administration leaders. I then read the telegram I had received that morning from Washington, which further confirmed the previous message, that Washington was opposed to armed intervention, except for the protection of the lives and property of American citizens from mob violence.

I had scarcely resumed my seat when a local American lawyer, Chauncy P. Holcomb, a Delawarean, and a former District Attorney attached to the United States Court for China, got up and made a fiery speech in which he denounced the "pusillanimous" policy of the United States Government and charged that the *China Weekly Review* "was largely responsible for the attitude of our home authorities in letting the Americans and other foreigners down." Before the vote was taken someone raised a parliamentary question by calling attention to the by-laws of the chamber, which provided that no member of the chamber could be expelled without due notice in writing being given and a certain number of days permitted to elapse so that a formal reply could be made. But the members present would not listen to opposition, even on constitutional grounds, and passed the resolution by a considerable majority. I immediately declared my determination to continue my editorial policy and refused to comply with the chamber's resolution demanding my resignation unless the chamber's action was confirmed at a meeting called for the purpose in accordance with the by-laws of the organization. No such meeting ever was held.

The correspondents for American and British papers who were covering the Shanghai crisis sent to their papers stories of the action of the American chamber, and as a result I was deluged by telegrams and cables congratulating me on my attitude and urging me to stand my ground in opposition to armed intervention. Among those who approved my stand were representatives of most of the mission boards.

Some days later I had confirmation of my suspicion that the American chamber's action had been instigated by members of the so-called "Raven Group" of local businessmen, who were deeply involved in speculative real-estate promotional activities in land located outside of the foreign settlements. This group stood to gain materially from an interventionist program. It was disclosed later that a member of this group had fostered the plan to create a so-called "Free City" at the mouth of the Yangtze River which would be independent of the Republic of China. The plan, which had been sent to the League of Nations at Geneva, was a thinly disguised scheme to carve a colony out of China's national domain which would, of course, include the Municipality of Shanghai. (For further comment on Raven, see Chapter II.)

American missionary groups in China, with few exceptions, took a position sharply in contrast to the attitude of the Chamber of Commerce, which was openly condemned as "gunboat" policy and contrary to the best interests of Americans and Chinese alike. Several of the missionary groups which had suffered in the Nanking incident refused to accept indemnities for losses of life or property.

The American chamber at Shanghai persisted in its opposition to the non-interventionist policies of the United States Government, and even went to the extent of appointing as its Washington representative a notorious Japanese propagandist, George Bronson Rea, editor of the *Far Eastern Review*, a paper which had served Japanese interests in the Far East for more than a decade. Mr. Rea once made a speech before the annual convention of the United States Chamber of Commerce in which he recommended a new policy for the United States in the Far East, which he called "benevolent intervention to save China from the Red influence of Moscow." Mr. Rea later became the diplomatic representative in Washington for the puppet state of Manchukuo with a salary of $25,000.

Robert Pickens, a member of the Washington Bureau of

the Associated Press, who was in Shanghai at the time of these events, compiled a summary of press opinion in the United States on the question of armed intervention in China. He called attention to the fact that ordinarily the American press is more or less dormant on the matter of China news, but largely due to the Nanking incident, even the most conservative papers printed long dispatches from their correspondents under heavy headlines. The China situation thus became a big story of first-rate importance, and as a result public opinion in the United States was mobilized to an unusual extent. The American press was almost unanimously opposed to intervention in China, and there was strong opposition to American cooperation with other Powers in a program which might involve widespread military action. According to a summary prepared by the *Literary Digest*, American editors had seldom been so unanimous in their endorsement of President Coolidge's policy. Mr. Pickens's survey, written for publication, declared that American editorial opinion in opposition to the Shanghai scheme of sanctions had led the State Department to follow a non-intervention policy.

XVI

China and USSR at War

ANTI-RUSSIAN SENTIMENT which developed in Central and South China following the split in the Kuomintang Party in 1927 quickly spread to North China. Here the Russians found their bitterest opponent in Marshal Chang Tso-lin, dictator of Manchuria and leader of the Northern military faction opposed to General Chiang Kai-shek (who became Generalissimo in 1928).

On April 6, 1927, Marshal Chang Tso-lin's police, assisted by guards from the Legation Quarter, which was controlled by the American, British, Japanese, French, Dutch, Spanish and Portuguese Ministers, raided the offices of the Soviet Embassy in Peking. Aside from the Chinese charge that the Russians were using the Diplomatic Quarter as a center for the propagation of communistic ideas, the foreign legations had their own grievances against the Russians through the discovery of a plot supposedly hatched in the office of the Soviet military attaché to secure access to the British Embassy compound. The Soviet Embassy occupied quarters adjoining the British Legation, from which it was separated by a high wall, and it was alleged that an entrance was being made through the wall from the Soviet side, with the aim of attacking the British guards and precipitating an incident. The Soviet Ambassador, then home on leave, was L. M. Karakhan, first diplomatic emissary sent to China by the USSR. A year previously, Marshal Chang Tso-lin had demanded Karakhan's recall.

Large quantities of communist propaganda literature and documents were seized in the raid, and several Russians and

Chinese found on the premises were arrested. The Soviet Government denounced the raid as "an unprecedented violation of the elementary rules of international law," but Marshal Chang ignored the protests and circulated to the press and the diplomats of the other Powers photographic reproductions of documents proving the existence of a widespread plot to communize China. The documents also indicated that members of the Soviet Embassy's staff were involved in the plot. This was a serious matter, as it constituted a violation of the stipulations of the Peking agreement of 1924 by which the Soviet Government bound itself not to disseminate communist propaganda in China. As a result of the disclosures the Soviet chargé d'affaires was recalled, and after a brief court-martial the Chinese ringleaders arrested in the raid were shot.

Chang Tso-lin's animosity toward the Soviet Russians was increased by the discovery of documents showing that the Russians were using the revenue and facilities of the Chinese Eastern Railway, which crosses North Manchuria, for the purpose of spreading communism throughout China. Following the Bolshevist Revolution in 1917, the Soviet Government offered to restore the Chinese Eastern Railway and other Czarist Russian interests in North Manchuria to Chinese control. Later Moscow withdrew this offer, and after the relinquishment of Allied administration of the railway at the end of World War I, the Russians took over complete control of the railway. In 1924 the USSR signed an agreement with China for the joint control and operation of the railway, but this agreement was not carried out, according to the Chinese, who alleged that the Russian general manager refused to consult with the Chinese co-manager of the board on matters of important policy.

Recently large numbers of Russian agents had been sent to Harbin under the guise of engineers and railway technicians, who were devoting their time and energies to the furtherance of communism. Schools operated by the educational department of the railway in Harbin and other cities inside the ten-mile-wide railway "zone" were used to disseminate communist propaganda in violation of the 1924 agreement.

A further cause of Marshal Chang's animosity was the knowledge that his arch enemy Marshal Feng Yu-hsiang was receiving both arms and financial supplies from Russia. Marshal Feng Yu-hsiang, well known Northern military leader, formerly affiliated with Marshal Wu Pei-fu in the Anfu Party, went to Russia in 1926, and studied military tactics for a year. When he returned to China in 1927 he established himself in Kansu Province, adjacent to the area now occupied by the Chinese Communists. With money and arms supplied by the Soviets he built up the so-called Kuominchun or "National" Army, and joined the Nationalists at Nanking. Shortly afterward he broke with General Chiang Kai-shek and organized a coalition against Nanking. He was defeated by General Chiang, and after a period of retirement again rejoined the National Government. Curiously, the rifles which the Soviets supplied to Feng's troops bore the trademark of the Remington Arms Company. The rifles had been manufactured in the United States for the Czarist forces in World War I and had been taken over by the Bolsheviks after the revolution of 1917.

Although General Chiang Kai-shek had established his nationalist capital at Nanking, foreign ministers, including our own, were still accredited to the Peking Government and maintained their headquarters there. They were reluctant to give up the comfort and protection of the old legation quarters, although some of the legations had sent unofficial representatives to Shanghai in order to maintain contact with the new government.

After the death of Marshal Chang Tso-lin, in June, 1928, his son, the "Young Marshal" Chang Hsueh-liang, took command and soon announced his adherence to the new National Government at Nanking. The Young Marshal also continued the anti-communist activities in North China and Manchuria which had been initiated by his father.

Shortly after he assumed office in Mukden the Young Marshal learned that the Communist International had called a secret regional conference to be held in Harbin, North Manchuria, on May 27, 1929. While the meeting was in progress the Chinese police staged a raid and arrested some forty Russian consular officials and practically the same number of Chinese Communists from various parts of Manchuria. The Chinese also seized two truckloads of papers and documents. Claiming that the documents confirmed their suspicions that officials of the Chinese Eastern Railway were taking an active part in the propagation of Bolshevist ideas, the Chinese took drastic action.

On July 10 they seized the railway, dissolved all Soviet unions of railway workers and arrested some 1,200 railway officials and union leaders, whom they interned in abandoned railway buildings several miles from Harbin. It was the first time the Chinese Government had ever acted so energetically and decisively against a foreign Power.

Accompanied by a number of other correspondents, including Wilbur Forrest of the *New York Herald Tribune*, Jim Howe, Associated Press, and William Philip Simms of the Scripps-Howard newspapers, I arrived in Harbin about a week later. We found that the Chinese had seized the railway telegraph system and all offices of the Soviet Far Eastern Trading Corporation, the Naphtha Trust, and the Soviet Mercantile Fleet, which was owned and operated by the railway. The Mercantile Fleet owned a number of large paddle-wheel steamers which operated on the Sungari and Amur rivers, reminiscent of steamboat days on the Mississippi and Missouri rivers.

The Soviet Government acted with equal energy. Minister Karakhan, who had in the meantime been appointed Assistant Foreign Minister in Moscow, denounced the Chinese action as a "gross violation of treaties" and gave China an ultimatum of three days to return a satisfactory answer, failing which the Soviet Government threatened "to resort to other means for the protection of its lawful rights."

Fighting soon broke out along the Chinese Eastern Railway at both the eastern and western borders of Manchuria, resulting in heavy casualties to the Chinese forces at the town of Manchouli, where some 8,000 Chinese soldiers were killed. The Chinese town of Pogranichnaya, at the eastern end of the railway, was badly shattered by Soviet artillery fire and air-bombs. A Chinese town known as Lahasusu at the mouth of the Sungari River, opposite Khabarovsk on the Amur, was bombed and burned, and two Chinese gunboats stationed there were sunk by Soviet planes.

The country about the junction of the Sungari and Amur rivers interested me very much, as there are numerous villages in the vicinity inhabited by some of the most primitive races of Northeastern Asia. We visited a village inhabited by a tribe of Tatars, most of whose clothing was made from the skin of the sturgeon, the fish which also produces the famous Russian "black" caviar. This particular tribe was locally known as "Fish-skin" Tatars.

I covered the battle of Lahasusu from the deck of an ancient Chinese paddle-wheel steamboat upon which I had traveled down the river from Harbin for about 600 miles. I was accompanied on the trip by Paul Wright of the *Chicago Daily News*, and Baron Taube, a Swedish nobleman, who represented Reuter's. By this time the weather was getting cold and ice had begun to form in the river. We wondered whether we would be caught by the river ice and captured by the Soviet troops. We were anchored at a little river town called Fuchin when a courier arrived stating the Russians were coming, after having captured and burned Lahasusu the preceding night. The captain hurriedly got up steam and we started upstream only five hours before the Reds arrived. The Chinese told us that the Russians always followed the practice, on capturing a Chinese town, of opening all the stores and granaries and distributing their contents free to the populace as a "communist" gesture. Another boat, carrying Chinese officials, which followed us, was badly shot up by Soviet planes. We managed to reach Harbin safely, but with the paddle-wheel and rudder of our steamer so covered with ice that we had difficulty in moving against the current.

It was while covering this war that I made the acquaintance of two important items of attire for Siberian travel. One was a blanket, formerly manufactured in Warsaw, Poland, and made of sheep and angora wool. It was nearly an inch thick, but light and flexible and practically impenetrable by wind, snow or rain. I paid $50 for it in a Harbin store. The other item was a pair of Siberian boots made by a Russian bootmaker in Tientsin. They were made of double-ply leather with a layer of camel's hair between, while the inch-thick soles contained a layer of asbestos. The soles were sewed and wood-pegged, as the bootmaker assured us that metal pegs carried the cold through the soles to one's feet. The shoes had one defect—they squeaked to high heaven. This, I was informed, was no objection in the eyes of the Russians, as it advertised the newness of the shoes.

The Far Eastern Soviet army invaded Chinese territory for about 200 miles at each end of the Chinese Eastern Railway and also bombed and occupied most of the Chinese towns along the border. But the Russians did not press beyond the Hinghan Mountains, due, it was reported, to a warning from the Japanese not to advance into their sphere of influence.

I heard one gruesome story of this warfare from a White Russian woman and a boy who ultimately reached Harbin. They had belonged to a White Russian community of several hundred families, located in the so-called Three Rivers District on the Argun River of North Manchuria. This area had been developed by Russian Cossacks, who had emigrated with their families across the border, following the revolution in 1917. The land they occupied was rich and suitable for farming and cattle grazing, and the colony prospered through the sale of dairy supplies to the large Chinese cities. The Soviet authorities in Siberia resented the activities of the White Russians just across their border and, after fighting broke out, charged that the White Russians with Chinese "Fascist" help were attempting an invasion of Siberia.

Fearing for the safety of their families, the White Russians sent their wives and children and all elderly males across country in a long wagon train to the railway at the town of Hailar, about 500 miles west of Harbin. The caravan, accompanied by a Russian Orthodox priest, had reached a point about fifty miles north of the railway when it was attacked by a force of Red Mongolian cavalry, allegedly led by Red army officers.

The woman and boy to whom I talked and who claimed to be the only survivors of this caravan, having escaped into the forest, told me that the Mongols had slaughtered every other member of the caravan. They then built a vast funeral pyre of the wagons and their contents, consisting of firkins of butter and large fifty-pound cheeses. Upon this pyre they piled the bodies of their victims, with that of the priest at the apex. They ignited the pyre and, yelling and shooting their rifles, rode their ponies in a wide circle about it as it burned. I could picture the troops of Genghis Khan in a similar victory celebration seven centuries ago.

After about six months of fighting, mostly of the guerrilla variety, the Young Marshal was forced to capitulate and to restore the control of the railway to the Soviets, since General Chiang Kai-shek was unable to send him reinforcements. Later there was a peace conference in Moscow, but it broke up without reaching an agreement, and the major issues between the two countries remain unsettled to this writing.

Three years later, after the Japanese had occupied Manchuria and Inner Mongolia and were threatening Siberia, Moscow sold the Chinese Eastern Railway to Japan for approximately $50,000,000—about a quarter of its real value. In 1937, when it appeared that the Japanese were making more definite plans to attack Russia, Moscow offered to join China in a military alliance against Japan, but she withdrew the offer and conciliated Japan in the face of the approaching war with Germany.

I had never before seen the vast expanse of North Manchurian farm and grazing lands, its forests, and the Sungari-Amur river system, which rivals the upper Mississippi and its tributaries. I realized that here was an empire worth fighting for, and I was not surprised that China's two powerful neighbors had had difficulty in keeping their hands off this rich terrain.

Here was a territory capable of absorbing a considerable portion of the excess population of China's congested seaboard provinces, a fact which was well known to the Chinese peasants of Hopei and Shantung provinces south of the Great Wall, who for a number of years had been migrating to Manchuria at the rate of more than a million a year. The Governor of Heilungkiang, the most northern Manchurian province, told me that Chinese farmers who arrived in North Manchuria completely destitute were usually able in less than ten years to purchase their farms outright and to refund loans advanced to them for the purchase of farm machinery. In a motor-car ride across the plain from Anganchi Station on the Chinese Eastern Railway to Tsitsihar, capital of the province, a distance of forty miles, I was constantly reminded of the fertile farm lands and the deep black soil of northern Missouri, Illinois, and Iowa. I was told by George Hanson, United States Consul-General at Harbin, that in his opinion Manchuria and Inner Mongolia could produce enough corn, wheat, soya beans and live stock to feed most of the people of East Asia. In order to participate in the expected agricultural development of this region, a large American manufacturer of farm machinery had already established a branch in Harbin. It was the only section of the Chinese Republic where heavy farm machinery could be used.

The city of Harbin, metropolis of North Manchuria, was established at the time when Czar Nicholas II was extending the Trans-Siberian Railway system through the mountains and forests of eastern Siberia and Manchuria to the Sea of Japan. In 1929 it could not equal the commercial and industrial development of the Europeanized China ports, but in many respects it seemed to me one of the most interesting cities in China. It resembled in many ways the earlier frontier cities of our own Northwest. The outfitting of hunters and trappers was a chief business. There were more fur stores than any other type of retail business, and it was possible to purchase any kind of fur there from Mongolian squirrel and silver fox to Russian sable, Siberian bear, or Korean tiger. In a small town near Harbin I saw a large compound or enclosure filled with Mongolian dogs, large shaggy canines with long silky black hair. I asked the Russian kennel man why the dogs were being kept in the enclosure. He replied in halting English, "Sell skins New York $50 one piece." I later learned that the Mongols were superstitious about their dogs, believing that they harbored the spirits of dead-and-gone ancestors, and hence would not kill them. The Russians, however, had no compunctions about raising them for the American market. I wondered what transformation these Mongolian dog skins passed through before they reached Fifth Avenue, and also what became of the spirits of past Mongolians who may have inhabited the original wearers of these skins.

One observed many Mongols, descendants of the followers of the great Genghis and Kublai Khans, on the streets of Harbin and in the towns along the railway. These men of the Gobi, whose forebears once ruled from the China Sea to the Danube, are probably still the world's best horsemen and also the cleverest horse traders. No words are spoken when horse trading is in progress at their periodic fairs. The buyer and seller face each other and each slides his hand into the other's sleeve. The buyer indicates the price he is willing to pay by pressing his fingers against the seller's forearm; the seller indicates approval or disapproval by pressure of his fingers on the buyer's other arm. After much nodding and shaking of heads, the two principals finally reach a bargain. The advantage of this method of bargaining is that others standing by have no way of knowing what price has been agreed upon.

The Mongols are fond of horse racing with their little Mongolian ponies, which resemble somewhat our mustangs of an earlier age. But one can never see both the start and the finish of a Mongolian horse race, because their race tracks stretch straight across the prairie. The Mongols line up their ponies, place their bets, and at a signal are off in the distance in a cloud of dust.

There are today only about a half million Mongols, most of them nomads, scattered over a territory about four times the size of Texas. Before the Japanese invasion of Manchuria and Inner Mongolia in 1931, the Mongols were about evenly divided between those giving grudging loyalty to China and those under Soviet rule. Now the Japanese have taken over Inner Mongolia and have added to it a considerable portion of western Manchuria where many Mongols feed their herds of cattle, horses and sheep.

Practically everything in Mongolia is linked traditionally with the "Great Ruler of All Men," Genghis Khan. This is true of a series of springs lying in symmetrical fashion on the opposite slopes of two hills several miles from Harbin to which, according to Mongolian folklore, the great Genghis often came. The water from the springs flows down the slopes of the two hills and converges in a main stream in such manner as to resemble, in the minds of the superstitious Mongols, the brain, spinal cord, and nervous system of the human body. The water in the different springs varies from boiling hot to tepid and is strongly impregnated with minerals from the volcanic rock through which it flows on its way to the surface. The Mongols and Russian peasants regard the waters from the springs as having miraculous healing powers, but believe that the uninitiated must exercise great care in using them and obtain the expert advice of the local medicine man. For example, the waters from two springs on opposite sides of the valley are infallible cures for eye ailments, with which the Mongols are widely afflicted.

But one must be careful to use the water from the spring on the right side of the valley for diseases of the right eye, and from the spring on the left side for treatment of the left eye. This treatment consists of pouring the water, which is nearly at the boiling point, from a rusty tin kettle directly into the infected eye. It usually is necessary for the patient to be held firmly on his back on the ground by two assistants, while a third pours the water from the kettle, which is held several feet above the patient. Practically all of the springs have pools walled with rough stones in which those receiving treatment sit and soak by the hour—usually unencumbered by clothing and with no segregation of the sexes.

Harbin, in 1929, had a population of somewhat more than a half million, about equally divided between Russians and Chinese. Unlike the China coast ports, where Chinese and foreigners live together in the foreign settlements, in Harbin the Chinese lived in one section, the old Chinese city near the river, while the Russians lived in "New Town," which the Czar's city planners had laid out with wide streets and ample parks. The city had changed little since the days of the Czar, as the Russian community was predominantly "White," despite the influx of Soviet agents in connection with the Chinese Eastern Railway. It was literally a city of Russian Orthodox churches. I was surprised to discover, however, that there was also a community of Russian Protestants, Baptists and Methodists. The Baptist pastor was the Reverend Charles Leonard of South Carolina, whose wife was famous in the community for her fried chicken, Southern style, and genuine Dixie corn pone. The Reverend Leonard had formerly been stationed in Shantung, but had followed his Chinese communicants when they emigrated to North Manchuria. There was a flourishing American Y.M.C.A. in Harbin, which had formerly been located in St. Petersburg but had withdrawn to Harbin following the revolution.

There was also a large, prosperous community of Russian

Jews, who dominated the retail business of the city, particularly the flourishing fur trade. Most of them had emigrated from Russia during the revolution of 1917.

Many White Russians, in view of the unstable political situation, had incorporated their businesses under the laws of Delaware and flew the American flag. This caused the American Consul many sleepless nights, because these pseudo-American firms, which had little or no American capital, were constantly demanding American protection from excessive Chinese taxes.

There were probably 350,000 White Russians living in Harbin and other Manchurian towns along the railway, and in general they continued to lead the life which they had known before the 1917 revolution. There was no curfew, and a half dozen cabarets with dozens of Russian girl dancers and entertainers—all "princesses"—kept open till daylight. Harbin also had its quota of gypsy entertainers. The leading hotel, the Moderne, was the social center for the more prosperous Russians and the foreign community. It was owned by a Russian emigree, who superstitiously believed that he would go bankrupt unless he rebuilt a portion of the building each year. As a result, there were always carpenters and stone masons at work somewhere on the premises, much to the annoyance and inconvenience of the guests.

XVII

"Real" Start of World War II

WE FOREIGN CORRESPONDENTS and newspapermen stationed in China were less surprised than the rest of the world when "all hell broke loose" in Manchuria in 1931. The world was told by Japanese spokesmen and propagandists that Japan's invasion of the Chinese northeastern provinces, and her subsequent military occupation of some 365,000 square miles of Chinese domain, had been precipitated by an attack on the Japanese-owned South Manchuria Railway by soldiers wearing the uniform of the Chinese Government. But the Japanese people at home had been prepared for developments by the circulation of an entirely different story.

Early in July, 1931, about two months before the Mukden affair, the Japanese newspapers carried sensational reports of the murder of a Japanese army officer, a Captain Nakamura, at an undisclosed point in Inner-Mongolia, an extensive area controlled by China and extending from the western border of Manchuria to Outer Mongolia, where Soviet Russia was dominant for several years. The Japanese had long had their eyes on Inner-Mongolia, as it was valuable grazing land and supplied North China with beef and mutton and their by-products, hides and wool. It was also a source of valuable furs. What Captain Nakamura was doing in Mongolia was never officially explained, but an account of the incident published in the *Japan Chronicle*, a British-owned and -edited paper at Kobe, stated that Captain Nakamura was accompanied by another Japanese army officer, a sergeant-major, whose name was not given, and also by a White Russian and a Mongolian guide. The passport which was issued to Captain Nakamura by the Chinese authorities at Mukden described him as an "educationalist engaged in historical and geographical studies." The captain carried with him a large sum of money, said to have amounted to 100,000 yen, or about $50,-000 in United States currency. The Japanese press, under military inspiration, stirred up a tremendous commotion over the murder of Captain Nakamura and charged a lack of sincerity on the part of the Chinese in their efforts to apprehend the murderer. China's investigation, as reported in the Chinese papers, alleged that the Japanese party, headed by Captain Nakamura, had been engaged on a mysterious mission along the border of Soviet-controlled Outer Mongolia, and that Captain Nakamura had in his possession a large quantity of heroin, a drug for which the Mongols have an inordinate desire. Fearing more serious complications, the Chinese authorities in Manchuria hastily expressed official regret and offered to pay an indemnity for the death of the Japanese captain. But the Japanese army rejected the Chinese offer, and the excitement mounted. We who had been following carefully the accounts of the Nakamura case in newspapers were therefore not surprised when the real storm broke at Mukden on the night of September 18, 1931.

But there was another important group which was not prepared, namely, the Institute of Pacific Relations. The Institute is made up of groups from various nations who spend their time between conferences in making investigations of special subjects which are likely to cause complications between nations and thus lead to war. The biennial conferences are not open to the public or press, but carefully censored reports of the various delegations attending the biennial meetings are published and now make up an extensive library. National groups participating in the Institute include Americans, Britons, Frenchmen, Canadians, Australians, New Zealanders, Russians, Chinese, and (before Pearl Harbor) the Japanese. The Institute among other things had been engaged for two years in compiling reports and documents pertaining to the crisis in the relations of China and Japan,

and all was in readiness for the biennial conference of the organization, which was scheduled to meet in Shanghai in the fall
of 1931. A large staff under a director was sent to Shanghai
to prepare the ground for the conference. At a tea and reception
which the American committee gave for the local Shanghai press,
the director introduced the members of his group, most of whom
were graduate students of Columbia University, as experts in
various phases of international relations. The work of the Institute is financed by private contributions, chiefly from the
large foundations in New York which are interested in promoting the study of international affairs.

Chester Rowell, well known San Francisco editor and publicist, was also sent to Shanghai with a staff of secretaries to make
preparations for the meeting, which was to be held in the Cathay
Hotel in the International Settlement. Mr. Rowell also gave a
dinner for the local press which was attended by some fifty
editors and correspondents. In his address, following the dinner,
Mr. Rowell explained the objectives of the Institute. He said that
national groups composed of key men and women had been
formed in various countries about the Pacific to study particular
questions of international concern so that in the event of complications arising between any of the countries the Institute
would have a body of experts available who were familiar with
the situation and who could immediately go into action and
bring pressure on their respective governments to maintain a
peaceful attitude until the particular problem could be adjusted
peacefully. In this manner, Mr. Rowell carefully explained, the
Institute planned to prevent the outbreak of another major war,
at least so far as the nations of the Pacific were concerned.

When Mr. Rowell had finished his address, he invited the
newspapermen to ask questions. Since I had been following the
reports from Manchuria rather carefully and realized the seriousness of the growing crisis there, I asked him the only logical
question: "What will the Institute do if China and Japan are at
war when the conference assembles?" For once, Mr. Rowell,
long rated as the best after-dinner speaker on the West Coast,

was stumped for a reply. After some thought he exclaimed, "Well, war ends everything," and sat down.

That remark was prophetic: By the time the conference of the Institute opened, in late September, at Shanghai, the Manchurian incident had occurred, and Japanese troops were in occupation of Mukden, the capital of Manchuria, and were in bloody conflict with the Chinese at several points in Chinese territory. At the opening session of the convention, Chinese and Japanese delegates sprang at each other and it was necessary to adjourn the meeting to Hongchow, a city where a more peaceful atmosphere prevailed. Although the press is always excluded from the meetings of the Institute, this particular row leaked out and received wide publicity.

The first reaction of the Powers to the Manchurian incident, following the futile American protest, was to send their military observers to the scene to make an investigation and report. America sent four, two from the Embassy at Tokyo and two from the Legation at Peiping.* Britain sent three military observers, France two, Italy one, and the Assembly of the League of Nations, then headed by a representative of the Spanish Republican Government, also sent an observer, the Spanish Consul-General at Shanghai, Señor Farrar, who had previously served as a colonial official in Spanish Africa. Newspaper correspondents, representing leading papers and press associations in the United States, Great Britain, France, and other countries, who were stationed in the Far East also flocked to Mukden to cover a story which all seemed to recognize instinctively as one of tremendous importance. There were also at Mukden the regular consular staffs of the United States and Great Britain, and some two hundred foreign residents who were engaged in business in the Manchurian capital.

Tokyo's nervousness over the action of the so-called "Kwantung" faction in the Imperial Japanese Army which had perpetrated the Manchurian "incident" led to the belief on the part of many correspondents in Manchuria that a vigorous protest

* In 1928 the name of Peking was changed to Peiping.

by the Washington Conference Powers, or even by the United States alone, would have caused the Japanese to withdraw. It was known that there was a strong faction in Tokyo which was opposed to the army's action, and there was indisputable evidence of Tokyo's indecision in connection with the Japanese army's ludicrous action concerning the occupation of Chinchow, important Chinese town and railway junction point marking the division of territory between the three northeastern provinces, or Manchuria, and China proper, south of the Great Wall. When the Powers realized that the Japanese had committed themselves too far to be recalled from a general invasion of Manchuria, they set about devising means to prevent the invasion from spreading into the vicinity of the Great Wall, which included the province of Jehol to the north of Peiping and the towns of Chinchow and Shanhaikwan in the vicinity of the eastern end of the Great Wall. The Japanese were, therefore, pressed not to extend their military activities into this area.

The Japanese Ambassador in Washington, acting supposedly with the authority of his Government, promised that Chinchow would be neither bombed nor occupied. In order to see that the agreement was observed the United States, Great Britain, France, and Germany (Germany was then on the side of law and order in the Orient) sent their respective military attachés to Chinchow, where they were quartered in a Chinese school, only a few hundred yards from the railway station.

A few days later the world was electrified by a report that "Chinchow has been bombed, despite the promise of the Japanese Government." General Honjo's headquarters at Mukden immediately denied the report, but became silent when a Swiss correspondent, Walter Bosshard, who represented the liberal Ullstein Press of Germany, made a trip to Chinchow and brought back with him a large collection of scraps of Japanese shrapnel shells which he had picked up in the Chinchow railway yards. When he dumped the shrapnel fragments on the table before the Japanese army spokesman, that worthy nearly had a heart attack; he adjourned the press conference. That night

Major Watari, the army spokesman, staged a geisha party for the correspondents, in which he consumed so many whiskey-sodas that he told the "whole inside story" of the bombing of Chinchow. He said that the army staff, made up of older generals at Honjo's headquarters, had received instructions from Tokyo not to interfere with Chinchow. But the younger officers would not listen, and staged a secret meeting at the private home of Major Watari, the army spokesman, where the bombing of Chinchow was framed.

I was among the group of correspondents invited to Major Watari's home that night. As we sat about a small table in the living room, Major Watari tapped on the table, a flimsy wooden affair about a foot square, and exclaimed dramatically, "This is a historic table; we sat around this table when we framed the bombing of Chinchow last night." After the die was cast the army "had" to send a force to Chinchow to occupy the place. The army dispatched a large force from Mukden over the Peiping-Mukden Railway, but the troops had proceeded only about half way when they were suddenly withdrawn. The reason for the withdrawal was a statement by the President of the United States at the White House press conference that the Japanese army "had run amok." The Japanese seriously believed at that time the United States meant business, but when they discovered that we were only bluffing again, they proceeded with their program.

I had been covering the war from the Mukden end, but now decided to take advantage of the lull incidental to the withdrawal of the Japanese army to make the trip to Chinchow for a first-hand inspection of the situation. I arrived at Chinchow a few days before Christmas, 1931, and found that all the military attachés except the American and British had cleared out. I also observed several bomb craters on the campus of the Chinese school where the League of Nations observers had their headquarters. The bomb craters showed that the Japanese had not only bombed the railway yards but had also tried to bomb the headquarters of the League of Nations Mission, composed of military observers, which was stationed there.

Early one morning between Christmas and New Year I visited the railway telegraph office to file a message, and found the operators unscrewing their instruments from the bench, a sure sign of impending evacuation. One of the men excitedly explained that "Japanese come soon." I hurried back to the headquarters with the news. A young American army intelligence officer, Lieutenant Aldrich, who commandeered an engine and went up the line to investigate, was taken prisoner by the Japanese and held for several hours. I caught the last train out of Chinchow, which was loaded with evacuating Chinese railway and civil officials. Most of the Chinese army had already withdrawn. I stopped over in the little border town of Shanhaikwan, where the ancient Great Wall of China comes down to the sea, and observed the Chinese army of Marshal Chang Hsueh-liang pass through the Great Wall from Manchuria into China proper, thus marking the end of Chinese authority in the northeastern provinces. A dispatch I sent, describing the final evacuation of Manchuria, was suppressed by the Chinese commander at Shanhaikwan.

It was five years before the Japanese were ready to extend their conquest into China proper, south of the Great Wall— five years of futile haggling and inactivity on the part of the Western Powers, while Japan, now in alliance with Germany, proceeded with her ambitious plans for Oriental and world conquest.

The Manchurian war and growing unrest in the Far East brought to the attention of American newspaper readers the dispatches of a new group of correspondents, whose names heretofore had been unfamiliar, as they had not been stationed in Europe. Among them were several who later came to be rated as experts on Far Eastern affairs, including Edgar Snow, who represented the *London Daily Herald*; Victor Keen, *New York Herald Tribune*; Reginald Sweetland, *Chicago*

Daily News; Edward Hunter and John Goette, International News; Glen Babb and Morris Harris, Associated Press; Frank Oliver, Reuter's Service; Hallett Abend, *New York Times;* John Morris, United Press; I represented the *Manchester Guardian* and *Chicago Tribune.* Later, when the situation grew more serious, the United Press sent Frederick Kuh from Berlin and International News sent Floyd Gibbons.

The situation was enlivened by the arrival of Will Rogers, who worried the Japanese censors with his daily fifty-word syndicated wisecracks, which were directed chiefly at the Japanese. One particular message was delayed several hours while the Japanese censor took it around to various Americans in Mukden for an explanation. It read as follows: "I have just heard that the League of Nations has decided to send a mission to Mukden to investigate the Manchurian Incident. It reminds me of a familiar scene in early days in Oklahoma when the sheriff arrived to inspect the stable after the horse had been stolen." It required considerable diagramming before the Japanese military censors and staff officers could understand that!

With regard to the Manchurian incident itself, we correspondents found plenty of evidence as to what had occurred. Japanese troops, previously stationed within the zone of the Japanese-owned South Manchurian Railway and in Korea, were in occupation of the Manchurian capital. When we arrived, the press representative of the Japanese military headquarters, Major Watari, who spoke English with an Oxford accent, explained that "there had been an incident—Chinese soldiers wearing the regulation uniform of Marshal Chang Hsueh-liang, head of the Chinese administration in the three northeastern Chinese provinces [Manchuria], had blown up a section of track of the Japanese railway on the outskirts of Mukden—the Japanese army was forced to take action against the Chinese troops in the vicinity of Mukden." In order that we might see exactly what had taken place Major Watari escorted us to the "scene of the crime," a section of track of the Japanese-owned South Manchuria Railway a few miles from Mukden.

There we and the military observers were shown the bodies of three Chinese soldiers lying alongside the track where, allegedly, they had been shot while running away from the place "where they had set off a charge of dynamite which had shattered three cross-ties and blown away a section of the rail on the outside of a curve." The damage had of course been repaired, Major Watari explained, as he pointed to three new ties and a new rail which had been placed in position. He also called attention to the fact that the position of the bodies of the dead Chinese soldiers indicated that they had been running away when killed. One small circumstance, however, was overlooked by Major Watari: there were no blood-stains on the ground where the bodies were lying. Since the Japanese had made a surprise attack on the Chinese garrison in the vicinity at the same time, it had been comparatively easy to produce the bodies. In order to overcome scepticism the Japanese military, some days later, produced a list of some three hundred cases of alleged Chinese infringements on Japanese "rights" in Manchuria.

Later when the League of Nations sent an international commission under Lord Lytton to investigate Japan's seizure of the Chinese provinces, an American expert, Ben Dorfman, who was connected with the mission, checked the train schedule and found that an express train, traveling at approximately fifty miles an hour, had passed over the scene of the alleged explosion within twenty minutes after the time when the Japanese army authorities said it had occurred. When faced with this evidence the Japanese army produced a brakeman from the train crew who testified he had "felt a slight jar" when the train passed over this point. But the army carefully preserved the three shattered ties and some three or four feet of twisted rail and a bent fish-plate, which were on exhibition for several weeks in the Mukden office of General Honjo, Commander-in-Chief of the Japanese forces in Kwantung. One wondered why the Japanese army went to such pains to justify its seizure of this Chinese territory when their larger activities and objectives were so obvious.

There was further evidence in Mukden which indicated the

Japanese methods used in seizing the capital city of Manchuria. In searching through the files of Japanese photograph shops I found a large collection of pictures showing Japanese in plain clothes bearing rifles and wearing arm bands. Foreign business-men testified that Mukden had been over-run for several days prior to September 18, 1931, by large groups of Japanese "tourists" wearing civilian clothes. The Japanese army had smuggled thousands of camouflaged soldiers into the city in readiness for the prearranged signal to occupy all strategic places—which they carried out according to plan at about 10 o'clock on the night of September 18, 1931. It is well to keep this date in mind, as it was the real beginning of World War II.

I wrote a story about Japan's occupation of Mukden by an army in plain clothes which I illustrated with the pictures I had picked up in the Mukden shop. Within a few hours following its publication in my paper in Shanghai, Japanese army representa-tives searched all shops in Mukden and confiscated all pictures showing "plain-clothes" soldiers.

An analysis of Japan's technique in seizing the Manchurian provinces shows that Hitler was an imitator rather than the originator of this particular method of stealing other people's territory. Japan claimed that the action at Mukden was pro-voked by the hostile act of a body of Chinese troops, but long before the "incident" occurred, Mukden was filled with Japa-nese troops in plain clothes; and further evidence showed that trains carrying large bodies of Japanese troops *in uniform* had already crossed the Korean border into Manchuria several hours before the Mukden incident occurred.

The Japanese also had a battery of field guns of the howitzer type mounted on concrete foundations in Mukden and long held in readiness for the attack. The guns were located in a closely guarded Japanese compound and were covered with large barn-like structures with corrugated iron roofs. The guns were trained on the Mukden arsenal. The Chinese claimed the guns had been smuggled in many months before in packing cases

labeled "mining machinery." On the day following the occupation an American acquaintance of mine, a businessman named
Kendall Graham, who resided in the neighborhood, observed
that the ends had been knocked out of the "barns" and most of
the corrugated roofs had been blown off by the concussion of
the guns. My friend, who was connected with an American oil
company, took me around to see these guns when I arrived
in Mukden.

It was in connection with Japan's campaign in Manchuria
that the world first began to hear stories of Japanese atrocities,
but generally they were disbelieved. We received frequent reports of Japanese wiping out entire villages which were suspected of harboring guerrillas, and the representative of the
League of Nations, Señor Farrar, kept a record of these reports
and telegraphed a full account to Geneva. An account of one
atrocity which I myself investigated and filed was denied by
the Japanese Consul-General in Chicago. He disputed my figures
that 3,000 Chinese villagers had been massacred, and said there
had been no massacre, "because only three hundred had been
killed."

The Japanese had a staff of American and British propa-
gandists, headed by an Irishman, George Gorman, and an
American, Henry Kinney, who were on the job disputing all
correspondents' stories of which the Japanese disapproved.
Kinney, a former resident of Honolulu, who was married to a
Japanese woman, had long served as publicity agent for the
South Manchuria Railway. Gorman had served as editor of
Japanese propaganda papers in Peiping and elsewhere. Gorman's
nominal job was that of correspondent for the *London Daily
Telegraph*, which got him into all of the press conferences, but
his main job seemed to be that of apologist for the Japanese
army.

XVIII

Russia, China, and Japan

IT IS APPARENTLY not generally known that Soviet Russia was willing, in 1932, to enter into an agreement with the United States and China for the purpose of preventing Japanese expansion on the continent of Asia whereby in the event of war between Japan and any one of the three Powers, the other two were to come to the rescue of the victim of Japanese aggression.

The proposed agreement was discussed informally by Russian, American, and Chinese delegates at Geneva when the League of Nations was considering the Manchurian question. The chief Soviet delegate was Maxim Litvinoff, Foreign Commissar, and the Chinese delegation was composed of Dr. W. W. Yen, Dr. Wellington Koo and Quo Tai-chi.

Since America at that time had no diplomatic relations with the Soviet Union, the attitude of the United States Government toward the proposal was not expressed. But the discussions between China and Russia resulted in two significant developments. The first was that the two governments agreed immediately to resume diplomatic relations, which had been in abeyance since 1927, when Chiang Kai-shek broke off relations with the Soviets because of Russia's propagation of communism in China. The second result of the informal conversations between American and Russian delegates at Geneva concerning their interests in the Far East was that they paved the way for a resumption of relations between the United States and Russia.

It is idle to speculate on what might or might not have happened if certain actions had or had not been taken on specific occasions in the past. Whether the proposed agreement between America, Russia, and China would have stopped Japan can only be guessed at, but if it had succeeded, it might have caused other nations with ambitions similar to those of Japan to hesitate before embarking on their subsequent adventures.

The disclosures concerning the proposed agreement were contained in a manuscript written by Thomas F. F. Millard and entitled "The Watch on the Pacific," but never published. Mr. Millard was present at the Geneva meeting as an adviser to the Chinese delegation to the League of Nations.

The fact that, as stated above, Russia and China—particularly Russia—were willing, in 1932, to join with the United States in a tripartite pact to block Japan is of tremendous interest in World War II, because of Russia's position of neutrality in the first four years of the war in the Pacific, involving Russia's partners, the United States, Britain, and China. That Russia's neutrality constituted America's most serious handicap in our war with Japan is generally recognized. The Soviet Government, in April, 1945, served notice on Japan of its intention to abrogate the neutrality treaty upon its expiration in April, 1946.

According to Mr. Millard's disclosures, the purpose of the proposed agreement, as stated in the preamble, was "to preserve peace in the Far East and establish and maintain political and economic stability in the Far East and the Western Pacific." The text provided that if any of the territorial possessions of America, Russia, or China, or their commercial and property rights within the region covered by the agreement or the political rights and safety of their citizens residing in these regions, were invaded or encroached upon by any Power outside of the agreement, the signatory Powers would consult about measures to be taken to preserve the status quo.

In addition to the main agreement providing for common action in the Far East and the Western Pacific, provision was made for three supplementary agreements to come into effect automatically in the event of an outbreak of war with Japan. The first of these, between the United States and Russia, provided that each should respect the existing territory of the other, and that of China as well, unless otherwise agreed upon with

China's consent. Upon the satisfactory conclusion of the war certain readjustments of territories held by Japan were to be made. The southern half of Sakhalin Island was to be returned to Russia. An equitable readjustment of Russia's railway interests in Manchuria was to be made. The islands in the Pacific mandated to Japan at the Versailles Conference were to be at the disposition of the United States Government. Any arrangements in regard to the Philippines agreed upon by the United States and the Philippines Government were to be respected. And finally, the territory of Japan proper was to remain intact, provided Japan agreed to a satisfactory limitation of her naval power.

In the proposed agreement between the United States and China, each country was to respect the territorial and political independence of the other. The United States would support China in abolishing special privileges and concessions within her borders as well as all agreements with Japan which impaired or infringed on China's sovereignty. The United States would supply China with military and naval advisers to assist in organizing China's military forces, and would supply aviation and other military experts together with munitions, supplies, and the financial assistance necessary to prosecute the war against Japan. China would agree to cooperate in all ways, including the use of China's ports for United States naval bases. She would also respect in the peace terms the territorial allocations agreed upon in the pact between the United States and Russia.

China and Russia would come to an equitable agreement between themselves on all matters in which the United States was not directly interested, but such agreements were not to qualify or contradict the terms of the United States pacts with Russia and China.

A memorandum embodying the proposed U.S.A.-Russia-China pact which was submitted to the State, War, and Navy departments expressed the opinion that the agreement would checkmate any schemes of the Japanese military party to conquer China or take Russian territory in the Far East. It was thought that the Japanese militarists would scarcely dare to challenge such a combination.

The reason the British Government was not included in the tentative agreement was two-fold. First, it was not thought at that time that Japan's program included an invasion of the Southwest Pacific, where Britain's colonial sphere existed; and secondly, Great Britain, when approached, raised objections to certain phases of the proposed pact which she thought might adversely affect certain efforts on her part to bring pressure on Japan through the League of Nations, which had the Manchurian question under consideration at the time.

One of the Soviet delegates at Geneva also proposed that China should recognize Russian sovereignty in Outer Mongolia and cede to Russia all Manchurian territory north of the Chinese Eastern Railway. This would give the Russians a short cut to the sea at Vladivostok and would permit Russia to develop nearby Poset Bay at the junction of eastern Siberia, Manchuria, and Korea, which is free from ice in winter. The section of North Manchuria referred to, sparsely populated except by Russian emigrants, had always been regarded as a Russian sphere of influence in Manchuria.

It was obvious that Russia could not remain undisturbed in the face of military activities in Manchuria, which by 1932–33 had reached the northern and western borders of Manchuria and were being extended into Inner Mongolia, which flanked Soviet-controlled Outer Mongolia on the east and south.

The Japanese did not conceal their animosities toward the Soviet Union and its citizens resident in North Manchuria. Russian Jews residing within the zone of the Chinese Eastern Railway, many of whom had Soviet citizenship certificates, were singled out for special attention of kidnapers in the pay of the Japanese gendarmerie. The most notorious case was that of Simeon Kaspe, son of Joseph Kaspe, owner of hotels, moving-picture houses, and a jewelry store in Harbin. The elder Kaspe had served as a cavalry officer in the Russian army in the Russo-

Japanese War, and afterward settled in Harbin. He prospered and sent his children to Paris for their educations. The youngest son, Simeon, became a talented pianist, and while in Paris adopted French citizenship. He was well known in the Far East, and had given recitals in Tokyo, Shanghai, and Manila. In 1933, after the Japanese occupied North Manchuria, young Kaspe was kidnaped by a gang of White Russian bandits in the pay of the Japanese gendarmerie. The leader of the gang was a White Russian named Radzoyevsky, who was head of a so-called "Fascist Club" in Harbin, which cooperated with the Japanese. The kidnaping plot was organized by the secretary-interpreter of the gendarmerie, a Japanese named Nakamura, who was assisted by a White Russian named Martinoff, who was connected with the Harbin police department. After young Kaspe was kidnaped and taken to a secret hiding place on the outskirts of Harbin, a letter was sent to the father demanding a ransom of $300,000. The father countered with an offer of a smaller amount, and notified the French Consul-General.

The French Vice-Consul, M. Chambon, demanded young Kaspe's release and presented the Japanese consular authorities with indisputable evidence of the connivance of the Japanese gendarmerie in the kidnaping plot. The White Russian fascist papers in Harbin, under Japanese inspiration, immediately started a campaign against the French consular official, calling him a "communist Jew." The Japanese authorities procrastinated and did nothing to apprehend the kidnapers, who, fearing complications, reduced their ransom demand. In previous kidnaping cases the payment of ransoms had not always resulted in the release of victims, and often had merely led to further demands for money. Hence, upon the advice of the French Vice-Consul, the elder Kaspe refused to pay the ransom—whereupon the bandits cut off their victim's ears and sent them to the bereaved parent. After holding and torturing young Kaspe for ninety-five days the bandits shot him.

The case aroused such widespread indignation among the people of Harbin that almost the entire community, including

Russians, Chinese, and Koreans, turned out for the funeral, the largest ever held in that city. The case received so much publicity in the Far Eastern press that the Tokyo Government, under French pressure, ordered the arrest of the six White Russian criminals who were involved in the kidnaping plot.

Since the Japanese had just occupied the district, the Chinese judicial authorities were still functioning in Harbin, which was within the railway zone. Despite attempts to intimidate the court through attacks published in the fascist papers, the Chinese court courageously found the six White Russian bandits guilty and sentenced four of them to death and two to life imprisonment. Harbin rejoiced at the verdict; but the rejoicing was short-lived. The head of the Japanese gendarmerie intervened, had the presiding Chinese judge arrested and ordered the sentences set aside. Six months later a special panel of three Japanese judges dismissed the case and ordered the criminals released, on the ground that they had "acted from patriotic motives." The Japanese-controlled fascist paper, published in the Russian language, commenting on the verdict, described the kidnapers as "honest and excellent citizens, real Russian patriots, who acted not from motives of personal gain, but purely for the purpose of obtaining funds for anti-communist organizations to continue their fight against Bolshevism."

Two papers run by Britons in Harbin, the *Harbin Herald*, edited by Lenox Simpson, and the *Harbin Observer*, edited by B. Hayton Fleet, which criticized the Japanese court action, were confiscated by the Japanese authorities, and the editors were expelled from Manchuria.

The reign of terror which followed the Japanese occupation spread all over Manchuria and was accompanied by wholesale kidnapings of Russian Jews and Chinese. The Russian Jews were invariably charged with communistic activities and membership in the Third International.

Japanese animosities against the Soviet Union were further increased by the action of the Soviet authorities in permitting a Chinese general and his army to "escape" from Manchuria, with their arms, into Soviet territory and later to re-enter Chinese territory in Sinkiang, far to the northwest. The Chinese general in question was a picturesque figure named Ma Chanshan. General Ma had first held up and defeated the vanguard of the Japanese invaders at the Nonni River, on the southern border of the Russian sphere in North Manchuria. Owing to a shortage of ammunition General Ma was compelled, however, to withdraw his forces into the Hinghan Mountains along the Amur River. Since this territory was practically inaccessible until roads could be constructed, the Japanese decided to try diplomacy. General Kenji Doihara, known as Japan's "master of intrigue," was sent to Harbin to negotiate with General Ma. After several meetings General Ma consented to "go over" to the Japanese, providing the Japanese would appoint him Minister of War in the new Manchukuo Government, and in addition provide him with a million dollars in gold bullion with which to re-equip his army.

In the meantime I had made a trip with a group of American correspondents to the frontier town of Tsitsihar, capital of Heilungkiang Province, to interview General Ma, who in fighting his rearguard action against the Japs had crossed the Chinese Eastern Railway to the west of Harbin.

We made the trip from Anganchi, the junction point on the Chinese Eastern line to Tsitsihar, over a narrow-gauge railway and reached General Ma's headquarters only about an hour before his evacuation of the city for a further withdrawal toward the Hinghan Mountains. He told us he planned ultimately to establish his headquarters at the town of Aigun, which is opposite the old Russian outpost of Blagoveshchensk on the upper Amur.

General Ma was small in stature, and unlike most Chinese he had a heavy beard with the ends of his mustache drooping down two or three inches.

Since we had only about an hour to interview the general, and our questions and his replies had to be alternately translated into Chinese and English, we were anxious to get on with the interview. We had proceeded only about ten minutes and were looking nervously at our watches when our conversation was made inaudible by the striking of a large "grandfather's" type clock standing in the corner of the room. The clock was equipped with a heavy sonorous gong, with chimes, and it seemed to take an interminable time to strike the hour, which was midnight. All questions ceased and the interview was in abeyance as we looked helplessly at each other until the clock had finished. It finally ceased striking and we revived the interview for a couple of minutes, when we were all startled again by another "boom" as a similar clock in an adjoining room started striking. Once more we sat helplessly until it had finished, a matter of several minutes. Again we resumed the interview— and again we were interrupted by another clock in another near-by room. The interview finally had to be cut short, as six clocks in various parts of the large compound struck; they had obviously been set to strike two or three minutes apart. Before we left the room I went over to the first clock to examine its mechanism. Across the face in English were the words "Made in Germany."

The Japanese finally agreed to General Ma's terms, and he went to Hsinking (old name Changchun), the new Manchukuo capital, but when he had received the money he secretly rejoined his troops in the Hinghan Mountains and again defied the Japanese invaders. The Japanese at once sent a large force into North Manchuria and succeeded in defeating a contingent of General Ma's troops. In checking over the Chinese bodies left on the field, following the Chinese withdrawal, the Japanese found a corpse attired in the uniform of a general. Near the body was a dead Mongolian pony similar to that usually ridden by General Ma Chan-shan, and, what was even more convincing, the Japanese found a saddle-bag containing papers bearing the signature of the general, and several of the gold bars which the Japanese army had given him to use in equipping his troops.

Japanese army officers were so elated that they sent a group of high officials bearing the uniform and other accouterments of the "deceased" Chinese commander to Tokyo where they were pridefully exhibited before Hirohito, the Son of Heaven. These formalities, in which General Doihara participated, gave General Ma the time he needed to transfer practically his entire army across the Amur to Blagoveshchensk on the Soviet side of the line, where the Chinese soldiers were entrained for Sinkiang Province. General Ma then dispatched a telegram to Generalissimo Chiang Kai-shek at Nanking apprising him of the incident.

Aside from the embarrassment caused the Japanese by General Ma's sensational exploit, the Japanese army was placed in a curious predicament involving the prestige or "face" of the Emperor. Since Hirohito had been told that General Ma Chanshan was dead, the Son of Heaven, obviously, could not be told that the Imperial Army had made a mistake and that the foxy Chinese general had outwitted them and escaped to Russia. The Japanese solved the impasse by permanently banning the use of General Ma's name in any Japanese paper. In the meantime, General Ma had long since been actively opposing the Japanese in Suiyuan Province, but with no mention whatsoever in any Japanese communiqué. General Doihara, whose intrigue back-fired, lost face and after suffering near defeat by the Chinese forces on the Yellow River, was transferred to the Japanese Air Force.

XIX

Vladivostok

WHEN THE JAPANESE had eliminated the last organized Chinese resistance in Manchuria and the "story" was dead so far as the American and British newspapers were concerned, I decided (in 1935) to investigate the possibility of making a trip to the Soviet Far East.

I had become acquainted with Soviet Ambassador Bogomolov and his Counsellor of Embassy, Spilvanek, through my coverage of a White Russian attempt to seize the Soviet consulate in Shanghai in 1928. Emboldened by Chiang Kai-shek's action in breaking off relations with the Soviets, a group of about 150 former Cossack soldiers who resided in the French Concession at Shanghai attempted to seize the Soviet consulate and set up a "White" Russian government in the International Settlement.

The news that an attempt was to be made to seize and occupy the Soviet consulate spread through the city, and a large crowd gathered, many of them being Russian women emigrees. The consular building was located directly across the street from the Astor House, and the lobby and windows of the hotel were filled with guests watching the show. The excitement began when a Russian woman hurled a brick through one of the windows of the consulate and at the same time uttered a loud scream. This apparently was the signal for action, as the mob closed in and bombarded the building with rocks, bricks, and other missiles, breaking most of the first-story and basement windows.

Despite the fact that neither the British nor the French police authorities interfered, the plot failed, thanks to the determined resistance of Soviet Consul Koslovsky and a handful of Soviet consular officials who barricaded themselves in the building. At the height of the rioting a member of the White Russian contingent, all of whom were attired in their old Czarist uniforms, managed to reach the door of the consulate and attempted to wrench the sickle and hammer from the iron grillwork. He received a bullet through his chest—it was fired through the door by one of the defenders—and died in the street. This took the fight out of the "White Guards," and after breaking a few more windows they dispersed before the belated arrival of the police. No arrests were made.

The Soviet Ambassador was pleased with my coverage of the story, and became a good source of news throughout the remainder of his stay in the Far East. I decided to capitalize on my acquaintance, and asked the Ambassador for a passport visa to visit Vladivostok and Khabarovsk, respectively metropolis and political capital of Soviet Siberia. Bogomolov promised to cable Moscow, but did not hold out much hope. The cable cost me $50, and after a wait of nearly a month I was informed that my application had been rejected.

In expectation of making the trip, I also applied to the Japanese for a visa to travel across the new state of Manchukuo; this was necessary in order to reach the Trans-Siberian Railway at Chita. The Japanese Consul said he also would have to cable the new Manchukuo capital at Hsinking for permission. When I called a few days later for a reply, the answer was an emphatic "No." I then learned that the Japanese army had kept a "blacklist" of all correspondents who had criticized the Japanese occupation of Manchuria, and had permanently barred them from visiting the puppet state. The way seemed to be blocked for my contemplated trip to Siberia.

Some weeks later the Shanghai manager of the Soviet official travel agency, Intourist, told me that I might be able to visit Siberia if I would apply for a six-month tourist traveling permit to visit the November anniversary celebration of the Soviet Union in Red Square, Moscow. He told me that if I could obtain a visa to visit Moscow, it might be possible to stop over in

Siberia on the way. He also told me that a Chinese cargo ship, being loaded with tea in Shanghai Harbor, was shortly sailing for Vladivostok. I decided to make another attempt, and sent another $50 cable to Moscow. This time the reply was favorable, and I received my passport visa and a six-month travel permit. The fee for the visa was $65, making the total cost of my admission to Russia $165. Previously I had regarded our State Department's charge of $10 for a passport as exorbitant.

Before sailing I was told by the Intourist representative that it was customary for travelers in Russia to purchase in advance books of coupons for use in payment for service in hotels, dining cars, and sleeping cars. I discovered later that the charges for hotel and express-train services were made at "official" exchange rate, whereas it was possible for travelers, after entering the Soviet Union, to purchase "cheap" roubles at black exchange markets for as many as seventy or eighty for an American dollar. The official rate was about eight roubles for an American dollar. Later, in Vladivostok, it was whispered to me that I could exchange my American dollars for roubles at the rate of seventy roubles for one United States dollar, but I refrained from patronizing the black market. Despite the fact that it was a criminal offense to purchase "cheap" roubles, I was frequently approached by Russians who offered to sell them at rates ranging from thirty to fifty for one American dollar. Once I was approached by a dealer in cheap roubles during the intermission at the ballet at the Bolshoi Theater in Moscow.

I did not realize the extent of Soviet nervousness regarding the crisis with Japan until I was aboard the Chinese cargo ship, loaded with tea, scheduled to sail immediately for Vladivostok. The cargo holds of the 10,000-ton freighter were not only filled with cases of tea but thousands of additional cases were piled on the decks and covered with tarpaulins almost to the tops of the smokestacks. The Russian taste for tea, which dates from the time of Ghenghis Khan, is almost equal to that of the Chinese for their native drink. The Russians were taking no chances on being cut off from their favorite beverage in the

event of a war with Japan. But there was further evidence
aboard the ship of Soviet expectancy of war with the Nipponese.
The limited passenger space was filled to overflowing with
Soviet officials and families who were hurrying home so as not
to be cut off in the Far East.

Among the passengers were several members of the Soviet
oil trust who had assisted the Chinese in establishing a Chinese-
Soviet oil monopoly, which had failed because the monopoly
could not compete with the American and Anglo-Dutch companies which obtained their oil from California and the Netherlands Indies. The big installation which was built at Shanghai
had been taken over by the Standard Vacuum and Dutch Shell
at a bargain and the Soviet oil men [and their families] were
going home.

Even more convincing evidence of the jittery state of
Soviet nerves developed after the ship sailed. I asked the captain,
a native of Sweden, how long it would require us to make the
trip from Shanghai to Vladivostok. He replied, "Ordinarily
about five days, but much longer this time." He then whispered
to me that the Japanese imperial fleet was holding maneuvers
in the Japan Sea, and in consequence he had received instructions not to sail directly for Vladivostok but to make a wide
detour into the Pacific around Japan and northward in the direction of the Aleutians, thence westward between Hokkaido, the
most northern Japanese island, and Sakhalin to the Siberian
coast, and then southwestward again within Russian territorial
waters directly to Vladivostok, thereby skirting the main Japanese islands. The sea was calm and the trip was uneventful, but
instead of the five days ordinarily required for travel by sea
from Shanghai to Vladivostok, this voyage required twelve days.

I know of no more delightful trip in the world than a peacetime cruise about the Japanese islands. For most of the coastline
the tree-covered mountains come down directly to the sea, with
occasional breaks in the wall through which one obtains a
glimpse of narrow green valleys and often little doll-house
villages and temples. On two or three occasions we observed

waterfalls cascading down the steep cliffs into the sea. One waterfall in particular will always remain in my memory. Seen from the sea, it appeared to be no more than a few yards in width but hundreds of feet in height. In the early morning it looked like a strand of white silk or molten silver waving in the breeze. It fell directly into the sea, sending up a cloud of spray in which a rainbow played.

I found that Vladivostok apparently had changed little, physically, from the appearance of the city when the American troops evacuated the port following our Siberian expedition in World War I. Although many years had passed, the sidewalks and streets contained the same holes, only deeper perhaps, which were there when our boys marched down to the jetty to embark for home following America's first adventure into Russian politics. The store fronts along most of the streets were still boarded up.

My first shock upon the landing of our steamer was to observe that most of the stevedores or dock workers were women. They were much better physical specimens than were the men working on the job. The foreman was a woman. My next shock came when a customs officer asked to see my passport, and examined my baggage. The official was also a woman. When I recovered my composure I addressed her in my very best (but limited) Russian; I had been studying the language, with indifferent success, for about three months. I noticed a puzzled look on her face, but she laughed and said (in English), "Please tell me what you want, and I will help you."

Most of the shops were closed; only one department store had been opened. I noticed that practically all of the customers who jammed the one department store were Koreans; they seemed to be the only residents possessing any money.

The shabby appearance of the town, however, did not mean that it was dead. On the contrary, Vladivostok was a hive of military activity. After resuming control of the city following the evacuation of the Japanese in 1922–23, the Soviet authori-

ties did little to improve the port for more than ten years. Then
they suddenly awoke to the realization that pious wishes and
propaganda would not stem the Japanese tide of conquest which
was sweeping across Manchuria and pressing against the Siberian
frontier from the Ussuri and Amur rivers to the deserts of
Mongolia.

The old fortifications which the Czar had constructed at
Vladivostok for the defense of Russia's "Jewel of the Eastern
Sea" became worthless after the Allied (Anglo-American-Japa-
nese) intervention in Siberia. The Japanese, who overlook
nothing, had thoroughly mapped the terrain, particularly that
facing Korea and Manchuria. After the Japanese troops finally
evacuated the area as a result of American pressure at the Washington Arms Conference of 1922, the Soviets, in order to show
their peaceful intentions toward both China and Japan, dismantled
all of the old Czarist fortifications and shipped the guns inland to
serve as scrap in the new iron foundries of European Russia.

Now the Soviet authorities were trying to make up for their
delay in rebuilding Vladivostok's defenses. Voroshilov, Minister
of War, went to Vladivostok and surveyed the situation. The
old Vladivostok iron works and ship-building plant was taken
over and rejuvenated. Long rows of wooden barracks were
constructed to house thousands of technicians and workers
shipped to the Far East from European Russia. Renamed the
Voroshilov Iron Works, the plant was converted to the construction, or rather the assembly, of submarines. They were
built in sections in European Russia or in Germany and shipped
over the Trans-Siberian Railway, or by sea to the Voroshilov
Iron Works, where they were put together. I counted a half
dozen of these sleek under-water craft cruising and maneuvering
in the harbor. I was told in Tokyo several weeks later when I
returned from Russia that the Russians had thirty subs based at
Vladivostok at that time. The Japanese were watching the situation closely, and visitors arriving in Tokyo from Europe by the
Trans-Siberian Railway were subjected to near third-degree
questioning by Japanese newspapermen and government offi-

cials in an effort to find out what the traveler had seen while crossing Siberia.

Since the Russians are experts in the art of psychological warfare, I often wondered whether much of their war preparation was not purposely displayed for its effect on the Japanese. For example, travelers along the Trans-Siberian Railway between Vladivostok and Khabarovsk always reported seeing large numbers of giant planes standing on air fields near the railway. I probably saw a half dozen of these giant planes, but I could well imagine that when the reports reached Tokyo the half dozen planes became hundreds.

The initial impression created upon the visitor newly arrived at Vladivostok was the nervousness, verging almost on hysteria, which prevailed among the 208,000 population of the port. Practically every man, woman, and child carried a gas mask or kept one within reach. At night groups of people could be seen standing at street intersections under the heavily shaded street lamps listening to instructions by OGPU officers, on "what to do in the event of a Japanese air raid."

One night the manager of Intourist took me in his new Soviet-made "Ford" to a high hill overlooking a deep valley on the outskirts of the city. Powerful searchlights trained on a large excavation project gave the impression of an inferno as thousands of laborers were driving a fifteen-mile tunnel under the Vladivostok hills. The announced purpose was to facilitate rail communication from the hinterland through the city to tidewater. In Moscow a few weeks later a German Embassy attaché, whom I had known previously in Tientsin, told me that the tunnel was being constructed for another purpose, to serve as a bomb-proof shelter for the population in the event of war with Japan. Elsewhere I was assured that the "tunnel" was actually an underground airdrome.

On another trip to the outskirts of the city my Intourist guide pointed out to me a large clearing on the wooded slopes of Russian Island in the harbor. My guide said it was the site of new fortifications being rushed to completion. Numerous long-range coast-defense guns had been installed in the hills, and special attention had been paid to the defenses on the land side, to prevent an attack from that direction. A large radio station on Russian Island, originally built by General Graves for the use of our American troops during the intervention, had been reconstructed and was in operation.

Visits to other hilltops disclosed numerous cuttings for new railway sidings and other larger clearings for air fields. Planes were constantly in the air, day and night, on patrol duty. I once counted 160 Soviet planes in the air at one time. A new refrigeration plant in the harbor area provided facilities for preparing and preserving fish in ton lots, obviously for feeding an army. An American company was also constructing a large modern cannery for the Soviet Fishery Bureau. Large cellars were under construction, for storage of vegetables, fruits, and dairy products.

One morning I was astonished to see thousands of workers engaged in transforming the street-railway tracks to broad gauge in order that they could be used for railway transport in an emergency. I was told that the workers, including many women welders armed with blow-torches, were from the Voroshilov Iron Works and that they had "donated" their holiday in order that the street railway could be changed to railway gauge.

All water and gas mains were being sunk to eight or ten feet underground as protection from air-bombing by the Japanese, and an underground aqueduct eighteen miles long was under construction to provide an auxiliary supply in case of need. Two electric power plants were under construction. I was also shown the ruins of a once-imposing church which had been dynamited to make way for a projected summer hotel and resort for workers and soldiers. The most ambitious project of all, the double-tracking of the Trans-Siberian Railway from the Urals to the Pacific, had not yet reached Vladivostok. This monumental job was being pushed through with forced labor—political prisoners from the Ukraine.

Mr. Melinkoff, representative of the Narcomindel or Foreign Office, complained, when I visited him, that he could not get the roof of his house repaired because all carpenters were employed on the tunnel job. "In Manchuria I could get a Chinese carpenter to do the job in a few hours," he said. But in Vladivostok there was no provision in the "five-year plan" for such small private jobs. Everything had to be subordinated to the main job. On one occasion it was necessary to import Chinese laborers from Manchuria to repair and pave a street about the railway station in preparation for the November Tenth Celebration. There were not enough Soviet laborers available even for this job.

Thousands of men, women and children, enforced emigrants from the Ukraine, were camped in primitive shacks and lean-tos for several blocks about the railway station, awaiting the construction or repair of houses. Similar scenes were presented at practically all railway stations along the route as far as Lake Baikal. All railway stations were jammed with people who had no other place to sleep.

Siberia was practically without modern roads, and worse, was without the mechanical means or trained engineering personnel with knowledge or experience in modern road construction. Having lived in China for many years, where modern roads were almost unknown until 1927, I was astonished to find that Russia, particularly Siberia, was even behind China in modern roads. When I mentioned the lack of roads the average Russian would shrug his shoulders and say that since the ground was frozen for a considerable part of the year "roads really were not necessary." However, some roads were being built; one twenty-five miles long was under construction to a town on the Vladivostok peninsula. Some weeks later I was standing next to a high German diplomat viewing the November Tenth military show in Red Square when a number of the new heavy Soviet tanks or "land battleships" lumbered by. I asked the German what he thought of them. He replied, "They would bog down in the Russian mud ten miles outside of Moscow." He appeared to be unaware of the Russian custom of waging war in the winter when the ground and rivers are frozen.

I was told that major effort in Vladivostok was being exerted in the field of popular education, but I was shown only two schools, one for children whose mothers worked at the Voroshilov Iron Works. The modern residence where this school was located had previously belonged to a member of the old American consulate. The other school, known as the Korean University, to which I was taken, was said to be the only one in existence where the ancient Korean language was taught. This statement was not strictly correct, however, as American missionaries in Korea, despite Japanese military opposition, used the Korean language in their schools until the Korean language was definitely outlawed by the Japanese Governor-General, some time before World War II. While visiting the Korean University at Vladivostok I was shown one room where some fifty students were engaged in translating articles and pamphlets into the Korean language. I was told that the booklets were being smuggled into Korea. Later, after Stalin signed the four-point non-aggression pact with Japan in 1941, the Russians not only closed the Korean University but moved a considerable portion of the Korean population from the Vladivostok area further west to some undisclosed point in Central Asia.

One day I visited a parade ground, and was surprised to see a regiment of Korean troops drilling and maneuvering under Soviet officers. I was told that the Korean regiment was part of the Soviet border-defense force. Later, in the vicinity of Lake Baikal, I observed even larger bodies of Oriental troops wearing the uniform of the Soviet army.

A vacant block near the hotel was jammed every morning

by thousands of men and women engaged in bartering articles of clothing, shoes, underwear, and occasionally a shabby fur coat, for a few kopeks of depreciated paper currency with which to purchase bread and vegetables. This "market" was apparently winked at by the authorities or was not considered "trading for profit" under the Soviet law.

The ancient Versailles Hotel still bore the name and some remnants of the opulence it had possessed in more prosperous Czarist days. It reminded me of a once aristocratic hostelry in an American town which had enjoyed and then been by-passed by an oil or mining boom. The condition of the sanitary plumbing was something to be forgotten as soon as possible after use. As for the wash-basins and bathtubs, I am willing to wager that I didn't find in all Siberia a half dozen that possessed plugs. On my first morning in Khabarovsk I asked the maid about facilities for taking a bath. She went away and returned with a tin can containing about a gallon of hot water. Motioning to me to remove my pajamas, she started to pour the water on my head so it would run down over my body in the fashion of a shower. I decided to forgo the luxury of a bath until I reached Moscow.

Every hotel was compelled by law to keep a large black book for use of the guests in making complaints. The manager said that the official inspector of hotels from Moscow was accustomed to drop in unannounced and demand the "black book" for a perusal of complaints noted down by the guests. While in Vladivostok I complained on several occasions of the lack of fish, although several varieties were always listed on the menu. The head waiter immediately produced the familiar black book. Finally I took it, and selecting a blank page wrote down all of the statistics I could remember that the Fishery Bureau had given me about Vladivostok's fish production. Under the figures I wrote, "In view of Vladivostok's great fish production, why can't I have some fish for breakfast?" Later I was visited by a delegation, including the manager, dining-room steward and chief bookkeeper, who explained to me that there had been a breakdown in the fishery delivery service. I was assured that the matter would be rectified when the inspector arrived from Moscow.

Vladivostok has a delightful spring, summer, and autumn climate, but the same cannot be said of winter, which is cold, blustery, and changeable. A balmy, invigorating morning might be followed by a cold, raw afternoon that made a fur-lined overcoat a necessity. The officials at Vladivostok had elaborate plans for developing Vladivostok as a summer resort, similar to the famous resorts on the Caspian and Black seas, but war preparations doubtless intervened.

While in Vladivostok I listened to many accounts of ambitious development projects, one of which nearly caused complications with the Japanese. It also had its humorous elements.

This project was for the construction of a causeway or dam connecting northern Sakhalin Island with the mainland, just north of the mouth of the Amur River. The engineer claimed that the cold weather which prevailed along the coast of the Maritime Province of Siberia was due to a cold ocean current from the Sea of Okhotsk which flowed southward along the coast of the Maritime Province. He argued that this frigid current was responsible for the disagreeable climate which prevails along the southern Siberian coast, and that by damming the narrow strait between Sakhalin Island and the coast, the cold current would be diverted away from Siberia and would flow down along the east side of Japan. The effect of this, according to his analysis, would be to produce a warmer climate along the Siberian coast and at the same time to transform the Japanese islands, particularly the northern islands of Hokkaido and Honshu, into arctic territories which the Japanese population would find unendurable.

News of this novel Russian solution of the Japanese problem, which would congeal them wholesale, naturally reached Japan and created a tremendous commotion. It was only one of many such rumors which were constantly coming out of Siberia and circulating among the Japanese in exaggerated form.

I often wondered if this was not an astute form of Russian psychological warfare.

Also, there was no questioning the fact that the Japanese were using these alleged threats from Siberia to stimulate their own war psychology and divert the minds of the Japanese people away from the critical economic situation then prevailing throughout most of Japan.

XX

Across Siberia

THE AWAKENING OF THE Russian Bear to the necessity of defending Siberia now was evident on all sides. The activities of every individual and the use of every resource in the land were directed, voluntarily or forcibly, toward the major objective, the saving of Siberia from the "makakas," the Russian word for monkey, used as a slang name for the Japanese.

I was amazed to observe at first hand the Soviet Union's method of handling labor. I inquired of my Intourist guide, a young woman member of the Komsomols, or Communist Youth Organization, why all of the labor groups, often numbering as many as a thousand men, engaged in double-tracking the Trans-Siberian Railway, were always bossed by armed guards of the OGPU. These armed guards were always recognized by their black leather coats and trousers and Cossack-style high leather boots, and they always carried a sub-machine gun. The clothing worn by the laborers was shabby, and in many cases showed evidence of a former more opulent existence on the part of the wearer. This was particularly true of fur caps, and fur lapels on their threadbare coats, from which most of the hair had been worn away. A fur cap has always been a sure sign of luxury in Russia, whether in Czarist or modern Communist days.

When the train stopped, as it often did, where work was in progress, the men would swarm about me as I stepped from the express car; they seemed to know instinctively I was an "Amerikansky," and beg for "toboc." My extra supply, bought in Shanghai, was quickly exhausted. Once a man who knew some English and obviously had seen better days dropped to his knees, kowtowed, and begged me for some tobacco, and when I handed him my half-empty tin he embraced me so enthusiastically that all the passengers cheered.

When I asked my Intourist guide for information about the armed guards, she always shrugged her shoulders and in her limited English replied, "political criminals." And so they were —largely, as I was later informed, from the Ukraine, where there had been mass opposition to Stalin's collective farm program. I was told that the farmers had slaughtered their cattle and staged a great feast, rather than surrender the cattle to the state, and that a vast and devastating famine had resulted. The usual charges against these men were ownership of land and employment of labor for profit. They were the famous "kulaks," now constituting an oppressed class in the "classless" society of the U.S.S.R.

In the railway yards at Chita, junction point where the Chinese Eastern Railway branched off toward Manchuria from the main or Amur line of the Trans-Siberian, I saw long lines of freight cars, literally thousands of them, flat cars, gondolas, and closed cars. The flat cars and gondolas were loaded with trucks, tractors, combines, and miscellaneous military equipment. The closed cars were filled with human cargo, largely men, who were being shipped from European Russia to Siberia to work on various construction and defense jobs. I noticed that all of the closed freight cars were locked on the outside and that the faces which jammed the little windows in the upper corners were wan and pale. Armed OGPU guards constantly patrolled between the long lines of cars. I was told that the prisoners could regain their citizenship by conscientious work for a certain period, usually five years. But thousands, particularly those of advanced years, obviously would not be able to live out the five-year period. I frequently saw bodies of those who had dropped from exhaustion or illness lying alongside the railway track.

A study of Russian history reveals that there have been many forced mass migrations of peoples within the borders of the country. The Yakut nation or tribe, which occupies most of the rich Lena River Valley in Siberia, has a tradition that its people are of Turkish origin and were moved in a mass from Central Asia by some early conqueror, perhaps Genghis Khan or Tamerlane. Present-day Yakuts, who number some 300,000, claim that they are "cousins" of American Indians, whom they greatly resemble. Yakutsk, the capital of the Yakut nation, is on the Alaska-Siberian air route connecting the United States and Canada with the Soviet Union, and in the early years of World War II had aroused the interest of American travelers. They have reported that the Yakuts are an enterprising race and control within their "republic" much of the gold, platinum, furs, and other valuable raw products of Siberia which are shipped abroad to help balance Russia's war economy. Educated members of the tribe, whom I met on the train in the vicinity of Lake Baikal and also in Manchuria, were friendly toward Americans and constantly asked questions about their American Indian "cousins."

There was still another example of forced "mass migration" of thousands of Russians in the triangular area fronting on Manchuria, located to the west of Khabarovsk, capital of Siberia. The territory, known as the Biro-Bidjhan district (named for two rivers), was set aside by the Soviet Government as a self-governing "colony" for the resettlement of Russian Jews. Most of the Jews in the district had been transported there from the towns and villages of the Ukraine and White Russia. But they fared better than the labor gangs along the railroad in that they retained their political rights and enjoyed autonomy in the direction of the local administration of the district. The editor of the party newspaper in Khabarovsk told me that the Jewish colony "was similar to the Palestine colony which Great Britain had fostered," and that a chief object of the Soviet Government in establishing the district was to divert the attention of Russian Jews from the British-fostered Zionist movement in Palestine, which had profoundly impressed the millions of Russian Jews. The secretary of the Siberian Jewish colony informed me that

Jewish organizations in New York had contributed considerable sums to the Russian project. Incidentally, the official Handbook of the Soviet Union, printed in English, listed more than a dozen types of Jews, some of them classed among the most primitive tribes of the country.

I learned from a Soviet army officer, whom I met on the train, that the chief objective of the Government in establishing the Biro-Bidjhan Jewish colony was strategic. Due to its location directly to the west of Khabarovsk, capital of Siberia, the district was intended to provide an important agricultural and industrial base for the support of the Far Eastern Red Army, headquartered in eastern Siberia. Due to the location of the Jewish colony along the Amur adjacent to the new Japanese state of Manchukuo, it would be impossible for a Japanese army to attack Khabarovsk without invading the Jewish colony, causing repercussions throughout the Jewish world somewhat similar to Hitler's attack on the Jews in Europe. Later when the Jews showed a disinclination to engage in "collective" farming in the new colony, the Soviet Government moved into the area several thousand Korean farmers from the Vladivostok area. Russian officials at Khabarovsk said there was considerable intermarriage between the Jewish colonists and the Koreans, leading inevitably to the creation of a new race, as was happening in North Manchuria and the Lake Baikal district, where there was considerable intermarriage between Russians, Chinese, and Mongolians, a process which had been going on since the arrival of the Russians in the Far East several centuries ago.

This vast area, stretching from the Pacific to the Urals, constituting one of the world's last frontiers, is a "melting pot" of races to such an extent that one hears a common statement in Russia that the complexion of the population shades off from white to yellow as one travels eastward from Moscow toward Siberia, and from white to brown as one travels southward toward the Caucusus, and that there is no perceptible dividing line between the colors. I was told by a well educated Russian woman in Harbin who had traveled extensively in Mongolia and eastern Siberia that there are eighteen more or less distinct racial groups or "tribes" within the present confines of the U.S.S.R., and that the non-white groups predominate in numbers over the white population. The existence of this situation had made it necessary for the Soviet Government to pay special attention to so-called "racial" issues and to enact legislation designed to prevent racial clashes. However, any suggestion that the Soviet Union has solved the racial issue is a statement of a hope, rather than an actuality. There are deep racial animosities in Russia, particularly in Asiatic Russia, which, for the present, are somnolent but require only a spark to ignite.

Siberia is a vast treasure house of natural resources, comparable to Canada, with the top tier of our northwestern States added for good measure. From the standpoint of agricultural and dairying potentialities, North Manchuria and parts of Mongolia greatly resemble northern Michigan, Minnesota, and the Dakotas. At the time of Japan's seizure of Manchuria, White Russian communities along the Siberian border were supplying butter and other dairy products to the large China coast cities of Dairen, Tientsin, Tsingtao, and Shanghai. For a distance of 3,000-odd miles from the Urals to the Pacific, the country is largely wooded. It is a common saying in Siberia that in the never-ending struggle between man and trees, the trees always seem to be winning. As one travels westward from Vladivostok, the forests are chiefly of birch, which the Russians have learned to carve into innumerable articles. The birch forests along the Ussuri shade off to limitless forests of virgin pine and spruce, resembling the forests of North America before they were devastated by the lumber and pulp mills. At intervals one sees little clearings, chiefly in the river valleys, with villages of log or sod houses, similar to our early West. Generally the country is as primitive as our early explorers and settlers found the upper Mississippi and its tributaries. In many places the forests have encroached so closely on the railway that the branches sweep the train windows.

In Khabarovsk I visited an agricultural fair which might have been held in one of our Middle Western county seats a quarter of a century ago. There were long rows of tables and booths displaying agricultural products and preserved fruits and vegetables. Most of the fruits were of the small or berry variety, including cranberries which grow in abundance in the Vladivostok area. I was intrigued by several species of small apples similar to the wild crab-apples of our Middle West, which we called "Siberian" crab-apples. It was noticeable that most of the exhibits belonged to members of the OGPU, to whom Stalin had entrusted the responsibility of looking after the food supply for the Far Eastern army.

I was impressed by the large numbers of soldiers in evidence at all points along the railway. At a tea and reception given by Commissar Krutoff, head of the Far Eastern Politburu, or Communist Party organization, I was cautioned against asking any questions about military affairs, particularly concerning the number and distribution of troops along the border. However, as usually happened at Russian parties, the flow of vodka quickly loosened tongues, and before long everybody was discussing the subject uppermost in our minds, Soviet measures of defense against the expected Japanese invasion of both Siberia and Outer Mongolia. The Russians feared an attack at two points: a combined land, air, and sea attack designed to cut off Vladivostok and the maritime province, and a major land-and-air attack on Outer Mongolia aimed at cutting off all Siberia east of Lake Baikal. For years the Japanese had conducted a propaganda campaign among the White or emigree Russians to the effect that Japan planned to "liberate" Siberia from communist influence and would "restore" Siberia to the White or Czarist Russians. The Cossack leader, Ataman Seminov, whose forces once fired on American troops in the vicinity of Chita during the American intervention in Siberia in World War I, had long been a resident of Dairen in South Manchuria within the Japanese zone, and was regarded as Japan's future puppet in Siberia. When asked about

Japanese intrigue among the emigree Russians in the Far East, Soviet officers always smiled and repeated their assertions that the Far Eastern Red Army, led by General Galen (or Bluecher), would be able to sweep the Japanese from Manchuria in short order.

A Soviet officer at Khabarovsk told me laughingly that an outbreak of war on the long Siberia-Manchukuo border would be preceded by a thousand dog-fights. When I asked him what he meant he said that the Soviet frontier defense guards had, for several years, trained police dogs for use in trailing Japanese spies. He said that when the Japanese learned of the Russian use of dogs, they immediately imported vast numbers of police dogs, with trainers, from Germany. Hence the expected dog-fights should hostilities break out.

Gregori Krutoff, the highest civil official in the Khabarovsk Government, made the following statement in reply to a question I put to him regarding the prospect of war between the U.S.S.R. and Japan: "War with Japan is inevitable so long as Manchuria is dominated by a crowd of Japanese military adventurers who think they must continue in possession of this territory to cover their past crimes."

Krutoff asserted that there were many sober-minded Japanese who favored the withdrawal of their military forces from Manchuria if it were possible, to "save the face" of the Kwantung army. But since this was impossible, owing to the methods the army had used in occupying the territory, the Soviets were going on the assumption that war was inevitable. The Russians were convinced that the Japanese army would be forced to stage another military adventure similar to that of 1931 in Manchuria if Japan experienced another serious economic crisis such as prevailed in Japan in 1929–31.

On the wall of Commissar Krutoff's office, which occupied an entire floor of the only modern building in Khabarovsk, was a large map of Manchuria upon which were indicated the many new railways and highways which the Japanese were driving through the sparsely populated areas of the country straight toward the Soviet border. Pointing to the map, Krutoff exclaimed: "These roads are not being built for peace. They are built for war."

But there was no indication of fear or of any desire to appease the Japanese. I was informed that the Russians had flatly rejected a recent Japanese proposal for a mutual withdrawal of armed forces for twenty-five miles. The Japanese proposal was clever, because such a withdrawal would have exposed the Soviet Trans-Siberian Railway to Nipponese attack, as much of the track along the Amur skirts the border.

Then there was the problem of the Chinese Eastern Railway, which the Czarist regime had built directly across North Manchuria to provide a short-cut to Vladivostok. The Russians were in daily fear that the Japanese would seize the railway and precipitate hostilities before Russia was ready. By means of clever propaganda they forced the Japanese, from consideration of "face," to agree to purchase the road. But even then the Russians did not breathe freely until the sale agreement was signed. The price finally agreed upon, approximately $50,000,000, was regarded as far below the real value of the 1,500-mile line, half of which legally belonged to China.

Although the Japanese occupation and the cutting of both ends of the line where it crossed the border into Soviet territory had destroyed the economic importance of the railway, there never had been any disposition on the part of the Soviets to surrender possession. The stagnation in the trade of Vladivostok caused by the Japanese occupation of Manchuria was evidenced in the long lines of empty rusting tank cars standing idle in the railway yards at Vladivostok. Ordinarily these cars would be in use transporting soya-bean oil, the chief Manchurian agricultural product, to market. The Chinese strongly protested against the sale of the Chinese Eastern Railway but were powerless to prevent it, as the Japanese were in occupation of Manchuria.

I was particularly interested in appraising Soviet policy toward Japan in this period of crisis in the Far East, which I felt instinctively would ultimately involve my own country. Even a superficial inspection of the vast area of Far Eastern Russia, which reaches around Japanese-controlled Manchukuo to the Sea of Japan, indicated the deep determination of the Soviets to fight for every inch of their territory. As one high official put it, "Our Far Eastern Red Army today matches the Japanese Manchukuan military machine, soldier for soldier, gunboat for gunboat, and plane for plane, along the entire Amur River frontier."

The feeling which prevailed among Soviet officials in Siberia that war was inevitable cooled perceptibly as I approached Moscow from the Far East. Relations between Moscow and Berlin were becoming more strained, and that situation naturally overshadowed the menace of Japan in Manchuria. While reiterating the oft-repeated statement that Russia "would not permit Japan to occupy a single inch of Siberian territory," the leaders of Moscow were undoubtedly speculating in their minds as to what they could do to keep the situation from getting out of hand in that quarter, while building up their "front" against Germany on the west. Thus we had the interesting triangular diplomatic spectacle of both Russia and Germany wooing imperial Japan for cooperation in the event of an outbreak of war in Europe, in which the U.S.S.R. and Germany, in all probability, would be on opposite sides.

Later I had cause to remember a chance remark of a Soviet official who, when I asked him the usual question about the relations of the Soviet Union and Japan in the Far East, replied rather impatiently: "Why doesn't America fight Japan? It's your job more than it is ours!"

And so indeed it turned out to be.

When I was in Khabarovsk I asked Comrade Krutoff if there were any Americans in the vast territory under his jurisdiction. He replied in the negative, and then as an afterthought he suddenly asked me if I knew where he could employ an American engineer. He said the Government would pay the engineer's travel expenses and a good salary. Thinking they had some special engineering project in mind, I asked about the character of the work they expected the American engineer to perform. Krutoff smiled and said, "Oh, the engineering part is not so important; we want an American to help us practice English conversation, but of course we will use his engineering knowledge too." The commissar then told me that practically every Soviet official in the Far East was studying the English language, but they could not find a single American in the Soviet Far East with whom to practice English conversation.

I was thinking of Krutoff's suggestion about employing an American engineer "who was also a good conversationalist" as I got into Krutoff's bright new Buick limousine to return to the Khabarovsk Hotel in order to pick up my baggage and then proceed to the railway station to catch the train for Moscow. Imagine my surprise when Krutoff's chauffeur, a middle-aged Russian, turned and said to me in good American English, "You're an American, aren't you?" I could not conceal my astonishment as I replied in the affirmative and asked him where he learned to speak the American language. He replied, "I lived in Honolulu for ten years after the revolution, then I returned home to Siberia." He then added, with a shrug of his shoulders, "But I never speak English here."

There was a time when Americans were deeply interested in large development plans in Siberia—in the period following our purchase of Alaska from Russia in 1867. Curiously, Alaska has occupied a significant place in the relations of Russia and the United States. When Secretary of State William H. Seward purchased Alaska from Russia in 1867, the agreed purchase price was $7,200,000 in gold, which figured out at about one penny an acre. But the actual purchase price was much less—only $1,400,-000—the balance, $5,800,000, was to reimburse Russia for the cost of a naval demonstration in New York Harbor during the United States Civil War, at a time when England favored the Confederacy and the Yankees needed a friend. The reason

Russia was willing to sell Alaska, and at such a bargain price, was the fear that Britain was planning to seize the territory.

I met several young Komsomols, or members of the Communist Youth Party, in the Russian Far East who knew far more about Alaska than I did, and all seemed to be under the impression that America had "tricked" the Czar into selling Alaska at too low a price. I wondered whether present-day Soviet school-books contained passages about Russia's "loss" of Alaska, but could not obtain any information on the subject.

The Russians in the period between 1860 and 1870 were anxious to obtain the assistance of Americans in the development of Siberia. The Grand Duke, a brother of the Czar, who was Governor-General of Siberia at the time of the sale of Alaska, made a contract with a group of Americans for the development of all railway and other transportation facilities, telegraphic communications, mining, forestry, and agricultural resources between the Pacific Ocean and the Ural Mountains. It probably was the greatest development concession granted by any government since the English King turned over India, Malaya and China to the East India Company. Nothing came of the American concession to develop Siberia, because the Czar feared it would result in a loss of prestige on the part of the throne. As a result Siberia remained dormant, a vast camp for political prisoners of czarist regimes, and more recently, the Soviet regime.

During this early period of American interest in Russian Siberia, an attempt was made to link the two countries by a combination land and submarine cable starting at Seattle and passing along the coast of Alaska, across the Aleutian Islands and Bering Sea to Kamchatka Peninsula, and thence across Siberia to Russia and Europe. The cable was to be operated by a private company, enjoying a government subsidy which would make it independent of the monopoly which controlled the Atlantic cables. The company interested in the project, after surveying the route along the Aleutian chain, landed a corps of surveyors on the coast of Kamchatka. The surveyors finally made their way entirely across Siberia to Europe, but nothing came of the project. The greatly needed trans-Pacific cable was not built until after the American occupation of the Philippines in 1898.

In 1920 the Soviet Government granted to the American oil promoter, Harry F. Sinclair, a concession to develop the valuable oil resources of northern Sakhalin Island, but Moscow was forced to cancel the contract and refund the bargain money because of Japanese pressure. The Soviet Government ultimately turned over the concession to the Japanese navy, which has since used the wells of Russian Sakhalin as a chief source of fuel for both navy and air force.

When I was in Siberia at the beginning of Soviet industrial development in the Lake Baikal region, I was told that Moscow's intention was to duplicate as far as possible the vast Japanese industrial development centered at Mukden in South Manchuria. I frequently speculated on what might have happened in Russian Asia had the great American development concession of the early 1870's gone through. There is sufficient pulpwood in Siberia to feed the world's presses for many generations.

XXI

Moscow in '35

I ARRIVED IN MOSCOW early in October, and was taken by my Intourist guide to the Novo Moscotia (New Moscow) Hotel, located at the approach to one of the bridges which span the Moscow River, only about a block from Red Square and the Kremlin. The excellent view of the Kremlin from the upper floors of the hotel was the chief feature offered its patrons in exchange for the high rates charged. I found that this hotel was the one in which the Communist Party put up its labor delegation guests from abroad. Many American engineers and technicians of various kinds employed in the Soviet Union also made the Novo Moscotia their headquarters while in the capital.

One unusual thing about the hotel, of which I became aware the next morning at breakfast, was that the dining room was divided by a temporary railing into two sections. People who dined at tables on one side of the railing, chiefly tourists or businessmen, were on a "valuta" basis, meaning that they paid for their service in foreign money, usually American money or its equivalent. For example, my breakfast came to practically one dollar in American money, and I paid the bill in American money. I gave the waiter a five-dollar bank note, and received in change a handful of miscellaneous small coins from practically every European country—except Russia.

On the other side of the railing the diners paid their bills in Soviet paper roubles which ranged in value at that time all the way from forty to eighty to the American dollar. The food served on both sides of the railing was exactly the same, so that the breakfast for which I paid a dollar in American money, if eaten on the other side of the railing, would only have cost from eight cents to twelve cents. The next time I visited the dining room I selected a table on the "paper rouble" side of the railing, but the waiter motioned me back to the "valuta" side as I, being a foreign traveler, was expected to pay my bill in American money. Later I learned of a new "American-style" restaurant where it was possible to pay the check in paper roubles, and as a result my bill for food went down miraculously.

A few days after I arrived in Moscow I found, in a second-hand bookstore, a small volume containing English translations of a number of Stalin's earlier speeches. The book was a lucky find, because a perusal of the addresses provided me with a valuable key to an understanding of what was happening in Russia. In the first place, I was impressed by the bitterness of Stalin's attacks on the Trotskyites. His hatred of his former political rival and of Trotsky's internationalist theories seemed to exceed his animosity toward the imperialists and capitalists. On several occasions Stalin expressed admiration for the efficient organization and management of American industrial establishments, repeating with enthusiasm the stories which Russian engineers had brought back from the United States.

However, the paragraphs in Stalin's published addresses which seemed to me of most significance in view of what was happening in Russia were his descriptions of conditions which prevailed in the Czarist army and military establishment which Stalin was trying to rectify. He told of instances where poorly trained and totally unarmed soldiers were driven into front-line trenches by officers who always carried whips (knouts) in their hands. The soldiers without arms were expected to pick up the rifles of their fallen comrades who were fortunate enough to possess them. Stalin said that much of the old Russian army's rifles and ammunition was purchased by the Government from dishonest contractors and was defective. He said that Russia in the past had to depend on foreign arms manufacturers for most of her military supplies; he attributed Russia's defeat in the war with Japan, and in World War I, in large measure, to these conditions and declared that never again would the Russian army serve as a "door mat" for foreign enemies to walk over in invading the country.

I was greatly impressed on my eleven-day trip across Russia by the great number of soldiers and officers, usually in new uniforms, who crowded the railway stations and trains and were seen in large numbers on the streets in every city and town I visited. I naturally was curious to know the size of the Russian army, and made frequent inquiries of Russian officials whom I met, as to the number of men under arms. I was always given the standard number, 600,000, which Russia supplied officially to the League of Nations when the League collected statistics on this subject from all countries. It seemed obvious to me that this number was a gross understatement, because the large numbers of men in new uniforms indicated that recruiting on a large scale had been going on for some time. Before I left Russia the truth was out. An official statement indicated that the army had been expanded to well over a million men. The expansion was apparent at the November Seventh Celebration in Red Square, where contingents from the various military branches, including light and giant tanks, were displayed. The same was true of the aviation corps.

A notable feature of the celebration in Red Square was an exhibition flight of the giant plane named Maxim Gorky, said to be the largest plane constructed up to that time. The plane was equipped with a radio and a giant amplifier for disseminating Government propaganda. The parade of military forces through Red Squre lasted from 10 o'clock in the morning to late afternoon. Stalin and members of the cabinet stood behind a stone balcony on the top of Lenin's tomb, only their heads and shoulders being visible from the diplomatic reviewing stand, which was only about fifty yards distant. I was told that the Russian infantry units which marched through Red Square that day were among the best drilled and equipped soldiers in Europe of the time. No one who observed the exhibition could leave without the impression that the Russian revolution had taken on a pronounced military complexion. The parade of civilian workers through Red Square that day was enlivened by numerous caricatures of Germans and Japanese. The various unions of workers, including women, also marched with a military precision that indicated widespread military training.

In addition to the military development which was obvious on all sides, the country seemed to be undergoing a rapid industrialization, and the personal comfort of the people was being sacrificed to the development of heavy industry. The only luxury article I was able to discover was a cheap brand of perfume which seemed to be on sale everywhere. Several amusing stories were told about the perfumery industry. Proponents of the communist system always argued that there could never be over-production under the Russian system, because the prices of surplus products would be automatically lowered by the Government, thus enabling the lower-income strata of the population to purchase the goods. Surplus stocks would be consumed in this manner without causing a depression in the industry. However, it didn't work out that way in the perfumery industry, because no one seemed to want the perfume, even though the price had been reduced to what seemed to me to be a fraction of its cost.

Another thing which impressed all tourists in Russia at that time was the selling methods used in the official stores. The addiction of the Russians to standing in queues was nowhere more in evidence than in the stores. On entering one always observed two long queues of customers, one headed toward the counters where goods were for sale, and another leading to the cash register. You first joined the queue leading to the merchandise counters, and after attracting the attention of the hardworking clerk, you indicated the article you wished and were told the price. If you decided to purchase the article, the clerk would lay it aside and hand you a small slip of paper with the price noted on it. You then took this slip of paper and joined the other line leading to the cash register. When you reached the cash register you handed the cashier the slip, with the amount of money noted thereon. The cashier then rang up your purchase and handed you a receipt. You then took this receipt and joined the first line again. After you reached the counter you presented the slip and received your package.

When I was preparing to leave Moscow, I visited one of the more modern food stores to purchase some supplies for the long railway trip. After going through the queue procedures, which required more than an hour, I found the clerk greatly embarrassed because the store was out of wrapping paper. I also was embarrassed, because the article I had purchased was a Russian sausage about four inches in diameter and about three feet long. I had estimated from its length that this sausage would be sufficient to supply me for the eleven-day return trip to Vladivostok. I now look back upon the incident as my most embarrassing experience in Moscow, as I had to carry that naked three-foot length of sausage in my hand all the way back to the hotel, a distance of more than a mile, through streets crowded with people, most of whom looked hungrily at the sausage, and suspiciously at the foreigner who carried it. The fact that the store was out of wrapping paper was no new experience to residents of Moscow, for the paper shortage in that country was almost unbelievable. People would ask for a small scrap of paper, whether newspaper or of the wrapping variety, for use in making cigarettes. They had a way of rolling the paper into a small funnel and then filling it with tobacco, which they smoked at a 45-degree angle in order to keep the tobacco from spilling out. The almost complete absence of practically all types of paper, in a country possessing the largest potential supplies of wood-pulp, led to many embarrassing situations.

The chief worry of newspapermen whom I met in the various towns, particularly in Siberia, was over their paper supplies. The organizations in charge of supplying paper to the various publishing plants were constantly falling down on the job, with the result that the papers either had to publish reduced editions, or had to skip an edition entirely. Since I had traveled for days through Siberian forests, the largest in the world, I naturally was surprised at the paper shortage. I was told by the editors that the Government did not regard the production of paper as an industry sufficiently important to have priority over other heavy industries.

Members of the correspondents corps in Moscow were astonished to learn that I had traveled to Moscow by way of Vladivostok and the Trans-Siberian Railway, as for several years none of them had been permitted to travel in the Ural area or Siberia. The cause for this seemed to me obvious. The Soviet authorities did not want either of their potential enemies, Japan or Germany, to know the details of the industrialization program which was being pushed in these regions. Also, the Soviet authorities were unwilling to have foreigners observe the forced-labor program which was being used in the industrialization process. Most foreigners in Moscow were familiar with the forced labor which had been used in the construction of the White Sea canal, but they had little conception of the extent to which it was being used in the development of Siberia.

I, along with other foreign visitors, was shown a number of modern industrial establishments, but very few foreign visitors observed another class of establishments with which we were once altogether too familiar in the United States. I refer to the sweat-shops where one observed, through dirty windows, crowded rooms with sweaty men, women, and children working over sewing machines or doing hand needle-work. I imagine that many of the uniforms for the new army, and much of the clothing sold to civilians came from these sweat-shops, despite the production of the new plants of which the authorities were so proud.

The famous Moscow subway was nearing completion; it turned out to be the Soviet's most baffling job, due to the soft, sandy nature of Moscow's soil. I was astonished one day to see a large crowd of workers emerging from one of the entrances, each carrying a shovel; all of the laborers were women. They wore overalls and caps, similar to the men's, and could be distinguished only by their voices. I was told by other correspondents that it had become so difficult to obtain men for work on the subway that the authorities appealed to the women of the country to complete the job, which they did with enthusiasm. I was also told that the chief object in rushing the construction of the subway was to provide air-raid shelters in the event of war.

I learned about the official censorship of news dispatches one night when I was invited to dinner at the home of one of the correspondents, Demaree Bess of the *Christian Science Monitor*. There were eight guests, all of them representing leading American and British papers. We had just been seated at the table when there was a telephone call for one of the guests, who was correspondent for a New York paper. After a few minutes the guest returned, tendered his apologies, and said that he had to go to the censor's office to talk about certain alterations in a cablegram which he had just filed. In a few minutes there was another telephone call, and another guest departed on a similar errand. Within an hour almost everyone had departed for the censor's office to discuss some statement or other in messages filed before dinner. This was repeated almost every day. Occasionally the correspondents were able to beat the game by sending copies of their messages by air mail and also by ordinary mail, hoping that one of the three would get through. Another way of getting messages out was to hand them to travelers leaving on the night train for Warsaw and Berlin, with instructions to file the message after crossing the border. But the Government was sure to retaliate against the correspondent who used such methods to elude censorship. A favorite device was to refuse the correspondent a visa to return, should he leave the country for any reason.

I met Karl Radek, editor of *Pravda*, at a dinner party given by some members of the official Tass News Agency, whom I had met in the Far East. Radek had previously been a follower of Trotsky, but managed to get on the Stalin band-wagon after the Trotsky purge. He was a brilliant journalist, and his editorials were frequently quoted in the Tass Agency reports. The chief topic of conversation at the dinner I attended was a book written by William Henry Chamberlin, former Moscow correspondent of the *Christian Science Monitor*. Chamberlin's book was strongly critical of the Soviet regime, particularly Stalin's "collectivist" agricultural program in the Ukraine, where tens of thousands of small land owners had been dispossessed when Stalin put through his communist agricultural program. It was this program which produced most of the forced labor which the Soviet authorities were using in their railway construction and industrialization program in the Far East. Radek could not understand why Chamberlin had written such a book "after being so well treated by the authorities during his ten-year residence in the Soviet Union." Radek also referred to other correspondents who had lived in Russia and had been "well treated," but had later written "unfriendly" things about the Soviet Union. He referred particularly to a New York columnist who had once been associated with Trotsky in the early days of the Soviet revolution, but after returning to the United States had written unfavorable things about the Soviets. Radek himself was a victim of the next purge.

The political situation in Moscow at the time was tense. Fascism in Italy and Germany was riding high, and Moscow was also worried over the possibility of war with Japan. The U.S.S.R., one of the most primitive countries in the world, with a population estimated at 160,000,000, consisting of well over a hundred nationalities speaking 180 different dialects, was being welded into a modern state capable of defending itself under arms against the world's most powerful nations. In its early days the Soviet regime had withstood interventionist movements participated in by Britain, France, and America on the European front, and Japan and America in Siberia. While the foreign interventionists and the White Russian reactionaries had been defeated, suspicion engendered during these conflicts still remained. Russia suspected everybody, and foreigners were constantly watched, as were Russians who associated with foreigners. The Japanese were under the closest surveillance.

Unlike Japan, which had started its industrialization program by tackling light industry first, Russia began with the heavy industries and was building tractor plants, and machine plants, was developing iron, coal, and copper mines and building blast furnaces at the expense of all but the most essential consumption goods. Serious mistakes were being made, partly due to the fact that the Russians were sorely lacking in workers possessing mechanical skills.

I heard frequent complaints on the part of the directors of various state-owned industries of their apparent inability to make consumption equal production. One obvious reason for this was the low economic status of the people, but there were other reasons. I took along with me a number of American magazines, including several popular publications for women. There was a tremendous interest in these papers, even among those who could not read English, and most of the interest was centered in the advertisements. I was constantly questioned about the products advertised, particularly articles of clothing, personal adornment or service. I soon reached the conclusion that the Russians are an advertisement-starved people and that the lack of advertising had much to do with the complaint that consumption did not keep up with production. The official abhorrence of advertising as part of the hated capitalist system undoubtedly had an adverse effect on the distribution of the limited amount of consumption goods which were produced, but apparently could not be sold.

Interest in the advertisements in my magazines on the part of people I met on the trains and in the hotels was eclipsed only by interest in some phonograph records I had purchased in Shanghai for a friend in Moscow, and of all the records, the ones that most delighted the Russians were two Hawaiian hula pieces. They nearly wore them out on a squeaky portable phonograph someone had on the train.

I heard an amusing story concerning Soviet prohibition of commercial advertising. The Soviet Government decided to establish a canned-goods industry. Machinery was purchased, a factory was set up, and an American woman, an authority on canning, was brought to Russia as an instructor and technical expert in the organizing of the plant. The finished product, consisting of tinned tomatoes, string-beans, fruits, and other products, was shipped to the retail stores; but there the product stayed on the shelves, because the Russian public was not familiar with this method of preserving food. An American resident who had heard of the predicament wrote a letter to one of the Moscow papers suggesting that the products be advertised in the customary American fashion. The letter aroused a storm of indignation with a flood of correspondence in all the newspapers reprimanding the bumptious American and condemning all advertising as the work of the devilish capitalistic system. The surprising outcome was that the correspondence appearing in all the newspapers constituted the best possible advertising, and as a result of the interest aroused, the canned-goods stocks began to move fast.

Aside from the large number of military men on the trains, it seemed to me that the remainder of the space in the passenger coaches was taken up by civilians, young and middle-aged men carrying brief cases. These earnest individuals were connected with the hundred and one government enterprises, factories, engineering projects, railway construction, etc., scattered over the country. In Moscow one saw these men in the hotels, on the streets, sitting or standing in long rows in the reception rooms in government offices, waiting for appointments with government officials.

The concentration of supreme authority in practically every field of human endeavor in the hands of a few officials in Moscow had created an almost unbelievable congestion in the Soviet capital. It was said that Moscow was the most crowded city on the continent, and I was willing to wager that at least half the population was composed of earnest young men carrying brief cases and waiting for appointments with the heads of government bureaus.

This congestion was observable particularly in the old-fashioned apartment buildings with which Moscow abounds. The Government carefully regulated the size and rents of apartments, but it could not regulate the number of friends and relatives who moved in on the household. The wife of a Soviet official told me that the only intimacy she enjoyed with her husband was when they went to the theater. She said they had a dozen friends and relatives living with them in their two-room apartment.

Moscow is a notable city of theaters, opera, and the ballet, most of which I visited while in the Soviet capital. The importance of the theater in the lives of the people was also evident in other cities and even in the smaller towns of Siberia and North Manchuria. In many of the latter the theaters also served as community centers or clubs. When I was in Moscow the leading state theaters were presenting plays depicting incidents from the lives of past great rulers, Peter the Great and Ivan the Terrible. My knowledge of the Russian language was insufficient to enable me to understand all the fine points of the dramas, but I did comprehend the fact that the plays emphasized and glorified the importance of the "strong man" in the affairs of state.

One day as I was walking from Red Square to the Novo Moscotia Hotel, I heard voices and saw a dim light through a door leading to a semi-basement room in an old stone building. I stopped and was surprised to hear a religious chant, the chant of the old Russian Orthodox Church, which I had heard at special New Year and Easter services at the various White Russian churches in Shanghai. I entered the little room and found a regular service in progress with about a dozen elderly persons present. The walls were covered with ikons. This church, little and poor but a church for all that, was located just one block from the walls of the Kremlin. Unfortunately the language difficulty prevented me from obtaining from the venerable priest the history of this service conducted within the shadow of the Kremlin in "godless" Moscow. It was the only religious service I observed in the country during my trip.

I learned a great deal from my official guide, whom I nicknamed "Siberian Anna," about the status of women and young people in the U.S.S.R. Anna was twenty-two years old and a member of the Young Komsomols. Despite her youth she had worked three seasons on a floating salmon cannery off the Kamchatka coast and had also helped construct the new town of Komsomolsk on the Amur. Soviet publications contained much about the new freedom enjoyed by women in the Soviet Union, and I was shown the "abortion clinic" in Moscow, where it was claimed any woman could go if she did not wish to give birth to her baby. I also met young women, particularly in Siberia, who had babies but were quite indefinite about the whereabouts of the husband and father.

In Vladivostok I was shown the official bureau where divorces were granted to either party for the asking, the only charge being the cost of a postage stamp to notify the other party. The official in charge, after showing me the records, offered to grant me a divorce if I desired one. He said the charge would be about twenty cents, due to the higher cost of foreign postage, and emphasized the point that the services of attorneys were unnecessary.

Threatening war clouds in both east and west shortly put an end to cheap and easy divorces. Stalin closed the Moscow abortion clinic before I departed from the country. The threat of war and the reality of war have caused the Soviet leaders to take steps safeguarding the stability of the family and home. The parentless children who were still roaming the streets and countryside even in the towns of Siberia and North Manchuria were rounded up and placed in trade schools. The latest step was an order abolishing co-education and providing for separate schools for the sexes throughout the country. Specialized education for girl students, designed to encourage home-making, was also decreed. Complete "freedom" for women had not worked out in actual practice.

XXII

Home, Via Japan

SINCE THE JAPANESE had refused to permit me to travel through Manchukuo on my way from the Far East to Moscow, I knew it would be futile for me to apply for a visa for the return trip through that province. I was apprehensive that the Japanese would not even give me permission to return by way of Japan. I knew that when one's name gets on the Japanese military blacklist, regardless of the reason, it never comes off the list. I wondered whether the animosity of the Japanese military authorities over the articles I had written about their Manchurian invasion was shared by the civilian government in Tokyo. I decided to find out, and called at the Japanese Embassy in Moscow.

The streets for a half block on each side of the Embassy appeared completely deserted, but as I approached the building I noticed two or three Russian OGPU guards standing in the alleyways and glancing at me curiously. I rang the bell at the front door several times without receiving an answer, so went around to the side door, which was finally opened by a Japanese servant, who took me upstairs. There I was happy to recognize a legation secretary whom I had previously known in Mukden, Manchuria. His name was Maori. He had gone to school in the United States and had been friendly and helpful to me despite the animosity of the military authorities. I questioned Maori regarding the possibility of getting a visa to return to Shanghai by way of Japan. Without hesitation he made the proper entry on my passport, and in addition gave me a personal note to the Japanese Foreign Minister who, he assured me, would be interested in talking to me about my trip across Russia, and particularly about the situation in the Soviet Far East, which the Japanese were watching closely.

My return trip to Vladivostok was uneventful, but a namesake of mine, Bonney Powell, had to suffer in my stead. He and I had previously worked together on several assignments, including the Manchurian invasion, and had frequently experienced complications with mail and telegrams due to the similarity of our names. He had without difficulty obtained a visa from the Japanese embassy in Berlin to return to Shanghai by way of Manchukuo, as the Japanese authorities had no black marks against him. We therefore traveled across Russia and Siberia at the same time but on different trains, and without either being aware of the other's presence, he returning by way of Manchukuo and I by way of Japan.

When Bonney reached the border town of Manchouli on the Siberian-Manchurian border, the Japanese and Manchukuo border guards immediately pounced on him and escorted him with his baggage, including his newsreel camera and several reels of pictures, to a private upstairs room in the railway station on the Chinese side of the border. Bonney was held there for nearly forty-eight hours while the Japanese examined every scrap of paper and every inch of the several newsreels that he carried. He had no idea why he was being detained, or why he was subjected to this indignity, until one of the Japanese gendarmes produced a memorandum he had received from Tokyo which referred to an article in the *China Weekly Review* dealing with the Manchukuo situation. Bonney then realized what had happened; the Japanese secret-service men apparently had been tipped off by the Japanese embassy in Moscow that I was traveling to the Far East, and they had mistaken Bonney for me. After he had convinced the Japanese that they had the wrong man, they were profusely apologetic and immediately returned all of his papers and film, although much of the latter had been ruined in the process of examination.

While I was in Vladivostok awaiting the boat for Japan, I

went to the Japanese consulate, but could raise no one, despite repeated knocks at all the doors. The window shutters were closed and the building appeared to be deserted, although I saw smoke coming from the chimney. I later learned that the Russian Embassy in Tokyo was being picketed by the Japanese and that the Soviet Ambassador and other members of the Embassy were unable to show themselves in the streets or at hotels without being followed or spied upon. The Russians in Vladivostok and elsewhere had been paying the Japanese back in their own coin, the only kind of treatment which they understood.

The little boat upon which I traveled from Vladivostok to Japan stopped at Rashin, one of the new ports which the Japanese were developing on the upper east coast of Korea. I decided that it was not safe for me to go ashore in Korea, but the captain of the ship assured me it could be managed. In fact, he urged me to do so in order to see the construction work which was going on there, and gave me a note to the customs officer of the port. I was met at the jetty by a Japanese newspaperman, correspondent for a Tokyo paper, who I suspected was also a member of the gendarmerie. He was quite accommodating and took me all over the new port, while at the same time asking me all sorts of questions about what I had seen in Russia.

In the little port everything was new, including the jetties, upon which new railway tracks had been built to enable freight cars to be loaded directly from army transports. Japanese engineers and contractors, utilizing the labor of thousands of Chinese and Korean coolies, were blasting off the face of the precipitous Korean mountains, in order to provide space for the docking of ships and for railway tracks. My Japanese newspaperman guide assured me that the port of Rashin, together with two neighboring ports, Seishin and Yuki, were being rapidly developed in order to enable the Japanese army to transport troops by rail and sea from the Tokyo district to Central and North Manchuria within sixty hours. When he said this he nodded significantly toward Vladivostok, and it was obvious that what the Japanese had in mind was the encirclement of Vladivostok from the land as well as the sea.

Immediately following the Japanese invasion of Manchuria in the fall of 1931, the Japanese army put a large force of laborers to work on a short stretch of track connecting the Chinese railway system in Manchuria with the Japanese railway which skirts the upper east coast of Korea.

I spent several hours investigating Rashin, which had the appearance of a boom town with hastily built shacklike stores and houses lining each side of the new streets. Finally I asked my volunteer guide to take me to some Korean houses and stores where Korean goods were sold. He shrugged his shoulders and said, "Koreans dirty people—live back in valley." I persuaded him, however, to take me to the Korean section, which I found most interesting, particularly the native markets, where I was able to purchase several articles of Korean embroidery and native jewelry.

Our ship finally landed at the little Japanese port of Takaoka on the west coast of Honshu Island of Japan, where the customs inspector accepted my passport visa without question. However, he devoted considerable time to an inspection of several books I had purchased in Moscow. I doubted whether his limited English enabled him to understand the contents of any of the books, and was confirmed in this belief when he selected a book and inquired, "What kind of book, this? Ancient, present or future history?" I glanced at the title (it was Victor A. Yakhontoff's "Russia and the Soviet Union in the Far East") and replied, "Mostly ancient, very old." This seemed to satisfy him and he stamped all my books and permitted me to go to the train. However, he confiscated my last remaining tin of tobacco, which I had obtained from a friend at the American Embassy in Moscow.

I found civilian authorities in Tokyo friendly and anxious to talk to me about conditions in Russia, but I had no luck whatever with the military, the spokesmen being cold and uncom-

XXIII

The Philippines in '36

THERE WERE DEVELOPMENTS in 1936 which caused international attention, previously centered on China and Japan, to be shifted to the Philippines.

I went to Manila in November of that year, planning to cover two important events. One was the inauguration of General Douglas MacArthur's program for the defense of the Philippines. The other was the meeting of the thirty-third International Eucharist Congress, a most important gathering of representatives of the Catholic Church from all parts of the world. It was the first time the Congress had ever met in the Philippines, the only Catholic country in the Far East. The Congress attracted a half million Catholics from Far Eastern countries, chiefly from China and the Philippines, and was concerned primarily with the position of the Church in the face of the gathering clouds of war in the Far East.

The prospect of early independence lent importance to the position of the new Philippine Commonwealth in Far Eastern politics. Within recent months Manila had been visited by the commander of the British fleet in the Far East, who had fired the first official salute on behalf of a foreign Power in honor of the new President. Other visitors included the British commander-in-chief at Singapore and the Governor-General of the Netherlands Indies. On the President boat on which I traveled to Manila were several children who were refugees from the civil war in Spain. I was told they had been adopted by a wealthy Spanish resident of Manila who was one of the chief financial supporters of General Franco, the Spanish dictator.

It struck me as an anomalous situation that the United States Government was embargoing shipments of arms and munitions to the Spanish republican government while wealthy Spanish residents of the Philippines, an American possession, were remitting large sums to Franco which he was using to purchase military supplies from Hitler and Mussolini. It also struck me as significant that Spanish merchants who never were able to prosper when the Philippines were under the Spanish Crown had become highly successful after the United States took possession of the islands. According to the latest census, there were some 2,000 Spanish residents of Manila, with several hundred more residing in the provinces. Several were rated among the wealthiest residents of the islands. After Congress passed the Independence Act a considerable number took out Philippine citizenship. In addition to those of strictly Spanish blood there was also a large and influential population of Spanish mestizos, that is, persons of mixed Spanish and native blood. Since the Philippines had been a Spanish possession, repercussions from the civil war in Spain were felt in the islands, where many of the issues involved in the Spanish conflict were also present.

In an address delivered in the Manila Stadium before an audience of 10,000 students on the eve of the Eucharistic Congress, His Grace, the Most Reverend Michael J. O'Doherty, Archbishop of Manila, referred to the agrarian problem as the chief cause of unrest among the masses of the 15,000,000 Filipinos. He stressed particularly the problem of the large landed estates owned chiefly by the Dominican, Augustinian, and Recollecto corporations. This problem extended back into the Spanish regime, which had lasted for nearly four centuries from the discovery of the islands by Magellan, 1519–1522. It was said that Magellan converted the first Filipino, a chieftain of the island of Cebu, to the Catholic faith. According to the Philippine *Handbook*, more than ninety per cent of the population are members of the Church, which was described as "the most potent organization which had materially and spiritually shaped and built the Filipino nation for 375 years."

Spanish cultural influence in the Philippines as spread

through the Catholic schools and churches had decreased noticeably in recent years, due to the influx of large numbers of American priests and nuns, who are specially trained for service in this field.

William H. Taft, the first Civil Governor, sent out to the Philippines by President William McKinley, made the initial attempt to solve the friar-land problem by purchasing large tracts and then selling small holdings to the native tenants on easy payments extending over a period of twenty-five years. But this had not solved the problem, as it was reported that the large Church corporations still owned 400,000 acres of the best rice, tobacco and copra lands, plus large realty holdings in the city of Manila.

President Manuel Quezon told me of his plan to use a balance of $30,000,000 belonging to the Philippines, which was held in the United States Treasury, to continue the land-purchase plan inaugurated by Taft a third of a century previously.

That the matter was urgent was indicated by a summary I made of news reports of uprisings of peasant tenants which had appeared in the three leading newspapers, the *Bulletin*, *Tribune*, and *Herald*. I found reports of twenty-five such clashes between tenants and the police, some involving bloodshed, within a period of approximately one month. I was also told that some 60,000 tenants on lands of the three big Church orders were in open rebellion. I was informed that there was little or no trouble where the lands were administered by the Church societies directly, but the most serious complications had developed where Church lands had been turned over to third parties, chiefly American and British real estate corporations, to exploit.

Of greatest seriousness was the organization of a radical party known as the Sakdalistas, composed largely of tenant farmers and laborers. The name of the party, "Sakdal," in the leading native dialect, the Tagalog, meant "we protest." It was alleged that the Sakdals were behind most of the recent uprisings, and it was significant also that the communist slogan, "United Front Against Fascism," was beginning to be heard in Philippine politics. The situation reached a crisis when the

Sakdals organized widespread rioting on the occasion of the inauguration of Manuel Quezon as President of the Commonwealth. An investigation was immediately launched, but Benigno Ramos, leader of the Sakdals, did not wait for the investigation to get under way; he fled to Japan, where he resided for several years and continued his propaganda against the Administration of President Quezon, and the Americans in the Philippines. Some old-time residents remembered back to the days of the insurrection of Aguinaldo against the American forces, when it was discovered that the rebels of that day were also receiving their supplies from Japan, the middle-men being renegade Americans who operated out of Shanghai.

Bishop Paul Yu Pin, Vicar Apostolic of Nanking, the leading Catholic delegate from China at the Eucharistic Congress in Manila, was appointed head of the organization of Chinese Catholic Youths and Catholic Action in China. Upon the recommendation of Archbishop O'Doherty, so-called Vigilante Committees of Catholic Action were set up in every Catholic parish for the purpose of studying social and economic problems. As to the strength and influence of the Church in China, it was reported that the present membership of 3,000,000 was increasing at the rate of 100,000 a year.

In view of the growing social unrest, it appeared that the decision to develop a strong military force in the Philippines was motivated as much by the desire to control social conditions as it was to meet the urgent demands of national defense.

A small army of carpenters was working night and day putting up temporary barracks. General MacArthur explained his program, which called for the training of 40,000 native troops a year, extending over a ten-year period, providing an army of between 400,000 and 500,000 men by 1946, the year when independence for the islands would come into effect. The men were to receive five and a half months' training the first year, with briefer periods each year thereafter.

The original Filipino trainees under the MacArthur-Quezon program later became the guerrillas and the Philippine underground, many of them led by American officers, who gave the Japanese so much trouble after their invasion of the islands. They also greatly facilitated General MacArthur's re-conquest of the archipelago.

The islands had been divided into ten defense districts, each with its mobilization center where equipment for the troops was stored. It was expected that by the end of the period the Commonwealth would have a well rounded force of thirty infantry divisions. A beginning also had been made in the training of an aviation corps, and there was talk of developing a fleet of speedy torpedo boats. Considerable difficulty was experienced in obtaining supplies, even out-moded equipment from the United States. Apparently few persons in the United States realized the necessity of defending the Philippines, and there was much disparagement of MacArthur's program. One powerful home newspaper syndicate advocated cutting the islands adrift or even giving them to Japan, as though that would end our responsibilities in the Pacific.

At that time the only armed forces entrusted with the defense of the new Philippine Commonwealth, consisting of some 1,400 far-scattered islands, was a small unit, less than a full division, of the United States Army. About half of this force consisted of the celebrated native Philippine Scouts.

I found General MacArthur and members of his staff, as well as President Manuel Quezon, seriously concerned with happenings on the Japan-Russia and China-Japan fronts. Since I had often visited Manchuria and had recently been in Siberia and Japan, I delivered a half dozen addresses before various groups at Manila dealing with my experiences in these countries.

In various talks I had with leading Americans and Filipinos, I gained a fairly complete idea of the outstanding problems of the new commonwealth, from the standpoint of defense against a powerful enemy such as Japan, and I was informed of the main features of General MacArthur's plan for the defense of the islands. It was based on the fortification of the Inland Sea, the connected bodies of water lying between the two main islands of Luzon on the north and Mindanao on the south. This important body of water, somewhat comparable to the famous Inland Sea of Japan, is bounded on the west and southwest by the important islands of Mindoro, Panay, Negros, Cebu, and Bohol, and on the east by Masbate, Samar, and Leyte. With the six entrances to this inland sea fortified with batteries of long-range defense guns, an enemy, even a powerful one, would find the Philippine fortress a hard nut to crack, particularly if the land batteries were supported by an adequate air force with sufficient bases and a fleet of speedy torpedo boats with enough auxiliary craft to carry military equipment and food supplies to the garrisons on southern Luzon. The rich islands to the south of Luzon, including the large island of Mindanao, constitute the bread-basket of the archipelago. If the inland sea route to these islands could be kept open, large forces operating on southern Luzon could be supplied almost indefinitely.

Practically everyone agreed on the wisdom of this phase of Philippine defense, but I did not find such unanimity on the question of defending Manila, the capital, located on Manila Bay in southern Luzon, the most northern island of the Philippine group. The island of Luzon, only a few miles south of Formosa, is vulnerable to attack from practically all sides, in this day of the long range bomber.

Since earliest times Manila had depended for defense upon the rocky fortress of Corregidor, located on an island at the entrance to Manila Bay. Before the era of the bomber, Corregidor was impregnable, but in the 1930's, with its exposed roads, communication lines, and power plant it was practically undefendable. However, west of the city, between Manila Bay and the China Sea, there was a rocky peninsula which our army engineers believed could be defended for a considerable period. This peninsula, covered with tropical vegetation, was known as Bataan, and was destined, a very few years later, to become a household word in America.

There was one question about the Philippines to which I

never was able to obtain a satisfactory answer. This concerned the fundamental problem of population. Why are the Philippines, probably the richest territory in the Far East from the standpoint of natural resources, the most sparsely populated Oriental country? With a total land area approximately the same as that of Japan and an arable land area probably twice that of Japan, the Philippines have a population of only about one fifth that of the Japanese islands.

To the visitor from such densely populated countries as China and Japan, Malaya, and the Netherlands Indies, the sparseness of the population is the most noticeable feature of the Philippine Islands. I asked many educated Filipinos for an explanation, and the reasons which they gave ranged from the high infant mortality rate to the effects of the peonage system which had prevailed on the big landed estates. In pursuing my inquiry I had one amusing experience. I asked the Filipino superintendent of schools in one of the districts of southern Luzon for an explanation. Instead of replying he called his wife and asked her how many children they had. She replied, "Fourteen now, next month fifteen." The superintendent told me that there was no race suicide among the upper strata of the population, where large families are the rule, and he felt that the proposed agrarian reform, which would provide the peasant farmers with their own land holdings, would result in a rapid increase in population.

It had often been suggested that a quick way to rectify the dearth of population would be to lower the immigration restrictions against the Chinese. There is already a large Chinese population in the islands, but they are chiefly of the merchant and professional classes. On occasion there has been strong opposition to Chinese businessmen due to their monopolistic control in retail trade and the rice industry. On several occasions attempts have been made to levy discriminatory taxes on Chinese businessmen. Once during the Spanish regime there were serious anti-Chinese riots in Manila, resulting in the death of many Chinese, but in recent years the relations of the Chinese and the

Filipinos have been friendly and there has been considerable intermarriage between Chinese men and Filipino women. The number of Chinese mestizos greatly outnumbered those of Spanish nationality. It is said that many of the more prosperous gold mines in the Islands were opened by Chinese, some of them dating back to the twelfth century, as evidenced by specimens of Chinese pottery and implements found in the mines.

Accompanied by an American familiar with the school system, I visited a number of schools on Luzon Island. The progress which had been made in popular education since the landing of the original shipload of some six hundred American school teachers soon after the occupation in 1898 was evidenced in the well filled schoolhouses, which usually occupied the most prominent buildings in the towns and villages.

The original American teachers had long since passed from the scene, and their places had been taken by Filipinos, themselves a product of the early schools established by the Americans. The terms of the Independence Act passed by Congress required all instruction to be conducted in the English language. I had to admit, however, after visiting several of the schools, that I was unable to understand much of the English which was taught by the native teachers. I did notice, however, that many of the children were reading the American comics in the Manila papers during the recess period.

It was while visiting the schools that I came to realize the complications which the language problem presented. During the long Spanish regime all educated Filipinos learned the Spanish language, which is still taught in some of the Church schools. After the American occupation, English became the official and commercial language. The rapid growth of nationalism in recent years caused the Filipino leaders to advocate the use of Tagalog, chief native dialect on the island of Luzon, as the official and general language. I was told by an official of the Department of Education that there were more than sixty dialects spoken by the natives of the various islands, and that many groups were opposed to the Tagalog dialect, which was spoken chiefly in the Manila district.

The public school system and the use of American textbooks were undoubtedly largely responsible for the development of the democratic system which prevails throughout the nation. It was also undoubtedly our policy of initiating local self-government at the very beginning, with a view to ultimate independence, that caused the Filipinos, alone among colonial peoples, to side with us in the struggle with Japan following Pearl Harbor. However, the influence of the Church, in this same connection, should not be overlooked.

I was invited to deliver an address before one of the classes at the University of the Philippines, and was astonished at the students' knowledge of American history, particularly information concerning outstanding events of national significance, and information pertaining to the lives of outstanding characters in America history. It occurred to me that the present generation of home American high school, college and university students, as well as their teachers, could benefit from the American educational program originally introduced in the Philippines.

XXIV

The Sian Incident

CHINA HAD EXPERIENCED many crises since the overthrow of
the Manchu Dynasty in 1911, but none which had more repercussions, domestic and international, than the Sian Incident of
December 12, 1936. I was still in the Philippines, but, realizing
the seriousness of the crisis, hurried back to China. Excitement
was running high both at Shanghai and at the national capital
at Nanking when I arrived there a few days before Christmas.

The kidnaping of Chiang Kai-shek, commander-in-chief of
the Nationalist armies and head of the National Government,
practically paralyzed the Nanking Administration and provided
an opportunity for political dissension and intrigue, which had
been held in check only by the firm hand of the Generalissimo.

The confusion in the Government was aggravated by the
critical political situation prevailing throughout the Far East.
The countries most deeply concerned, aside from China, were
Japan and the Soviet Union. Germany and Italy were also involved, as they were signatories, with Japan, of the so-called
Anti-Comintern Pact which preceded the later Japanese-German-Italian military alliance. The Anti-Comintern Pact, directed
at the activities of Soviet Russia and the Third International,
had been signed in Berlin on November 25, 1936, less than a
month previously, hence played its part in precipitating the Sian
Incident as the three Powers, Japan, Germany and Italy, had
been exerting strong pressure on China to become a member of
the anti-communist accord.

The relations between Japan and China, and between Japan
and Russia, were already at the breaking point, due to Japan's

occupation of Manchuria and the extension of Japan's military activities westward into Inner Mongolia, which bordered on Soviet-controlled Outer Mongolia.

The terms "Inner" and "Outer" as applied to the northern and southern sections of Mongolia did not come into general use on Chinese maps until after Soviet Russia's occupation of the northern or undeveloped section of the territory, shortly after the Soviet Revolution in 1917. Inner, or Southern Mongolia, had already been cut up into the frontier Chinese provinces of Chahar, Suiyuan, and Ningsia, and were settled largely by Chinese farmers. Outer, or Northern Mongolia, which was still populated by nomadic Mongolian tribes, had been organized by the Soviet Russians into the "Mongolian People's Republic" and incorporated into the Soviet Union.

The Russians, long apprehensive, were becoming increasingly restless because the Japanese in their advance westward would shortly be in a position to cut the overland routes through Suiyuan and Sinkiang which connected China and the Soviet Union.

The Soviet Union had already begun to take steps to counteract Japan's invasion of Inner Mongolia by sending troops into Sinkiang or Chinese Turkestan. The Soviet troops were dispatched from the Outer Mongolian province of Altai, which the Russians had occupied in 1918 and renamed Tannu Tuva. The troops were originally stationed in eastern Sinkiang directly on the overland trail and motor road leading from Lanchow, Kansu Province, to Urumchi (Tihwa), capital of Sinkiang, and thence to the Russian border.

The United States also had increasing cause for uneasiness regarding the situation in the Far East, because of the expiration of the Naval Limitation Treaty with Japan and Great Britain, negotiated at the Washington Arms Conference in 1922. Japan had finally denounced the treaty and asserted her right to construct a navy "adequate to her needs." Our naval experts were aware that the naval treaty had long been a dead letter, as the Japanese had secretly exceeded their building quotas in certain types of fighting craft and had completed strategic bases and fortifications in the Pacific Islands which they had agreed not to fortify.

As for the British, they were involved in an unexpected domestic crisis which overshadowed even their vast interests in the Far East. Edward VIII had just relinquished his throne and had been succeeded by George VI. Reports of ominous developments in the Far Eastern situation were overshadowed by a story on the front page of the *North China Daily News,* leading British paper in Shanghai, which carried the headline, "British People Stunned with Disappointment; Deep Resentment that Country Had Been Sacrificed for a Woman." Obviously the British were in no frame of mind to worry about developments in the Far East, when their King-Emperor had relinquished his throne in order to marry an American woman.

Shanghai was seething with rumors concerning the welfare of Generalissimo Chiang Kai-shek. The now Chinese-controlled *China Press,* in an attempt to make the best of a bad situation, expressed the hope that the mutiny of General Chang Hsueh-liang and the Communists at Sian would result in further consolidating national unity. The same sentiment was expressed by Dr. H. H. Kung, Minister of Finance, who temporarily succeeded Chiang Kai-shek as director of political affairs of the government. He declared in an interview that "those who unfurled the anti-Japanese banner as a pretext for shielding their own questionable political behavior would shortly realize the seriousness of the crisis which they had precipitated."

The Shanghai papers also published a brief dispatch from Tokyo which stressed the critical relations between Japan and the Soviet Union. The dispatch referred to the arrest of two Japanese editors, Katsuhei Zama and Hirokichi Otake, on a charge of turning over confidential documents concerning the situation in Inner Mongolia to a Russian named Boris Rodov, who was an attaché of the Soviet Embassy. The documents allegedly dealt with the activities of a certain Mongolian Prince

Teh, who recently had gone over to the Japanese and had been appointed chairman of the new puppet Government which the Japanese army had set up in Inner Mongolia. Prince Teh, it appeared, also had connections in the Russian sphere in Outer Mongolia.

The secret pact which Japan and Germany were pressing China to sign provided for the employment of special Japanese advisers to the Chinese Government to watch over communistic activities and to exercise control over "unlawful" activities of Koreans in China. It also specified the suppression of all anti-Japanese activities in China and the appointment of a joint Sino-Japanese commission to revise all Chinese schoolbooks. In addition to these demands, which were presented to the Chinese Foreign Minister, Chang Chun, by the Japanese Ambassador, S. Kawagoe, the Japanese were also pressing Generalissimo Chiang Kai-shek to agree to what amounted to Japanese suzerainty over the political and military affairs of North China. A tentative understanding on this subject, known as the "Tangku Truce," which had been agreed upon by the Minister of War, General Ho Ying-chin, and Japanese General Umetzu, on May 31, 1933, had provoked violent anti-government demonstrations by the students in Peiping. Generalissimo Chiang Kai-shek had continuously sidestepped the Japanese demands, while working strenuously to strengthen China's military position for the showdown which he realized was inevitable. His trip to the northwest for a conference with General Chang Hsueh-liang and other officials in that area was made in an effort to consolidate the situation there in the face of the coming clash with the Japanese.

It was the Generalissimo's second trip to Sian in recent months in connection with the critical situation in the northwest, arising from the conflicting interests and ambitions of Japan and the Soviet Union in Mongolia and the rebellious attitude and political intrigue of the Chinese Communists, who were gradually extending their influence in the northwest, chiefly in northern Shensi and Suiyuan.

The Chinese communists had increased their army from

about 25,000 in 1928 to approximately 100,000. Opposed to the communists were General Chang Hsueh-liang's army composed of some 130,000 former Manchurian troops and some 40,000 Shensi provincial troops under General Yang Hu-cheng. Both groups were underpaid and disgruntled, and an easy prey for communist propaganda.

In order to understand the position of the Chinese Communists from the standpoint of domestic Chinese politics, it is necessary to go back to 1927, when the Communists were expelled from the Kuomintang Party and the Government. Unlike the situation in other countries where civilian communist movements exist, the Red faction in China is not only a political party but also possesses a well equipped army.

When Chiang Kai-shek expelled the Communists from the party, overthrew the Soviet regime they had set up in Hankow, and broke off relations with the U.S.S.R., the Red forces withdrew into the inaccessible mountainous districts between Kiangsi and Fukien provinces, south of the Yangtze River. Other Red forces which had operated in the Canton district and had tried (without success) to establish a Soviet Government at the port of Swatow, near Canton, had also withdrawn into the mountains between Kiangsi and Fukien provinces, where they joined the other groups.

The intention of the Communists to continue their defiance of the Central Government was indicated in interviews with various Chinese Red officials and their Soviet advisers, and with American sympathizers who had fled to Moscow after the overthrow of the Red regime at Hankow. Among those who attempted to paint an optimistic future for communism in China were Eugene Chen, former Foreign Minister at Hankow, and Michael Borodin, the former Soviet adviser at Hankow.

But official Moscow had tired of the costly Chinese adventure, and furthermore, the U.S.S.R. could spare no military or naval forces in the Far East capable of dispatching relief to the Chinese Communists at their headquarters in the Kiangsi mountains. The Chinese Soviet regime was therefore forced to shift for itself, which it proceeded to do in characteristic fashion by issuing paper money, collecting taxes, and instituting a land-redistribution program among the farmers in Kiangsi Province, where extensive land holdings by the gentry had long been responsible for popular discontent among peasant farmers and villagers. I still have in my possession a silver dollar minted by the Chinese "Soviet Government" which contains the profile of Lenin on one side and the sickle and hammer on the other.

Throughout most of the period from 1928 to 1934, Generalissimo Chiang Kai-shek and his associates were occupied in consolidating the position of the Nanking Government and fighting off rival military factions.

The Red factions in Kiangsi thus had a breathing spell in which to reorganize their Soviet Government and re-establish connections with Moscow. But the land-redistribution program which the Communists initiated in Kiangsi precipitated a disastrous famine in Northern Kiangsi and led ultimately to their undoing. Strong opposition developed among the land-owning gentry of Central China and the Chinese bankers in Shanghai, whose loans were defaulted as a result of the socialization (confiscation) program. Generalissimo Chiang, whose Government was also under heavy obligations to the same bankers, was again forced to take action against the Chinese Reds. He finally accomplished their evacuation of the Kiangsi mountains by blockading the coast of Fukien Province, building a chain of blockhouses on the land side which cut off their access to the Yangtze River, and air-bombing their mountain bases.

In mid-October, 1934, the Reds, now numbering approximately 90,000 men, quietly slipped out of their mountain hiding places and set out in search of a new location. Following the mountainous regions along the provincial boundaries in South and Southwest China, their trek developed into an epochal march of approximately 4,000 miles before they reached their new location in the northwest. They were able to make the long trip through generally hostile territory, by marching in small groups and sticking to the provincial boundaries. In this manner they passed through Kweichow and Yunnan provinces in the southwest, then turned north along the narrow mountain valleys of the Upper Yangtze to Szechwan Province, thence over the mountains to Kansu Province, and finally reached northern Shensi, where they re-established their Soviet Government at the town of Yenan, in territory adjacent to Russian-controlled Outer Mongolia. The Reds were led on their long migration by two well known Communist leaders, Chu Teh and Mao Tseh-tung, both of whom had been trained in Moscow under Trotsky and Radek.

Another Red group under the command of General Ho Lung, which had been established in northern Hunan Province, also withdrew and joined the Red Government at Yenan. A third Red force, which styled itself the "anti-Japanese Fourth Army," and had established itself in the mountains of Anhwei Province on both banks of the Yangtze River, was broken up by Generalissimo Chiang Kai-shek, and part of it was incorporated into the Nanking forces.

The remnants withdrew to the northwest, but not before they had perpetrated one of the worst atrocities against American missionaries since the Nanking Incident in 1927. Two youthful missionaries, the Reverend and Mrs. John Stam, were seized with their two-weeks-old baby girl and were publicly beheaded. The Stams, both recent graduates of the Moody Bible Institute of Chicago, had only recently arrived in China and had been assigned to Anhwei Province. Mrs. Stam, while being led to the hill where execution took place, hastily wrapped her baby in a bundle of old rags and tossed it into a Chinese house along the route of march to the execution ground. The baby was cared for by friendly Chinese peasants and was later restored to its grandparents, the Reverend and Mrs. Charles Ernest Scott, veteran Presbyterian missionaries in Shantung Province.

The execution of the Reverend and Mrs. Stam was staged on a hill before a large crowd of country people and was accompanied by an outburst of posters, banners and oratory, with the bound victims standing by. The speeches and posters denounced the United States and world capitalism, and extolled the Soviet Union. After the helpless victims had been beheaded, the Reds responsible for the atrocity issued a bombastic statement declaring the execution of the young missionary couple had been carried out in retaliation for the action of an American company in selling to the Nanking Government airplanes which Generalissimo Chiang Kai-shek had used in bombing the Reds out of their base in the mountains of Kiangsi.

It was estimated that not more than 25,000 out of the original Red Army numbering some 90,000 survived the long trek to northwest China. However, their strength was quickly replenished, despite the barren, mountainous, and thinly populated nature of the country to which they had migrated. By the winter of 1936–37 they again claimed to have 100,000 troops.

Indications of impending trouble in the northwest had already appeared in the Shanghai newspapers in the form of dispatches from Sian telling of student parades and demonstrations demanding a cessation of pressure against the Chinese Communists and the formation of a "united front" against the Japanese. The Chinese Reds also utilized the services of an American woman leftist, who delivered speeches which were broadcast in both English and Chinese over the Communist radio stations. The Chinese Communists were desirous of diverting Japanese pressure from their own front and hoped that Chiang Kai-shek could be forced to bear the weight of the Japanese onslaught. In the background was undoubtedly also the hand of Moscow desirous of diverting Japanese pressure from Siberia and Russian-controlled Outer Mongolia. The Russians were anxious for Japan to become involved still more deeply in China, knowing full well that such involvement would ultimately lead to complications with the United States and Great Britain. Although disavowed in Moscow, evidence pointed to Russian influence as a vital factor in the Sian incident.

I first met Chang Hsueh-liang (who played the unheroic role of cat's-paw in the Sian Incident) at Mukden, in 1929 on the occasion of the brief war between China and the Soviet Union. Chang was then known as the "Young Marshal" to distinguish him from his late father, Marshal Chang Tso-lin, who, as I have told, was assassinated by the Japanese in 1928.

The Young Marshal was only thirty years old when he fell heir to his father's vast fortune and the position of commander-in-chief of the Government forces in Manchuria. He was ill prepared for this responsible post, the most precarious administrative position in the Chinese republic, as most of his life had been spent as a playboy in Mukden, the Manchurian capital, and at the old capital (Peking), or in his father's army. He spent one year in military school in Japan, and upon his return was appointed commander of one of the Manchurian armies. Somewhere along the line he acquired the opium and morphine habits, which remained with him for several years and greatly handicapped his career. He was finally cured by Dr. Miller, an American Seventh Day Adventist missionary physician at Shanghai.

Despite this, Chang Hsueh-liang was an ardent Nationalist and devoted a considerable portion of his fortune to the development of education in the Manchurian provinces. He endowed the National Northeastern University and the Manchurian Military Academy at Mukden, and was in process of developing a system of general education throughout Manchuria when the Japanese intervened in 1931. The Young Marshal had already defied the Japanese in 1928, when he unfurled the Nationalist flag over Government offices throughout Manchuria and announced that the Manchurian provinces had joined the Nationalist Government at Nanking. Again in 1929 he intervened at Peiping to break up a coalition of disgruntled militarists and politicians led by Wang Ching-wei which opposed General Chiang Kai-shek and the new Government at Nanking.

The Young Marshal was a patient in a Peiping hospital when the Japanese staged the so-called Manchurian "incident" and seized Mukden on the night of September 18, 1931, hence his troops in the vicinity of the Manchurian capital offered little resistance to the invaders on that fateful occasion. After serving in various posts under the Nanking Government, the Young Marshal was appointed director of the so-called "bandit-suppression" headquarters in southern Shensi Province, where his chief job was to watch over the activities of the Chinese Communists, who were again becoming troublesome in the northwest. The Young Marshal had a force of 130,000 troops, made up largely of remnants of defeated Manchurian armies. There were also collected at his headquarters several hundred students and teachers who had been forced to leave Manchuria, due to the wholesale closing of the schools by the Japanese. Since most of his fortune was invested in Manchurian lands, forests, and mines which had been seized by the Japanese army, the Young Marshal soon found himself in straitened circumstances and forced to depend upon the Nanking Government for funds. The result was that his troops were poorly paid and his schools and governmental departments impoverished.

It had been known for several months that instead of opposing the Reds, the Young Marshal's forces were fraternizing with them and permitting them to spread anti-Nanking propaganda among the people in his territory. Generalissimo Chiang Kai-shek had consistently opposed a policy of conciliation toward the Chinese Communists since the original break between the Kuomintang and the Reds at Shanghai, Nanking, and Hankow in 1927. The Generalissimo regarded the Chinese Reds as creatures of the Moscow Comintern and refused to negotiate with them so long as they maintained their Russian connections and their independent position in the northwest. It was thought that the Generalissimo intended to dismiss the Young Marshal as commander of the anti-Communist headquarters at Sian, and to replace him with another member of his staff who would continue opposition to the Reds. Three days before the departure of the Generalissimo for Sian, the Nanking Executive Yuan (Council) had adopted a resolution reaffirming that the Chinese foreign policy laid down by Generalissimo Chiang Kai-shek should remain as the guiding principle of the Central Government and that the anti-Communist campaign in Northwest China should be continued. Generalissimo Chiang was accompanied on the trip to Sian by ten other high government officials, some of them army commanders, and a small bodyguard. Among the military officers was General Chiang Ting-wen, Pacification Commissioner for Fukien Province, who was scheduled to replace the Young Marshal as commander of the anti-Red forces in the northwest.

The northwestern frontier town of Sian where the dramatic kidnaping of the Generalissimo and his staff was staged is about seven hundred miles inland, due west from the shores of the Yellow Sea. Aside from its strategic location on the ancient northwest road connecting China and Central Asia, Sian is important historically as it was the seat of the Chou Dynasty, which had its beginnings about 1122 B.C. and continued more than eight centuries. The classical period of Chinese history, which produced the famous scholars Confucius, Mencius, Lao Tzu, and Mo Tzu, fell within the Chou era, and many of the world's finest examples of ancient bronze art have come down to us from the graves of Chou rulers in the vicinity of Sian. In this area also were staged the wars between the houses of Chou and Shang (1400 B.C.) for supremacy over the valleys of the Yellow River and its tributary, the Wei, wherein dwelt the ancestors of the Chinese people of today.

It was a fitting stage for the enactment of a modern drama of Asiatic politics involving the political interests of China, Japan, and Russia, and ultimately of the entire world.

Generalissimo Chiang Kai-shek arrived at Sian by airplane on December 7, and established his headquarters at a hot-springs resort a short distance outside the city. The Generalissimo was welcomed by Shao Li-tze, Civil Governor of Shensi, a former newspaper editor from Shanghai, who had been appointed to the position by the Central Government. Civil Governor Shao had charge of the local police force, which remained loyal to the Generalissimo in the complicated developments of the following days. It was the first important political mission undertaken by the Generalissimo in many months when he was not accompanied by his wife, Mei-ling.

The days immediately following the Generalissimo's arrival at Sian were occupied in conferences between the Generalissimo and his staff and the Young Marshal, Chang Hsueh-liang, and General Yang Hu-cheng, the provincial military chieftain. Little was accomplished, as the Young Marshal and General Yang constantly insisted on bringing into the conference local groups which demanded immediate war against Japan. After four days of futile conversation, the Generalissimo informed the Young Marshal of the Government's determination to press the campaign against the Communists. He insisted that it would be suicidal to face war with Japan while the Communist army remained in an independent position in the northwest. The Young Marshal and his associate, General Yang, insisted that it would be better to accept the Reds' terms and form a "united front" of national resistance.

The Young Marshal insisted that the Central Government assume responsibility for the financial support and munitioning of some 270,000 troops in the northwestern territories. He was not, however, in a position to give assurances that the "united front" would accept the orders of the commander-in-chief of the Nationalist Government. This may explain why the Young Marshal had decided to bring the representatives of the Communists into the negotiations with the Generalissimo.

Following a heated discussion which left the situation at a deadlock, the Generalissimo retired to his private quarters on the outskirts of the city, where he was protected by his small bodyguard and a contingent of local police.

The Young Marshal immediately called a meeting of the divisional commanders of his forces and those of General Yang Hu-cheng, and issued secret orders to move a division of his own

troops and a regiment of General Yang's troops into the environs
of the city during the night, and by daylight the coup d'état was
complete and the city entirely surrounded. The only resistance
encountered was from the Generalissimo's small bodyguard and
a contingent of loyal police at the hot-springs resort where the
Generalissimo was staying. Aroused by the firing, the Generalissimo and one of his guards escaped from his sleeping quarters and climbed over a high wall which surrounded the compound. He might have succeeded in getting away had he not
sprained his ankle and been forced to hide in an abandoned
tomb. Here he was found by a young Manchurian officer, who
escorted him back to the building and ultimately to the city,
where he was confined in the private quarters of General Yang
Hu-cheng. The Civil Governor, Shao Li-tze, who with his
police remained loyal to the Generalissimo, was also arrested
and detained with Generalissimo Chiang's staff officers.

The announcement of the detention of the Generalissimo
created intense excitement throughout the city and was the
signal for demonstrations, mass meetings, and parades. The city
was quickly placarded with banners and posters denouncing
the Japanese-German-Italian Anti-Comintern Pact and demanding a "united front" against Japan. The radicals were for a
Soviet-style public trial of the Generalissimo on the charge of
prosecuting the war against the Reds and failing to declare war
on Japan. Others favored taking the Generalissimo to some secret
hiding place in the northwest and holding him as a hostage until
Nanking called off the anti-Red war.

Up to this point there was no outward manifestation of Red
participation in the plot to kidnap the Generalissimo. But the
hand of the Chinese Communists was soon in evidence after the
Young Marshal dispatched a plane to the Communist head-
quarters at Yenan and transported three of the Red leaders to
Sian. They were Chou En-lai, Political Commissar of the First
Front Red Army and Deputy Chairman of the Red Military
Council; Yeh Chien-ying, chief of staff of the East Front Red

Army; and Pao Ku, head of the Red Secret Police. They were accompanied by several secretaries and assistants. Of the three Communist envoys, Chou En-lai was remembered as the organizer of armed laborers, strikers, and pickets in the plot to seize Shanghai on behalf of the Communists at the time of the Nationalist Revolution in 1927. Chou was arrested by Generalissimo Chiang Kai-shek but was released, whereupon he went to Moscow for several months, later returning to join the Red regime in Northern Shensi.

Not many hours elapsed before the perpetrators of the Sian outrage realized the seriousness of their action. Of particular significance were simultaneous disavowals from Moscow and Tokyo, each denying any complicity in the plot, but at the same time charging each other with the responsibility. The Moscow papers printed bombastic reports denouncing the kidnaping of the Generalissimo as the work of Wang Ching-wei and the Japanese. Government officials in Tokyo charged that Marshal Chang Hsueh-liang's action had been inspired by the Communists, and declared it was an "object lesson" demonstrating the necessity of China's joining the Anti-Comintern Pact immediately.

The Tokyo paper, *Hochi*, declared that communist propaganda for a "united front" was the same, whether in Spain or China, and threatened that Japan would take action if Chang Hsueh-liang attempted to form an anti-Japanese front with Soviet Russia. The liberal Chinese paper, *Ta Kung Pao*, charged that the Japanese had taken advantage of the Sian crisis to increase their pressure on China to sign the anti-communist defense agreement. The Tokyo *Nichi-Nichi* declared that the Chinese Communist Army of Chu Teh and Mao Tseh-tung was steadily gaining in strength and was watching for an opportunity to seize the central power in China.

XXV

A Bear by the Tail

IN NANKING I SAW A COPY of a circular telegram said to have been dispatched from the Young Marshal's headquarters in Sian to all important government offices and newspapers in the national capital. The telegram explained that the detention of the Generalissimo was necessary "in order to stimulate his awakening to certain national and international problems." The telegram was not signed by any of the principals in the affair, and carried only the signatures of divisional commanders of the Young Marshal's and General Yang's troops. While it contained no signatures of Communist leaders, it embraced all the demands which the Communists had previously made on the Central Government, including a cessation of civil war, the formation of a "united front," and the release of political prisoners at Shanghai who had been arrested for inciting strikes and for financing seditious publications. The telegram demanded a reorganization of the governmental offices to admit "all political parties." Finally the telegram demanded that a military alliance be negotiated with the Soviet Union.

Nanking was seething with excitement and unrest, which the Government was having difficulty in holding in check. Certain military groups were urging the Government to take drastic action, including the bombing of Sian and the moving of government troops against the Young Marshal's forces in southern Shensi. It was suspected that some of those urging drastic action were less interested in rescuing the Generalissimo than in inciting the recalcitrant troops to murder him. There was criticism of the Generalissimo for having gone to Sian with only a small bodyguard to negotiate with the Young Marshal, "when he should have ordered the army to move against him." The excitement grew when a telegram, purporting to have been sent by the Generalissimo, was received, stating that he had been wounded and warning Madame Chiang Kai-shek against attempting to come to Sian to assist him.

Never had the Nanking Government been faced with such a predicament, as a hostile move against Sian might well result in the assassination of the Generalissimo—and at a time of crisis when he was practically the only military man in the country around whom all factions could rally.

But help came from an unexpected quarter.

W. H. Donald, an Australian newspaperman, who had lived in China for many years, was in Nanking serving as an adviser to the Generalissimo. As soon as he learned of Generalissimo Chiang Kai-shek's predicament he went to Dr. H. H. Kung, who had been appointed acting head of the Government, and volunteered to fly to Sian to investigate the situation and offer his services to the Generalissimo. A few years previously Donald had served as an adviser on the staff of the Young Marshal, then head of the Manchurian Administration, and knew him well.

Donald had a wide acquaintance with other Chinese officials and foreign diplomats, for whom he had performed many important and confidential services, but in all his many years of experience he had never been faced with the problem of rescuing the head of a government from a rebellious faction determined to use this extraordinary method to force an alteration in fundamental state policies.

Donald had been a cub reporter on a Hong Kong paper when James Gordon Bennett of the *New York Herald* sailed into the harbor aboard his palatial yacht on a trip around the world. Bennett formed a liking for the youthful reporter, and appointed him as the *Herald's* correspondent in the Far East.

I first met Donald at the old capital, Peking, during World War I when he was serving as the director of a bureau of information which the Chinese Government had set up, its first attempt at international public relations.

Due to his long acquaintance with the Young Marshal and his familiarity with the complicated political situation, Donald was in a position to offer sound advice to both the Young Marshal and the Generalissimo. Donald stopped over night at Loyang, headquarters of government troops in Honan, where he conferred with the commander in charge and also dispatched telegrams to the Young Marshal apprising him of his expected arrival the next morning at Sian. While in Loyang Donald also familiarized himself with the location of the nearest troop concentrations and air bases. The largest garrison was at Tungkwan, the narrow gorgelike pass along the Yellow River leading from Honan into Shensi. This pass was held by Nanking troops, which could march on the Young Marshal at a moment's notice. The same was true of the air base at Loyang, where several bombers were available. Donald knew that the presence of the Government's forces would have a sobering effect on the Young Marshal's officers and on the Communist-inspired students and teachers who were advocating drastic action against the person of the Generalissimo.

Donald was met at the Sian air field by a representative of the Young Marshal, who escorted him to the latter's headquarters. Before leaving the air field Donald had an opportunity to observe that the Generalissimo's planes were undamaged. After a short talk with the Young Marshal, Donald was taken to the Generalissimo's quarters, where further discussion took place.

Donald then wrote a brief report, which he sent to Nanking. The report stated that Chiang Kai-shek was not seriously injured, and that he desired a competent government official to come to Sian to negotiate; it asked that troop movements along the Honan-Shensi border be delayed.

According to Donald's later report, the Young Marshal and his associates quickly realized that they "had a bear by the tail," for the Generalissimo was adamant in his original position that the Communists must be suppressed by force unless they were willing to submit to Government control of their army and territory. Whenever the Generalissimo tired of listening to the arguments of his captors he would retire to his quarters and read his Bible. In reply to criticisms of his policy toward Japan he handed over to his captors a copy of his private diary. Here the rebel leaders learned for the first time of Chiang's innermost thoughts on Japan and of his efforts to unify the country in preparation for the inevitable reckoning with Japan. His captors were particularly impressed by a passage in the diary in which the Generalissimo uttered a prayer that he might be given ten years in which to prepare the country for war. The prayer had been made five years previously, hence only half the time he regarded as necessary had elapsed.

When he had received assurances that the Generalissimo would not be harmed, Donald returned to Nanking, bringing with him General Chiang Tung-wen, who was to have taken over the command at Sian if the Young Marshal had refused to move against the Communists.

After hearing Donald's report, the standing committee of the Central Executive Committee (or yuan) of the Nanking Government adopted resolutions branding the Young Marshal a rebel and stripping him of all of his official posts and honors. They also demanded the immediate release of the Generalissimo and ordered a military expedition against the Sian rebels in case this demand was not complied with immediately.

Acting under these instructions General Ho Ying-chin, Minister of War, ordered the mobilization of twenty divisions of troops along the Honan-Shensi border and directed that several squadrons of bombers be concentrated at Loyang in western Honan to conduct demonstrations over Sian and other border cities controlled by the Young Marshal and General Yang Hucheng. It was rumored that the Minister of War had issued orders for the bombing of the outskirts of Sian but that the orders were held up at the urgent request of Madame Chiang Kai-shek, who insisted upon going to Sian to join her husband.

A serious controversy developed over this delay, some officials urging that, after all, Madame Chiang Kai-shek was only a wife arguing for the life of her husband and that this should not be permitted to interfere with vital matters of policy. She was charged with using her influence with her brother-in-law, Dr. H. H. Kung, to prevent the Government from moving against the rebel factions.

Another controversy developed as to which official of the Government should accompany Donald back to Sian and what instructions should be given him concerning negotiations, if it was decided to negotiate instead of fight. The Young Marshal demanded that Dr. H. H. Kung, Finance Minister, be sent to Sian with power to negotiate a financial settlement. Donald stated that the Generalissimo was adamant in his refusal to negotiate under duress, and had merely shrugged his shoulders when informed that a powerful faction in Nanking was advocating military action, including the bombing of Sian. Donald also reported privately that the dissension which prevailed in the rebel camp had prevented the radical factions from getting together on any scheme for exploiting the Generalissimo's predicament politically; some groups advocated public trial in the Russian fashion, while others demanded the staging of a public execution of the Generalissimo. Neither the Young Marshal nor Yang Hu-cheng wanted the Generalissimo to suffer personal injury or to be executed, as such an action would certainly precipitate open warfare with the Central Government. The delegates from the Communist camp when they arrived at Sian concurred in this view, as they likewise did not wish to kill the goose which was expected to lay golden eggs.

When Donald flew back to Sian he was accompanied, not by Dr. H. H. Kung, but by Madame Chiang Kai-shek, wife of the Generalissimo, and her brother, T. V. Soong, former Finance Minister, who was then chairman of the board of the Bank of China. Both Soong and his sister were authorized to conduct negotiations for the release of the Generalissimo.

After a brief stop-over and conference with government military leaders at Loyang in Western Honan, the planes carrying the Nanking party arrived at Sian on the morning of December 17.

The representatives of the Nanking Government at Sian, aside from Generalissimo Chiang Kai-shek, were Madame Chiang, T. V. Soong, W. H. Donald, and several assistants. On the side of the rebels were the Young Marshal Chang Hsueh-liang and the provincial militarist, Yang Hu-cheng, and their assistants, including a young Manchurian officer, Lieutenant Sun Ming-chiu, who probably saved the Generalissimo's life on the night of the Sian rebellion. Also in Sian at the time were the three representatives of the Communist Party, Chou En-lai, Yeh Chien-ying and the mystery man, Pao Ku. They had just arrived from the Communist Army headquarters at Yenan in Northern Shensi, on a private plane supplied by the Young Marshal.

The only personal account of the happenings at Sian which took place between December 17 and Christmas of 1937 which has not been published is that of the Young Marshal. He returned to Nanking on the same plane with the Generalissimo, but he was a prisoner, and has remained a prisoner since, somewhere in West China. Of the other participants in the "political drama" of Sian, both the Generalissimo and Madame Chiang have issued complete reports of their side of the controversy. Generalissimo Chiang declared in his diary that he did not sign any agreement and insisted throughout the conference on the submission of the northwest political and military elements to the Central Government.

The Communist angle as well as the Red situation in general in Northwest China has been presented voluminously by several American writers.

W. H. Donald, the Australian newspaperman, who served in the important role of mediator in the Sian Incident and who probably knows more than anyone else about the innermost details of the incident, was a prisoner of the Japanese in the Philippines. He was engaged in writing his memoirs when the

Japanese took over the islands, together with his yacht which he had built in Hong Kong for a South Seas cruise. He was released following General MacArthur's capture of Manila early in 1945.

T. V. Soong, former Finance Minister and Shanghai banker, who also played a prominent part in the negotiations for the Generalissimo's release, has likewise remained silent. The size of the check he is said to have handed over in exchange for the release of his illustrious brother-in-law has never been disclosed.

Since the Sian negotiations were conducted in secret and no official report of the outcome was published, there is still speculation as to what actually happened. The most obvious result of the Sian Incident was apparent just seven months later at Peiping. It was written in letters of blood for the world to read—war! War between China and Japan, and ultimately involving the entire world.

One result of the Sian Incident was an unexpected trip abroad for Dr. H. H. Kung, Minister of Finance in the Nanking Government. Dr. Kung's trip resulted from a confidential proposal of the Soviet Government that China take steps to form a military alliance against Japan. Moscow was especially anxious that the United States be brought into the alliance, but Soviet officialdom realized it would be futile for them to make the proposal. The Russians therefore urged China to send a mission abroad to sound out the various Powers. Russia, in fear of a Japanese attack, promised China full military support and agreed to send ample military supplies to the Chungking Government by way of the ancient highway across Sinkiang. Moscow also promised Nanking that there would be no further conplications concerning the Chinese Communists, who would give their full support to the Central Government in its resistance to Japanese aggression. Dr. Kung did not realize the full import of his mission until he reached Berlin and was apprised of Germany's plans to wage war against the Soviet Union. Dr. Kung was told by the Nazi leaders to advise his government to join the Anti-Comintern Alliance of Germany-Japan-Italy without delay.

When Dr. Kung reached Moscow he found the Russians had cooled on their proposal for a Chinese-United States-Soviet anti-Japanese alliance. Moscow now realized that war with Germany was inevitable, and did not want to do anything to provoke the Japanese to attack Russsia on the eastern flank. It was not long until the Chinese Communists also ceased their attacks on the Japanese army in northwestern China.

XXVI

Sequel of Sian

CONTRARY TO EXPECTATIONS in many quarters the outcome of the Sian Incident greatly enhanced Generalissimo Chiang Kai-shek's prestige. Influential political and military leaders, particularly in the South, who had refused to give active support to Nanking, now declared their readiness to cooperate with the Generalissimo in opposing the Japanese. One of the Southern politico-military leaders who declared their readiness to support Generalissimo Chiang was General Tsai Ting-kai, famous Cantonese commander who had resisted the Japanese invasion of Shanghai early in 1932, following the Manchurian Incident. Later, General Tsai broke with Nanking and retired to the British Colony of Hong Kong. Two other important military commanders, General Pai Chung-hsi and General Li Tsung-jen of Kwangsi Province, both of whom had distinguished themselves in the Nationalist Revolution, also declared their readiness to support Chiang Kai-shek in resisting Japanese aggression. General Li Tsung-jen declared that in his opinion China could hold out against Japan for ten years.

The Japanese interpreted the outcome of the Sian affair as further evidence of the growth of communism in China, and urged that stronger pressure be exerted on Nanking by the Japanese Government to force China to join the Anti-Comintern group. Since the Manchurian Incident the Japanese had confined their activities south of the Great Wall to diplomatic pressure at Nanking; but there were hints of more ominous moves. The Japanese navy had landed sailors and seized the harbor area at Tsingtao on the Shantung coast in retaliation for the action of the Chinese customs authorities in attempting to break up a gang of Japanese smugglers. There also were strikes of large numbers of Chinese laborers in Japanese cotton mills at Tsingtao. Since the settlement of the Shantung Question at the Washington Arms Limitation Conference in 1922, the Japanese had greatly increased their investments at Tsingtao, particularly in cotton manufacturing. Relations between the Chinese and Japanese at the Shantung port had been generally peaceful up to the time of the Manchurian Incident.

The Japanese army newspaper *Shanghai Nippo*, commenting on the outcome of the Sian rebellion, declared that the Nanking Government should now be willing to accept Japan's proposal for "joint action against the Russian-supported Chinese Reds." The paper declared, "Nanking has now reached the cross-roads and must decide the Government's future course. . . . Should the Nationalist Government continue to avoid giving a definite answer to Japan's proposals and should Generalissimo Chiang Kai-shek attempt to carry out the agreement by which his release was effected, then the Japanese Government will harden its attitude toward China. . . . The Sian episode has made Chinese-Japanese relations more critical than before the incident." The paper declared that the civil war in Spain was a prologue to a new world war, and the Chinese would have to decide their attitude toward Japan "according to developments in the international situation. . . . Should Chiang Kai-shek utilize the new world war for a fight with Japan, he will become China's grave-digger."

In mid-January of 1937 there was a report from Sian stating that an American woman "with communist sympathies and having connections with leftist groups in the United States" had arrived in Sian and had delivered several addresses before mass meetings of students. The report said that several Chinese Communist leaders, including Chu Teh, Mao Tseh-tung, Chou En-lai, and others had arrived in Sian to confer with her. The report alleged that the Shensi War Lord, Yang Hu-cheng, had sent an ultimatum to Nanking declaring that if Generalissimo

Chiang Kai-shek "did not open war immediately on Japan, the Communist army would attack the Nanking Government."

There were further ominous reports from North China, leading to the belief that Japan was actively preparing for further adventures south of the Great Wall into China proper. Japan had been in control of Manchuria for five years, and had converted that rich Chinese territory into a tightly controlled Japanese war base. Using the forced labor of tens of thousands of Chinese, the Japanese had built strategic railways and highways to vulnerable points on the Siberian and Outer Mongolian borders. The League of Nations at Geneva, after investigating the Manchurian Incident and condemning Japan for stealing her neighbor's territory, had lapsed into a silence from which it never awakened. Both Hitler and Mussolini extended diplomatic recognition to Japan's puppet state of Manchukuo. They chose the time of the Sian episode for their gesture of contempt for both China and the Comintern.

In view of the large number of reports indicating growing uneasiness in North China, I decided to make a trip to Peiping and Tientsin, where trouble seemed to be brewing.

The Japanese were feverishly pushing their plans for further military moves, but whether southward into China proper or northward into Russian Siberia, or whether in both directions, could not be determined. It was no longer a question whether the Japanese would strike, but where and when.

From Peiping I went on to Kalgan, the strategic frontier city at the gateway in the Great Wall northwest of the ancient capital, Peking, now Peiping. Kalgan is on the border between North China and Mongolia, and is located at the intersection of two important ancient highways, one leading from Peiping to Urga, capital of Mongolia, and the other leading from Peiping westward to Russia and Central Asia. The railway leading from Peiping to Kalgan crosses the famous Nankow Pass in the Great Wall, a few miles south of Kalgan.

Immediately after I arrived at the dusty Mongolian town, I

went to the yamen or headquarters of General Sung Cheh-yuan, who commanded the border defense troops. The Chinese word *yamen* means, literally, "flag-gate," indicating the headquarters of the chief military commander. As I entered the compound filled with low brick- and mud-walled buildings, I involuntarily thought of the long procession of Mongolian conquerors, beginning with the greatest of all conquerors, Genghis Khan, who had ridden their horses through that gateway in the ancient mud-walled official compound and held audiences with other equally fierce horsemen from the plains, deserts and steppes of northern and central Asia. Shortly another conqueror, less picturesque than the dashing horsemen of the plains, was destined to pass through the same flag-gate.

The situation in Kalgan became tense as the Japanese completed their conquest of Jehol Province, ancient summer home of the Manchus located to the north of Peiping, and prepared to move westward into Chahar and Suiyuan provinces, which, with the province of Ningsia, make up Inner Mongolia.

There had already been serious fighting between the Japanese and General Sung Cheh-yuan's troops on the border between Jehol and Chahar. In reply to my questions General Sung assured me of his intention to oppose Japanese military penetration into Inner Mongolia. I noticed, however, that General Sung appeared nervous and apprehensive, and evaded most of my questions. That night as I boarded the train back to Peiping, I was surprised to see General Sung's secretary on the train. The secretary admitted that General Sung was also on the train; that he had received instructions from Nanking to transfer his headquarters to Peiping, where too the situation was becoming critical. General Sung was one of the few commanders who put up even weak resistance to the Japanese in Manchuria. Most of the other subordinate commanders under the Young Marshal had simply withdrawn their troops without offering battle, saying that they were obeying orders from the Nationalist Government at Nanking, that the question of Japan's invasion of Manchuria had been referred to the League of Nations, and that China had agreed to abide by the League's decision. General Sung, however, had put up a fight at the Hsifengkow Pass in the Great Wall directly north of Peiping.

The struggle for the control of Inner Mongolia centered about the town of Pailingmiao, located about three hundred miles northwest of Kalgan on the northern edge of Suiyuan Province adjacent to the Outer Mongolian border. The town was important as a communications center, and also was the headquarters of the Mongolian branch of the Buddhist religion. There were numerous Lama temples and monasteries and a large congregation of Lama priests from both Inner and Outer Mongolia and Tibet. I had already observed evidence of the fighting at Pailingmiao at Peiping, where the curio shops were filled with religious pictures, jewelry, and other articles which had been looted from the Lama temples in the vicinity of Pailingmiao. According to information supplied me by General Sung Chehyuan, the Japanese had plotted with the young and ambitious Mongolian Prince Teh (official name, Teh-Mu-Chu-Keh-Tung-Lu-Pu), to establish a so-called "Great Mongol Empire," which was to extend westward from Jehol Province to Sinkiang in central Asia. Pailingmiao, because of its location and religious significance, had been selected as the political capital of the new puppet state. Large quantities of military supplies and provisions secretly purchased by the Japanese had been sent there in preparation for a coup d'état, Japan's ultimate objective being to establish a buffer state which would cut off China from direct contact with the Soviet Union.

When the Chinese commander in Suiyuan, General Fu Tso-yi, learned of the Japanese plan, he sent troops to Pailingmiao and after some fighting occupied the city, including the Lama temples. A number of Japanese agents and spies found in the city were executed.

The penetration of the Japanese army into Chahar and Suiyuan provinces from the Japanese base in Jehol was finally blocked at Paotow, at the end of the railway, which is about four hundred miles west of Peiping on the upper reaches of the Hwangho, or Yellow River. This had marked the most western point of Japanese penetration, and probably indicates the mutually agreed-upon line of demarcation between the Japanese and Russian spheres of influence in China's northwestern territories. The Chinese Communist Army's territory is directly west of this area, within the Russian sphere.

With their position thus consolidated in both Manchuria and Inner Mongolia, the Japanese army leaders were ready for further ambitious moves. Would their next advance be north or south? I did not have to wait long for an answer.

In his new position as head of the Political Council at Peiping, General Sung Cheh-yuan had to face the new Japanese onslaught on China proper south of the Great Wall. The Japanese had already begun the "softening" process preliminary to more drastic moves. An ultimatum was presented to the Peiping Political Council forcing that body to consent to the demilitarization of twenty-two hsiens or counties of the northern area of Hopei Province lying directly south of the Great Wall. Following the withdrawal of Chinese troops, the Japanese formed a puppet administration in the district, which they called the "East Hopei Anti-Communist and Autonomous Government."

I interviewed the head of the puppet set-up, a Chinese named Yin Ju-keng, at his headquarters a few miles east of Peiping. He admitted his role without shame, and disclosed interesting details of Japanese procedure in dealing with the inhabitants of territories occupied by the Japanese army. First, the Japanese army appointed advisers to serve with each county magistrate throughout the area. The advisers were specially trained in schools set up for the purpose in Tokyo and in Manchuria. The Japanese army then ordered the gentry or property owners of the district to raise a "peace preservation corps," which was trained and officered by Japanese army men. All Chinese farmers were compelled to join cooperative societies, which were controlled by the Japanese. All textbooks in the school had to be purchased from the "Sino-Japanese Cultural Society," and every school was required to subscribe to and keep on file certain specified puppet newspapers. All middle schools were ordered to employ Japanese teachers to give instruction in the Japanese language, and the Japanese teachers had orders to deliver daily "advisory speeches" to the pupils. There was established in each city and town a Japanese-language "research council" for the purpose of teaching and interpreting the Japanese language to Chinese adults.

As a result of the expulsion of Chinese police and customs officials, the district became the center of vast smuggling and narcotic enterprises participated in by Japanese, Koreans, and Chinese criminals.

When I arrived in Tientsin early in June, 1937, I found the Chinese population absorbed in what the newspapers called the "corpse mystery." The sensation completely eclipsed local interest in the approaching war.

Prominently displayed on the front pages of the Chinese papers was an announcement by the Provincial Governor, General Sung Cheh-yuan, that a reward of $5,000 would be paid to anyone supplying information concerning 107 corpses which had been found floating in the Hai-ho, the tidal river which connects Tientsin with the sea. The bodies were all of the male sex, and ranged from twenty to forty years of age. None of the bodies, it was said, showed evidence of physical violence.

When I called at the local Defense Commissioner's office to inquire concerning the mystery, I was shown a number of pictures of bodies which had been removed from the river. My attention was directed to a particular group of six bodies, one of which had "come alive," after being dragged from the water. It appeared that this man had fallen, or had been thrown, into a shallow place where his face had not been submerged. He was sent to a hospital and, upon regaining consciousness, disclosed the mystery of the 107 corpses. This man, named Chia Yung-chi, thirty years of age, was found to be suffering from heroin poisoning. All he remembered was that he had accompanied a number of fellow peasant laborers from the interior, to a resort in the Japanese Concession where opium and heroin were being smoked. He had considerable money in his pocket, representing his savings from a season's work in Manchuria. His money and most of his clothing were gone when he was dragged from the river. The last he remembered was that he had smoked some heroin cigarettes which a girl had sold to him in the resort.

Investigation disclosed that all of the corpses which had been fished out of the river probably represented victims of heroin and opium dens operated by the Japanese in their Concession at Tientsin. The 107 bodies recovered were probably a small percentage of the actual number of victims, as the tide in the river was strong at that point and might have swept most of them out to sea. It was disclosed that it had long been the practice of the police in the Japanese Concession to send a truck through the streets and alleys of the section where the dope dens were located, to pick up the bodies of victims, transport them to the river bank, and dump them in when the tide was running out to sea. It was said that the police who collected the bodies paid little attention to whether the victims were alive or dead. In the winter when the river was frozen, the bodies were dumped through a hole in the ice.

As a result of the disclosure, the Chinese municipality and provincial authorities established cheap hostels where the laborers were looked after until they could be sent back to their homes. Tientsin had always served as a vast labor camp where coolie laborers from the interior provinces congregated while waiting for employment by labor contractors who transported them to Manchuria for work on railroad, mine, or forestry projects. After the Japanese occupied the Manchurian provinces they restricted the influx of Chinese laborers and farmers from North China, but this had little effect on the number which flocked into Tientsin looking for jobs.

I visited several of the cheap hostels which the local Chinese authorities set up to take care of the laborers, and careful inquiry showed that a large percentage had become addicts of the Japanese heroin traffic which had practically superseded the older opium-smoking habits of the wealthier classes of the Chinese. The Chinese administered heroin in two ways, by hypodermic injection in the forearms, or by smoking the powder in cigarettes. In many of the low-class heroin dives which I inspected I observed Chinese young men purchasing small packets of heroin in the form of white powder for as low a price as ten or twenty cents. They would take an ordinary cigarette and shake out about a quarter of the tobacco, then fill the empty part with heroin powder. In smoking they would carefully hold the cigarette at a 45-degree angle in order to prevent the heroin from spilling out. Japanese dealers also sold patent cigarette holders with the bowl or receptacle set at an angle on top of the stem in order to facilitate the smoking of heroin cigarettes. The Chinese name for this type was "airplane smokes."

I was told that the heroin habit acquired in this way was practically impossible to break. I visited the streets named Hashidate, Hanazowa, Kotobuko, Komai and others in the Japanese Concession, where practically every shop was given over to heroin manufacture or sale. I was accompanied on the trip by a New York business acquaintance, and when we reached one of the streets our taxi was practically mobbed by "runners" from the various houses soliciting our trade. The shops, which usually had sleeping quarters upstairs, were easily distinguished by a sign extending out from the wall upon which were written two Chinese characters reading "Yang Hang," meaning "Foreign Firm." The Japanese and Korean proprietors used the name "Foreign Firm" supposedly for the purpose of creating the impression among the customers that the shops were owned by Europeans.

A further type of heroin-dispensing resort which was prevalent in Manchurian cities and was also found in Tientsin consisted of an ordinary type of residence, on the front of which was constructed a boxlike structure resembling a large vestibule. Heroin addicts would enter the vestibule and knock on the door leading into the house. A small sliding panel would be opened, and the customer would be told to thrust his bared arm through the aperture, with the appropriate amount of money in his hand. The money would be taken, and the customer would receive a hypodermic jab in his arm.

The production of heroin in Japanese factories in Tientsin and Dairen had grown to enormous proportions, but prepared opium for old-fashioned smoking purposes was still in sufficient demand to enable the Japanese to maintain an elaborate establishment consisting of a large hotel which had been adapted for the purpose. The furniture was removed and in its place were substituted cheap wooden platforms or bunks covered with grass matting and a small hard pillow or head-rest at the end. A narrow aisle extending down the center of the room provided access to the beds or divans. The smokers would come in, usually in pairs, frequently a man and woman. They would recline on the matting bunks facing each other, with the opium paraphernalia between them. An attendant, usually a little Korean girl about ten or twelve years old, would then bring two pipes, a small alcohol lamp, and a small tin or porcelain container holding the opium, which resembled thick black molasses. Taking a small metal wire resembling a knitting needle, the girl attendant would dip one end into the sticky opium and turn it about until she had accumulated a considerable portion on the end of the wire. She would then hold the opium over the flame and revolve it rapidly in order to prevent it from igniting into a blaze. After the little ball of opium had begun to smoke the girl attendant would quickly remove it and hold the smoking ball on the end of the wire directly over the small aperture in the metal bowl of the pipe. The smoker would draw a deep breath, filling his lungs with the sickeningly sweet fumes of the opium. They would repeat the process two or three times, until they fell asleep. Each process was called a "pipe" or a "smoke," and usually cost one dollar in Chinese currency, equivalent to about thirty cents in American currency. If the house also supplied the woman companion, the charge was usually five dollars.

The establishment which I visited was located on Asahi Road, the chief street in the Japanese Concession. There were probably two dozen rooms on each of the six floors, and each room contained divans for ten or fifteen smokers. There was no privacy for the smokers, and there was no attempt at concealment, as the house was open the full twenty-four hours and was brilliantly illuminated. Fumes of the burning opium in hundreds of pipes could be smelled a block away.

The Chinese authorities, unable to prevent the wholesale debauchery of their citizens who resided within the Japanese Concession, adopted drastic regulations, including the death penalty, for opium smokers and dealers in the surrounding Chinese-controlled territory. But the Chinese fight against the narcotic evil was a futile struggle, because opium and its derivatives, morphine and heroin, were as much a part of Japanese aggression as were the rifles in the hands of Japanese soldiers. Japanese laws against the use of narcotics in Japan were rigorously enforced. No Japanese subject was permitted to use or dispense narcotics in Japan, but thousands of Japanese and Korean subjects of Japan are encouraged to engage in the traffic among subject peoples in occupied territory on the continent and insular possessions. The intimate connection between the Imperial Japanese Army and the drug traffic probably will not be disclosed until Japan has her overdue revolutionary housecleaning, but it was alleged that the morphine and heroin factories at Tientsin and Dairen were operated directly by the Special Service Section of the army. (In Shanghai the opium-smoking resorts which operated in connection with the gambling establishments were certainly controlled by the S.S.S.)

Heroin and morphine were not the only products being smuggled in by the Japanese at that time. W. R. Myers, an American citizen, who occupied the post of Commissioner of the Chinese Maritime Customs at Tientsin, told me that Japanese merchandise smuggled into North China from the Japanese zone and Manchuria amounted to about $10,000,000 monthly, despite the fact that the Chinese authorities were able to seize about one-third before it reached its destination. The merchandise, consisting of cotton goods, rayon, sugar, kerosene, and cigarettes, usually arrived at isolated customs stations on armed trucks about midnight. After driving away the guards the trucks would proceed to inland points where the materials were sold at bargain prices. An American merchant at Tientsin showed me a circular he received from a Japanese customs broker offering his services in smuggling in American goods at fees far below the Chinese customs rates.

Of most serious import, the "demilitarized zone" served as a concentration and training base for Japanese soldiers brought in from Manchuria and Japan.

Most persons thought the Japanese blow would fall at the port of Tientsin, where the situation had been strained for many months, due to widespread purchase of land and industrial property by Japanese speculators in violation of Chinese orders against the sale of real estate to aliens. Tipped off by friends in the army, hordes of Japanese adventurers flocked to Tientsin to purchase land and developed property, in expectation of handsome profits following the Japanese intervention.

A member of the staff of the American consulate at Tientsin called my attention to a report he had translated from one of the Chinese papers, stating that an organization of Japanese known as the "Sacred Farming Society" had purchased a large tract of land a few miles from Tientsin, and that serious opposition had developed among the Chinese farmers in the vicinity. The land was unsuitable for agriculture, but despite this and the opposition of the Chinese, the head of the Japanese group, one Eizo Shima by name, declared that he possessed a secret method for removing alkali from soil and that his object was to promote Chinese-Japanese friendship by teaching the Chinese improved methods of farming and gardening. Accompanied by my friend Mr. Ward, of the American consulate, I visited the Japanese farming project which the Chinese designated as "God's Farmers." We found the place in confusion. A number of small houses which the Japanese had constructed in the manner of squatters' huts were smoking ruins. The Japanese claimed that Chinese marauders crept up at night and poured gasoline on the thatched roofs and set them on fire. All of the Japanese wore semi-military uniforms and were of the ronin type. Ward and I looked at each other and exclaimed involuntarily, "frame-up," as it had all the earmarks of a planted incident and we could imagine headlines in the Japanese papers charging the Chinese with interfering with a Japanese enterprise.

The "sacred farm" affair occurred on June 12, less than a month before the actual outbreak of hostilities, which did not occur at Tientsin, after all. The exposure of the "sacred farm" affair in the *China Weekly Review* and other papers may have caused the army to change its plans.

Late in June the Japanese Government presented a secret ultimatum to the Peiping Political Council demanding that it join in a "Central Economic Council" embracing the territories of Manchukuo, Korea, and North China. Peiping was asked to send delegates to a conference at Dairen, Manchuria, which was scheduled to create an "organic continental bloc," the first objective of which was to promote heavy or war industries. Other subjects on the agenda included elimination of trade barriers, coordination of production, standardization of products, coordination and linking-up of similar industries in the three continental territories with those in Japan. It was the Japanese conception of a "cartel" arrangement. News of the ultimatum was disclosed in the press of Tientsin on July 4. Fighting broke out between the forces of Japan and China near Peiping three days later, or on July 7.

The Japanese army followed its usual procedure and prepared an "incident."

Since the Boxer Rebellion in 1900, when Chinese fanatics besieged the foreign diplomats at Peiping, the various foreign Powers had maintained small "token" forces in the old Chinese capital for the purpose of guarding the legations. The force at the American Legation usually consisted of some 250 Marines. The British, French, Italians, and, occasionally, other powers, maintained similar small forces, as also had the Germans, Austrians and Russians prior to World War I. The Japanese, however, maintained a considerably larger force, usually a full regiment.

It was the custom of the various foreign units to conduct their exercise drills and maneuvers on the glacis surrounding the wall about the Legation Quarter in Peiping. But not so the Japanese; they insisted on holding their maneuvers in the countryside several miles outside the city—and at night.

On the evening of July 7, at about 10 o'clock, the Japanese troops were staging a sham battle near the village of Lukouchiao (Marco Polo Bridge), about twenty miles west of Peiping. The scene of the maneuvers was near the intersection of the two important railways which serve Peiping. Japanese officers claimed their troops were fired on by soldiers of the Chinese 29th Army, which was under the command of General Sung Cheh-yuan. The Japanese immediately made drastic demands; that Chinese troops be withdrawn from strategic points about Peiping; that the Japanese be permitted to search villages in the vicinity of the Marco Polo Bridge; that the Chinese troops were inspired by Communists, hence the Chinese authorities should cooperate with the Japanese in eradicating them; that the Chinese military authorities should apologize, and punish the culprits. The Japanese claimed that one of their soldiers had been kidnaped in one of the villages, but the man was later found in a "sing-song" house.

The Chinese agreed to appoint members of a joint commission to investigate, but fighting broke out before the commission got started. Japanese military planes flew over the district and dropped leaflets ordering the Chinese troops to withdraw from the area. Both sides brought in reinforcements, and the clashes grew in intensity. The Chinese seized the airport where Japanese planes from Tokyo landed, and the Japanese retaliated by seizing the railway junctions. Martial law was enforced in Peiping, and the city gates were closed. There were intermittent clashes and truces, until the commanders agreed to withdraw their troops to opposite sides of the small Yungting River. Suddenly the Japanese barricaded the gates to their quarters in the Legation Quarter and manned them with machine guns. By July 13 large bodies of troops began to arrive from Manchuria, and fighting about the city grew in intensity. The Tokyo papers demanded a "show-down" in North China, claiming that North China was "swept" by anti-Japanese propaganda inspired by the Communists.

The war was on.

XXVII

Mounting Tension

1—*End of "Wait and See"*

IN THE SUMMER OF 1937, after the Japanese had intervened in North China but before they attacked Shanghai, I boarded a little Chinese steamer, the *Sanpeh,* for a week-end trip down the China coast to the Chusan Islands. I was accompanied on the trip by James Howes, secretary of the American Chamber of Commerce, and his son. Much to our surprise the boat, which belonged to a well known Chinese company, had a German captain and flew the Nazi swastika flag after it cleared the harbor limits. The captain told me that all the coastal steamers belonging to this particular Chinese company had been taken over by a German concern. I noticed, however, soon after the ship was under way, that the German captain had practically nothing to do with its operation, which was still controlled by the Chinese officers and crew. The Nazi captain emerged from his cabin and showed himself on deck, in his new uniform, only when the boat was in port, or when it was passing a Japanese warship. He received a handsome salary for this service, and the reason was obvious: the Chinese expected the war to spread to the Yangtze Valley, and had made a paper transfer of their ships to a German company in the expectation that the Japanese would not seize the ships if they were under the Nazi flag.

As the little *Sanpeh* slowly steamed down the Whangpoo to the Woosung breakwater and the broad muddy mouth of the Yangtze, we passed an unusually large number of Japanese destroyers parked in groups of two, three, and four along the river with a half dozen more anchored just outside the breakwater at Woosung. As the officers of the Japanese warship carefully inspected the *Sanpeh* through their glasses as we passed alongside in the narrow river, it was impossible to escape a feeling of apprehension; and I wondered whether the little Chinese ship with its Nazi camouflage would be able to run the Japanese gantlet on the return voyage up the Whangpoo.

We landed at Chusan, which is the largest of a group of islands scattered about the mouth of Hangchow Bay, a wide, shallow, V-shaped estuary which cuts into the China coast about 150 miles south of Shanghai. It is approximately thirty miles long and fifteen miles wide, with a fairly good harbor. In the middle of the Eighteenth Century, when the Chinese rulers would have no dealings with foreign barbarians, the East India Company was compelled to establish bases for trading on islands off the China coast. One of these bases was later destined to become the Crown Colony of Hong Kong, famous center of international trade and politics. The other, now practically unknown, even to the map-makers, was the island of Chusan. For many years Chusan was a hive of business and naval activity, resounding to the shouts and tread of British sailors, soldiers, and traders. Its importance ceased after the opening of Shanghai to British and world trade in the middle of the last century, and at the time of my visit it was little more than a sleepy fishing village.

I had a letter of introduction to the principal of the Chusan Middle School, one of several educational institutions on the island which were supported by the American Baptist mission. I was not surprised when Professor Fong told me that a squadron of Japanese destroyers recently had called at Chusan and had taken soundings in the harbor. This information provided the first clue to future Japanese activities along the coast to the south of Shanghai. I had cause to remember my visit to Chusan after I was thrown into prison and the Japanese gendarmes had rifled the files in my office.

Professor Fong took me to see the old cemetery where several hundred British and French soldiers and sailors were buried.

Some of the graves dated back to the days of the old British East India Company, in the middle of the Eighteenth Century, but most of the European occupants of these forgotten graves lost their lives through disease or wounds suffered in the Anglo-French wars with China in the middle of the last century.

The East India Company had selected Chusan Island as a trading base for Central China on account of its location near the port of Ningpo, chief city of Chekiang Province, which was, at that time, the main source of Chinese tea. Since opium bulked large among the products exchanged for tea, this was an added reason for the selection of Chusan as a trading post, as the location of the island facilitated smuggling.

Ningpo was once a household word in the United States. Much of the tea carried on the fast-sailing clipper ships came from that city and was sold in American stores as "Ningpo" tea. It was one of the early centers in China for Protestant missionary work. Many of the early American Consuls who served at Ningpo were missionaries; one, named Cunningham, died in Ningpo, and his body lies today in the old Ningpo cemetery surrounded by the graves of his six wives. Many of his reports to the State Department were appeals for an increase in salary, as he found it difficult to live on the salary of $1,000 a year which the department allowed him. Another early American Consul at Ningpo, Townsend Harris, negotiated our first commercial treaty with Japan, following the opening of that country, by Commodore Perry, to American and world trade. The Harris treaty with Japan was signed in 1858, following which Harris became a teacher of political economy to the Japanese. In one of his early dispatches to the State Department, Harris made an interesting observation. He said that the common people of Japan were well disposed toward foreigners, but "the officials are the greatest liars on earth."

The suspicion of the Chusan professor and myself concerning further Japanese activities in that region was borne out by later events, for shortly after my return to Shanghai I received a letter from Professor Fong stating that a Japanese naval contingent had taken over the island. He stated that he had barely managed to escape with his wife and children to Ningpo aboard a junk. Later he informed me that history was repeating itself at Chusan, as the Japanese had converted the island into a base for a vast smuggling trade extending along the China coast as far south as Canton. As one might suspect, opium and Japanese narcotics were again chief articles of the new trade. The Japanese navy established a base at Chusan, and after the passage of a century the island has again become a hive of military activity.

In the meantime, at Nanking, Generalissimo Chiang Kai-shek was being attacked and ridiculed for his "wait and see" policy. Some reactionaries were demanding that, as a means of appeasing the enemy, Chiang resign and withdraw completely from participation in national affairs. Faced with dissension at home and attacks from abroad, the head of the National Government could no longer delay action. The Generalissimo announced, in an interview with the *Central Press* on August first: "I declare again that China does not seek war, but we will accept war if it is forced on us. We have reached the limit of our endurance."

Chinese troops in North China, evicted from Peiping and Tientsin, had withdrawn to the "last line of defense" along the Yellow River and the Lunghai Railway. The Japanese were bombing this line daily, and their future intentions were indicated by massing of troops and mechanized equipment in the evacuated districts. At Tientsin the Japanese bombed and completely destroyed Nankai University, one of the leading Chinese educational institutions of North China. The Japanese charged that the university had been a center of anti-Japanese activities. The real reason was that the Japanese had discovered that two sons of the president of the school, Dr. Chang Po-ling, were aviators in the Chinese Air Corps. On August 3 a flotilla of nine Japanese warships entered the harbor at Swatow, near Canton, and demanded the resignation of the local Chinese commander, on the ground that he had encouraged a strike of Chinese wharf coolies who were loading a Japanese ship in the harbor. Chinese military commanders in Central and South China met at Nanking to consider the threatening situation, and the National Government decided to evacuate all Chinese residents from Japan. On August 7 the Japanese ordered the evacuation of all Japanese nationals from Hankow and other points in the Yangtze Valley and South China.

Early in August the *Shanghai Nippo*, a Japanese mouthpiece, charged that the Chinese had violated the neutrality agreement of 1932 by bringing in 2,000 men to strengthen the local Peace Preservation Corps. On August 9, General Sugiyama, Japanese War Minister, declared that China "must be chastised for her insincerity" and that Japan's non-aggression policy must be abandoned.

That evening an officer and a sailor of the Japanese navy were shot and killed as they were trying to enter the Chinese airdrome at Hungjao on the outskirts of Shanghai, and a Chinese guard at the airdrome was also killed. The Japanese Consul, Okamoto, declared the incident was of a "grave nature" and had been reported to Tokyo for appropriate action. A huge exodus of Chinese residents of the Hongkew and Chapei districts of northern Shanghai began, as a result of rumors that the Japanese were contemplating military action in the next few days. Thousands of Chinese from the country districts to the north of Shanghai poured into the International Settlement and the French Concession.

The situation at Shanghai became rapidly worse. Japanese troops landed at Woosung, ten miles north of Shanghai, and also in the northern or Hongkew section of Shanghai itself. Heavy fighting of a hand-to-hand nature broke out in the northern district of Shanghai when Chinese troops attacked the invading Japanese. The Japanese battleship *Idzumo*, which was regarded by the Chinese as a symbol of Japanese aggression, was moved up the Whangpoo and anchored alongside the Japanese consulate, directly in front of the International Settlement. Japanese naval authorities at Shanghai announced that they would be "compelled to adopt defense measures" because of numerous Chinese acts of aggression, including the murder of the Japanese naval officer and his chauffeur on the evening of August 9. They also announced that they were prepared to take "any necessary steps if the situation was further aggravated."

The Chinese mayor of the city, O. K. Yui, demanded that America and Great Britain prevent Japan from using the northern or Hongkew sections of the city as a base of operations against China. Great Britain requested that Shanghai be excluded from the zone of Japanese-Chinese hostilities, but Japan's answer was that the request was "clearly unacceptable—Britain has asked us to do the impossible." Instead, the Japanese expelled the International Settlement Police, including the British, from the Hongkew section. Japanese bombers had already raided Hangchow, Nanchang, Nanking, Soochow, Chinkiang, and the Shanghai-Nanking Railway. The Chinese had curtailed railway traffic and declared martial law in all cities and districts adjacent to the railroads. At the same time, they ordered the lower Yangtze closed to navigation.

2—Black Saturday

In recalling, as I just have, the mounting tension of those early August days, I am surprised that we in Shanghai were so unprepared for the tragic events of "Black Saturday," August 14, 1937.

The regular issues of the *China Weekly Review* usually contained from forty to sixty pages. I have before me a thin, sickly number of August 21, 1937, of only sixteen pages, greatly reduced in size, and resembling the miniature editions of American magazines put out for United States soldiers abroad; but this issue of the *Review* was so poorly printed that it is difficult to read. Our regular printing plant happened to be in the line of fire between the Chinese and Japanese forces, and the entire printing staff hurriedly evacuated the building and fled to places of safety. It looked as though we, as well as several other papers in the downtown section, might not be able to continue publication. A heavy shell from a Japanese battery had penetrated the composing room of the *North China Daily News,* leading British paper, and caused heavy carnage. A day or two later one of our Chinese printers turned up and told me he had a friend who owned a little printing plant located in a basement somewhere that was not likely to be hit by Japanese bombs. He insisted that his friend could print a small edition on a little hand press. The result was a genuine "underground" edition of the *China Weekly Review.*

In this miniature edition appeared a condensed account of the bombing incidents which resulted in the killing of nearly 2,000 persons and the wounding of some 2,500 more, nearly all being Chinese civilians—men, women and children—and all of them refugees who were fleeing from terrorism created by the Imperial Japanese Army in its invasion of the Shanghai area. Most, but by no means all, of the bombs responsible for this slaughter were dropped by crippled Chinese planes flying over the International Settlement. It was estimated that a million and a half Chinese, most of them farmers, villagers, and factory workers, had fled into the International Settlement, and for many days the streets, roads and bridges leading into the Anglo-American administered area had been jammed with Chinese carrying their worldly possessions, including innumerable children, the great majority seeming to be babes in arms. Chinese charitable organizations had established relief centers at various points in the International Settlement. Bombs falling among the crowds at these congested relief centers or in the vicinity were responsible for the heavy casualties, said to be the greatest among civilians anywhere up to that time.

The worst carnage occurred at a street intersection between the International Settlement and the French Concession, about a mile from the Bund, where some 5,000 refugees had assembled to receive free rice dispensed by an amusement concern known as the "New World." The streets which crossed at this corner were main thoroughfares known as Yu-ya-ching Road and Avenue Edward VII. The traffic light in the center had just turned from green to red when a small motor car with three passengers, a man, woman and little girl, came to a stop, waiting for the traffic light to change. Hearing planes flying low over-head, just skimming the tops of the business buildings, the driver of the car opened the door and stepped out in the street to investigate. Just as his feet touched the ground he uttered a cry, threw up his arms and dropped dead on the pavement. A ma-chine-gun bullet had passed through his heart.

The victim, the first foreigner to be killed in the China-Japan war, was the Reverend Dr. Frank Rawlinson, editor of the *Chinese Recorder*, leading magazine of Protestant missions in China. Dr. Rawlinson was born in England and received his education in the United States, where he became a naturalized citizen. He was the outstanding pacifist in the missionary com-munity in China. He was a strong and fearless opponent of Japanese militarism, and was also opposed to the militarization of China as a means of settling international differences in the Far East. Mrs. Rawlinson and their daughter were stunned at his collapse and, not realizing what had happened, they lifted him into the car and drove to a hospital. The car had just turned the corner when all hell broke loose in the wide crowded plaza at the street intersection behind them.

A Chinese plane, carrying two heavy bombs, had attempted to drop them on the Japanese battleship *Idzumo*, anchored in the Whangpoo harbor directly in front of the downtown section of the city. Before the Chinese plane could get in position for the delicate bombing operation, it was attacked by a Jap fighter. Badly wounded, the Chinese pilot attempted to return to the Hungjao Airdrome on the outskirts of the city, which was still held by the Chinese forces. Realizing his inability to reach the Chinese base with his damaged plane and heavy load, he at-tempted to loose the bombs as he flew over the local race course. But the heavy explosives fell short of their mark by about three hundred yards, striking almost in the center of the plaza, crowded with the normally busy noon-time traffic of Shanghai streets, consisting of motor cars, rickshas, and pedestrians, plus the thousands of Chinese refugees who had gathered there for their free bowls of rice and tea.

The first bomb, exploding as it struck the asphalt street, apparently had detonated the second a few feet above the street level, causing its load of death-dealing explosives to spray across the crowded plaza. Dozens of motor cars and their occupants were riddled with shrapnel or incinerated by their exploding gasoline tanks, while hundreds of pedestrians were dropped in their tracks for a block in all directions. The worst carnage was among the crowd of refugees massed in front of the New World Amusement Center, where the food was being dispensed. Mangled bodies of men, women and children, with most of their clothing burned away, were heaped against the building to a height of five feet.

I was standing on the roof of the American Club, about ten blocks distant, watching the fights between Chinese and Japanese planes when the bombs struck the plaza. The explosion shook the entire city. I hurried to the scene, and for the first time in my extensive coverage of battles, I actually saw human blood running in the gutters. When I got home late that night after covering the story, my shoes, socks, and trousers were caked with blood. I assisted the police and Red Cross in removing numerous charred bodies from motorcars which had been caught as the drivers of the cars moved around the circular island where the traffic signals were located. One car, a Ford, attracted my particular attention, as it was standing within twenty feet of the yawning crater in the asphalt where the bombs had fallen. There were three charred bodies in the car, two in the front seat and one in the rear. The driver, or rather his charred skeleton, sat perfectly erect with the blackened bones of his hands still grasping the wheel. When the bodies were removed from the car, the driver's license, upon which the owner of the car was sitting and which had thus escaped incineration, established his identity as a well known American businessman in Shanghai. The other figures in the car were his wife and the Chinese chauffeur.

After the police and Red Cross workers had finally removed the last truckload of bodies from the scene, they sent back another truck which they loaded with legs and feet which the explosion had severed from the bodies of the victims and scattered over the plaza in grotesque array. Among those killed at this street intersection were ninety Chinese printers out of a staff of one hundred employed by the Seventh Day Adventist mission in the production of their church magazine. The office of the magazine had previously been located in Chinese territory, but it had been moved into the Settlement for safety on the day preceding the bombing.

The other tragic happening of Black Saturday occurred within a few minutes of the first bombing. These bombs, five in number, were also aimed by Chinese aviators, flying Northrop bombers, at the Japanese battleship *Idzumo* in the harbor, but missed their mark by about five hundred yards and crashed into the busiest block of Nanking Road, Shanghai's main street, and directly in front of the city's two leading hotels, the Palace and the Cathay. This street was also crowded with Chinese refugees, several hundred being killed and wounded. Several foreigners were killed and others wounded at this point.

The same afternoon, another bomb struck the roof of the six-story office and warehouse of the United States Navy Purchasing Bureau, also located in the downtown section of the city and only about a block from the American consulate. This bomb, a freak hit, crashed through the concrete roof and five concrete floors and landed on the cement floor of the basement of the building without exploding. It contained the mark of a munitions house in Czechoslovakia. The nationality of the plane which dropped this bomb was never established. Some days later, another high explosive missile, either a bomb from a plane or a shell from a naval gun, struck the fronts of, and seriously damaged,

Shanghai's two largest Chinese department stores. Here the casualties were numerous, both within the crowded stores and in the streets.

Two nights following Black Saturday I was working late in my office when the door opened and an American woman, Mrs. Eleanor B. Roosevelt, wife of Theodore Roosevelt, Jr., entered. She explained that she was visiting in Shanghai and had been horrified by the slaughter of innocent civilians caused by bombs falling in the streets of the city. She wondered if something could be done to induce both combatants to withdraw their troops and naval craft from the borders of the International Settlement. After some discussion Mrs. Roosevelt decided to send telegrams to the leaders of the opposing sides, stating she had personally witnessed "casualties and destruction terrible beyond realization among innocent defenseless peoples," and appealing to them to order a discontinuance of bombings in the Settlement. One telegram was addressed to Madame Chiang Kai-shek, asking her to bring the matter to the immediate attention of the Generalissimo.

We then considered the names of various Japanese leaders to whom the other telegram could be sent. I urged that it be sent directly to Emperor Hirohito, who was personally responsible for the acts of his military commanders, but a local American resident who had accompanied Mrs. Roosevelt to my office said he had discussed the matter with a member of the American Embassy and the fear had been expressed that addressing the telegram directly to Hirohito might be considered "disrespectful."

It was finally decided to address the Japanese telegram to Prince Konoye, the premier. The text of the telegram was as follows:

PRINCE KONOYE, PREMIER OF JAPAN:
I have today telegraphed Madame Chiang Kai-shek that bombing be withheld until arrangements can be made for protection of lives of innocent people in the concessions. On account of the presence within and along the boundaries of the International Settlement of an extraordinary number of Japanese army and naval forces, the

Chinese claim they must take necessary military measures and precautions. I urge your excellency to devise ways and means to neutralize the situation and permit safeguards for non-combatants. I feel I may cable you on account of the evidences of friendship shown me in the past by their Imperial Majesties.

ELEANOR B. ROOSEVELT

(Mrs. Theodore Roosevelt, Jr.)

This telegram had unexpected results, particularly in view of the fact that the Japanese had ignored strong protests by both the American and the British governments. The Japanese never replied to Mrs. Roosevelt's telegram, but the following day the Japanese naval commander ordered the warship *Idzumo* removed from its anchorage in front of the city. The withdrawal of the *Idzumo* removed the chief target of Chinese aviators from proximity to the congested downtown section of the city. The Japanese did, however, continue to fire projectiles from their heavy naval guns over the city, and many residences in the outlying districts were struck. A Japanese plane also dropped an incendiary bomb near one of the United States Fourth Marine barracks, but no injury was done. Other Japanese air bombs were dropped on an American cotton mill which was protected by a contingent of United States Marines, but none was injured.

Madame Chiang Kai-shek in her reply said that the Generalissimo had ordered an investigation of the incidents and had authorized a relief appropriation for the victims.

XXVIII

American Ships, Japanese Bombs, in 1937

AFTER JAPAN'S WAR IN CHINA had been in progress for several months, two young Japanese officers, former schoolmates at the Tokyo Military Academy, met in Nanking, capital of Nationalist China. Nanking had just fallen to the Japanese. The time of the meeting was a few days before Christmas. The young officers were Sub-lieutenants Tashiakai Mukai and Iwao Noda. The meeting of the two officers in the Chinese capital was a matter of considerable popular interest in Japan as their exploits had been heralded, together with their pictures, in the daily editions of the Tokyo *Nichi Nichi Shimbun*, leading newspaper in the Japanese capital.

The following is a brief translation of the account of the meeting of the two Japanese officers in the Chinese capital, which a translator in my office handed me one morning: "After formal bows the two Japanese officers drew their swords and pointed with pride to the badly nicked edges of the long blades. Said Lieutenant Noda, 'I have killed 105—how many have you killed?' Lieutenant Mukai replied, 'Aha-ha, I have killed 106—so sorry!'"

Mukai had won by one on a matter of points, but, the *Nichi Nichi's* correspondent explained, it was impossible to settle the bet between the two officers because there was no way of determining which of the two had passed the 100 mark first; it was therefore decided to call it a tie and extend the competition to determine which officer could first pass the 150 mark, that is, kill 150 Chinese.

The report in the Tokyo *Nichi Nichi* stated that the race "started with renewed vigor December 11 for the goal of 150."

It appeared that the two officers had first met in a night club in Shanghai, when the original bet had been made to determine which of the two could first kill 100 Chinese. It was not specified that the victims had to be Chinese soldiers; as a matter of fact the Chinese army had withdrawn from most of the towns between Shanghai and Nanking, a distance of some 200 miles, through which the Japanese army advanced on its way to Nanking. It was assumed therefore that most of the victims of the competition in mass murder by the two Japanese officers had been Chinese civilians.

Some time after the occupation of Nanking on December 13, 1937, the Japanese army spokesman at Shanghai announced that the army had decided to establish a factory in Shanghai for the repair and reconditioning of swords.

The report of the competition of the two Japanese army officers shed considerable light on the orgy of looting, murder, and rape which took place following the entrance of Japanese troops into the Chinese capital. There had been some looting by the defeated and retreating Chinese troops, and Nanking had experienced serious rioting and disorder, with atrocities against Chinese civilians and foreigners, at the hands of the Communists in 1927, but the residents of the Chinese capital had never experienced such an ordeal as marked the occupation of the city by the Japanese army. Japanese occupation of the native sections of Shanghai and other cities of the lower Yangtze region had been accompanied by murder, looting and the rape of civilians, and the Chinese generally were familiar with the stories of Japanese atrocities in Manchuria, where entire populations of villages had been wiped out and all of the houses looted and burned by the Japanese because the villagers were accused of harboring guerrillas.

The rape of Nanking was almost like that of Carthage in the barbarity shown to its inhabitants. The accounts of foreign missionaries, many of whom had witnessed the atrocities, and even obtained pictures of them, indicated that there was a collapse of all discipline among a considerable section of the Japanese forces. It seemed as though all of the pent-up hatred for foreigners with which the Japanese army had been indoctrinated by years of teaching and training in brutality burst forth in an orgy of terrorism following the occupation of the city. An authenticated report by an international group of foreign missionaries stated that large numbers of Chinese civilians were wantonly shot or bayonetted and left to die in the streets. People who attempted to flee the city were rounded up, robbed and machine-gunned indiscriminately. So-called safety zones which were created and supervised by missionaries were invaded by Japanese soldiers during the reign of terror, which continued for several days. Large numbers of men were bound together and shot in bunches, or their clothing was saturated with kerosene and they were burned to death as human torches.

The Japanese charged that the Chinese victims were soldiers who had discarded their uniforms for civilian attire and were trying to escape from the city. Japanese soldiers singled out 400 males of various ages from one refugee safety zone, which was supervised by Christian missionaries, and marched them outside the city wall in groups of fifty, to be mowed down by machine guns. Other Chinese were tied to posts and used as dummies for bayonet practice. Japanese soldiers invaded the premises of mission schools and seized Chinese women and girls, who were dragged away. Not a single prisoner was taken by the Japanese army. Japan's propaganda that her sole purpose was to "liberate" the Chinese people was made to mean in actual practice their "liquidation." John Allison, an American consular official who accompanied a missionary to the Japanese army headquarters for the purpose of urging the Japanese commander to control his rioting troops, was slapped and insulted by the Japanese sentry at the gates of the compound. Most of the private homes in the city were plundered, and refugees passing through the city gates were robbed of their meager possessions.

I inspected numerous photographs snapped in mission hospitals showing Chinese with deep gashes in their heads, necks, shoulders, and arms caused by Japanese soldiers, who were putting into practice an ancient and popular Japanese military exercise in which soldiers, wearing heavy leather headgear, wire masks and shoulder guards, beat each other over the heads with heavy clubs until they drop from exhaustion. I had frequently watched these exercises at Japanese barracks in Manchuria and in Japan, and marveled at the ability of the soldiers to stand such brutality. I did not realize that the exercise would ultimately be put to practical use with real swords against unarmed civilians. I saw one picture, taken by a missionary doctor, of a Chinese man who had a deep crease across the back of his neck where a Japanese officer had struck him with his sword. Luckily the sword was dull; almost miraculously the spinal cord had not been severed, and the man lived.

I also saw numerous pictures snapped by the Japanese themselves, showing Chinese being beheaded by Japanese soldiers, and I possessed one revolting picture of a Chinese woman who had been raped by two Japanese soldiers who were shown in the picture standing by the body of their victim. The Japanese have a weakness for photographing each other, and could not resist photographing even their own barbarous acts. I obtained the prints from a Korean photograph shop in Shanghai, where the films had been sent to be developed. The soldiers apparently wanted the prints to send to their friends at home in Japan. Japanese soldiers seemingly had no feeling whatsoever that their inhuman actions transgressed the tenets of modern warfare or common everyday morals.

There have been two occasions since Japan abrogated the Four-Power Naval Limitations Treaty when it is possible that Japan might have been brought to terms without resort to arms on the part of the United States and the other Powers which were parties to the Washington Arms Limitation treaties. The first was in September, 1931, when the so-called Kwantung (Manchurian) faction in the Imperial Japanese Army staged the coup d'état or Mukden Incident, and invaded China's Manchurian provinces. On that occasion governmental leaders at

Tokyo were so fearful that the United States would take action to enforce the treaties which guaranteed China's territorial integrity, that they went to great lengths to disarm suspicion and criticism by the American people. Large sums of money were expended in propaganda and in other ways to influence public opinion and prevent Washington from taking a strong stand. Their efforts were so successful that we even continued our shipments of war materials to Japan.

One of the most effective propagandists for Japan was an American, a former teacher and newspaperman of Honolulu named Henry W. Kinney, who was employed by the South Manchuria Railway at Dairen, Manchuria. Kinney made a trip to the United States, following the Manchurian Incident, and interviewed editors, columnists and radio commentators. Following his return he made a long written report to his Japanese superiors in which he listed those who had expressed sentiment favorable to Japan's policy of aggression. Unfortunately for Kinney his confidential report fell into the hands of an American, who turned it over to me. I published it—it still makes interesting reading, particularly the list of pro-Japanese publicists, though more than a dozen years have elapsed. After the Japanese discovered the leak they gave Kinney an extended vacation, which he was still spending with his Japanese wife on the French island of Tahiti in the South Pacific when the war broke out.

Many influential citizens urged our Government not to take a strong stand, in the mistaken belief that pacifically inclined civilian elements in the Japanese Government might be able to get the upper hand over the military. Even Ambassador Joseph C. Grew at Tokyo recommended a moderate policy, in the belief that a strong stand by Washington might provoke the Japanese militarists to an "even more intransigent attitude."

The second time when a strong stand on the part of the United States Government might have forced a change in Japanese policy was when the Japanese deliberately bombed, machine-gunned and sank the United States gunboat *Panay* in the

Yangtze River above Nanking in December, 1937. Instead, the weak, vacillating policy of our State Department encouraged the Japanese to play fast and loose with Americans and their interests in the Far East, and ultimately encouraged the Japanese militarists to plot the sneak attack on Pearl Harbor four years later.

Americans in Shanghai and Nanking had a private joke which they repeated to each other, usually in low tones if a non-American was within hearing. The joke was brief but very much to the point: "Did you know that Ambassador Nelson T. Johnson now lists the expenses of the American Embassy at Nanking as 'running expenses'?" The wisecrack had a special meaning for Americans because it exemplified the unusual activities of the American Embassy staff at Nanking for several weeks prior to the Japanese occupation of the Chinese capital. Documentary dispatches exchanged between Ambassador Johnson at Nanking and the State Department covering this period have not been published, but most persons were aware of the fact that the American Ambassador was worried as much by his instructions from the State Department as he was by the aggressive attitude of the Japanese. As soon as the Japanese began to direct their attention toward the Chinese capital at Nanking, following their occupation of Shanghai, Ambassador Johnson employed a Chinese contractor to dig a bomb-proof shelter in the small rectangular garden which faced the Embassy offices and quarters of the staff. The shelter aroused considerable interest in diplomatic circles because of its elaborate interior fittings and the fact that it was the first to be built in Nanking. Descriptions and pictures of it were forwarded to the Secretary of State, but those in Washington who were responsible for the protection of American interests and prestige in the Far East were not satisfied. They feared the shelter would furnish insufficient protection, and they wanted nothing to happen that could possibly involve the United States with Japan. Ambassador Johnson was therefore instructed to take extraordinary precautions against being hit by Japanese missiles.

As a result he instructed the commander of the United States Yangtze Patrol to station a couple of small river patrol boats, including the *Panay*, at the Nanking jetty, a short distance from the Embassy premises. Whenever word was flashed from Shanghai that Japanese bombers were on their way to blast Nanking, the entire Embassy staff, consisting of secretaries, Consuls, Vice-Consuls, and stenographers, led by the Ambassador, would sprint to the jetty, board the gunboats, and steam, under forced draught, upstream. After they had proceeded a few miles, the boats would anchor in mid-stream and wait until they received word that all was clear, then they would return to their quarters at the Embassy. In order that there could be no mistake about the overpowering desire of great and powerful America to avoid all suspicion of courting danger, the American Embassy supplied both the Japanese army and navy with detailed maps showing the exact location of the Embassy, the river gunboats, and the exact point on the Yangtze where the boats bearing the Ambassador and his staff were to be anchored on each trip. Also, large American flags were painted on the top decks and awnings of the boats, which were clearly visible from the air.

The near panic at the American Embassy soon spread to the other foreign embassies, even to the Germans, who arranged to travel up the river on British ships. Finally word came that the Japanese were planning a mass bombing attack on the Chinese capital, using bombers based in Formosa and which they had purchased in the United States. As soon as I heard the report I arranged with another correspondent, Victor Keen of the *New York Herald Tribune*, and Joseph Pearson, president of Press Wireless, to make the trip to Nanking to see the show. At midnight we slipped around the Japanese lines in my Ford car, and by driving all night over terrible roads we managed to reach Nanking before noon of the day the Japanese had selected for the bombing.

Nanking was a dead city so far as the streets and shops were concerned, as the civilian population had either fled or gone into hiding. We immediately drove to the American Embassy, which we also found completely deserted except for one secretary, J. Hall Paxton, who was born in China of missionary parents and had joined the consular service several years before, after his graduation from college in the United States. Paxton told us that other members of the staff had hurriedly departed at daylight on the daily trip up the Yangtze in order to avoid injury by Japanese bombs. Paxton added: "But damned if I'm going to run away from the little . . ." Ambassador Johnson, however, was not there that day, as he and most of the staff had departed for Hankow, about six hundred miles west of Nanking, where the National Government was planning to transfer its headquarters. I had lunch with Paxton, which was prepared by his Chinese cook and house boy who also had remained on the job. After luncheon I drove to the building of the Chinese Officers' Moral Welfare Association, a sort of Chinese army Y.M.C.A., where I interviewed Generalissimo and Madame Chiang Kai-shek. I asked the Generalissimo what he thought of the action of the American Ambassador in running away every time there was a rumor of a Japanese bombing. He smiled, shrugged his shoulders, and replied, "You see, we are still here."

We remained in Nanking all afternoon awaiting the Japanese bombing attack, but it didn't happen that day, and since important developments were expected at Shanghai, we decided to return to that city immediately, leaving shortly after dark by a roundabout road in order to avoid the Japanese troops who were then consolidating their position in preparation for the advance on Nanking. Fortunately for us they had not yet entirely encircled Shanghai.

Shortly after daylight we ran into the worst mudhole I have ever seen. A section of the highway for about a mile had been converted into a loblolly three to four feet deep. Heavy military trucks had cut the road into a series of deep parallel ruts resembling trenches. Numerous cars and trucks preceding us had driven into the morass in the hope of getting through, but had mired down helplessly in the soft earth. Fortunately, before leaving Nanking I had purchased several feet of rope in a Chinese store, thinking that I might find some use for it. It was lucky I had brought along the rope, and it was also lucky that I had a bright new Chinese ten-dollar bill in my pocket. Noticing a number of Chinese farmers, men, women, and children, in a field watching the show, I waved the ten-dollar bill and asked them to pull us out of the mud. They responded immediately and with enthusiasm, and some twenty men, women, and children, accompanied by much "heigh-hoing" and singing, pulled us out of the mudhole to dry ground in short order. But while we were in the midst of it someone yelled, "Jap planes coming," and they were—a whole squadron of heavy Japanese bombers. We dropped everything and dived into the nearest ditches. Since more than a dozen large Chinese army trucks and as many more cars were stuck in the mud, we provided an excellent target. But the Jap bomber pilots paid no attention to us—they were on a more important mission, the bombing of Nanking.

We had missed the bombing of Nanking, and wondered if the remaining members of the Embassy staff had managed to escape. After the Japanese bombers had passed and our Ford had been dragged to dry ground, there was a tremendous outcry among the Chinese truck drivers and occupants of other motorcars who charged us with demoralizing coolie labor by paying them $10—whereas $1 would have been sufficient, in their opinion. Since the foreigners had paid the farmers $10, they obviously would not work for the Chinese for a lower price, as such action would cause a "loss of face." I was told that $10 remained the standard price for pulling victims out of that particular mudhole.

On the afternoon of December 12, the U.S.S. *Panay* was bombed, machine-gunned and sunk by Japanese planes, together with a small tanker, the *Mei-an*, and two launches belonging to the Socony Vacuum Company. The bombing occurred while the boats were anchored in the stream about twenty-five miles above Nanking, adjacent to the village of Hohsien, where they had proceeded in accordance with State Department instructions. The bombing of the ships and subsequent machine-gunning of launches carrying survivors ashore resulted in the killing and wounding of several naval officers, servicemen, and civilians, including the captains of the two larger ships.

A few hours before the bombing of the American ships at Hohsien other Japaneses forces attacked two British river gunboats, the *Ladybird* and the *Bee*, and five British river steamers, the *Suiwo, Tsing-teh, Tuckwo, Wangtu* and *Tatung*. All of the British ships were clearly marked with large painted replicas of the Union Jack. Several British naval ratings and civilians were killed and wounded, as the British boats not only were bombed from the air, but also were shelled by Japanese shore batteries. The British ships at the time were anchored in the Yangtze off the town of Wuhu, about fifty miles above Nanking. Wuhu was the headquarters of Colonel Kingoro Hashimoto, commander of the Japanese troops in this region. Hashimoto's first anti-American gesture upon arriving at Wuhu had been to remove the American flag from the gateway of the American mission compound, tear it into shreds and trample it on the ground with his hob-nailed boots.

Among the casualties on the American ships was a widely known Italian, Sandro Sandri, special correspondent of the well known Italian newspaper, *La Stampa*, published at Turin. Previously Mr. Sandri had been correspondent for Mussolini's personal paper, the *Popolo d'Italia* of Milan. Sandri had taken the lead in the organization of the branch of the Italian Fascist Party at Shanghai. He was aboard the *Panay*, was struck by both shrapnel and machine-gun bullets, and died the following day. Near casualties on one of the British ships, the *Wangtu*, were several members of the German Embassy at Nanking. None was hit by Japanese shells, but the boat was so badly damaged that it was necessary to transfer the German diplomats to a British gunboat. As a result of these incidents the Italian and German governments both lodged protests with the Japanese Government at Tokyo, despite the fact that both countries were in alliance with the Japanese and were members of the Anti-Comintern Pact.

There was a curious reaction in Washington when Hiroshi Saito, the Japanese Ambassador, appeared at the State Department early on the morning of December 13, only a few hours after the incident, tendered the apologies of the Japanese Government, and offered to make restitution. Except for a brief radio flash, the State Department had as yet received no details of the incident. Ambassador Saito admitted that "since the Japanese had been informed of the position of the American ships, the bombing of the *Panay* was a grave blunder . . . of course it was completely accidental and a great mistake." He was very sorry!

Admiral Harry E. Yarnell, commander-in-chief of the United States Asiatic Fleet, who was in Shanghai, acted immediately, in confident expectation that the Government would take a strong stand on the sinking of the *Panay*, and canceled the sailing orders of the United States cruiser *Augusta*, which was anchored in Shanghai harbor. The ship had previously been ordered to proceed to Manila. Admiral Yarnell also repudiated a statement, allegedly made by the Japanese naval spokesman, that all American naval craft would be withdrawn from the Yangtze River. He declared, "United States naval vessels are in Chinese waters for the protection of American citizens, and will remain here as long as the necessity exists." Admiral Yarnell said further that if the Japanese demanded the withdrawal of American ships from China waters, the demand would be ignored.

But Admiral Yarnell's stand was not supported by Washington. The Senate launched upon an involved debate concerning the withdrawal or non-withdrawal of all American gunboats and forces from the Orient, and there were charges that Great Britain was trying to get the United States "to pull her chestnuts out of the fire in China." One Senator declared, "If Japan has accepted the responsibility and apologized, there is nothing more the United States can do about it." Senator Key Pittman made the only logical suggestion, that the United States Government should demand that all Japanese army and navy officers concerned in the bombing and machine-gunning of the *Panay* and other American ships should be punished. He pointed out that the series of "accidents" to neutrals was becoming intolerable, and that there was little satisfaction in having the Japanese Government express regret on each occasion. Senator Pittman pointed out that it was the practice of the Japanese Government to grant broad discretionary powers to its army and navy commanders in the field, "hence the United States Government should obtain the names of the high Japanese officers who were responsible for the outrages and demand that they be punished." He declared that only such punishment would demonstrate the good faith of the Japanese, and would halt the series of violations of international law. He pointed out that the Japanese Government had subjected itself to the suspicion that such incidents were deliberate and were designed to frighten neutrals into withdrawing all representatives and nationals from China.

But the Administration took no such determined stand. It only demanded an apology and compensation and a guarantee against repetition, which the Japanese Government, through Ambassador Saito, had already offered to carry out voluntarily. There was no demand for punishment even of the chief culprit, Colonel Kingoro Hashimoto, the army commander at Wuhu, who was allegedly responsible for the outrage. The issue was further confused by President Roosevelt's personal insistence that the American note be presented directly to Emperor Hirohito. This, Koki Hirota, the Japanese Foreign Minister, refused to do, and there was considerable puzzlement in the Far East as to who had thought of this strange diplomatic gesture. In Tokyo, Ambassador Joseph C. Grew was described as being deeply touched by the sight of Japanese school children soliciting pennies on the streets adjacent to the United States Embassy, with which to purchase a nice new gunboat to replace the *Panay*, when as a matter of plain fact the Japanese Government quibbled a long time over the matter of paying for the sunken *Panay* and finally, when the Japanese could no longer sidestep the issue, they offered to construct a ship in a Japanese dockyard and present it to the United States. This offer, of course, was refused by the Navy Department.

The responsibility of Colonel Kingoro Hashimoto, commander of the Japanese troops stationed at Wuhu in Anhwei Province, for the bombing of the U.S.S. *Panay* and other American ships, as well as the shelling of the British ships, was disclosed in the course of a controversy between the Japanese army and navy spokesmen over the incident. The Japanese military attaché in China, General Kumakichi Harada, in the course of a press conference at Shanghai, went to great lengths to disavow any connection on the part of the Imperial Japanese Army with either the air bombing of the American ships or the machine-gunning and shelling of both American and British ships by Japanese troops on the banks of the Yangtze. As a result of General Harada's attempt, by implication, to place sole responsibility on the Japanese navy, the Japanese naval spokesman made some sensational disclosures regarding Colonel Hashimoto and his army connections.

It appeared that the Colonel, who had previously served as Japanese military attaché in France and Turkey, had been involved as one of the leaders in the February 26, 1936, army rebellion in Tokyo. On that occasion Hashimoto denied that he was either fascist or socialist, but claimed that he represented the "new spirit in the Far East," the chief objective of which was to eliminate all American and British influence from Asia. He denied that he had any connection with the bombing of the *Panay*, but it was disclosed that he had issued orders to the Japanese troops to fire on all ships on the Yangtze "regardless of nationality," despite the fact that he had been advised of the locations of the American and British boats. The actual shelling of the British boats and the machine-gunning of the sinking *Panay*, as well as the launches carrying survivors ashore from the *Panay*, apparently was ordered by one of Colonel Hashi-

moto's subordinates, allegedly in the belief that they were con-
voying ships loaded with Chinese troops.

The Japanese army authorities at first charged that the *Panay*
had fired on Japanese troops along the banks of the Yangtze,
but when this was disproved and the Japanese authorities were
presented with indisputable evidence that the *Panay* and other
American ships had been both bombed and machine-gunned by
Japanese planes, the Japanese naval authorities admitted their
responsibility. Some days later they announced that Rear Admiral Teizo Mitsunami, chief of aerial operations, had been
recalled from China and would be relieved of his post. The Navy
Department also stated that it would "punish" all naval fliers
implicated in the bombing of the *Panay*. The Japanese army
authorities finally apologized to the British for firing on the
British ships, claiming that they had mistaken them for a convoy
transferring Generalissimo Chiang Kai-shek's troops from Nanking to Hankow, following the Chinese withdrawal from Nanking and transference of the seat of government to Hankow.

Survivors from the ill-fated *Panay* did not arrive in Shanghai
until December 17, five days after the sinking of the ship. They
were brought down the river aboard the British gunboat *Ladybird* and the U.S.S. *Oahu*, a sister ship of the *Panay*, which had
been anchored at Nanking and had not been damaged. The seriously wounded were immediately transferred to local hospitals,
while the less seriously wounded were carried on stretchers
aboard the *Augusta*, flagship of the United States Asiatic fleet,
where they received treatment by naval physicians.

The bombing and shelling of the American and British ships
and the arrival of the survivors, including wounded, and the
flag-draped coffins of those who were killed, created a deep
impression on Shanghai's international community. The seriousness of the outrage and its international significance were attested
by the large number of correspondents, representing practically
every important newspaper and press association in the world,
who were present in Shanghai to report the story. Among the

few newspapermen who were aboard the *Panay* at the time of the bombing and thus obtained a first-hand eye-witness account, was Jim Marshall of *Colliers*, but Jim was in no condition to report the story, as he was seriously wounded in the shoulder and throat by Japanese shrapnel.

The most complete and connected account of the attack, showing unmistakably that it was deliberate, was given by a young Annapolis graduate, Lieutenant John Willard Geist, who was aboard the *Panay* at the time of the incident and accompanied the survivors on the long trek along the river bank at night until they were picked up several hours later by the surviving American and British boats. Lieutenant Geist said the *Panay* was bombed by two flights of Japanese planes, the first consisting of three planes and the second of six planes. He said the first Jap bombs were dropped with remarkable accuracy from an altitude of approximately 7,000 feet. Practically all of the bombs either hit their mark or fell so near as to cause serious damage to the ships. The second Japanese flight flew lower and machine-gunned the sinking ships as well as the lifeboats bearing the survivors ashore.

XXIX

Working for "The Trib"

DECEMBER 17, 1937, THE DAY ON WHICH the *Panay* survivors landed at Shanghai, was a memorable one for another reason in the Shanghai office of the *Chicago Tribune*, where the brass sign bearing the slogan, "World's Greatest Newspaper," had hung so long that the metal was nearly worn through by the polishing given it by the office coolie.

Aside from editing my own paper in Shanghai, I had served on occasion as correspondent for leading American and British papers and press associations throughout most of my residence in the Far East. Among the papers I represented for considerable periods were the *Manchester Guardian*, leading liberal paper in Great Britain; the *Daily Herald*, London, organ of the British Labor Party; and the *Chicago Tribune*, owned by Colonel Robert R. McCormick, outstanding exponent of isolationism in the United States. I also cooperated on various occasions with the correspondents of the *New York Herald Tribune* and the Associated Press in covering important events when it was impossible for one correspondent to be in two places at the same time.

For several years I represented the *Chicago Tribune* and the *Manchester Guardian* simultaneously, which prompted one newspaper friend to inquire how it was possible for me to cover developments in such a controversial field as China for two newspapers which in their policies were as far apart as the two poles. My reply was that I never gave much thought to the matter of policy of a paper when I was covering a story, but always tried to the best of my ability to get the underlying facts and leave the interpretation to the editorial staff. I do not remember ever having any of my dispatches altered because they did not conform to the policy of the paper. However, the editors, on occasion, took issue with me in the editorial columns.

My connection with the *Chicago Tribune* dated from my first trip to old Peking in 1917, when the Japanese presented their second ultimatum to the Chinese Government concerning the so-called Twenty-one Demands. At that time I received a cable from Edward S. Beck, managing editor of the *Chicago Tribune*, asking me to cover the story. I had been in China only a few months, and had never written a newspaper cable in my life, but Mr. Beck apparently liked my story, as he displayed it on the first page under a banner head. Several weeks later I received a check for $25, and thus began a connection with the *Chicago Tribune* which lasted, with a few intermissions, for nearly twenty years.

On a part-time basis at first, I later became the *Tribune's* regular foreign correspondent in China. During the long era of China's civil wars, the brief war between China and Russia in 1929, Japan's intervention in Manchuria in 1931, my trips through Russia, and the early months of war between China and Japan in 1937, I filed regular dispatches and sent mail stories to Chicago. Since the difference in time between Shanghai and Chicago is about twelve hours, it was necessary for me to do most of my work at night, and in consequence I became the chief night-owl among the foreign correspondents, frequently not getting to bed before three or four o'clock in the morning for long periods. For several years I was the oldest man, in point of service, on the *Tribune's* foreign staff, and had I remained on the staff a few months longer I would have been eligible for retirement on pension.

I was the only man on the foreign staff of the *Tribune* who had never worked in the home office in Chicago, hence was spared contact with office politics except by hearsay. Occasionally a correspondent would pass through Shanghai with the latest gossip and advice on "how to get on with the Colonel." Floyd Gibbons, ace *Tribune* man in World War I (where he lost an eye), was in the Far East on several occasions and used to advise me by the hour, usually in some hotel bar. Once in Mukden, after several drinks, Floyd got down to fundamentals and told me how to be a success with the *Tribune*. "You must always 'write down'—don't be 'intellectual,' the people who buy the *Tribune* in Chicago don't understand or give a damn about Far Eastern politics—they want hot stories about battles and bandits." I soon learned, however, that my not having worked on the local staff in Chicago resulted in a serious handicap, as my salary was always lower than that of other correspondents who had previously worked on the local staff.

On the morning of December 17, 1937, Captain Corpening, personal representative of Colonel Robert R. McCormick, arrived in Shanghai from Chicago by Pan-American Clipper with instructions to close up all *Tribune* offices in China. I had been apprised by cable of Captain Corpening's impending arrival and the purpose of his trip, but I was completely in the dark as to the reason for the sudden decision. Corpening was sitting on the edge of his bed eating his breakfast when I burst forth:

"Why in heaven's name is the *Tribune* closing its offices in China at this time? Here is the *Panay* case, China and Japan are already at war, and real world news is beginning to break in Asia."

Looking up, he said between bites, "The Colonel thinks China is no longer important as a source of news—he says China will soon be taken over by the Japs—hence the *Tribune* will cover China news from Tokyo in future."

My knees suddenly became so weak I slumped into a chair. All I could do was repeat, "But this is no time to wind up."

While we were talking, a cable arrived, addressed to Corpening. It was from the Colonel, instructing him to "Cover the *Panay*." The *Tribune* had just received the advance cables from A.P. telling of the expected arrival in Shanghai of the *Panay* survivors.

Passing the cable to me, Captain Corpening said, "You come along."

"But I have been fired," I exclaimed.

"Oh, don't worry about that—I'll see you are taken care of," he replied. The captain then became communicative and told me he was the only man in the whole *Tribune* organization who could enter the Colonel's quarters at any hour, day or night.

Later, after we had gone to the Shanghai Country Hospital to interview the *Panay* survivors, I discovered why Captain Corpening wanted me to accompany him. We first approached Frank H. Vines, an official of the British-American Tobacco Company from Roanoke, Va., who had been aboard the oil tanker *Mei-an* when it was bombed and whose arm had been paralyzed by the concussion of the Jap bomb which had sent the tanker, along with the *Panay*, to an ignominious grave in the mud of the Yangtze. I naturally stood back in order to permit Corpening to conduct the interview, but Corpening motioned me to go ahead. As we were leaving the hospital, he explained: "You know, I never interviewed anybody in my life."

Corpening told me that he had never had any newspaper experience other than serving as Colonel McCormick's personal assistant and secretary.

That night I went back to the office. The habit of staying up until 2 or 3 o'clock in the morning for practically twenty years was too strong to be broken off at once. About midnight Corpening came in, sat down at one of the office typewriters and after several minutes pecked out a few words on a cable blank which he handed me. He had written exactly three lines. I've forgotten the wording, but I glanced at it and exclaimed, "For goodness' sake, the *Panay* story is worth more than that."

He took the cable, tore it up and said, "You go ahead and write it, I'll take care of you."

I wrote the *Panay* story and filed it. It made Page 1—under Corpening's name, of course. Captain Corpening remained in Shanghai for a couple of days while we closed up the *Tribune* office and took down the old brass sign. It's surprising how quickly the outward evidence of twenty years of work can be eliminated. Colonel McCormick paid me three months' salary in advance.

The last I heard of Captain Corpening was a couple of weeks later when he turned up in Hankow, then the temporary seat of the National Government, where he tried to hire a special train from the Chinese authorities in order to "visit the fighting front." The Chinese demurred—they had never rented a train. Corpening assured the Chinese that the *Chicago Tribune* "could afford to buy the entire train outright if necessary." The Chinese finally made him understand that both of the railways out of Hankow had been cut and he couldn't get within five hundred miles of any front even if he had a half dozen trains. Corpening finally left China in disgust.

From 1937 on, for four years—up to the day and hour of the sneak attack on Pearl Harbor, the *Chicago Tribune* covered the Far East with one correspondent—Kimpei Sheba, a Japanese, stationed in Tokyo. Sheba was born in Honolulu, hence was technically an American citizen.

XXX

The Pressure Increases

DESPITE THE COMPARATIVE SAFETY of the International Settlement and the French Concession, where most British and Americans resided, Japanese pressure began seriously to be felt in 1938. The Japanese were in control of the entire territory about the city, and in addition had a large army within the northern or Hongkew section of the city. This meant that the Settlement authorities were no longer able to collect taxes or other revenues in this district, which previously had been their chief source of revenue, owing to the location there of most of the city's manufacturing enterprises.

Another cause of serious worry to the American and British administrators of the Settlement was the fact that the municipal power plant and water works were located within the Japanese area, hence the Japanese had the power to strangle the Settlement at any time by cutting off these facilities. And a constant source of trouble and annoyance was the Japanese military patrol, placed on the main bridge connecting the two sections of the city. All cars, trucks, and pedestrians were stopped and searched, and their Chinese chauffeurs had to dismount from the cars and bow almost double to the Japanese guards. Any chauffeur who refused was beaten and detained. Heavy toll was exacted on every load of material sent into or transported from the Japanese area. Most of this graft went to Japanese army and naval officers.

Shanghai University, one of the largest educational institutions in the Yangtze Valley, which was operated under the auspices of the American Baptist Mission, was closed and looted by the Japanese. Another Chinese educational institution, Kwanghua University, was completely destroyed, as also was Shanghai

Labor University, established following the 1927 revolution. Another Chinese school, Fuhtan University, established by a well known educator, Dr. John Y. Lee, was taken over and used by the Japanese as headquarters for the army staff. St. John's University, the oldest educational institution established by the American Episcopal Mission, was likewise closed, but later permitted to resume. Japanese soldiers paid regular inspection trips to dormitories and class-rooms.

The chief defender of foreign interests in the midst of these developments was an American citizen named Stirling Fessenden, who occupied the post of secretary-general of the International Settlement, a position resembling that of city manager in the United States. Fessenden was elected chairman of the Municipal Council of the International Settlement in the early 1920's, and was familiarly known as "Lord Mayor" of the city for nearly two decades. He was finally forced to resign, in 1939, as a result of failing eyesight.

Fessenden was born at Fort Fairfield, Maine, and after graduation from Bowdoin College he went to Shanghai as a young law school graduate in 1904 on a mission for the old American Trading Company of New York. He remained to become an important figure in the hectic politics of the International Settlement, wherein lived almost half of Shanghai's 3,500,000 people, including nearly 100,000 foreigners of various nationalities. Fessenden had a wide acquaintance in both the foreign and the Chinese communities and, of particular importance, enjoyed their confidence and respect. During the long period of anti-foreign agitations beginning in 1925, Fessenden was the only foreign official in Shanghai who was in constant contact with the Chinese leaders. On no less than three occasions he was credited with "saving" the Settlement from possible occupation by hostile Chinese factions. The most serious threat was in 1927, when he blocked the Communists' attempt to take over the Settlement. On another occasion he blocked an attempt of the Diplomatic Body in Peiping to "take over" the Settlement and abolish its elective form of government. The Peiping diplomats failed because they were no match for the Yankee lawyer, who knew more about the legal status of the Settlement than any other foreigner there. He had also the happy faculty of knowing when to compromise with Chinese Nationalist sentiment, which resented foreign activities within the country.

In 1938 Fessenden outwitted the Japanese when they attempted to stuff the ballot boxes at the annual election. The Japanese brought in a horde of new residents and provided them with credentials for voting in the annual election. Just what happened was never explained, but the Occidentals won out by a narrow margin. There were whispers of "Tammany tactics," and the Japanese claimed that several ballot boxes containing their votes were never opened.

When Fessenden retired from the municipal government in 1939, the Municipal Council gave him a tax-free residence for the rest of his life, but since he had antagonized the Japanese, they retaliated, after they took over the Settlement following Pearl Harbor, by evicting him from his house, and forcing him to live in a squalid Russian boarding house. He had become blind and was looked after by friendly Chinese servants, who remained with him until the end. He died tragically of a heart ailment on September 20, 1943, the day following the sailing of the exchange ship *Gripsholm*. He was sixty-eight years old. He was offered an opportunity to return on the *Gripsholm*, but knowing the end was near, he preferred to die in Shanghai, rather than at sea.

The Japanese always contended that the Americans and Europeans never granted them an adequate voice in the administration of the International Settlement; but when the Japanese by forceful measures obtained the upper hand, their control did not contribute to peace, order, or public welfare. It had all the earmarks of a marauding expedition designed to squeeze the last dollar out of the community and permanently to demoralize the population.

Early in 1939 I made a survey of gambling and narcotic dens which had been established on the borders of the International Settlement following the advent of the Japanese army. It was found that there were 125 institutions of this character which had been opened since the occupation of the territory by the Imperial Japanese Army. This populous area, corresponding to the suburban district of any large and growing American city, was administered by the so-called "S.S.S." (Special Service Section) of the Japanese fighting forces. The Japanese-controlled section was separated from the areas administered by the Anglo-Americans and the French by streets only; hence it was often difficult to determine exactly where the International Settlement and the French Concession ended and the Japanese-administered areas began.

The first of these Japanese "institutions of culture" which sprang up within a few weeks after the Japanese occupation were gambling houses with opium dens attached. They were operated either by Chinese of the criminal type who claimed to be adherents of the Wang Ching-wei puppet government, or by Japanese ronin, a type of gangster formerly in the entourage of the daimyos or feudal barons. The Japanese military police who patrolled the area at first made an effort to close the dens, but the S.S.S. quickly stepped in and created a so-called "Shanghai Supervised Amusement Department."

Gambling houses, opium-smoking and heroin-dispensing dens, and houses of prostitution grew up like proverbial mushrooms. Most of the places, in addition to the payment of a heavy license fee, were taxed at the rate of $150 a day for medium-sized institutions, with higher prices running up to $500 a day for the more elaborate "palaces." The walls of the alley-ways and streets adjacent to entrances of the resorts were plastered with advertising posters, while the more imposing places used neon signs. Each den had its own armed guards, most of them gunmen of the lowest types. Nights became hideous as a result of fights between gangs employed by rival houses, and there were frequent assassinations. One imposing institution, which carried the

name of "Hollywood," boasted that it had an "army" consisting
of 400 armed guards. The Hollywood house was located on
property belonging to Wang Ching-wei, the Japanese puppet.
Battles between armed guards of the rival houses frequently approached the seriousness of small wars.

There was considerable curiosity as to the origin of the
vast amount of gambling paraphernalia which suddenly appeared from nowhere, until it was discovered that an enterprising Japanese had established a factory where roulette wheels,
chuck-a-luck and fan-tan apparatus were manufactured. Considerable equipment also was purchased from a thriving gambling
institution which had been operated for years on the border
between British Kowloon and Chinese territory near Canton.
Many of the Cantonese previously connected with the Canton
gambling houses, all of whom claimed to be adherents of Wang
Ching-wei, flocked to Shanghai and were associated with the
Japanese ronin in operating the gambling houses and narcotic
dens in Shanghai. Many of the houses had previously been residences owned by foreigners who had been forced to move out
of the district. But the foreign residences were soon found to be
inadequate, and new buildings of flimsy materials were erected
almost overnight. Most of these houses consisted of large gambling rooms surrounded by smaller rooms, or cubicles, containing
opium-smoking divans.

Since the International Settlement had for many years pro-
hibited gambling and dealings in narcotics, the large native
population soon found itself almost overwhelmed with opportunities to indulge in all forms of commercialized vice without fear
of police interference. A few foreigners, not subject to exterri-
torial control by their own consular officials, also participated in
the operation of gambling houses, but they soon became involved
in complications with the Japanese, who had no desire or intention of permitting Europeans to cut in on the vice racket. One
foreigner, a Hungarian named Joe Farren, for a time operated
a fashionable gambling establishment in the residence district,
but he ultimately had complications with the Japanese military

and was sent to the notorious Bridge House Political Prison, where he committed suicide by hanging himself from one of the bars of his cell.

Along with these manifestations of Japanese enterprise there was a simultaneous introduction of the so-called Central China Religious League, the announced purpose of which was to unite all the religious sects of Asia into one composite group under Japanese direction. Protestant and Catholic missionaries were "invited" to participate in this movement, the leader of which was a Japanese Christian, the Reverend Sabrow Yasumura. Reverend Yasumura announced that he was delegated by the Japanese Government to open a central office through which all communications between Occidental missionaries and Chinese Christians should be transmitted. He declared that Japan's objective was to "build a strong and stable China and lay down new foundations for peace in East Asia in accordance with the spirit of imperial Japan." He exclaimed, "It is high time for all of us to lead the war-stricken Chinese masses, and strive for the spiritual advancement of China." The Japanese papers said that the Reverend Yasumura had arranged for some six hundred Japanese Christians and Buddhists to come to China to take over the work formerly conducted by Occidental missionaries. He announced that all Chinese Christian churches, Buddhist temples, and monasteries were to be taken over by the new Japanese-directed Central China Religious League.

All forms of Chinese business were taken over and reorganized into cartels coordinated with similar industries in Japan. For example, all communication facilities, including the foreign radio companies, the Chinese telephone and telegraph, were taken over and reorganized into the Japanese-controlled Central China Tele-Communications Company. All Chinese industrial plants such as machine shops, iron works, cement factories, and cotton mills, which the Japanese wanted continued in operation, were taken over and reorganized, usually by one of the large Japanese family monopoly groups in Japan. This applied particularly to the cotton and silk spinning and weaving industries. Factories which the Japanese did not desire to continue in operation were closed, and their mechanical equipment was junked and shipped to Japan as scrap.

The Japanese naval authorities paid special attention to the extensive Chinese fishery industry, which was conducted by thousands of picturesque junks, most of them owned by individuals or family groups and organized into guilds. Since fish is the staple diet of China's densely populated coastal provinces, the fishery industry provided employment for tens of thousands of people who lived on their junks and spent their lives on the sea. After the Japanese had established their blockade of the coast, the Japanese naval authorities announced their decision to "reorganize" the Chinese fishery industry. A Japanese monopoly corporation was formed and a central fish market was opened under Japanese supervision, which included the fixing of prices, for the various types and grades of fish. All Chinese fishing junk owners were ordered to bring their daily catch to the Japanese central fish market. Any junk owner who refused or attempted to elude the Japanese inspectors found himself in serious complications with the Japanese navy. Travelers along the coast told of seeing the wrecks of innumerable Chinese junks which had served as targets for Japanese destroyers or gunboats.

American and European businessmen thus saw their Chinese business associates and friends being dispossessed and robbed of their property on every side. The jetties in the Japanese-occupied Hongkew section of the city provided a visual demonstration of Japan's intentions regarding Shanghai, in the enormous piles of scrapped machinery heaped on the wharves, awaiting transportation to Japan. Early in the struggle many Chinese businessmen managed to transport essential parts of their machinery into the sections of the Settlement controlled by the Americans and Europeans, but their freedom from Japanese extortion was short-lived, for the Japanese seized everything after Pearl Harbor.

The State Department was frequently reiterating its stock

warning to all Americans in China who were not engaged in "essential" activities that they should return to the United States, but few became excited as a result of these warnings, which were always made every time there was a turnover in Chinese politics, local or national. Furthermore, there never was a time, even in 1932, when the Japanese made their first attack on Shanghai, when there was sufficient American or British shipping available on the Pacific to transport even half of the Anglo-American community home in any brief period of time. Also, it must be admitted, the Occidental population at Shanghai had been sitting on the rim of the volcano so long that it entertained little thought of the dangers involved for itself in the situation.

But it became more and more obvious to the Americans in the Far East, in the summer of 1939, that the Japanese were planning an attack on the United States. Japanese military leaders made no attempt to conceal their intentions, either in Tokyo or on the China front; many were quite open, or even boastful, of what they were going to do. For example, Admiral Mitsumasi Yonai, a Navy Minister, declared in the lower house of the Diet on February 5, "I feel extremely sorry for America when I hear that she is planning to fortify Guam."

Probably the frankest statement of Japan's intentions appeared in a book entitled "Nichi-Bei Sen Chikashi" (Japanese-American War Imminent), which was written by Lieutenant-General Kiyokatsu Sato, a well known commentator on military affairs. The book was issued in the late summer of 1939, and I printed a summary of it in the *China Weekly Review* of September 2, 1939, where it must have been read by our diplomats in the Far East.

I had been attracted by the startling picture on the jacket, which was in bright red and depicted the American fleet being decimated and sunk by the Imperial Japanese Navy and Air Force. The artist who drew the lurid picture must have been inspired by the Japanese war god, for the drawing was prophetic and could have been used quite appropriately to illustrate the Japanese account of the destruction of the United States Fleet at Pearl Harbor—two years later. The startling element in General Sato's book was the fact that he outlined Japan's plan of attack on Honolulu and also later campaigns which would eventually bring the Japanese army in triumph to Washington, having conquered the rest of the United States en route.

Although the American community in Shanghai, businessmen as well as missionaries, were convinced of the certainty of a general war in the Far East which would involve the United States, there was the equally definite feeling among the members of the community that our people at home did not realize the seriousness of the situation, or its implications from the standpoint of the future welfare and security of the United States.

As a result of this conviction, the American Information Committee was organized for the purpose of disseminating in the United States information regarding the threatening aspects of the crisis created by the Japanese occupation. Headed by a missionary named Edwin Marks, the committee included in its membership a large number of representatives of American business organizations and mission bodies, and two or three journalists. None received pay for his or her services, because everyone was prompted by an intense desire to contribute toward a better home understanding of the crisis. Members of the community who were familiar with various phases of the situation were called upon to prepare authenticated reports dealing with various phases of the Japanese occupation, and its effect on the lives and activities of both foreigners and Chinese. Thousands of booklets were prepared for distribution in the United States to newspapers, chambers of commerce, civic associations, etc. Funds covering the cost of printing and postage were raised in the American community, and members of the committee volunteered their services in smuggling the booklets aboard non-Japanese ships bound for the United States. We did not dare send them through the Chinese post office, which was controlled by the Japanese army.

XXXI

Bomb and Bayonet

I WAS RETURNING HOME late one winter evening early in 1940 when my chauffeur stopped the car and called my attention to a crowd of people grouped about an electric light pole near a street intersection in the French Concession. As the crowd shifted I noticed a man's head lying on the curb at the foot of the pole.

Thinking there had been an accident, I pushed through the crowd of foreigners and Chinese and called to my chauffeur to follow me and bring the flashlight we always carried in the car.

As my chauffeur switched on his light there was a cry of horror from the crowd and I started involuntarily, for there was no body attached to the head lying in the shadow. It was the head of a Chinese young man which had been cut from his body and propped up on the still bleeding stump of the neck against the foot of the pole. The head had been cut off so recently that there were drops of sweat on the forehead.

The crowd, which had now grown to considerable proportions, including several men and women in evening dress who were returning home from parties or the theater, drew back from the gruesome sight as my chauffeur continued to play the flashlight about the foot of the pole. Suddenly he uttered an exclamation and directed my attention to a slip of paper, freshly written in Chinese characters, which was pasted to the light pole about a foot above the detached head. The chauffeur swore again as he read and slowly translated into pidgin English the inscription pasted on the pole.

The inscription was a "warning to editors," stating that the head was that of a Chinese journalist who had written articles

334

against the Japanese and the puppet Wang Ching-wei regime. It threatened that all other editors would suffer a similar fate unless they discontinued their attacks on the Japanese or the puppet, Wang Ching-wei. The beam from the flashlight in the hand of my chauffeur switched back to the face of the latest victim of a new form of Japanese atrocity and he swore again, exclaiming in his limited English "belong Wong from *Shun Pao*." So it was—Wong, an assistant editor of one of the leading Chinese papers, who had disappeared mysteriously a few weeks previously. It had been rumored that he was taken to a notorious hang-out on the edge of the International Settlement known as "No. 76 Jessfield Road," in the center of the so-called "bad-lands" where the puppet Wang Ching-wei and his gangsters had their headquarters. The place, an old-style foreign residence, surrounded by a high wall with a heavy iron gate, had been taken over by the Wang Ching-wei crowd and fitted out with various forms of torture apparatus, including electrical devices for use in forcing victims to disclose the whereabouts of relatives and friends, or hiding places of jewelry or treasure.

It was the custom to hold wealthy or influential prisoners at "No. 76" and permit them to observe other prisoners being tortured; and after several days of this the victims would be offered their freedom on condition they would agree to join the puppet Nanking Government, or, if they happened to be wealthy or had wealthy relatives, to hand over a large sum of money. Jabin Hsu, graduate of the University of Michigan, and formerly a well known journalist who had served as press relations officer with the National Finance Ministry, was held prisoner for a month in a cell from which he could observe almost daily executions in the adjoining courtyard. To regain his freedom, Hsu was forced to hand over his family fortune, amounting to $300,000, and agree to join the staff of the puppet central bank. Hsu told me in an interview following his release that his captors had assured him that he could quickly recoup his fortune by becoming an officer of the puppet state bank.

The chief jailer at "No. 76" was an ex-chauffeur named Wu

Su-pao who had once driven the car of Stirling Fessenden, American chairman of the International Settlement administration. Due to his position as the No. 1 chauffeur Wu became fat, prosperous, and arrogant. He was engaged in numerous racketeering activities, including the secret sale of gasoline and tires from the municipal garage, to which he had access. When the Japanese organized the puppet Wang Ching-wei government, Wu Su-pao was placed in charge of the gangster hang-out at "No. 76." It was his custom to take the prisoners out for a walk in the evenings, the stroll ending up at a corner of the walled compound, where there were several freshly filled graves. Wu would then throw his arm affectionately over the victim's shoulder and tell him of the benefits to be derived from joining the puppet regime or contributing a liberal sum to its support. It was hardly necessary for him to mention the consequences of refusal.

But Chinese newspapermen almost to a man remained loyal to their government, despite the fact that the foreign settlements were entirely surrounded by the Japanese army and they were in constant danger of assassination. Also they had an almost fanatical faith in the ability of the Americans and Britons to hold the International Settlement.

As the situation grew more serious the Japanese and puppet assassins intensified their attacks on the Chinese papers. One evening as I was working in my office there was a heavy dull explosion in the vicinity, which shook the building. A bomb had been thrown into the office of the *Hua Mei Wan Pao*, a Chinese paper which had its office next door to the building occupied by the *China Press* and the *China Weekly Review*. Several newsboys and office coolies were killed. On another occasion six hand-grenades were thrown at the windows of the *Shun Pao*, resulting in the killing of one printer and the wounding of several others. Other bombs were exploded on the front steps leading to the office of the *Shanghai Evening Post and Mercury*, and on one occasion a bomb was secreted in the printing press, but there were no casualties, and little damage resulted.

Later, however, the *Evening Post* suffered a real tragedy when Samuel H. Chang, editor of the *Post's* Chinese edition, was shot in the back and killed by an assassin as he was sitting in a German restaurant on Nanking Road in the International Settlement. Sammy, who was well known among the foreign correspondents as a source of information on political developments, had been accustomed to stopping at the restaurant in the afternoons for a cup of coffee and a sandwich. The assassin was never apprehended, but the police discovered that Sammy's car had been trailed by a car belonging to Tang Leang-li, the Nazi-trained agent of Wang Ching-wei, but they were not able to determine whether Tang was the actual murderer.

Samuel H. Chang was born in Swatow, China, and was graduated from Haverford College in Pennsylvania. After his return to China he worked on three American papers, the *North China Star*, the *China Press*, and the *Shanghai Evening Post and Mercury*. His wife was a member of a well known Chinese family living in Salt Lake City, Utah. The assassination of Sammy Chang brought home to foreign newspapermen the seriousness of the Japanese attack on the free press which had existed in the International Settlement almost from its establishment in 1842. It also caused me to remember a threat by a Japanese gendarmerie officer that all American-educated Chinese would ultimately be assassinated or driven from the country after the Japanese had won the war.

The most serious gangster attack on any Chinese paper, however, was on the Chinese edition of the *China Press*, which was printed in a warehouse adjoining our office and reached from the street by a narrow alley-way. One night six armed gangsters attempted to enter the printing plant but were detected by the watchman, who slammed shut the heavy iron gate, blocking their entrance. A policeman was attracted by the commotion and fired several shots at the gangsters. The shots were returned, and as more policemen came up the fight grew to the proportions of a battle. An American ex-sailor named Tug Wilson, who owned a near-by bar and restaurant frequented by newspapermen, ran across the street to assist the police and was shot dead. One Chinese pedestrian was killed, several were wounded, and plate glass windows on both sides of the block were shattered. The gangsters managed to reach their car and escaped, but not before killing a policeman on another street who attempted to halt them as they sped toward the "badlands."

In July, 1941, there came the first attack on American and other foreign newspapermen. The *Central China Daily News*, organ of the Wang Ching-wei puppet regime, published a "blacklist" of local newspapermen who, it declared, were scheduled for early "deportation." The list contained the names of seven foreigners and some eighty Chinese newspapermen. It was rumored that Tang Leang-li had been assisted in compiling the list by a renegade foreign newspaperman who had been on Tang's payroll for two or three years but had suddenly left the city after the publication of the list.

The foreigners listed for "deportation" included my name at the top, followed by those of C. V. Starr, publisher, and Randall Gould, editor of the *Shanghai Evening Post and Mercury*; Carroll Alcott, member of the staff of the *China Press* and radio commentator over the American station XMHA; Hal P. Mills, editor of a theatrical journal and nominal editor of the Chinese paper *Hua Mei Wan Pao*; Norwood F. Allman, lawyer and registered owner of the *Shun Pao*; and a Briton, J. A. E. Sanders-Bates, manager of the University Press, which published several Chinese papers. At the top of the Chinese list was the name of Woo Kya-tang, a brilliant Chinese journalist, a graduate of the School of Journalism of the University of Missouri, who was managing editor of the *China Press*. Woo was married to an American girl, a former classmate at the university, Betty Hart of Kansas City. The names of more than a dozen members of the editorial and mechanical staffs of the *Shun Pao* were also on the list.

Immediately after the publication of the "black-list" the municipal police stationed guards at all of the newspaper offices, and in my case sent a plain-clothes Chinese detective to sit in my front office and accompany me as I walked home in the evenings. Several days later, in the afternoon, as I was walking toward the American Club where I had resided for several years, I was struck on my back below my shoulder by an object which I thought was a piece of wood about a foot and a half long and about two inches in diameter. I was nearly knocked down by the blow, and, thinking a piece of timber had fallen from a scaffolding where carpenters were making repairs, I glanced upward, but saw nothing. I then looked at the object which had glanced off my back against the wall of the building and was still rolling along the sidewalk a few feet from where I was standing. Noticing that it was wrapped in a newspaper, and not suspecting its nature, I reached down and picked it up. As my fingers closed on the missile I realized that it was a "potato-masher" type of hand-grenade used by both the Japanese and Chinese armies. I resisted the impulse to drop it, as I noticed that the cord which released the mechanism had only been pulled part way out; had I thrown it down the shock might have caused it to explode. It was nothing short of a miracle that it had failed to explode when it glanced off my shoulder and struck the building.

By this time my bodyguard, who was walking several feet behind me on the crowded sidewalk, came running up and I showed him the hand-grenade. He immediately drew his revolver and glanced around at the crowd which had begun to assemble. I told him to go to the corner and summon a policeman, in the meantime carefully placing the explosive on the sidewalk and motioning the people to keep away from it. Soon a Chinese policeman hurried up and after I had explained the incident he, with what seemed to me a singular lack of imagination, also picked up the grenade and carried it, held at arm's length in front of him, with my bodyguard walking ahead to clear the way, to the central police station, where it was immersed in a bucket of water. Examination showed it to be a live bomb, but the man who tossed it had been apparently in too great a hurry as he failed to pull the firing pin out sufficiently to cause the grenade to explode. It was suggested in some quarters that the intention might have been only to frighten me and cause me to discontinue my critical editorial policy regarding the activities of the Japanese and their puppets. The police, however, discounted this suggestion.

A few days after the attack on me a man having close connections with both the Japanese and the Nanking puppets called on me and suggested that I "sell" the *China Weekly Review*. I indignantly rejected the offer.

Japanese and puppet attacks on the press of the International Settlement were not confined to attempts to assassinate editors and news writers. Since the Japanese had seized the central Chinese post office when they occupied the Hongkew section of the International Settlement, they immediately banned the transmission through the mail of any newspapers of whose policies they disapproved. However, the presence of Japanese censors and inspectors in the post office was not sufficient to intimidate members of the loyal Chinese postal staff, who secretly cooperated with the newspapers in helping them elude the Japs. The practice was for the loyal clerks in the post office to telephone the circulation managers of papers at night and tell them when the Jap guards had gone out to eat, or were asleep or drunk. The circulation clerks would then rush the papers to the post office, where the sacks would be stamped with counterfeit seals indicating they had been passed by the Japanese censors. The loyal Chinese clerks became so skillful in eluding the Japanese postal censors that it almost amounted to the operation of dual post offices, one subject to Japanese censorship and the other operated by the loyal staff who defied the Japs. As proof of the skill of the postal staff, they succeeded in smuggling out of Japanese-controlled Shanghai and into Free China the last issue of the *China Weekly Review*, dated December 6, 1941, issued from the press only a few hours before the Japanese crossed the boundaries of the International Settlement.

Of the seven foreign newspapermen "black-listed" for deportation—or assassination—three, C. V. Starr, Randall Gould, and Carroll Alcott, shortly departed for the United States on one of the last American ships and thus missed the fury of the Japs after Pearl Harbor. Another, Norwood Allman, had gone to Hong Kong to arrange for shipments of print paper. He was caught there and imprisoned in Camp Stanley until repatriated on the *Gripsholm*. My son, John Wm. Powell, who had been a reporter on the *China Press*, also departed on one of the last American ships.

Why did I remain in Shanghai?

That question is difficult, because it involves both tangible and intangible factors. Among the tangible factors was my staff of loyal Chinese assistants in the front office and mechanical department who had stuck by me, some almost throughout the period of my residence in Shanghai. This loyalty extended down to the lowest coolie on the staff, who slept in the office and carried the mail past the Japanese pickets, who never spared their bayonets if anything aroused their suspicion. I had no intention of abandoning them to the Japanese, who would certainly take vengeance on them in case I departed.

Next among the tangibles was the fact that, in addition to my regular newspaper work, I was director of a secret radio station owned by Press Wireless, Inc., which had been operated under the nose of the Japanese censors who controlled all the other communication services, including the cable companies and the American R.C.A., and Mackay radio services. As the situation became more critical it became all the more vital that the last remaining uncensored radio service be kept in operation. We succeeded in accomplishing this seemingly impossible task up to 10 o'clock on the morning of December 7, 1941, and cleared all the messages telling of the occupation of Shanghai, before the Japs found our station and took it over.

Among the intangible factors was loyalty to the community. Although the State Department and the navy had provided means of transportation for many of the women and children and others whose work was not regarded as "essential," a majority of the Americans, both businessmen and missionaries, remained. There was another, a smaller group, who imagined they were on such good terms with the Japanese that they would be able to continue without molestation. One man boasted that he had entertained so many Japanese army officers, he was sure he wouldn't be interfered with. He also boasted of the handsome fees he had received as retainers from the Japanese (before Pearl Harbor). There were still others who "went over" entirely to the Japanese and accepted employment with them. This included several newspapermen, one of whom became a broadcaster and news commentator over the Japanese station and denounced several of his colleagues as "espionage officers who had worked against the Japanese." Other American and British newspapermen continued in positions on two newspapers, the *Shanghai Evening Post* (American) and the *Shanghai Times* (British), which had been taken over by the Japanese and continued in publication under Japanese editors.

XXXII

Shadow of the Hun

IF ONE COULD ONLY SEE into the future—for six months, three months, one month, one day!

Shanghai newspapers, read now, more than three years after the Japs landed on the Shanghai Bund, almost simultaneously with Pearl Harbor, show many signs of the coming storm. But at the time neither the readers nor the editors of the Shanghai newspapers realized the tragedy in store for them.

Of greatest significance perhaps were the accounts of the influx of German Nazis, many of whom had been expelled from the United States and Latin America. At the top of the list was Captain Fritz Wiedemann, former German Consul-General at San Francisco and aide to Hitler's master of intrigue, Propaganda Minister Paul Joseph Goebbels. Wiedemann arrived at Shanghai early in October, 1941. Reports issued by the German news agencies stated that Wiedemann was scheduled for the post of Consul-General at Tientsin, on its face quite a come-down from the important post he had occupied at San Francisco, speeding Nazi propaganda and propagandists from the New World to the ancient Orient and vice versa. But the dashing Wiedemann's talents were not to be wasted at the little North China port.

Wiedemann's arrival in the Orient was in keeping with his usual flair for the dramatic. He declared in an interview that the British had given him safe-conduct, whereas the British probably would have given a great deal to have apprehended him. He had tried to leave San Francisco secretly on a Japanese ship but was detected, taken ashore by the United States authorities, sent across the country under guard to New York, and back to Germany on a special ship along with other Nazi agents. However, he did not remain long in Germany and suddenly turned up, supposedly from a submarine, at the Nazi base in Latin America, Buenos Aires, capital of Argentina. Here he boarded a Japanese boat for Tokyo, bearing numerous briefcases and suitcases filled with documents for the Nazi Ambassador in Tokyo and other Nazi agents in the Far East, including Herr M. Fischer, German diplomatic representative to the Japanese-supported puppet Wang Chingwei in Nanking.

The reason for Wiedemann's appointment to the unimportant consular position at Tientsin was disclosed shortly after his arrival in Shanghai. The Nazis expected an early collapse of Soviet Russia, following an attack by Hitler in the East and Japan in the West, and were preparing an organization to accompany an expected Japanese invasion of Outer Mongolia and Siberia from Manchukuo. The Japanese had long been training a White Russian "army" in Tientsin for use in the Siberian adventure. The Russian army, consisting possibly of two regiments conscripted in the Russian communities in North China and Manchuria, was nominally headed by the old Cossack Ataman Semenoff, who had been in Japanese pay since the Russian revolution.

Wiedemann's arrival in Shanghai was rightly regarded as evidence of an active Nazi diplomatic offensive in the Far East, designed to offset Anglo-American efforts to force a Japanese withdrawal from China. Hitler had long since withdrawn all German military advisers from Generalissimo Chiang Kai-shek's headquarters, in deference to Japan's wishes, and had granted diplomatic recognition to the puppet state of Manchukuo and the puppet government of Wang Ching-wei at Nanking. Wiedemann had attended the celebration of the anniversary of the signing of the Anti-Comintern Pact in Tokyo on September 27, and had conferred with the growing colony of some 3,000-odd German experts who had arrived in Japan, chiefly from Mexico and other Latin-American countries, in mid-October. These experts included reinforcements for embassy and consular staffs in both China and Japan, but of even more importance were several specialists for service in key posts in the Japanese Government, particularly in the Home Ministry. German propagandists arriving in Shanghai gave out interviews, published in English in the Nazi propaganda organs in Shanghai, forecasting that the Japanese-American conversations in Washington "were certain to be disrupted."

The British had attempted to break the tide of Nazi agents and propaganda which was flowing into Japan and China from United States West Coast ports, chiefly San Francisco. A British naval vessel intercepted the Japanese liner *Asama Maru* outside Yokohama, and removed several high Nazi officials who were on their way to Japan and China from the United States and South America. Later, the British ship was forced to hand most of these officials back to the Japanese, following a strong protest by the Tokyo authorities. The German Ambassador in Tokyo, Eugene Ott, had participated in the Japanese protest from behind the scenes.

Other well known Nazi agents who arrived secretly in the Far East by way of Japan included Dr. Johannes Borchers, who was scheduled for the post of Consul-General in Shanghai. Borchers had previously served as Consul-General in New York. Another, who had arrived somewhat earlier and had inaugurated the Nazi-White Russian set-up at Tientsin, was Walther Fuchs. Reports in the papers stated that his primary object was to stir up anti-Russian unrest in North China and Outer Mongolia, and to lay the foundation for an Axis orbit in Asia that would facilitate the link-up between Japan and Germany following the anticipated collapse of Russia. The Germans also expected to take over the International Settlement and the French Concession at Shanghai following the outbreak of war between Japan and the Anglo-American Powers, and had the personnel ready for the various offices.

Upon Wiedemann's arrival in Shanghai there was a conference of all high Nazi officials in the Far East in the quarters of the Nazi "center," which included the German School, the Nazi drill hall, and a radio station, located in Chinese territory controlled by the puppet Wang Ching-wei Government, but directly across the street from the border of the International Settlement. The conference was attended by Dr. Martin Fischer, German Minister to the Wang Ching-wei Government; Ernst Wendler, German minister to Thailand (Siam), and Christian Zinsser, Acting Consul-General at Shanghai. Zinsser had previously been expelled from Guatemala and Honduras for Nazi intrigue. Another attendant at the conference was a Colonel Meysinger, allegedly a high member of the Gestapo who had been sent to the Far East for special work.

Other lesser-fry Nazi agents and propagandists who arrived in Shanghai in the weeks immediately preceding Pearl Harbor included Dr. Klaus Mehnert, who had long been a Nazi secret agent and propagandist while serving as a member of the faculty of the University of Hawaii at Honolulu. Soon after his arrival in Shanghai Dr. Mehnert started an English-language magazine which he called *The XXth Century*. Mehnert spoke English so perfectly that no one suspected he was German until he started the Nazi magazine. Another well known Nazi propagandist who arrived by way of Buenos Aires, San Francisco, Honolulu, and Tokyo was C. Flick or Flick-Steger, who had received his education in the United States and was thought by many to be an American citizen. Flick had gone to Germany, where he served for several years as assistant to Karl von Wiegand, Hearst's well known Berlin correspondent. Karl von Wiegand was also in Shanghai and had resided at the Park Hotel for many months, where he covered the Far Eastern situation in weekly dispatches to the Hearst press. Von Wiegand, an American citizen, had a wide acquaintance with both German and Japanese officialdom. He received almost daily communications from the Tokyo Foreign Minister, which enabled him to scoop the other correspondents. His daughter was married to a German physician who had resided in Shanghai for many years. Flick-Steger was manager of the Nazi radio stations XGRS and XHHB in Shanghai, broadcasting in English and Chinese. The chief English-language news commentator and broadcaster was Herbert Moy, a New York born and educated Chinese. He was assisted by another American citizen, Robert Fockler, who went to Shanghai originally as a jazz-band leader in a Shanghai night club. Another Chinese-American connected with the German Transocean News Service in Shanghai was Francis Lee, but he resigned after Pearl Harbor, and, accompanied by two other American correspondents, succeeded in escaping to Chungking.

Nazi propaganda in Shanghai was mainly anti-American and anti-Jewish in character, the two terms usually being linked together in Nazi references to American officialdom and State Department policies. The first distribution of anti-Jewish propaganda, probably the first in Shanghai's history, took place in a novel manner. When the German Nazi diplomats and agents began arriving in Shanghai in large numbers in 1940 and 1941, they found all of the British-owned hotels closed to them. They therefore took up quarters at the Park Hotel, a new Chinese-owned hostelry, which had been built on American lines. It was the tallest building in the city, sixteen stories, fronting on the Race Course, chief recreation center for foreigners in the city. One Saturday afternoon in late October when the Race Course was filled with people attending the fall race meeting, the sky was suddenly filled with leaflets as though distributed from an airplane. The leaflets contained anti-Jewish inscriptions printed in both English and Chinese. It was discovered that the leaflets had been distributed from the tower of the Park Hotel, and had been carried by the high wind over the Race Course.

There was a tragic element involved in the initiation of anti-Jewish propaganda, always a preliminary to anti-Jewish persecution, due to the fact that there had arrived in Shanghai in recent months some 25,000 Jewish refugees from Germany and Austria. Many of these refugees had arrived in Shanghai after months of travel about the world seeking a place to land. They had finally come to Shanghai, because it was the only port in the world where a passport visa was not necessary for landing privileges—in the International Settlement. The refugees were quartered in tenement property where they were supported by funds raised locally or transmitted from Jewish relief societies in New York and London. They were greatly assisted by two well known Jewish residents of the Settlement, Sir Victor Sassoon, British, and M. Speelman, Dutch, large property owners, who provided free quarters for the refugees. The Japanese seized all of the property after Pearl Harbor and forced the refugees to live in a squalid "ghetto" on the Nazi order. The New York committee sent a representative to Shanghai to supervise the distribution of food, clothing, and financial assistance.

Financial assistance took the form of small loans to individuals and groups to enable them to engage in business activities to which they had been accustomed before being expelled from their homes by the German Nazis. In some quarters it was thought that the advent of Jewish refugees from Germany and Austria might be beneficial to the commercial life of Shanghai, as the Jews, being adept at the management of small businesses, would tend to offset the influx of Japanese which had followed the military invasion in 1937. At any rate it was hoped that they might be able to bridge over the time until they could be located elsewhere or possibly return to their homes in Europe.

Thousands of the Jewish refugees had begun to gain a foothold in the Shanghai community as small merchants or in professional lines, when the fresh storm of Nazi propaganda broke about their heads. Most of the Nazi circulars followed familiar lines. One circular distributed early in November contained the names of 270 Shanghai Jewish firms or American and British firms which employed Jewish clerks or assistants. The list was accompanied by a letter ordering all "Aryans" to boycott the Jewish firms and threatening, in the event of non-compliance, that violators would have their names and photographs supplied to the head Nazi organization in Berlin for "appropriate action," the nature of which was left to the imagination. The long arm of German Nazism was extending into the Orient as it already had done in North and South America.

Previously there had never been any manifestations of anti-Semitism among either the Chinese or the Japanese. Most of the Jews already resident in the large cities of China and Japan had reached the Orient by way of Bagdad, Aden, Bombay, and Singapore. China in her ancient past had absorbed a large colony of Jews which had settled in Honan Province. The origin of the once numerous and thriving Jewish colony at the city of Kaifeng, Honan, has always remained a mystery, but modern investigation had proved the fact of its existence. Numerous descendants of the early Jews are to be found there today, speaking Chinese, wearing Chinese clothes, and living as other members of the Chinese community do. Other colonies of Oriental Jews which settled at Japanese ports, particularly Kobe, also had been absorbed into the local Japanese communities.

The list of business firms which the Nazi circular scheduled for boycotting was interesting, as it indicated the type of businesses in which the German refugees were engaged: fur stores, pharmacies, women's tailors, photographers, leather and handbag shops, children's garments, shoes and stockings, food and provisions, jewelers, art dealers, men's tailors also selling woolen cloth, beauty parlors, cabarets, theaters, night clubs. There were sixty-nine women's dress-making and tailor shops in the list. It was rumored that there had been considerable racketeering in connection with the compilation of the list, as the Nazi promoters had offered to omit names of particular shops where the proprietors were willing or able to pay bribes. The Nazi organization which had charge of this phase of the anti-Jewish "drive" occupied a suite in the Park Hotel Tower which rented for $2,500 a month.

When the Japanese occupation threw Shanghai's commercial life into confusion the refugee Jewish population enjoyed a temporary prosperity, for much of the merchandise which the Japanese looted from Anglo-American homes and offices was sold to the second-hand stores and pawnshops and then became a

matter of public barter. Hundreds of the refugees would con-
gregate at the corner of Nanking and Szechwan Roads, adjacent
to the Shanghai branch of the Chase Bank, reminiscent of the old
curb market in New York. Here one could buy anything from
a worn fur coat or a second-hand dress to a dozen aspirin tablets.
One heard of lucky individuals who had cornered this or that
article, and the prices in the inflated currency shot up to unbelievable heights. A suit of tailor-made clothes cost $4,000 or
$5,000 Chinese; a pair of shoes, anywhere from $500 to $1,500.
An amusing story was told about an enterprising Viennese who
went around to all the second-hand stores and pawnshops and
bought up all the garments containing "zippers," thus making
himself the controller of this important product, as no more
could be imported and they could not be manufactured locally.

The results of the German anti-Jewish propaganda were soon
apparent. Neither the Japanese nor their Chinese puppets were
interested in the ideological phases of anti-Semitism as spread by
Hitler's Nazi agents, but they were not averse to taking advantage of the movement for purposes of selfish gain. An English-
language paper, having Japanese and puppet Chinese backing,
published an editorial charging that wealthy Shanghai Jews had
extended financial assistance to the Kuomintang Party. The editorial contained the following revealing paragraph:

. . . there is not the slightest doubt that the situation in which
China finds herself today would never have been of such duration,
except for financial assistance extended to the Kuomintang Government . . . by the Jews. It is estimated that at least 75 per cent of the
revenues of most local commercial establishments go to the Jews
. . . this is also true in the biggest cities of the world, London and
New York. . . . Berlin is the one exception *now*.

The allegation that 75 per cent of the income of local industries and business establishments went to Jews was untrue, as
revenue statistics of the International Settlement showed that
approximately four-fifths of the local taxes were paid by Chinese
retail properties, industrial or large commercial interests. It was

true that the largest blocks of downtown real estate were owned by Jews, the Sassoons, Ezras, Hardoons, Shamoons, and others, most of whom were from Persia, Arabia, or India, and had British nationality. The Sassoons had made vast fortunes in India and had made heavy investments in Shanghai following the Nationalist Revolution in 1927. Most of the Sassoon investments were in hotels, apartment houses, and office buildings, and the Japanese and their puppets immediately saw the possibilities for profit through seizure of Sassoon properties in the event of war. The process was started by the Nanking Government when it confiscated the property of the Hardoon estate. After Pearl Harbor the Japanese Government seized all the Sassoon and Shamoon properties, announcing that the action had been taken in order to "protect" the properties.

Shanghai was flooded not only with anti-Jewish propaganda, but also with general Nazi propaganda, including every known type of booklet and circular. I made a collection of thirty separate types of Nazi propaganda literature distributed in Shanghai, and presumably in other Chinese cities, in the six months preceding Pearl Harbor. The collection ranged from illustrated magazines, with the usual quota of rotogravure German damsels in the nude, to books of 300 pages. One book, entitled, "How They Lie," consisted of excerpts from the American United Press and British Reuter's news services, skillfully arranged in parallel columns to emphasize the difference between official British statements and the final outcome of particular events referred to in the dispatches, such as Hitler's Balkan campaign, the drive into Greece, Crete, etc. Another booklet, "Two Men on a Boat," dealt sarcastically with the Roosevelt-Churchill "Eight Point Declaration." On the back page was the following reference to the President of the United States:

Surrounded by a group of rapacious financiers and money-sharks, resentful and vindictive Jews, armament profiteers, and other rogues, he sought re-election for a third term by deliberate lying. He solemnly promised to keep the United States out of war. So soon as the third term was secure, he all of a sudden discovered all manner of perils allegedly threatening the Western Hemisphere. When the American people still persisted in declining participation in Britain's war, Roosevelt cast away the mask. . . . His latest order to the American Navy to shoot on Axis vessels at sight, is a plain act of war. To pursue the selfish aims of his plutocratic war-clique, he will sacrifice American lives. . . . He feels no compunction at making all decent and peaceful Americans labour and toil for their own enslavement. . . . History will call it the greatest betrayal ever perpetrated by a President against the American people. . . . Look for the outcome!

Aside from the anti-American broadcasts over the Nazi radio stations, the Nazi organization also inaugurated extensive anti-American propaganda campaigns in Chinese through the puppet Wang Ching-wei vernacular newspapers. In this way they were assisted by Tang Leang-li, who was Wang Ching-wei's chief secretary and propagandist. The head of the Nazi press bureau in Shanghai was F. Cordt, who spent much of his time with officials of the puppet Government in Nanking.

Chief organ for dissemination of anti-American propaganda was the German Transocean News Service. The issue of the *China Weekly Review* for October 4, 1941, only two months before Pearl Harbor, contained a summary of anti-American reports which had appeared in Transocean. One dispatch from Stockholm said that "living standards in the United States were being impaired in order to supply Great Britain with adequate assistance." The summary in the *Review* follows:

A dispatch from Berlin on Sept. 4, distributed in Shanghai by Transocean under the heading of "Commentary," referred to President Roosevelt's Labor Day address as demonstrating all the characteristics of "brutal force and lust for power." [It] declared, "even the citizens of the United States must ask themselves whether it is not the policy of their President which, with its brutal penetration of South America, with its interference in the sphere of purely European interests, and with its continuous sabre-rattling, bears all the characteristics of brutal force and lust for power." In the third paragraph the German report dragged in its old favorite, "Jewish influence." The following statement appeared, ". . . it is known to everybody that under the regime of Franklin Roosevelt even in boom times 11 millions were unemployed in the United States. . . . Roosevelt, the 'Democrat' who is in his office as the paid servant of Jewry, has now entered a moral alliance with the deadly enemy of every democracy, with Bolshevism."

Transocean followed a consistent policy of reporting fully all anti-administration speeches of Senator Wheeler, Lindbergh and all comment against the Administration which appeared in such papers as the *Chicago Tribune* and the Hearst press. In this connection Transocean performed an interesting journalistic "stunt" by cabling back to Shanghai practically all of the dispatches *sent from Shanghai* to the Hearst press in the United States by the Hearst correspondent, Karl von Wiegand, who was stationed in Shanghai. In other words, von Wiegand, who obtained most of his information from Nazi and Japanese sources in Shanghai and wired his reports to the Hearst press, may, if he wishes, read his dispatches all over again in Transocean reports from Berlin and New York a few days later.

The German news service also displayed in its reports distributed in Shanghai, deepest compassion for the "unfortunate victims of American aggression in Iceland." One Transocean dispatch revealed the alleged contents of a letter written by an Icelander to a relative in South America—which, according to the report, "fell into German hands." The letter said that the Americans had "invaded our country like a swarm of locusts," a curious figure of speech to be used by a resident of an Arctic land. The Icelander expressed the fear that the Americans would consume all of the available food on the island and that the inhabitants would starve "because the effective German submarine blockade was sinking tonnage in our waters with greatest success."

On September 25, a Transocean dispatch referring to the proposal to arm merchantmen, quoted an editorial which had appeared in a Berlin publication and was headed "Roosevelt Running Amuck."

On September 28, there was a brief Transocean dispatch from Mexico City, which quoted a complaint that a Mexican tanker had to spend a week in the port of Houston, Texas, awaiting repairs, "because preferential treatment in U.S. dockyards is being given to damaged British ships."

Also, on September 28, there was another interesting dispatch quoting the world-famous Swedish explorer, Sven Hedin, as declaring that the war "which Stalin had been preparing in order to extinguish Western civilization and Christianity would be a thousand times worse than was the onslaught on western civilization by the Mongolian tribes in former centuries." Sven Hedin asked "whether Americans were without pangs of conscience in putting weapons in the hands of the Bolsheviks in order to assist them in their fight against Italians, Germans, Finns, Hungarians, Slovakians and Rumanians." Sven Hedin's article appeared in a new Berlin periodical named "Berlin-Rome-Tokyo" and described as an organ "close to the Wilhelmstrasse." This was apparently the first indication to reach the Far East that Sven Hedin, well known Swedish explorer in the Far East, had allegedly cast his lot with the Nazis.

Nazi propaganda against Americans and Britons in Shanghai displayed a viciousness which may have indicated that the Germans had not forgotten their animosities over the part played by the British, Americans and French in deporting them from Shanghai after the fighting ceased at the end of World War I. Since China, in World War I, had delayed declaration of war against the Germans, the deportation was not carried out until after the armistice. As the deportation, which was carried out by the Americans, British and French, involved a serious loss of face on the part of the Germans in the eyes of the Chinese, the Germans were deeply resentful. The deportation incident was later dramatized by several German writers in books and plays which were used by the Nazis to stir up hatred against the Allies.

XXXIII

History Punctuated

I WAS AWAKENED ABOUT 4 O'CLOCK on the morning of December 8, 1941, by what I thought was the explosion of three or four large firecrackers outside my window. I did not realize that the explosion marked the end of International Shanghai as it had existed for almost a century—since 1842.

The explosion seemed to come from the street just outside my window in the American Club, about two blocks from the Bund, the street which runs along the Whangpoo River, Shanghai's harbor.

When the blasts were followed by several more, I realized something had happened which I as a newspaper man should investigate. Hurriedly putting on my clothes, I ran downstairs. As I reached the front door the watchman, a White Russian, exclaimed, "Japanese come!"

I ran toward the Bund, overtaking on my way two other newspaper correspondents, who also lived at the club and had been awakened by the bombs. Our way to the Bund was blocked by a Japanese sailor in full war equipment. He pointed a rifle at us, with bayonet fixed. We turned back to the next cross-street, only to find that all of the streets leading to the Bund were barred by armed Japanese, who were gradually extending their lines into the business section.

Our curiosity was stimulated by the fact that the whole waterfront was suddenly illuminated by a large fire. Someone suggested we climb to the roof of one of the buildings back from the Bund, which we did, and discovered that the fire came from a ship which had been anchored almost directly in front of the International Settlement.

Two smaller fires, which seemed to be floating about the harbor, turned out to be launches. Near the burning ship was anchored the U.S.S. *Wake*, a river patrol boat which the United States Navy had used for several years on the Yangtze.

The *Wake* was brilliantly illuminated and appeared to be a hive of activity. We were joined by other newspaper men connected with the press associations, who told us news had just been received that Japan had attacked Pearl Harbor, had destroyed the American Fleet, had declared war on the United States and Britain, and was in the process of occupying Shanghai.

The blazing ship in the harbor was the British gunboat *Petrel*, which had been dynamited by its crew when the Japanese sent a destroyer alongside and demanded its surrender. We wondered what had happened aboard the *Wake*, because it carried a contingent of American sailors, who had previously retired from the navy and had been engaged in various occupations in Shanghai, prior to being called up for service in recent weeks.

It had been rumored among the foreigners in Shanghai that the Americans also had planted dynamite in the hold of the *Wake* and intended to sink the vessel in the event of Japanese attack.

The regular crew of the *Wake*, as well as all other American service men, including the Fourth United States Marines, had been transferred to Manila several days previously by order of Admiral Thomas Charles Hart, stationed in the Philippines. Admiral Hart, since retired from the navy and sent to the United States Senate by his home State, Connecticut, is a submarine expert and deserves much credit for our submarine campaign, a disastrous one for Japanese shipping.

The highest ranking American naval officer at Shanghai before the attack, Rear Admiral William A. Glassford, Jr., had taken all the American river patrol boats excepting the *Wake* to Manila, a somewhat precarious enterprise because the boats were not constructed for sea service and all would have been swamped had they run into a typhoon.

Since there had been a crew of some twenty-five aboard the

Wake, we wondered why they had not put up some resistance or sunk the ship, as the British had done with the *Petrel.* We learned later that the *Wake* was only left in Shanghai for radio communication purposes by the American consulate.

We also learned later that most of the American sailors on the *Wake* jumped overboard and swam to a Panamanian freighter anchored in the harbor, where they were concealed by the crew.

There was a valuable radio equipment on the *Wake* which the Japs seized.

The Japanese made a great to-do about the capture of the American vessel, which was exploited in Japan and in the Japanese-controlled press in China. One would have thought from the description of the capture that the *Wake* was a 10,000-ton cruiser rather than a gunboat of a few hundred tons. The Japanese incorporated the *Wake* into their navy and renamed it the *Tatara Maru.*

By 10 A.M. the military occupation of Shanghai had extended over most of the city. As controller of Press Wireless, I urged the correspondents to get their stories off as soon as possible, knowing the Japanese would quickly seize all communications. I followed my own advice by filing to the *Daily Herald,* London, and also assisted some of the other correspondents who had not yet arrived on the scene.

Press Wireless, a radio communication service devoted exclusively to news messages, is owned by a group of leading newspapers in the United States. All the stories telling of the occupation of the city which got to the world's press went out over this station, because the Japanese already had guards in all the other cable and radio offices, and no messages of any kind could be sent. They had the city securely bottled up, excepting the one "leak," which was the Press Wireless circuit to Manila and San Francisco.

However, there was one other American radio station in Shanghai, which the Japs did not get. It was located at the American consulate and was used for official messages. An American marine was guarding the station when a squad of Japanese soldiers arrived to take it over. When the Japs demanded admission, the marine barred the door and seizing a heavy iron bar he completely demolished the set while the Japs banged at the door with their rifle butts.

As soon as I could get away I hurried to my own office, the *China Weekly Review*, knowing well that it, and the *China Press*, in the same building, would be among the first newspapers to receive the attention of the Japanese. My Chinese staff realized this too, and was on the job before daylight, removing the typewriters, the price of which had mounted to unbelievable heights because of the embargo.

Before noon the Japanese army had occupied the building and placed seals on all doors. I decided to return to my room at the American Club to await developments, and I did not have long to wait.

Shortly after 10 o'clock a servant came running to my room, greatly excited, and said that Japanese sailors were in the lobby and had ordered everybody to leave the building in two hours. Since the American Club served as the center for American community activities, such as the Chamber of Commerce and other organizations, the enforced evacuation created a serious problem.

Many of the residents had lived there for years. Everyone started packing furiously, but few had enough trunks and bags to hold their belongings. This resulted in the loss of practically all personal effects on the part of many, including myself.

Before noon, two fully armed Japanese sailors carrying their rifles, with bayonets attached, slung over their shoulders, appeared at my door and demanded admission. Both were drunk, and their arms were full of bottles of beer looted from the club bar. They made themselves at home and proceeded to consume the beer, at the same time ordering me to hasten my departure.

The Japanese knew what they wanted in Shanghai, and proceeded to take it without delay. All properties belonging to the British-Indian millionaire, Sir Victor Sassoon, including hotels, offices, and apartment buildings, were seized, and the Japanese announced that they had been confiscated. The *North China Daily News*, leading British newspaper, which was almost as old as the Settlement, was also closed and sealed.

Since the Japanese wanted to take over Shanghai as a "going concern" they did not interfere with any of the public utilities such as the American-owned Shanghai Power Company and Shanghai Telephone Company, or the British-owned Shanghai Water Works and the Tramway Company. They did, however, seize all of the busses of the British Shanghai Omnibus Company. There was also, at first, little interference with the personal activities of American and British residents. However, one occasionally saw a foreigner being marched along the street by a squad of Japanese soldiers or sailors, presumably on the way to some internment camp in the Hongkew section, which the Japs had occupied in 1937. These scenes became commonplace after December 20.

The American diplomatic and consular staffs were concentrated on two floors of the Metropole Hotel in the downtown section for several days but later were moved to the Cathay Mansion, a residence hotel which was owned by the Sassoon interests. They remained there until they were repatriated on the first trip of the exchange liner *Gripsholm*. The British embassy and consular staffs were permitted to remain in their regular consular quarters on the Bund, or at the Cathay Hotel. They were repatriated about two months after the Americans.

Another British morning paper, the *Shanghai Times*, which always had followed a pro-Japanese policy, became openly Japanese and continued under the nominal editorship of the owner, E. S. Nottingham, although the real authority was vested in a Japanese army officer. The American afternoon paper, the *Shanghai Evening Post and Mercury*, was taken over and its policy "reformed." C. V. Starr, the owner of the paper, was in New York and the paper was in charge of the business manager, George Bruce. Bruce continued the paper for several months under the supervision of a Japanese army officer. Bruce, however, was later interned and died in a Japanese camp. According to reports of other American internees, the Japanese intercepted a note that Bruce secretly sent to his wife. Bruce was removed to another camp for "questioning." He was detained for two weeks and dropped dead shortly after he had returned to the first camp.

As the Japanese had been in control of the Hongkew industrial area, which included most of Shanghai's public utilities, since 1937, their occupation of the remainder of the International Settlement put the entire city, except the French Concession, in their hands. The composition of the municipal council, which had included five Britons, five Chinese, two Americans and two Japanese, continued to April, 1941, when a special election approved a proposal to change the representation to three Britons, three Americans, three Japanese, one German, one Swiss, one Netherlander, and four Chinese. After Pearl Harbor the Japanese ousted the Americans and Britons, and appointed Germans and Italians in their places.

Thus the Japanese moved in on one of the world's largest and richest cities, and the leading port on the continent of East Asia. They made the best of their opportunities. Among the confiscated properties were the foreign banks, including the Shanghai branches of the American National City Bank of New York, the Chase Bank, the British Hong Kong and Shanghai Bank, and Chartered Bank of Australia and India.

The manager of the National City Bank, J. A. MacKay, was interned and no transaction could be conducted without the approval of two Japanese officers, both of whom had formerly been employed in the New York office of the Yokohama Specie Bank and were familiar with American banking practice.

No gold deposits (United States dollars or British pounds) could be withdrawn, and only sufficient amounts could be taken from Chinese dollar accounts to meet urgent payroll requirements. A similar situation prevailed at the British banks.

The Japanese announced that all foreign banks were to be

liquidated, and none would ever be allowed to function in the future. The effect of this situation on the economic life of the city may well be imagined.

The large Chinese banks, such as the Central Bank, Bank of China, and Bank of Communications, which were already operating in a restricted manner, were likewise taken over, and later handed to the puppet Nanking Government. But the Japanese continued to maintain their control.

The Central Bank was transformed into the Central Reserve Bank and made the chief financial organ of the puppet Nanking Government. Shortly after the occupation the puppet bank put out a new note issue with which it bought up the notes previously issued by the National Government at the rate of one Nanking dollar note for two Chungking dollar notes.

However, all transactions with Japan had to be conducted with so-called military yen notes printed in imitation of regular Japanese currency, but containing no serial numbers. It appeared to be the intention of the Japanese to repudiate this currency or permit it to decline in value at some future date. The Japanese had followed that practice in the Russo-Japanese War, which was fought on Chinese soil in Manchuria; all Japanese purchases in the field were made with so-called "military notes" which were repudiated after the war, and later were bought up for a few cents on the dollar and destroyed. In the present instance the Japanese followed a similar procedure, as all purchases of Chinese cotton, food, and other products were paid for with "military yen," usually at the point of the bayonet.

The financial and currency situation at Shanghai, which had greatly improved following the organization of the National Government in 1927, became more complicated under Japanese control. In any financial enterprise of substantial size it became necessary to use American currency or its equivalent at an established rate of exchange, despite the fact that transactions in American or British currencies were also outlawed. Chinese exchange shops, however, continued dealings in American currency despite the ban.

When I left Shanghai, in June, 1942, the new notes issued by the Central Reserve Bank were down to about forty to the American dollar on the "black exchange." Notes of the legitimate Central Bank before Pearl Harbor had been stabilized at about three to the American dollar. A friend of mine who was repatriated on the second voyage of the *Gripsholm*, told me that he had exchanged an American one hundred dollar note for sixteen thousand dollars of puppet currency in the Shanghai black market.

Late in 1942 the Japanese announced their intention of abolishing the International Settlement Administration and turning the Settlement over to the control of the puppet Wang Ching-wei Government at Nanking. The Japanese also brought pressure, through the Germans, on the Vichy Government and forced the French to hand over their Concession, almost as old as the International Settlement, to the Nanking puppet regime. It used to be a common saying around Shanghai that the French would be the last Europeans to "hand over" their Oriental possessions to the native peoples. "The soft-hearted Americans and British might compromise, but never the French," was a common remark. As a result of this sentiment much Anglo-American property was turned over to the French for "protection." The large modern Development Building, owned by Chinese interests, was transferred to a French company a few weeks before Pearl Harbor. The building had been occupied for several years by the American Consulate and United States Court for China, and it was hoped to prevent Japanese seizure by transferring it to a French (Vichy) corporation. But the Development Building along with the American Consulate and Court and their properties were among the first seized by the Japs on the first day of occupation. The Japanese had lost any respect they may have held for the French as a result of Vichy's "sell-out" of French Indo-China to the Japs, who immediately set about converting it into a base for further adventures into British territories to the south.

While the Japanese have eliminated the western "imperialists" from their century-old control of Shanghai, and theoretically have handed the city over to the Nanking Government, they have continued to maintain their military hold on the city and have not permitted the Wang Ching-wei regime to function within the municipal area. The final adjustment of the Shanghai Question will provide one of the most serious of after-war problems, because of the extent of foreign holdings in the great Chinese port. The total American investment at Shanghai probably approximated a quarter of a billion American dollars. British investments were much larger, as the British possessed more industrial property. Since the extraterritorial system prevailed up to and after the Japanese occupation, many of the larger Chinese holdings in commercial and industrial property were incorporated under foreign flags. The unscrambling of these interests and the settlement of claims for losses will occupy the attention of an international commission for many years after peace has been restored.

An American professor, Dr. William Crane Johnstone, Jr., once wrote a book * in which he devoted 314 pages to a solution of the Shanghai Question which had worried China and the western nations for more than a half century. After discussing various methods of solving the problem, most of which Professor Johnstone dismissed as impractical, he added as afterthought, "Of course some nation might 'take' the foreign settlements." That is exactly what has happened, but obviously it has not permanently settled the Shanghai Question!

* "The Shanghai Problem," Stanford University Press, Stanford University California, 1937.

XXXIV

Japanese "Efficiency"

TWO OR THREE DAYS after the Japanese occupation of Shanghai, in December of 1941, there appeared a notice on the bulletin board of the Metropole Hotel, where I was staying, calling a meeting of Americans in the assembly room of the hotel for the purpose of "discussing problems incidental to the occupation." The notice contained the name of the Japanese officer in charge of the occupation. It struck me as strange that the Japanese should call a meeting to "discuss" problems when they were in undisputed military control of the city.

Only about two dozen Americans, including a few newspapermen, turned up for the meeting. Our curiosity regarding its object was soon satisfied, for aside from a few Japanese army officers, chiefly from the army spokesman's office, the room was filled with Japanese newspapermen and press photographers. No sooner had the Japanese officer in charge called the meeting to order than an American, owner of a small factory in the Hongkew district, was on his feet paying the Japanese fulsome praise for their efficiency and forbearance in the occupation of the Settlement. He even praised the Japanese for the consideration they had displayed toward the members of the American Club, who had been given only about two hours before they were kicked out of their premises. I myself had only about fifteen or twenty minutes to throw a few things into a suitcase and get out. I had to abandon practically all of my clothing and numerous pieces of carved ivory, and art treasures, including some rare Mongolian and Tibetan rugs, pieces of brocade and jewelry I had picked up on my newspaper travels in the Far East and in Russia and had treasured for many years.

I listened in silence to the speech of my fellow countryman as he praised the Japanese, even when he spread it on so thick that most of us wondered as to his real óbjective. Was it possible that he had "sold out" to the Japs in order to obtain protection for his factory, or for some other reason? We wondered. Japanese newspapermen present took copious notes on his address and before he sat down he was photographed repeatedly; in fact every American in the room was photographed.

After the Japanese chairman had called on others for their views on the occupation, it became apparent that their purpose in calling the meeting was to obtain complimentary statements from Americans for use in their propaganda in Japan and abroad. I naturally wondered what was in store for the thousands of American citizens, civilians, and servicemen in Shanghai and other ports of occupied China, the Philippines, and elsewhere in the Far East, now at the mercy of the invaders. I was well aware of the brutalities to which the Chinese had been subjected in Manchuria in 1931-32 and in China proper since 1937, but along with other foreigners I probably thought "They can't do that to us." I actually heard a prominent Englishman use that expression as he argued with a group of Japanese army officers who were evicting him, along with a number of other well known British residents, from the British Shanghai Club on the Bund.

As the meeting in the Metropole Hotel broke up one of the Japanese army officers recognized me and exclaimed, "Why, Mr. Powell, are you still here? We thought you had run away with Mr. Woodhead!" (H. G. W. Woodhead was a well known elderly British editor and commentator employed as a columnist on the *Shanghai Evening Post and Mercury*, who had gone into hiding immediately following Pearl Harbor.) He allegedly sent word to the Japanese that he would commit suicide if the Japanese attempted to intern him. I replied to the Japanese officer, whom I recognized as a member of the army spokesman's office, "No, I'm still a newspaperman and have decided to stay and see the end of the show—I don't suppose you can do worse than shoot me!" I soon discovered that the Japanese could do worse than shoot people. They could starve and torture them to a point where the victims would prefer death a thousand times to the treatment they received in innumerable prisons, scattered over the Far East, where Americans and Britons have been confined since Pearl Harbor.

As I think back over my experiences in the days immediately following the Japanese occupation, when I was still at liberty, the outstanding events and incidents which remain in my mind are a succession of queues in which I seemed to spend most of the daylight hours. First, there was the matter of money. I discovered that I had only a few dollars in my pocket, so I walked around to the Shanghai office of the National City Bank of New York, where I kept my personal and business accounts. As I neared the vicinity of the bank, I discovered that a considerable portion of the foreign and Chinese communities apparently had a similar idea, for a line had formed which not only extended around the block but overlapped. The line was made up not only of Americans, but of large numbers of other foreign residents, particularly Russians, Scandinavians, Portuguese, Jewish refugees and Chinese, all of whom thought that an American bank offered better protection than banks of other nationalities.

It took me about five hours to reach the doors through which depositors were admitted in groups of a dozen or so. After I finally was admitted to the private office I found the three American executives of the bank, MacKay, Reid, and Bates, standing with their hands in their pockets looking on more or less helplessly while two Japanese sat at the desk with the bank's books opened before them. One of the American officers whispered to me that both of the Japanese had been trained in the New York office of the Yokohama Specie Bank and "understood" American banking practice. They seemed to understand their job so well that I suspected they had been "planted" in New York for the purpose of "studying" the National City Bank. One of the Japanese explained to me that they were permitting all firms which employed Chinese labor to withdraw a certain percentage of their company deposits "in order to keep the workmen off the streets." The Japanese army apparently desired to avoid any disruption of business which might fill the streets with hungry, rioting laborers. Large employers of Chinese labor were told to advise their Chinese staffs to "go home" to the country districts. This applied to all concerns which were forced to close down or to curtail their activities because of the Japanese occupation. The public utilities, including the electric light and power plant, water works and telephone system, were continued—under Japanese supervision, of course.

The Japanese "liquidators" at the bank explained that no deposits in United States dollars could be withdrawn, which caused serious embarrassment, as most depositors had converted their savings into United States dollars in order to avoid losses resulting from the rapid depreciation of Chinese currency. Later the Japanese and the Nanking puppet administration announced that the national Chinese currency would be outlawed after a certain date, and replaced by new currency issued by the puppet central bank, the rate of exchange of old for new currency being two for one. It wasn't long, however, before the new puppet currency, printed in Japan to imitate the old national currency, had also slumped to forty for one American dollar.

I had ordered a suit of clothes from a Russian tailor just before the Japanese occupation. The agreed price was $150 in Chinese currency, or about $50 in United States money. When I obtained the suit after being released from prison five months later, just before the sailing of the first exchange ship, the price had jumped to $2,000. In the months following Pearl Harbor Shanghai passed through a period of currency inflation which was reminiscent of conditions in the large German cities following World War I. Mother Helen, the head Franciscan nurse at the municipal hospital, where I was a patient following my release from the Japanese internment camp, told me that the prices for hospital equipment had risen to fantastic figures. For example, a gallon of rubbing alcohol cost $600; iodine, so long as it was obtainable, cost $1,000 an ounce; sulfa drugs disappeared completely and were unobtainable at any price.

The most serious problem developed in connection with supplies of blood for transfusions. The Fourth Regiment United States Marines, which had been stationed in Shanghai for more than a dozen years, had constituted Shanghai's and China's almost sole source of supply of healthy blood. Hospitals in Shanghai and other coastal ports and even at interior points accessible to airplanes were accustomed to applying to the Marine Corps for supplies of blood. A number of marines had volunteered to supply blood at a nominal charge of $50 Chinese, or about $15 in United States currency. The donors had been examined as to health and blood-count, and constituted an invaluable "blood bank" for the community.

But when the situation became critical and the Fourth Regiment was transferred to Manila (later to fight at Bataan and Corregidor), Shanghai was left without any source of supply for blood transfusions. I was one of the first to suffer from this situation, as it was necessary for me to have a blood transfusion immediately after my removal from the Japanese prison camp to the municipal hospital. My doctor finally found an American who was willing to supply me with a quantity of his blood. Two weeks later, however, when I required a second transfusion, the American could not be found. My physician, Dr. W. H. Gardiner, made a canvass of the other doctors and finally found an Englishman who was willing to volunteer. The third time it was a Russian, and his blood caused a violent reaction in my veins. My fourth and last transfusion before leaving the Shanghai hospital was supplied by a Chinese, giving me the impression that I probably am the only person entitled to claim blood-relationship to the United Nations, as I actually have samples of American, British, Russian, and Chinese blood in my veins. My physicians in New York, Dr. Frank L. Meleney and Dr. Jerome P. Webster, gave me two further transfusions at the Presbyterian Hospital upon my arrival in New York; both came from the large bank maintained at the hospital, which Dr. Meleney assured me was strictly "anonymous" from the standpoint of race or nationality, as scientific tests have shown that it is all the same.

The problem of establishing blood banks in China is a serious one, due first to traditional Chinese prejudice against parting with blood, which they believe cannot be replaced. Secondly, the Chinese have been so impoverished physically, as a result of the long war, lack of health-building food, and prevalence of disease, particularly malaria and intestinal ailments, that it is difficult to find individuals sufficiently healthy to supply blood. Shanghai doctors found that a similar weakened situation prevailed among the Jewish refugees who had served long terms in Nazi internment camps in Hitler's Europe before they were sent to Shanghai and forced to undergo further privations at the hands of Tojo's emissaries.

XXXV

Horrors of Bridge House

MY FIRST CONTACT WITH the notorious Japanese Bridge House Prison was on December 20, 1941, following the occupation of Shanghai on December 8. The barbarities to which the Americans, Britons and Chinese were subjected in that prison were only a repetition of Japan's inhumane treatment of the Chinese and other Oriental peoples with whom they previously had come in contact. Like the Nazis in Europe, the Japanese regarded themselves as a "master race," to do with other peoples as they wished.

Early in the morning of December 20, six or seven gendarmerie officers in civilian clothes came to my room at the Metropole Hotel in Shanghai and informed me they had instructions to search the room. The spokesman referred to the fact that I was editor of the *China Weekly Review* and was a director of the *China Press,* both of which had been sealed on December 8.

They seized all papers, carbon copies of letters and other records which I had in my room. Since my offices had been sealed I had not been permitted to visit them, but I was informed that the gendarmes had repeatedly entered the building and removed various files and office records, and even the electric clock on the wall.

After they had searched my room one of the men told me I would have to accompany them to their headquarters for questioning. We went downstairs, where a motor car was waiting. One of the men suddenly remembered to ask me whether I had a box in the hotel safe. I told them I had one, containing only a small sum in Chinese money. After counting the money, the gendarme said, "We are not interested in money, only letters and papers."

I entered their car, and the officers drove across Szechwan Road Bridge and into the compound of the Bridge House Apartments, where I was taken to the third floor and introduced to the gendarme in charge. This was in the Hongkew section, and while located only two blocks from the central post office, the existence of the prison was not suspected by the foreigners. While I was being questioned a number of other foreigners who had been picked up that morning were brought in. The officers asked me to remove all articles from my pockets and place them on the table. The articles were put in an official envelope and labeled with my name. I was not permitted to have more than one handkerchief, and they even took away my suspenders and garters.

One of the men then produced a printed form and asked me a number of questions concerning nationality, place and date of my birth, and other personal matters. When this statement was completed I was asked to sign and fingerprint it.

I was then taken downstairs to the ground floor and into a section of the building which had been constructed for shops but later converted into a sort of stockade for prisoners. As my eyes became accustomed to the darkness I could see long rows of cells or stockades and could hear a dim murmur of voices. I was first taken to an officer sitting behind a rough desk in the corner. He, apparently, was the chief jailer, as the wall alongside his desk was covered with lists written in Chinese characters and also a considerable number of names in English, each on a little wooden tag; the tags were attached to metal pegs driven in the wall. Also there was a heavy metal ring on which were suspended a large number of keys, ranging from the small "Yale" type to large, ominous ones six or eight inches long. The gendarme who accompanied me opened one of the doors. It was double-locked and barred, and resembled a Hollywood property set. I was shoved into one of the cells. There was a hole about six inches square in the center of the door, through which the guards pushed the food. Occasionally when a prisoner had violated the rules the guards would order the man to come to the door and the guard would drive his fist through the hole and strike him in the face. If the prisoner was too slow in walking up to be struck, the guard would open the door, drag the man out into the corridor, and beat him with a club.

The room was already crowded to suffocation and there was no place to sit, even on the floor. Finally an American, Rudolph Mayer, a brother of the Hollywood movie magnate, who had been imprisoned some two weeks earlier, recognized me and asked me to join him. I made my way through the crowd to the corner where Mayer was sitting on the floor. He asked one or two of the Chinese prisoners sitting next him to move over to make room for me, and as a result I got a fairly comfortable seat in the corner of the room. I say "comfortable" because I could lean against the wall, and that was far better than sitting upright in the middle of the room.

Mayer told me he had saved that place because a Korean had died there of blood poisoning the night before. The Korean had been jabbed in the leg by a Japanese bayonet, and had been permitted to die in great agony. This did not increase my peace of mind, but I was nevertheless glad to get a corner place, even though it smelled to high heaven. Mayer told me he never was able to find out why the Japanese had arrested him, unless it was their intention to blackmail his wealthy brother in Hollywood.

The room or cell which we occupied was about eighteen feet long and twelve feet wide and could accommodate twenty to twenty-five persons sitting in rows on the floor, but for several days after my arrival there were more than forty prisoners in the room. For several nights it was necessary for many prisoners to stand up most of the night.

Events had occurred so rapidly that morning that my head was in a whirl. It was not long before a gendarme appeared at the door and called my name. The door was unlocked, with a great clatter of keys and bars, and I was told to accompany the man upstairs. Here I had my first experience with a gendarme examination.

I was told to write approximate dates of the entire history of my life, with special emphasis on what I had done since arriving in China in the spring of 1917. I do not know how many times this was repeated, but I believe I was told to write out my personal history at least a dozen times. The examiner then read it over laboriously, translated it into Japanese, and proceeded to question me on various points mentioned in the memorandum.

The man who questioned me on most occasions was named Lieutenant Yamamoto. His knowledge of English was not perfect, and he used an interpreter who was little better equipped. Later another interpreter was brought in, a man who said he had lived in San Francisco many years and had a wife and child still living there.

The questioning, which extended from December 20 through January to February 26, followed a general pattern and seemingly was designed to link me with American and British intelligence services. Once I was flatly accused of receiving large sums from the office of Major G. A. Williams, United States naval attaché, stationed at Shanghai. The examiner told me they had seized all of Major Williams's private papers and had the proof despite my denials. I told them I frequently talked to Major Williams about particular developments in the Chinese and Far Eastern situation, but it always was in the course of newspaper work and on no occasion had I received so much as a penny for my services.

Once the examiner told me they had found a record in the Major's office listing my name with those of Morris Harris of the Associated Press and Fred Opper and H. G. W. Woodhead of the *Evening Post*, as being on the Major's payroll. Several times they tried also to link me up with British intelligence, but since I did not even know the names of the persons in charge they finally gave this up.

They questioned me for several days about my trip to Chusan Island in the summer of 1937. On returning to Shanghai after that trip I had written an article suggesting the possibility that the Japanese were planning to occupy the island preliminary to naval operations along the coast between Shanghai and Hong Kong. Since the Japanese navy did this a few months later, the Japanese gendarmerie officer insisted this constituted definite proof of "espionage" activities directed against the Japanese navy. Chusan Island, south of Shanghai, was later used by the Japanese as a base for their invasion activities along the China coast to the south of Shanghai.

I imagine most of the American and British newspapermen were subjected to the same line of questioning, as the Japanese suspect all foreign newspapermen, particularly correspondents, of espionage activities on behalf of their home governments. Japanese gendarmerie officers who hang around the large hotels in Tokyo and other large Japanese cities for the purpose of spying on foreign residents and tourists always carry cards indicating they are connected with some newspaper.

All my statements were taken down by the chief examiner, in Japanese, on large sheets of Japanese ruled paper. These sheets were then perforated and folded into a sort of book, and I was asked to sign and fingerprint the last page. I always asked the examiner to give me a summary of the material contained in the manuscript, and on several occasions caught him in deliberate falsification.

It occurred to me that these statements, which probably filled half a dozen books, could easily be altered because it was possible to change or substitute pages and merely attach the last sheet which contained my signature and thumbprint.

I had no complaint of my treatment while undergoing questioning, except the wear and tear on my nerves. Moreover, I managed to keep my temper, except once or twice when I became exasperated at some of the seemingly nonsensical questions which they fired at me.

I once saw a big brutal gendarmerie officer with heavy thick hands slap a Chinese woman prisoner until her eyes were swollen shut and her face so inflamed that she was unrecognizable. They were trying to force her to disclose the whereabouts of her husband, a college professor whom they wanted on espionage charges. The Chinese woman refused to tell them where her husband was hiding, although she was subjected to the daily slappings until she became too weak to leave the cell, and lay weeping all day long on the floor.

The examiner produced a large number of copies of back issues of the *China Weekly Review*, extending over a period of several years, and asked me about certain articles or paragraphs which had been underscored. In most instances I was able to explain the circumstances and background of the articles.

There was an amusing development when the Japanese produced a recent copy of the *Review* which contained a brief article referring to the wholesale theft of motor cars in Shanghai. The article said the stolen cars were being turned over to the Japanese army authorities, who were at that time planning their campaign into French Indo-China. They wanted to know where I had obtained this information, so I told them it came from the police and the insurance companies, but I refused to give any names. I had a special interest in the subject, as the gangsters had also stolen my car.

Another article my inquisitors brought forward was one which had been reprinted from the *New York Herald Tribune*, the *Nation*, and *Asia Magazine*. It was written originally by Wilfrid Fleisher, former editor of the *Japan Advertiser* in Tokyo, and contained a reference to the plot of an army officer in Tokyo to overthrow the Emperor and establish a fascist dictatorship. They insisted that this article was disrespectful to the Emperor. My attention had been called to the same fact by the Japanese consulate some time previously, and as a result I had printed a statement that there was no intention to insult the Son of Heaven. This apparently did not satisfy them, as the subject was brought up several times.

They also dug up a further article which we had reprinted from a Chinese magazine in 1932, nine years previously, which referred to the "Emperor" Pu-yi of Manchukuo as a "puppet of a puppet." The article said that Pu-yi was a puppet of Hirohito, the Son of Heaven, who in turn was the puppet of the Japanese army general staff. My inquisitor insisted this article was also disrespectful of the Japanese Emperor. I called his attention to the fact that the article was nearly ten years old and had appeared in connection with Chinese comment on the Manchurian crisis. The explanation did not satisfy him, however, because of all the crimes classified under the general heading of "dangerous thoughts" in Japan, the worst that an editor can commit is to say something which the police censors can interpret as "disrespectful of the Son of Heaven." Large numbers of police censors are employed in every city for the sole purpose of watching the newspapers, foreign as well as native, for "disrespectful" references to Hirohito or the royal family. Had the Japanese succeeded in their program to "dictate peace in the White House," hundreds of American editors and cartoonists would have had a difficult time, as the Japs have long memories and their intelligence files are very complete.

Under Japanese military control of Hongkew since 1937, the existence of Bridge House Prison had been kept a profound secret. As there were a large number of Chinese prisoners, we realized at once that many Chinese who had disappeared from the International Settlement had been thrown into jail here. Several of the Chinese told us that they had been here for many months, so long, in fact, that they did not remember the cause of their incarceration. Many of the Chinese prisoners were boys not over fifteen years of age, probably high school students. It was rumored that Russians in the Settlement had been confined here also.

Bridge House Prison consisted of about fifteen cells which had been built inside the main building and in most cases were open only on one side, which was inclosed by heavy wooden bars six inches in diameter and set about two inches apart. I must have counted the bars a thousand times during my stay in Cell No. 5, which had been still further congested by the addition of some twelve more foreigners. These were mainly Britons but included in the group was Victor Keen, correspondent for the *New York Herald Tribune*, who was brought in shortly following my incarceration.

Many of the foreigners in the cells were Britons, including several well known businessmen, one being head of the China agency for Dodge cars and trucks. Another, named Ellis Hayim, was president of the Shanghai Stock Exchange. Another elderly man, named Brister, was connected with the British Ministry of Economic Warfare. A young man, only about twenty years old, told me he had been a member of the band of one of the British regiments previously stationed in Shanghai. Ellis Hayim and his wife, who was also imprisoned, were rated among Shanghai's leading socialites. He told me that the Japanese gendarme officer who questioned him and his wife was chiefly interested in obtaining information about the guests who attended certain dinner parties which Mr. and Mrs. Hayim had given in honor of Admiral Glassford and Admiral Hart. The Japanese also displayed great curiosity about the conversation at other dinner parties. In Japan the police always come around and quiz the servants about the guests who attend dinner parties given by foreign residents.

Another British prisoner was Bill Gande, head of a wholesale liquor house, whom the Japanese also accused of "espionage" and finally sentenced to jail for eight years on this charge. Gande had always taken a prominent part in the foreign special police and it probably was in this connection that the Japs suspected him of "espionage designed to undermine the Japanese Empire."

I learned later, on the exchange ship bound for home, that other American newspapermen, and a number of American businessmen and missionaries, had been confined in another part of Bridge House at the same time I was there. Among the busi-

nessmen were the managers of the National City Bank, Socony
Vacuum Oil Company, and the Singer Sewing Machine Company. Later, practically all of the Americans in the city, some
2,500 in number, were interned, but not in Bridge House.

The Japanese, in their haste to even scores with all the Americans and Britons against whom they had grudges, made many
ludicrous mistakes. One day a half dozen gendarmes dragged
into our cell an infuriated Englishman with his coat and trousers
badly torn, indicating that he had put up a fight against arrest.
After he became somewhat composed, I moved over to a place
beside him and asked him what had happened. He told me he
was an engineer employed by the Shanghai Power Company,
and was at a loss to understand why he was arrested. After he
had come back from his first session with the inquisitors upstairs, I noticed he had a puzzled look on his face. When the
sentry had walked to the end of the corridor the Englishman
turned to me and said, "I wonder what these bloody blighters
want—I never wrote anything about the Japs in my life." I
then realized why the Japs had grabbed the engineer, whose
name was W. R. Davies. They had mistaken him for R. W.
Davis, the managing director of the senior British newspaper,
North China Daily News. The situation struck us as having
amusing elements, as R. W. Davis, the newspaper publisher, was
in Hong Kong. However, W. R. Davies didn't consider it
amusing, and he was still threatening to murder some "bloody"
Jap when the gendarmes discovered their mistake and released
him. Up to that time the Japanese had avoided arresting anyone
who was connected with any public utility, as they wanted to
keep the city services operating.

A Spanish woman, wife of a banker in Manila, was held in
our cell for several weeks on suspicion that she had cooperated
with a foreign business firm in purchasing and monopolizing
all available supplies of quinine in Shanghai. The woman declared she knew nothing about the deal.

Many foreign businessmen who had dealings with the Japanese found themselves in serious trouble after the outbreak of war, as they were unable to make deliveries of the merchandise promised. Money they had received from the Japanese as advance or bargain payments had been remitted abroad, and "frozen," and hence could not be returned to the original Japanese purchasers. In the final months and weeks before Pearl Harbor the Japanese had embarked on a mad buying spree in Shanghai, grabbing up all available stocks of foods, medicines, gasoline, cigarettes, shoe leather, and what not. After Pearl Harbor they simply commandeered everything, including every motor car and truck in the city. After President Roosevelt announced the embargo on gasoline shipments to Japan, the Japs bought enormous quantities which they stored in secret underground storage tanks at Shanghai. Many foreign businessmen who had cooperated with the Japs, but couldn't make deliveries after the outbreak of war, found themselves in the Japanese internment camps.

Aside from the male foreigners, there were three foreign women, one British, one Spanish, and the other an unfortunate White Russian girl who shortly became hysterical. We thought her condition to be due to the fact that she had been deprived of her daily supply of heroin, for which many poor Russians possessed an appetite which the Japanese were glad to satisfy at very low prices. There were also two or three Chinese women in the cell for a part of the time. Once a Chinese man was brought in with his little three-year-old son. The little boy cried all night, his wails being heard throughout the prison.

Although I was impressed particularly by the congested condition of the cell, I soon discovered that there were other elements of even greater seriousness. There were no facilities for washing, and the toilet equipment consisted of a rough box in the corner which was open to the room and was cleaned out in the mornings by Chinese prisoners who were pressed into service.

The women prisoners had to use the same toilet facilities as the men, so the foreign men would stand with their backs to the toilet, forming a screen for the women. Finally, as a result of demands by everybody in the cell, the women were permitted to go to a toilet on an upstairs floor.

Since I had been informed I was being taken to the Bridge House only for questioning, I wore only a light overcoat and did not think of bringing along a blanket. The building was entirely without heat. At 9 P.M., however, the guard brought into the cell a large bundle of blankets, which created a near riot as the prisoners fought each other for possession of the heavier coverings.

I found the prisoners had formed groups of two to six, and by snuggling close together they were able to cover themselves with one blanket. We never removed our clothing, as we would have frozen.

There were vermin of all types, the worst being the body louse, or "cootie." The place was alive with them, and since the prisoners included several persons who were dangerously ill, we naturally expected everyone to die of some kind of epidemic, particularly typhus, which was prevalent. A friend who suspected the louse situation sent me a jar of ointment. The gendarme guard refused to permit it to be brought inside my cell until I had demonstrated by tasting it that it was not poison or dope. I learned afterward that the ointment was sent to me by Judge Milton J. Helmick of the United States Court, and I will never cease thanking him as long as I live. It probably was the first modern instance of a judge sending a prisoner a jar of ointment.

The gendarmes maintained a medical service of sorts among the prisoners. It usually consisted of an occasional visit by a Japanese woman nurse, accompanied by two petty officers. Anyone with a fever or any type of ailment got aspirin. Any who had boils, an epidemic of which swept the place, were treated with a red liquid resembling mercurochrome, of which the Japanese seemed to have a liberal supply.

I had a badly infected finger which swelled to about twice normal size. After about two weeks of begging for medical treatment, I was taken upstairs to the dispensary, where the

Japanese medical assistant, without administration of an anesthetic, literally trimmed all the skin off my finger with his scissors. Japanese soldiers stood about the room and appeared to enjoy my grimaces as the doctor performed the operation.

The worst phase of the daily visit of the Japanese nurse and her assistants was the treatment in the cell of several venereal cases among the Chinese prisoners. Since these cases had been neglected in some instances for many weeks or even months, the men were in a desperate condition.

The place was also infected with rats. The Japanese guards never interfered with them except to stamp their feet when the rodents became too bold in running about the corridors. One night a rat stuck its head out of a knot-hole in the partition next to my head and tugged at a strand of my hair which it apparently wanted for a nest.

I had not been in prison many days before I began to have severe pain in my feet, particularly the bones in my heels. As there was at that time no external indication of the ailment, the Japanese doctor just laughed at me when I told him that the pain was so severe I could scarcely put on my shoes. All prisoners were deprived of their shoes, which were piled in the narrow hallway outside. Whenever anyone was removed from the cell for questioning or for any other purpose there was a mad scramble for the right shoes. We had to lie with our bare feet on the cold floor, and they usually would be blue by morning. Our stockings had long since worn to shreds.

Only once did I succeed in getting the Japanese nurse to paint my feet with iodine, and this had little or no effect on the pain, which increased day by day. Several other prisoners also complained of pains in their feet, and many of the Chinese had large sores on their feet and legs. I did not know then that this was due to malnutrition caused by the poor quality of the food we received, plus the fact that we frequently were compelled for long periods to sit on our feet "Japanese style," which retarded the circulation.

Our food was of such a low order that no Japanese coolie

would have looked at it. In the morning there was a bowl of rice, which was fairly palatable because it was warm. Noon and evening meals consisted of a bowl of rice, which few of the foreigners could eat. It was stone cold, usually contained three dried herring heads, and apparently was prepared once a week and left standing in the hallway or courtyard.

Very few of us could eat this mess, so we made a deal with some of the Chinese boy prisoners whereby in exchange for our rice they agreed to search out the cooties in our undergarments every day. It wasn't long before the Chinese boys had organized a lottery based on the number of cooties found in the various undershirts of the foreign prisoners.

This arrangement proved satisfactory except that it left us with only one bowl of rice a day, obviously not enough to keep body and soul together. This was the cause of much of the illness which I later learned was beriberi.

Thanks to efforts of friends outside, we were finally able to obtain limited quantities of foreign food, chiefly sandwiches. The Japanese refused to let any canned food come into the building, but since our friends outside did not know this they continued to send tins of meat, fish, and fruit, which were consumed by our guards. Our distress was due, principally, to the lack of meat and fresh vegetables.

It was always difficult to eat the things which were sent in, because of the starving Chinese prisoners who sat watching us. Many times I cut my sandwiches into a dozen pieces and passed them around. On one or two occasions there were serious riots over food because the Japanese would not allow the Chinese to receive anything from friends outside.

Perhaps our most exasperating experience was on Christmas Eve, when friends sent us a roasted turkey. We only managed to get the scraps in our cell, and when we complained to the officer he came back with the excuse that they could not permit bones to be taken into the cells, as the prisoners might use them as weapons against each other or the guards.

XXXVI

"Dangerous Thoughts"

PRISONERS IN BRIDGE HOUSE were not permitted to talk to each other, were supplied with no reading matter, and were compelled to sit on the floor closely packed in rows, which facilitated counting when there was a change of guards, which was every four hours. Also we had to sit usually with our heads bowed, facing in the direction of Tokyo as a sign of our submission to Hirohito, Son of Heaven. Frequently Chinese prisoners who were caught talking were ordered to stand at the front of the cell, where they were beaten about the head by guards.

The only foreigner I knew of who was treated in this way was a Russian prisoner, who could speak neither English, Japanese, nor Chinese. He was severely beaten, allegedly because he failed to understand an order. The Russian's name was Chesnakoff; he was a young Soviet citizen, who had come to Shanghai on a ship from Vladivostok. The Japanese accused Chesnakoff of spying on some of their military activities in the Shanghai district.

Once I received a thermos bottle of tea from a friend on the outside. I had only begun to drink the tea when the guard came up and demanded I return the empty bottle. Quickly I gulped down all that I could and passed the bottle to some of my Chinese cell-mates. When I took the bottle to the front of the cell and passed it to the guard he was infuriated and ordered me to step up close to the hole in the door which was used for passing in food and for the return of empty dishes. He reached in and gave me a strong slap on the face.

This was the only time I was ever physically molested by

one of the guards. However, in other ways the foreign prisoners were usually subjected to the same treatment as the Chinese prisoners; that is, they were compelled to sit on the floor with their knees drawn up tightly in front of them. All prisoners were lined up and searched almost daily, and woe to anyone found in possession of so much as a piece of string or a piece of paper. There was dismay when the searchers found a small nail file, the only one in the prison, which everybody had been using in secret when the guard's back was turned.

When some of the prisoners had violated the regulations and the guards were unable to find the culprits, they compelled all of us to sit on our feet in Japanese fashion with our heads lowered. As we were always forced to face toward Tokyo during this operation, it became known as the "New Order Kneeling Posture."

Several times in my cell prisoners were compelled to sit on their feet as long as six or eight hours and, as a result, were not able to walk for several days.

The beating of Chinese prisoners by the guards was an almost continuous procedure. All through the night we would hear screams, indicating that some poor devil was being punished for a real or fancied violation of the rules.

In one case the guards caught a Chinese smoking a cigarette which had been smuggled into the cell. He was beaten to a pulp, and was not able to stand for more than a week. Later he developed beriberi and died in my cell shortly after the Japanese doctor had given him a hypodermic. We suspected the hypo had contained poison.

Another time a Chinese prisoner found with money in his possession was removed at midnight to the corridor and beaten over the head and face with a club. From curiosity I counted the blows, with a British prisoner lying beside me. There were eighty-five of them before the victim ceased screaming and lapsed into insensibility. When the guard had finished there was only about a foot of the former yard-long club remaining in his hands, the rest of it having been splintered away. The guards kept a pile of these cudgels handy in the corridor. They were rough pieces of one-inch board about four inches wide and about three feet long.

A significant element in the prison situation both at Bridge House and Kiangwan Prison, where I was sent later, was the presence of a considerable number of Japanese prisoners. These consisted of young men, employees of American and British firms, from whom the gendarmes were trying to obtain information regarding the activities of the foreigners. One of these Japanese prisoners in my cell, a young man named Ono, had been employed for several years by the Texas Oil Company and had made several trips to Port Arthur, Texas, on oil tankers. He did not hesitate to express his hatred of the Japanese gendarmerie officers, whom he always referred to contemptuously as the "big shots upstairs." The Japanese also threw into our cell a number of Japanese soldiers charged with drunkenness while on duty.

The Chinese prisoners who fraternized with the Japanese soldiers told us that the real reason for their imprisonment was their objection to being sent to Malaya, where fighting was then in progress. Later when I was taken to the Kiangwan prison I saw hundreds of Japanese prisoners, military as well as civilians, who were being held on charges of harboring "dangerous thoughts." I was told by a foreign newspaperman in Japan that there were more than 50,000 political prisoners of this class in Japanese jails at the time of the Manchurian occupation in 1931-32. Later they were released to join the army for further adventures to the south.

I talked to many of these prisoners and found their regard for the gendarmes was little higher than my own. Once a gendarme officer beat a Japanese soldier into insensibility in the cell adjoining mine because the soldier had called him the one profane word in the Japanese language, "bakka," which stands for anything from "fool" to the equivalent of some of the most profane epithets in the English language.

The Japanese gendarmerie, profoundly secret in its organization, corresponds in many respects to the German Gestapo. I think it is safe to say that it contains all the criminal elements in the military establishment. Their power appeared unlimited, and they often boasted they could arrest even high Japanese military officers, but I never heard of this happening. In Japan the gendarmerie is of all branches of the military establishment the most hated and feared by the civilian public.

One night the Japanese gendarmes brought in a new prisoner, an aged Britisher, so weak he could hardly stand. They pushed him into the corner alongside me, and I saw he was in severe pain. He was suffering from several boils on his neck; they had become so infected and swollen, because of lack of medical attention, that his head was pressed over against his shoulder. He grew worse and about midnight he nudged me and asked me if I knew a prayer. He said he had been born in a Catholic home, but had drifted away from the faith. "I think I am going to die," he said. We repeated the Lord's Prayer together, and as he grew calmer, he told me his life history. He was born in England and enlisted in the British army as a youth to serve in India. He was stationed in the Punjab for seventeen years, spending most of the time in the saddle. After retirement he came to Shanghai, where he served as head of the C. I. D. (Criminal Investigation Department) in the municipal police, later retiring to form a private detective agency. His name was Captain E. G. Clarke. He had married an Indian woman who brought him food in the prison every day. Their home was in the country and she rode a bicycle a distance of twenty miles in order to bring the food. The Japs seized Clarke after Pearl Harbor, and charged him with the usual "crime," espionage activities against Japan. He was thrown into a dirty cell in another part of Bridge House and left there to die of malnutrition and exposure.

I never did learn why he was transferred to my cell, but a few days later when I was taken upstairs for another session with Lieutenant Yamamoto, my official inquisitor, I told him of Captain Clarke's serious condition, that he was likely to die unless he was sent to a hospital. Yamamoto made a gesture with the edge of his hand across his throat, indicating that he thought Clarke should have his head cut off, but I could see that my words had impressed him. Late that night there was a commotion in the courtyard; an ambulance had arrived to take Captain Clarke to the municipal hospital. I learned several weeks later, just before I left Shanghai on the exchange ship, that Captain Clarke was recovering. Before leaving the prison that night he gave me his blanket, the most valuable article in the cold prison.

On February 26 a group of gendarme officers came to the prison cells and read the names of eight foreigners, including myself, who were told to go to the gendarmerie office. There we were informed that we were to be taken to another prison, at Kiangwan, where we would be subjected to a court-martial on a charge of espionage. The group included six Britons, the Russian Chesnakoff, and myself.

Each was given a shave and a haircut, and then we were taken in an open truck to Kiangwan, where a new prison had been built beside a main highway, near the new Chinese Civic Center Headquarters which the Japanese army had taken over. This prison consisted of solitary cells, each about five feet wide and ten feet long, entered by a door about four feet high. The door had a slot at the bottom through which food was passed to the prisoner.

There was a small window six feet above the floor. In the corner was the usual toilet, a box which was cleaned out once a week. The floors were wood, the walls fresh wet cement. Since the building was not heated, it became unbearably cold at night.

Every morning we were removed from the cells and taken across the courtyard to a wash-house where each man was provided with a toothbrush and told to use it and wash. We were not permitted to take the toothbrushes to our cells but had to

hang them on hooks, each labeled with our respective names—
in Japanese—which none of us could read. After the first day
the toothbrushes became hopelessly mixed and we lost our enthusiasm for this phase of the morning exercise. We were
warned not to talk.

This was the only time the prisoners ever got together,
except at rare intervals when we were permitted to take exercise in the courtyard under supervision of a military officer in
uniform. We were still permitted no reading matter. Also, we
were not permitted to have any of the medicines our friends
had sent us at Bridge House and which the guards had permitted
us to bring along.

The condition of my feet, which had pained me severely at
Bridge House Prison, rapidly became worse, due, I suppose, to
the freezing weather which prevailed all through March, when
Shanghai often has its coldest weather of the year.

I frequently complained and asked that a doctor be sent to
examine me, but this had little effect until my feet had swollen
to about twice their normal size and turned purple, making it
impossible for me to put on my shoes and leave my cell.

Meanwhile my weight had dropped from about 145 pounds
when I entered Bridge House Prison to about 70 or 75 pounds.
I was no longer able to stand, due to weakness and the condition of my feet.

One of the British prisoners also complained about pain in
his feet, and another Briton, Mr. Gande, had so many boils on
his neck that he could not lift up his head.

One day while I was still able to go out in the courtyard
with the other prisoners, I had a chance to talk to one of the
elderly British prisoners. He was very depressed and was certain
he never would get out alive. He felt sure I would get out, and
asked me to do a favor for him. He said, "I have a little daughter
living in the French Concession in Shanghai. I want you to
write to a certain bank in Australia and tell them to see that my

deposit there is handed over to my daughter after the end of the war." He mentioned the amount in English pounds, and it was so large as to surprise me. Later when I told some of the younger correspondents of the incident, they with one accord asked for the young lady's address.

The food at the Kiangwan prison was somewhat better, as we got a bowl of seaweed in addition to the rice, which was all that had been provided at Bridge House. The seaweed was fairly palatable at first, but after a while we became tired of it.

The food sent in from the outside came from the city by truck a distance of ten or fifteen miles, and usually arrived frozen. Since I could no longer put on my shoes the Japanese finally sent for a doctor, who made an examination of my feet. He gave me a daily injection for about two weeks, but this brought no relief, and I steadily grew weaker and no longer could eat anything. I could, however, drink the tea they occasionally brought me. One day as I was lying on the floor looking through the slot into the corridor, which was about four feet wide, I saw the slot in the door directly opposite my cell cautiously opened and a Japanese prisoner, a member of the "dangerous thought" brigade, motioned to me and then put his finger to his mouth. There were about fifty Japanese prisoners in that section, and they had noticed that I was not eating the food which the guards brought me. I quickly realized that the Japanese prisoner was motioning for me to give him my food. After that, I would watch until the sentry had walked around the corner on his beat and then I would push the aluminum pans containing the food as far into the corridor as I could reach. The Jap prisoner would then quickly reach out and grab the pan and pull it into his cell. After they had finished he would roll the pans back to my side of the corridor.

Since I was not permitted to read and couldn't even whisper to the other prisoners, I used to while away the time by composing an endless poem which started out,

I'm only a little Japanese,
But I'm wonderfully clever.
I slipped into Pearl Harbor seas,
And sank America's fleet forever.

Then I sneaked across the China Sea,
To proud Shanghai and Hong Kong.
I caught the Anglo-Americans fast asleep,
With both male and female pants down.

The poem became progressively worse and completely un-printable by the time I got to Singapore, Burma, and Batavia. But it did help me to forget the terrible pain in my feet. At night I would lie in the darkness and the deathly quiet, listening for an old-fashioned clock somewhere in the building to strike the hours and half-hours. Like the Americans and Filipinos at Bataan and Corregidor, I never gave up hope of release, and figuratively strained my eyes for the planes and battleships which I felt would surely come. But there was no disguising the fact that my physical condition was rapidly deteriorating, and I began to speculate on the matter of death. My thoughts would flit from a prayer beseeching divine assistance for my wife and children in the United States, who I knew were worrying about me, to the book I planned to write after I got out. I had no way of knowing that my family and friends in the United States were moving heaven and earth to see that I was included in the list scheduled for exchange. A Chinese prisoner who was brought into Bridge House Prison before I left there told me that a report had been circulated in Shanghai that Vic Keen and I had been executed as spies.

One day a gendarmerie officer came down to my cell and insisted that I write a letter stating I was in "good health." I was puzzled at the request, not knowing that the Swiss Consul-General, acting on behalf of the United States Government, had called at the Bridge House and demanded the right to see me. The Japanese refused the request, but attempted to side-step a diplomatic issue by showing the Swiss official my letter stating I was in "good health." Aware of the Japanese inability to understand Americanese, I wrote the letter in such a way as to indicate my real condition, but the Japs must have had expert advice, as they brought the letter back a half dozen times and finally threatened to punish me unless I wrote the letter as they directed. The Swiss Consul-General told me after I had been taken to the hospital that he suspected my real condition because of the time it took the Japs to produce the signed letter stating I was "all right."

I finally became so weak that I could only murmur "Take me to the hospital," when the Japanese officer came to my cell in the mornings to see how I was. One day when I had practically lost hope and would have welcomed death to put an end to my misery, I heard a commotion at the door, and as it opened and I looked into the corridor I was thrilled by the sight of two Japanese guards bearing a stretcher. The Japanese doctor, who accompanied them, gave me another shot in the arm and said, "You go hospital." He then turned his back and walked away as the guards rolled me on the stretcher. As they carried me out of the dark interior of the building into the bright sunlight, I made a supreme effort and rolled my head over to one side. My heart almost stopped beating, for there stood the municipal ambulance, and waiting at the door were Dr. Gardiner and my old journalistic collaborator, Vic Keen of the *New York Herald Tribune*. Both Gardiner and Keen looked at me searchingly, as though to make sure they had the right patient. At the General Hospital, when Dr. Gardiner was examining me, he laughed and said that I resembled Mahatma Gandhi following one of his extended fasts. I told him that my situation was really worse than Gandhi's as I had been provided with neither grape juice nor goat's milk.

XXXVII

Yankee Grain in China

A JAPANESE OFFICER accompanied me in the ambulance from the Kiangwan Prison to the hospital, and after a conference with Sister Helen, the French Franciscan nurse in charge, he pasted a notice on the door of my room. It stated with great formality that no one was permitted to enter the room without official permission of the Japanese army authorities. After the officer had departed Sister Helen told me that the Japanese officer had given her orders that only two persons, aside from the hospital staff, be permitted to enter my room. They were my physician, Dr. W. H. Gardiner, and Victor Keen, my newspaper colleague. Both Gardiner and Keen were in turn warned not to disclose my whereabouts or condition to anyone on penalty of severe punishment. Dr. Gardiner used to tell me about conversations he frequently overheard in which someone said that he knew positively that Powell had been shot.

The first problem, naturally, was to decide what to do with my feet, which were swollen twice their normal size and were almost black, due to "dry" gangrene. Should they be amputated above the ankles, the usual practice in such cases? I heard the doctors discussing the subject in the corridor.

The terrible pain my feet were causing me was almost unbearable and could only be borne when I kept them elevated to a height above my heart; but to lose them entirely, leaving me with two stumps! Even the thought of that was unbearable, and then came the inescapable thought of ultimately recovering and going home to my family and friends in that condition.

Finally we had a conference with the doctors, each presenting the pros and cons, whether to operate or not. Dr. Ranson, a Briton, who had studied surgery in New York, suggested a delay of a few hours to enable him to make an inspection of Chinese and poorer-class Russian hospitals to see whether he could find any similar cases. He found many cases in varying degrees of seriousness, the worst being those in which the ailment, because of neglect, had spread to the limbs and arms.

Another consultation, and it was decided to follow the most approved treatment, which consisted largely of building up the body by supplying artificially the missing elements, thus permitting nature to overcome the poisonous infection. This treatment was prolonged and painful, as it necessitated daily dressings and removal of dead tissue and infected bones. The treatments were usually preceded by a morphine injection, which mercifully deadened the pain as the doctor removed a toe here and a bone there. I finally lost practically the entire foreparts of both feet, which have been reduced to two stumps upon which I hope, ultimately, with the help of some specially designed shoes, to be able to balance myself and walk again. Since my arrival at New York Presbyterian Medical Center, my infections have been cured and I have had innumerable skin-grafting and "plastic" operations under the skilled hands of Doctors Frank L. Meleney and Jerome P. Webster, both of whom received three years of valuable experience in the Rockefeller Institute in Peiping. Due to their skill and the services of the nursing staff, I have made a miraculous recovery—in fact, I am on a reducing diet as this was written.

One day another patient was brought into the hospital room in Shanghai adjoining mine, and a Chinese orderly whispered to me that the patient was a "high Italian naval officer." After the officer had been there a few hours he came in to see me— and told me a strange story. He was a retired naval officer, captain of the Italian liner *Conte Verde*, which had been caught in Shanghai harbor when war broke. His ship carried a crew of about 350 Italian officers and men, who found themselves bottled up in Shanghai with no chance of getting home.

He said that about a month after the outbreak of war the Japanese asked him to assist them in transferring a large Yugo-slavian-registered ship, which was also marooned in Shanghai harbor, to Japan. The Japanese were anxious to have the ship in Japan for use as an army transport to carry troops to the South Seas. The regular crew of the ship had deserted after the outbreak of war, and the Japanese had no one available in Shanghai who knew how to operate it. The captain of the *Conte Verde* recruited two dozen members of his Italian crew and sailed the Yugoslavian steamer across to Japan. All went well until they were entering Kobe Harbor, when, without warning, there was a terrific explosion and the ship was blown out of the water. About a dozen of the Italian volunteer crew were killed, and the captain was hurled from the bridge into the water.

The torpedo which caused the havoc was fired by an American submarine which apparently had been lying in wait off the Japanese port.

The captain said that he swam until he was nearly exhausted, when he found a water-soaked board floating on the surface of the water. By gripping the edge of the board with his teeth and paddling with both hands he managed to keep his nose above the water and himself afloat for eight hours, when he was picked up by a Japanese fisherman and taken to Kobe and ultimately sent back to Shanghai.

To my surprise he seemed to have no resentment against Americans, despite the fact that he was suffering from a severe attack of arthritis as a result of exposure in the cold, dirty water of Kobe Harbor. Rather, he blamed the Japanese for all his troubles. The *Conte Verde* was later used to transport Americans, including myself, to Lourenço Marques, the little port in Portuguese East Africa where the first exchange of war prisoners between the United States and Japan took place. It required no perspicuity on the part of the American passengers on the *Conte Verde* to discover that the Italian crew to a man hated the Japanese and wished they could get away from them. Some of them thought they might be able to escape from the ship when it reached the African port, but there was no opportunity. The Japanese seized the *Conte Verde* and interned the officers and crew in Shanghai after the collapse of Italy.

The difficult food situation which quickly developed in Shanghai as a result of the Japanese occupation was soon observable in the hospital, where many common articles, domestic as well as imported, disappeared from the menu. Potatoes, for example, were out for a long time, the reason being the refusal of Chinese farmers to bring them to market because the Japs had taken over the municipal markets, and in addition to the extortion there the Japanese sentries along the roads leading into the city all exacted their toll. The Japanese had also seized the abattoirs, thus obtaining control over meat supplies.

The fact that the Japanese invasion of Chinese territory was a robber expedition was nowhere more evident than at Shanghai. Here it was observable that the robber instinct, previously restricted to higher officers, had seeped down through the ranks to the common soldiers, who were now filling their own pockets by "squeezing" the poor Chinese peasants. Previously the ordinary Jap soldier had been interested only in killing and torture, but when he saw his officers filling their pockets he quickly helped himself, either by looting the poor Chinese homes or by forcing the peasants to pay toll as they trundled their produce to market along the roads or the canals. As Shanghai was an old and wealthy city in the midst of a rich district dotted with innumerable family villages, it offered the Japs an opportunity for loot which had not existed in the open spaces of Manchuria or North China.

Once I was in the border town of Antung at the beginning of the war when the customs authorities, who still belonged to the Chinese regime, seized a Japanese army officer whose pockets and clothes were so filled with jewelry and money that he could scarcely sit down. How many people he had murdered or tortured to obtain this secret hoard of some rich Chinese or Russian family was never known.

It wasn't long before every imaginable line of trade, particularly foods, had been "organized" and monopolized by the Japanese. All of the Chinese railroads and telegraphs, previously government-owned, were taken over and handed to private Japanese companies to which monopoly privileges had been granted. In many cases the Japs went through the formality of appointing Chinese, usually friends of the Wang Ching-wei puppet Administration at Nanking, to minority positions in the Japanese monopolies. The Wang Government, at periodic intervals, would issue official notices legalizing the Japanese monopoly concerns.

As a result of the wholesale looting of Chinese resources, the Chinese farmers and food producers and processors ceased functioning, except for their own personal requirements. This explained why famine conditions developed in many sections of China which had been prosperous. In Kwangtung Province of South China the Japanese have followed the practice of raiding rice-growing districts, where they either seize or destroy crops of rice which are likely to be transported into Free China.

After having been starved in the Japanese internment camps for nearly four months, I naturally had to return to a normal diet by slow degrees. My stomach, long unaccustomed to normal food, rebelled against many articles which had constituted a chief topic of conversation among the prisoners during the period of incarceration. For example, we used to dream about thick juicy steaks, but after I was taken to the hospital I found I couldn't eat meat of any description except an occasional small piece of boiled chicken. The hospital managed to obtain supplies of eggs, which I could eat, and when I first arrived, there was ample oatmeal and hot milk. But the supplies of oatmeal suddenly stopped, and Sister Helen tearfully told me that no more was available in the Shanghai market. "I have searched everywhere, and there isn't a single package of any kind of American breakfast cereal in Shanghai," she said.

I was lying in bed thinking of this new crisis when I suddenly had an idea. For the past two years the American Red Cross Committee in Shanghai, of which I was a member, had been distributing "cracked wheat" and dried powdered skim milk to thousands of Chinese refugees who had been impoverished by the war. The Red Cross committees of businessmen and missionaries had been formed in the areas occupied by the Japanese army. Chinese businessmen in the foreign ports financed the transportation of the grain from Shanghai to interior points. The Japanese permitted most of the shipments to pass into territory controlled by their army, the reason being two-fold: First, the Japanese didn't want to do anything which might cause the United States Government to enforce the threatened embargo on vast shipments of scrap iron, oil, machinery, and cotton which were flowing into Japan; second, the Japanese army was purchasing (with worthless military notes) or seizing, all of the rice and other foods which the Chinese farmers produced, hence they were not averse to permitting American humanitarians to take over the job of feeding the starving victims of Japanese aggression. It also happened that the famine period in China, beginning with the Japanese invasion of North China and the Yangtze Valley in 1937, coincided with the period of surplus wheat in the United States. Enormous quantities of the wheat were shipped to China in "cracked" form, meaning that it had passed through the first milling process, chiefly in the big mills at Seattle.

Missionary organizations and their Chinese affiliates who had charge of much of the distribution originated numerous palatable menus which gradually changed the almost exclusively rice-eating habits of the Chinese in the Yangtze Valley and South China to a diet of American wheat.

In North China the population was already accustomed to grain diets, wheat, corn, or kaoliang, but in Central and South China the staple was rice, which, incidentally, is the most expensive grain of all to produce, as it must be hand-planted, hand-harvested and hand-threshed.

My "great idea" as I lay in the municipal hospital, after Sister Helen had told me of the drying up of the cereal supply, was concerned with the large quantities of cracked wheat which the Red Cross shipped to Shanghai, and much of which was still in storage. I dictated a letter for Sister Helen to send to the American Relief Committee, which was still functioning, suggesting that they intercede with the Japanese army to release some of the wheat for use of the patients in the hospital. As a result we succeeded in obtaining a considerable quantity of the cracked wheat for the hospital. I also learned that the American committee had induced the Japs to release a further quantity of the American cracked wheat and dehydrated milk for the use of a considerable number of Americans who found themselves in destitute circumstances as a result of the shutting down of businesses with which they were connected. Thus the American population in Shanghai unexpectedly became the beneficiaries of a charity enterprise which originally was intended for Chinese victims of Japanese aggression.

I wondered what became of the tens of thousands of starving Chinese who had subsisted on the American cracked wheat prior to Pearl Harbor, because the Japs immediately stopped all distribution to the Chinese and commandeered all stocks. They also did the same with regard to the large stocks of specialized foods such as evaporated milk, baby foods and medicines which the American Committee for Medical Aid to China, and other bodies, had sent to Shanghai for relief purposes. Presumably these unfortunate people joined the ranks of the thirty million Chinese refugees who fled from Japanese-occupied regions and joined the long trek to the west where they could be under the National Government of Free China.

XXXVIII

On the Exchange List

ONE DAY A YOUNG Japanese lieutenant from the army spokes-man's office came to see me at the hospital, and brought along a large parcel of cigarettes. He spoke American-English per-fectly, and said he had attended school in the United States. He disclosed to me in great secrecy the exciting information that there was to be an exchange of American and Japanese civilians, and that American newspaper correspondents were to be included in the exchange. He was certain that I would be permitted to sail on the exchange ship, providing my health would permit me to be taken on board.

Would the Japanese really permit me to sail, and would I be physically able to make the trip? I put it up to Dr. Gardiner. "You might be able to make the trip if you had daily medical attention, but I'm not on the exchange list!" There was no way of obtaining a copy of the sailing list to see whether any doctors were included. It turned out that there were thirty missionary doctors on the boat and more than fifty nurses, but we had no way of knowing it then. I had no assurance, aside from the word of the young Japanese army lieutenant, that my name was on the list.

Later I had another caller, the Consul-General for neutral Switzerland, who acted for the United States in the Far East. He told me of many attempts he had made to see me at both Bridge House and Kiangwan prisons, but he had always been put off with crudely written letters bearing my signature stat-ing "I am in good health and very satisfied," or similar ridicu-lous statements which I obviously had not written. The Swiss

Consul-General also told me of the report which had been circulated in the United States that I had been executed for "espionage," and of inquiries he had received from the State Department on the subject. The Swiss official assured me that my name was on the sailing list of the exchange ship, providing my physical condition would permit my being taken aboard, and providing also that the Japanese didn't change their minds at the last minute and decide to hold me in Shanghai.

A few days later Vic Keen came to see me, in great agitation, and showed me a copy of the *Shanghai Evening Post and Mercury*, former American paper but now a Japanese organ, which had a two-column story on the front page stating that a number of Americans and Britons had been convicted by army court-martial of espionage activities against Japan and had been given heavy sentences. My name was in the list. Keen felt certain that a group of the army which was known to oppose my repatriation had been able to countermand the previous order, and that I probably would be returned to the Japanese prison. I also learned that the report in the paper had been broadcast over the Japanese radio by an American journalistic renegade who had "gone over" to the Japs and was broadcasting Domei and Transocean reports over one of the former American stations.

Under the excellent care of the hospital staff my health had begun to show improvement; my weight was up to 79 pounds, and I was able to sit in a reclining chair in the sun on the veranda adjoining my room. The pain in my abbreviated feet had also decreased, thanks to the removal of many of the infected bones and tissues, and the receipt of further blood transfusions. The prospect of my being able to sail spurred the nurses and Chinese orderlies to increased effort in my behalf. Vic Keen's Chinese boy even smuggled into the hospital some delicious Chinese food of his own preparation, Sister Helen brought me a little charm which she pinned on my pajamas over my heart, with a prayer for my recovery. She was elated when I repeated to her from memory a prayer-poem she had given me a few days previously.

Then I received a report that Dr. Gardiner's name had been added to the sailing list, which brought me almost as much joy as it did him. I also learned that another long-time medical friend, Dr. J. C. McCracken of St. Luke's Hospital, and his wife, were scheduled to sail. So too was Dr. Randolph Shields of the Cheeloo Medical School in Shantung. The presence of such a large number of missionary doctors and nurses on the exchange ship was an indication of the extent to which the Japanese invasion of China had forced the suspension of hospitals and medical services.

In the midst of the joyful news and preparations for departure came the report in the renegade papers, supplemented by the broadcast over the Jap radio, that I would not be permitted to sail.

Of one thing I was certain—I would never go back to the Jap prison alive. I mentally calculated the distance from my bed to the veranda, and wondered whether I might be able to summon sufficient strength to crawl to the veranda and climb over the four-foot banister and throw myself to the street, seven floors below. The idea of suicide had never before entered my mind, although I suspected on several occasions that the Japanese gendarmes would have been greatly pleased if I had leaped over the railing of the narrow balcony which fronted the fourth-floor apartments in Bridge House Prison where the gendarme inquisitors had their offices. The Japanese guard who escorted me from my cell to Lieutenant Yamamoto's office and back, often, late at night, would point over the banister into the dark courtyard below and laugh significantly, but I pretended not to notice him and hurried along the dark passageway as fast as I could walk.

My thoughts involuntarily reverted to the case of my friend and former newspaper colleague at Shanghai, "Jimmie" Cox, correspondent for Reuter's, who jumped or was thrown from a fourth-floor window in the gendarmerie headquarters in Tokyo during the same kind of inquisition to which I was being subjected. Jimmie, well known in newspaper circles in the Far East, had been manager of Reuter's Tokyo office for some time when he was suddenly summoned to the gendarmerie headquarters and charged with espionage activities on behalf of the British Embassy. After he had been questioned for several hours, so the gendarmes alleged, Cox had confessed his guilt and jumped from the window to the concrete sidewalk below. He was not killed by the fall and was taken to a hospital in an unconscious condition. The British Embassy finally forced the Japanese to permit a British doctor to examine him, and it was found that his arms and legs were covered with marks indicating that he had been repeatedly pricked by a hypodermic needle.

There was no way of explaining the mystery, as Cox never regained consciousness. Were the marks of the needle evidence of some weird form of Japanese torture designed to make him confess to something of which he was not guilty? Some thought the gendarmes had repeatedly beaten him into insensibility and then revived him with a hypodermic, until they had forced him to sign a crudely written confession, following which they had thrown him from the window. After his death the Japanese turned over to Jimmie's wife the sheet of paper containing his alleged confession. Relman Morin, Associated Press correspondent in Tokyo, who sent a report of the incident, was himself summoned to the police station for questioning concerning his sources of information; but he was released after a few hours. James R. Young, I.N.S. correspondent in Tokyo, was also imprisoned for several weeks because of cables he had filed while on a trip to China, which had aroused the ire of the war lords. Other correspondents in Japan, including Otto Tolischus of the *New York Times,* were also imprisoned and mistreated after Pearl Harbor.

The day following publication of the report of my "conviction" the young Japanese lieutenant came to see me again, and when he saw the distressed look on my face he smiled reassuringly and said, "Don't pay any attention to that story or the broadcast; you are certain to be on the *Conte Verde* when it sails next week." I asked him why the story had been printed. His reply was only one word, "Face." It continued to puzzle me, but after I reached New York a friend told me he had heard in Washington that the Japanese had made a last-minute attempt to hold me but had been forced to permit me to sail when the State Department allegedly threatened to hold a Japanese banker whom the Tokyo Government was anxious to have repatriated.

Two days before the *Conte Verde* sailed my Japanese officer acquaintance came to tell me good-bye—and he had a request, which explains why I cannot divulge his name. He told me he was a graduate of a well known American university—and "if I happened to see any of his classmates, would I explain to them that he entertained no hatred for Americans and had joined the Japanese army not from choice." He was one of the only two Japanese among several scores I met in the course of many years of newspaper work in the Orient who expressed such sentiments.

Sister Helen and the head Chinese orderly at the hospital came to my room early one morning and announced that the ambulance had come to take me to the *Conte Verde*. Dr. Gardiner arrived a few minutes later, with his hands full of vaccination and inoculation certificates, and testimonials to my "good health" and complete freedom from any "contagious ailments." These were all necessary in order to obtain a sailing permit. Also there was an order permitting me to draw from the ship's purser the sum of $100 to cover my expenses on the voyage. The money was a loan from Uncle Sam, advanced through the State Department and the Swiss consulate. I needed it greatly because I had disposed of most of my worldly possessions which had escaped Japanese seizure, including my office typewriters, in order to pay my hospital and medicine bills. My office, including a large stock of precious print paper and my office library, the most complete newspaper reference library and "morgue" in the Far East, and also my business and personal accounts in the bank, were of no use to me now, as they were sealed by the Imperial Japanese Army. When I was finally carried aboard the ship the strain of the last few days which had buoyed me up was suddenly relaxed and as the bearers set my stretcher down on the floor in the corridor to my stateroom, I fainted—for the first time.

When I came to I found a slip of paper someone had slipped into my hand. It was from a personal friend, a young American woman journalist formerly employed on the *China Press*. She wished me a pleasant trip and expressed her faith in my final recovery. She asked me to tell her parents not to worry, and expressed the hope she would be able to sail on the "next voyage" of the *Gripsholm*. Unfortunately she was not permitted to sail on the next voyage, and as I write is still in Shanghai. As the *Conte Verde* drew away from the jetty I strained my eyes to see her among the hundreds of Americans standing on the jetty, all trying to be brave, but holding back their tears with difficulty. I couldn't hold mine back! All of them prayed to be able to sail on the "next exchange ship," but none dreamed that more than a year would elapse before the stubborn Japanese would agree to another sailing, or that in the intervening time all Americans in Shanghai and elsewhere in the Far East would be interned and that many would not be able to survive the ordeal. There has been no further exchange of prisoners with Japan.

XXXIX

Homeward Bound

THE PASSENGER LISTS of the first voyage of the *Conte Verde*, which carried refugees from China ports, and of the *Asama Maru*, which carried refugees from Japanese ports, Manchuria and Korea, included five distinct groups: first, diplomatic and consular officials; second, newspaper correspondents; third, "out-port" missionaries; fourth, Canadians; fifth, Latin-Americans. The term "out-port" is a familiar one in the Orient, referring chiefly to missionaries who reside in the interior parts of the country, not in the coastal cities. In addition to these five classifications, there were also a few businessmen on board. The missionaries, who were the largest group, included both Protestants and Catholics. The details of the exchange concerning feeding and medical care of passengers were arranged through the International Red Cross at Geneva, Switzerland.

We had one stowaway on the *Conte Verde*, an American young man who came on board to tell his friends good-bye and who lingered too long over a drink in the friend's cabin. Unfortunately for him, he was discovered by the Japanese before our ship passed the last customs boat at the mouth of the Yangtze. An hour more and he might have been safe, but he was transferred from our ship to the customs boat and sent back to Shanghai. We never heard what happened to him, but imagined the worst.

The *Conte Verde* was a crack Italian liner before the war, operating between Italian ports and the Orient. It was manned by an Italian crew numbering some 300 officers and men. The *Conte Verde* was caught in Shanghai at the time of the Japanese attack on Pearl Harbor, but since Japan and Italy were part-

405

ners in the Axis the Japanese could not seize the ship, despite Japan's dire need of ocean tonnage. Since the *Conte Verde* was used for repatriating Americans from Japanese-occupied territory, the ship was subject to Japanese governmental orders, which were carried out by a contingent of Japanese naval officers and Foreign Office officials aboard. Fortunately the Japanese remained in their quarters, and we saw little of them. The situation was a curious one, because it was obvious that the Italian officers and crew were on friendlier terms with the passengers than they were with the Japanese. The Italian head steward on the deck where my cabin was located quickly assured us that he had little love for the Japanese, and wished that Italy was on our side in the war.

The officers and men of the *Conte Verde* had an opportunity, not many months later, to demonstrate the truth of this statement. On the morning of September 8, 1943, the day when Italy dropped out of the war, Americans who had been interned in an old factory building in the Pootung section of Shanghai were astonished to see the *Conte Verde*, which had been anchored just off shore, slowly changing its position. There were a large number of sailors and officers on the main deck, and they were waving and shouting at the interned Americans, who had been attracted to the windows of their "jail" by the shouts of the Italians. The Americans were astonished, however, to see the proud Italian liner, instead of moving forward as they expected, slowly turn over on its side in the muddy harbor. The Italian crew had received a tip-off by radio from some source in Italy telling the news of their country's withdrawal from the war. They immediately opened the valves in the hull and scuttled the ship. The Japanese were infuriated, as they would have seized the ship to help balance their losses of ship tonnage caused by American submarine action. Within a few minutes a Japanese destroyer, with its guns trained, sped up to the *Conte Verde*, but it was too late—the ship was already lying on its side, and the Italian officers and men were clinging to the rail, cheering the interned Americans on shore. The commander of the Japanese destroyer removed the Italian officers and crew, and placed a Japanese guard on the sloping deck. The Italians were interned for the duration.

Later the Japanese, pressed still more for shipping, floated the *Conte Verde* and prepared to take the ship to Japan for repairs. But they were frustrated again—this time a lone American plane, attached to the Fourteenth Air Corps at Kunming, flew over and dropped several bombs directly on the ship— which slowly settled back on the muddy bottom of the Whang-poo, where it lies with its deck awash.

The first stop of the *Conte Verde* bearing our party of war refugees was off shore at Singapore, where we were joined by the *Asama Maru*, which had preceded us, stopping at Hong Kong harbor, to pick up a number of Americans and Canadians who were on the repatriation list. From Singapore both ships sailed southward, practically within speaking distance of each other for the entire voyage down the coast of southwestern Asia and then across the Indian Ocean to the little Portuguese port of Lourenço Marques, in the southern tip of the Portuguese colony of Mozambique on the east coast of Africa.

Since both ships had been granted safe passage by all belligerents, they were plainly marked and were brightly illuminated at night, so there would be no mistake on the part of some submarine commander. On the entire voyage from Shanghai to Africa, approximately thirty days, we sighted only one small cargo boat, and that was in the Indian Ocean. After leaving Singapore we passed through the dangerous waters of the Netherlands Indies and through the Coral Sea, the scene of the memorable victory of the American warships over the Japanese, which will probably go down in history as the battle that saved Australia from Japanese invasion.

When the *Conte Verde* first crossed the equator, several of the younger passengers planned a celebration in honor of Father Neptune, God of the Sea, in accordance with ancient custom. The ceremony usually consists of ducking, hair-cutting, beard-trimming, or worse, but the celebration was called off when it was learned that the point where our ship crossed the equator was quite near the graveyard of the American cruiser *Houston*, which had been torpedoed by the Japanese and went down with practically her entire crew of more than 600 officers and men. Both the *Houston* and the sister cruiser, the *Augusta*, were well known in Far Eastern ports.

The spirits of the passengers improved as we traveled farther and farther away from Japan. We had evidence, however, of the nervousness which still prevailed among the passengers one Sunday when Bishop Gilman, the speaker at the church service, referred to the Japanese in his sermon. Several of the passengers feared that the Bishop's reference might arouse the indignation of the Japanese officers aboard, and an attempt was made to induce the Bishop to make an apology, or at least an explanation, which he naturally refused to do.

We had not sailed far before the problem of a nurse became paramount, as I was practically helpless. My friend, Dr. J. C. McCracken, decided to appeal for volunteers. As a result eight missionary nurses offered their services. The young ladies were Miss Beulah Bourns, Somerset, Manitoba, Canada; Miss Ruth Danner, Bloomington, Ill.; Miss Helen Dizney, Boston, Mass.; Miss Isabel Hemingway, New York City; Miss Vera Ingerson, Battle Creek, Mich.; Miss Geneva Miller, New York City; Miss Irene Moore, Chatham, Ontario, Canada, and Miss Edith Myers, New York City. Another missionary to whom I owed much on the trip was Mr. Don Faris of Tapino, British Columbia, Canada. Mr. Faris was connected with Cheeloo University, Tsinan, Shantung, where he had charge of rural life work. He came to my cabin every day and carried me to the deck, where the brilliant sun and bracing sea air worked wonders on my emaciated body.

All of the young women had been in charge of mission hospitals at interior points in China, in some cases more than a thousand miles from the coast. They had remained on the job up to the Japanese occupation of the territory where they were located, and each had a thrilling story to tell of her experiences in trying to care for the Chinese patients and protect the property after the Japanese had taken over. In some cases their Chinese patients were literally thrown into the street and the hospital closed. At one hospital in Shantung the nursing staff was confined to the building, and for a considerable period no one was permitted to enter or leave. They ran out of food, and had it not been for the loyalty of the Chinese staff, who managed to smuggle in rice and vegetables, they would have starved. In other cases, however, they received better treatment and were not subjected to any indignities. Most of these young ladies plan to return to China to resume their work in sections of the country under control of the National Government. All are engaged in useful service in the United States and Canada.

There apparently were no cases in North China similar to the atrocities described by Miss Gwen Dew, correspondent for *Newsweek*, who was at Hong Kong when the Japanese captured that British port. Miss Dew described to me how the Japanese soldiers shot the British doctor who attempted to prevent them from entering his hospital, following which they bayonetted the wounded British and Canadian soldiers and capped their brutalities by raping the nurses.

The passengers on both the *Conte Verde* and the *Asama Maru* received their first genuine thrill and sense of relief when we entered the harbor of Lourenço Marques. Since Portugal is neutral, Lourenço Marques provided a welcome port of call on the East African coast for allied ships of every description. Here we had our first glimpse, since Pearl Harbor, of American and British flags. They were flying from the masts of rusty tankers, but they could not have brought more joy had they been on a palatial liner. There were several American and British tankers and cargo boats in the harbor, and as soon as the captains of those ships recognized us they began sounding the victory signal with their sirens, while the officers and crews cheered. Immediately the whole harbor and surrounding hills were echoing to the sounds of the sirens giving the V signal at full blast. We realized for the first time that we were at last free from the barbarian of the East.

We knew that we were scheduled to meet at Lourenço Marques the Swedish liner *Gripsholm*, which carried the same number of Japanese repatriates from the United States as there were North and South Americans on our ships. As our ships drew near the jetty we noticed that the *Gripsholm* had already preceded us into the harbor and was anchored at the dock. As arranged previously, the *Asama Maru*, carrying refugees from Japan, Manchuria, Hong Kong, and Korea, and the *Conte Verde*, carrying our party from China, drew up on each side of the *Gripsholm*, which was loaded with Japanese. After our ships had been made fast at the dock, a conference was held as to the actual method of making the exchange. All passengers were instructed to pack their bags and stand in the corridors, and when the signal was given two lines of Japanese from the *Gripsholm* moved down the gangplank of their ship to the jetty, while similar lines from our ship and the *Asama Maru* moved down our gangplanks to the same jetty, where the lines passed each other, the North Americans and South Americans then proceeding up the gangplank to the *Gripsholm*, while the Japs took our places. Since the total passenger list on the *Asama Maru* and *Conte Verde* numbered approximately 1,600, we quickly discovered that the *Gripsholm* was to be much more crowded than had been the case on either of the other ships on the outward voyage. Some American children, not being as aware of the seriousness of the war situation as were their elders, began fraternizing with the Japanese boys on the *Gripsholm*. Since the Japanese boys had attended school in the United States, they all spoke the same language, hence there was considerable amusement aboard our ship when a Japanese kid yelled across to the American boys hanging from the rail of our ship, "What kind of food have you got on your ship?"

One of our youngsters immediately replied, "Rotten, but have you got any ice cream on your boat?" To which the Japanese replied, "Plenty!" We were told that many of the Japanese were none too enthusiastic about returning to their homeland after long residence in the United States.

There were innumerable reunions as the passengers from our ships, which had sailed within sight of each other for thirty days, finally got together on the *Gripsholm*. There were several cases where American and Canadian husbands, who had been interned at Hong Kong and were passengers on the *Asama Maru*, were reunited with their wives who had been in Shanghai and in consequence were passengers on the *Conte Verde*. Among the American newspapermen in Japan who were passengers on the *Asama Maru* were Robert Bellaire, head of the United Press at Tokyo; Max Hill, head of the Associated Press, and Relman Morin, also of the Associated Press at the Japanese capital. Another well known American correspondent in Japan who had been interned and had suffered severely at the hands of his Japanese captors was Otto Tolischus of the *New York Times*.

There also were numerous reunions of American diplomats from Japan and China. On the *Asama Maru* were Ambassador Joseph C. Grew and his staff, including Mr. Eugene H. Dooman, Counsellor of Embassy, and Mr. Frank Williams, commercial attaché. On our ship were Mr. Frank Lockhart, Consul-General at Shanghai and concurrently Counsellor of Embassy, and his staff. Also on our ship was Miss Jacobson, acting manager of the office of the United States Treasury at Shanghai. The director of the China office of the United States Treasury at Shanghai, Mr. Martin R. Nicholson, died suddenly of a heart ailment in his office only a few days before Pearl Harbor, and his body was still unburied at the undertaker's when the Japanese took over the city. Nicholson's friends, including myself, felt that it perhaps was fortunate that "Nick" had escaped the Japs, as he probably had tracked down more international dope smugglers, including many Japanese, than any other man in

the narcotic-suppression division of our Treasury Department.
I had known Nicholson for many years and had spent many
evenings in his home, when he recounted his adventures with
desperate smugglers of narcotics. Three notorious gangsters recently executed at Sing Sing, who owed their convictions on
a murder charge to Governor Thomas E. Dewey, were exposed
as members of an international dope ring by the unadvertised
activities of Martin Nicholson, Treasury agent at Shanghai.

Several of the American consular officials left our ship at
Lourenço Marques, upon instructions of the State Department,
which transferred them to other posts in Africa, the Near East
and India. Mr. A. Bland Calder, acting commercial attaché in
China, was transferred to Moscow. Other American newspapermen aboard the *Gripsholm* were Morris J. Harris, former chief
of the Associated Press bureau in China; Jimmy White, also
with Associated Press at Shanghai; John Goette, International
News Service at Peiping, and "Hank" Ford, International
News Service at Shanghai.

Since several days were required to make the transfer of
passengers and other arrangements at Lourenço Marques, time
was provided for an inspection of this attractive little Portuguese port, a jewel on the east coast of the dark continent. Although located in Portuguese colonial territory, Lourenço
Marques served in peacetime as an outlet for a rich and rapidly
developing hinterland extending for thousands of miles across
Africa and south to Cape Town, Union of South Africa. Many
of the passengers took side trips to view the sights of East Africa
in the vicinity, particularly the giant hippos in a nearby river.

Lourenço Marques is famous for two things—its excellent
fruit, which rivals that of Florida, and native-made bronze cruci-
fixes and sacred images. My nurse bought me a beautiful crucifix
which I shall always treasure. As for the famous fruit of
Lourenço Marques, I gave one of my nurses a dollar and asked
her to purchase for me a supply of African grapefruit. She
came back with two large baskets, one on each arm. There were

more than a dozen, of excellent flavor and considerably larger than either our Florida or California brands. As none of our passengers had eaten any fresh fruit for weeks, we practically cleared the shops of their supplies.

I was too ill to leave my cabin except to be carried on deck, hence I had to enjoy the scenery at second-hand. Fortunately I met an old newsreel acquaintance from the civil war days in China, Merle LaVoy. Officials who took charge of our party at Lourenço Marques had issued strict orders against any newsreel men being permitted to come on board the *Gripsholm*, but LaVoy had been up against censorship too long to permit that to bother him. One day LaVoy appeared in my stateroom, dressed in a heavy overcoat which bulged in all directions. He looked as though he weighed three hundred pounds. But the excess avoirdupois quickly disappeared when he divested himself of at least a half dozen cameras, including newsreels. With the help of Dr. Gardiner, LaVoy immediately proceeded to take my picture from all points of view, including the lacerated and swollen remains of my feet. One picture which he snapped, showing me lying on the bed with one of my injured feet extended, he labeled "Gandhi" Powell because, he explained, of my resemblance to the wasted frame of the Indian Nationalist leader. My weight then was about eighty pounds. This particular picture later appeared in *Life,* and must have been seen by most of my old classmates, teachers, neighbors, friends, and relatives, because when I landed at New York I found more than six hundred letters awaiting me.

Since LaVoy had been stationed for a considerable time in South Africa, he told many interesting stories of conditions on that continent. I was particularly interested in his description of the large game preserve, largest area in the world where the native animals of Africa are protected and live as if in their native haunts. Within the park are innumerable African animals such as lions, elephants, giraffes, wildebeests, gorillas, and so on, living in their natural state. He said that it was possible for one to travel in a motor car through the native haunts of these animals without molestation. LaVoy declared they wouldn't even look up when the motor cars passed by.

Practically all of the newspapermen aboard received cables at Lourenço Marques asking for stories of their experiences and descriptions of conditions in the Far East following Pearl Harbor. As a result there was a great scurrying about for typewriters, paper, carbon paper, and cable blanks. The little Portuguese telegraph office at Lourenço Marques was swamped with news messages, some of them several thousand words in length. I received a cable from Mr. Charles G. Ross of the *St. Louis Post-Dispatch* bureau in Washington asking me to write a series of articles for the *Post-Dispatch*. As I was physically unable to sit up in bed and type, I was at a loss to comply with Ross's request. Two of my nurses who had stenographic experience volunteered their services, and soon my stateroom resembled a newspaper office, with me dictating and the nurses typing the stories. I succeeded in sending one story by cable before the *Gripsholm* sailed. The others I dictated in more leisurely fashion on the voyage from Lourenço Marques to Rio de Janeiro. Consul-General Lockhart read my report, and asked me for a copy to be incorporated in his report to the State Department. When the *Gripsholm* reached Rio I dispatched the stories by air mail, and they reached their destination in a few hours and without censorship. The articles were later syndicated to newspapers all over the United States and Latin America by King Features. *Reader's Digest* also summarized the article in an early issue after I landed.

After the *Gripsholm* had rounded Cape of Good Hope on the return voyage, our fear of Japanese torpedo attack changed to anxiety about Nazi submarines, as they were then active in the South Atlantic. We sailed directly across the South Atlantic to Rio de Janeiro, our first stop in the new and free world of the Americas. Since we had a large number of Latin American diplomats aboard, we spent several days in the Brazilian metropolis, which has one of the most beautiful harbors in the world.

High above the city on a commanding mountain peak is a gigantic statue of Jesus with arms outstretched. The statue rivals in size and beauty the famous statue of Christ of the Andes, which stands on the peak of a mountain on the border between Chile and Argentina, symbolizing many decades of peace between the two important Latin American countries.

At Rio our ship was joined by a number of officials of the State Department, and other departments of the government, including the F.B.I., who were interested in checking up on our passenger list and obtaining the latest information from the Far East. Among them was Dr. Carl F. Remer, an old resident of Shanghai and a contributor to the *China Weekly Review*. He had been Professor of Economics at St. John's University in Shanghai, and author of books on economic and financial conditions in China, but later returned home and joined the faculty of the University of Minnesota. He is now serving as an executive in the State Department at Washington. Professor Remer brought me the first news of my family; that my wife, son, daughter, son-in-law, and three-year-old grandson would be in New York when our ship reached the home port. I also had another welcome visitor on board the *Gripsholm* in Rio Harbor—Dr. Shao-Hwa Tan, Chinese minister to Brazil, whom I had known in Nanking. He brought me messages of greeting and good-will from the then Chinese Ambassador in Washington, Dr. Hu Shih, as well as other members of the Chinese diplomatic and consular staffs in New York and elsewhere, including Mr. T. V. Soong, Foreign Minister, and Generalissimo Chiang Kai-shek. Of my many Chinese friends, I have the greatest esteem for an unknown restaurant owner in New York who notified me that I could always dine at his place without charge. He said that he had read of my experiences at the hands of the Japs, and wanted to show his appreciation of my service for China in a practical way. He assured me that no Chinese restaurant would charge me for a meal if I would identify myself, but I haven't tried that out.

Although the danger of Nazi submarines was still an ever present one, the voyage home from Rio almost resembled a pleasure tour, thanks to the smoothness of the sea. As we were on the last lap of our voyage, the restraint under which we had lived so long gradually lifted. Many of the "godless" passengers, including most of the newspapermen and businessmen, and several of the diplomats, resorted to the well known American games of poker and craps, and while we had only a few days left, the time was nevertheless sufficient for most of them to lose the sums which had been advanced by the State Department to cover incidental expenses. A doctor friend of mine was the chief winner.

On the voyage to New York the *Gripsholm* swung out to the mid-Atlantic, to avoid German submarines which were active along the Brazilian Coast and the Caribbean Sea. One day there was considerable excitement when we passed the burning wreckage of a ship, supposedly a tanker which had been torpedoed. We felt that the captain of the *Gripsholm* should have stopped to see whether there were any survivors clinging to the wreckage, but he had instructions to proceed directly without stopping for anything because there might have been a German submarine lurking in the vicinity, ready to blow us out of the water had we stopped to investigate.

XL

China's Future

MY CHIEF WORRY on the long homeward journey had been the question of medical attention and hospital service upon landing at New York. Due to my long absence from the United States, I was unfamiliar with doctors and hospitals, and I frequently discussed the matter with various physicians whom I knew aboard the *Gripsholm*. Most of the missionary doctors recommended the Columbia Presbyterian Medical Center of New York, which had long maintained connections in the Orient, particularly with China, through the dispatch of medical missions of physicians and nurses. I was told that several members of the medical center staff had served on the faculty of Peiping Union Medical College (Rockefeller Institute) in North China.

A further source of worry, as the *Gripsholm* neared New York, was how I would get off the boat in my helpless condition. In the general excitement as we entered the harbor, I was almost forgotten in the rush of passengers to the decks. However, one faithful nurse remained to watch the passing scene from the window of my stateroom and describe excitedly the never-to-be-forgotten landmarks of New York's harbor and the famous skyline of lower Manhattan. She exclaimed, "Oh, there's the Statue of Liberty," and we both wiped the tears from our eyes.

The *Gripsholm's* propellers had scarcely ceased revolving, as the ship came to a stop alongside the pier, when I heard someone hurry along the corridor leading to my room. A familiar figure entered the door—it was my son, John William, who had departed from Shanghai only a few weeks before Pearl Harbor, after a year on the staff of the *China Press*.

Luckily he had decided to return home in order to complete his course at the School of Journalism at the University of Missouri, and thus had escaped the Japs. As he strode into my stateroom he was accompanied by a marine corporal, who solved my problem of leaving the ship by picking me up bodily and carrying me ashore in his arms. He commented humorously on my light weight and Gandhi-like appearance as he carried me with little effort down the gangplank and directly to a waiting ambulance, driven by a young woman in the uniform of the American Red Cross Ambulance Corps. I saw another young woman standing beside the ambulance, who introduced herself to me. She was my daughter, Bunny, whom I had not seen since she departed from Shanghai when she was ten years old. After completing the journalism course at Missouri, she had joined the *Post-Dispatch* in St. Louis, but shortly afterward had married and was living in Washington, where her husband, Malcolm Stewart Hensley, was acting director of the foreign broadcast monitoring service of the Federal Communications Commission. He is now manager of the United Press in India.

I was taken temporarily to the Marine Hospital on Staten Island, where my wife was awaiting me. This hospital is under the supervision of the United States Public Health Service, and I was told that emergency cases resulting from enemy submarine attacks on our merchant ships were taken there. I stayed in the Marine Hospital only about twenty-four hours, when arrangements were made to transfer me to Harkness Pavilion of the Columbia Presbyterian Medical Center. There I still am as this is written, over two and a half years later.

After a careful examination by staff physicians at the Medical Center, I was told that the original diagnosis of my condition made in Shanghai had been correct. My ailment was a serious case of gangrenous infection of both feet, resulting from malnutrition, exposure, and the stoppage of circulation in my feet and legs, due to the Japanese habit of forcing Occidental prisoners to sit on their feet "Japanese fashion" for long periods at a stretch.

Every effort was made at once to check the infection in my feet. This and further difficult surgical tasks were undertaken by Dr. Frank L. Meleney and Dr. Jerome P. Webster, and their assistants. At the some time I was put on a diet of enriched milk and other foods with large doses of vitamins in order to build up my general resistance and restore my starved, emaciated body.

During my long stay in the hospital I have also had innumerable blood transfusions. I was immediately impressed by the ease with which blood or plasma transfusions are made in this country, in comparison with the difficulties I experienced in Shanghai on my release from prison. There was no such thing as a blood bank in all China at the outbreak of the war, and it is only since I have been a patient at Presbyterian Hospital that the hospital authorities, in cooperation with Chinese interests in New York, have sent a complete blood-bank unit to China. A Chinese nurse, Mrs. Liu, who received her training at the S.D.A. Sanitarium at Shanghai and at Presbyterian Hospital in New York, has charge of the bank, the first in China.

As the infection in my feet gradually cleared up, the exposed surfaces were covered with grafts of skin, transplanted from my upper thighs. This is known as pinch grafting, and is done by the removal of small pieces of skin about the size of a nickel, which are then grafted on the exposed surfaces so that the edges meet and, if the graft is successful, grow together. About sixty pinch grafts of skin from each of my thighs were required, a process which lasted for over a year.

By the fall of 1943 I was beginning to regain my strength and even to leave the hospital for a few hours at a time in a wheel chair to speak at bond rallies and on the radio. One or two spots of infection, however, seemed to resist every resource of modern science, with the result that after every sortie one or another of the grafts would break down. Special shoes had been made to enable me to stand erect and eventually to walk, but evidently the skin grafts were not sufficiently strong to bear the pressure when I stood on my feet.

It was finally decided, early in 1944, that more drastic surgical treatment was necessary to adequately cover with flesh the stumps of my heels and the bones of my feet. This, a type of grafting known as plastic surgery, in which Dr. Webster is particularly skilled, involves the removal of a considerable section of skin, together with about a half inch of underlying tissue. The earlier pinch grafts had often been painful, as the spots from which the skin was taken were sometimes slow in healing on account of my general physical condition, and, in addition, I suffered constant pain and discomfort in my feet. I was ill prepared, however, for what I was to experience now.

A flap about four inches wide and twelve inches in length was cut loose from my right thigh and a piece of skin from my chest was grafted on the exposed wound. The flap itself was brought downward and left attached just above the knee. My left knee was bent and my left heel was attached to the under side of this flap just above my right knee. A plaster cast held the graft tight, with my left knee suspended from a framework built above my bed. I remained for six weeks lying on my back in this position. I was then put on the operating table once more. The flap was cut off at the knee, my left leg was stretched out, and the other end of the flap was grafted to my right heel. I understood that it was necessary to hold down my left leg by force to encase both legs in a plaster cast. As a result of the second operation following the six weeks' ordeal I had been through, I sank lower than I had been at any point since my return, and for the first time I felt that perhaps I should have urged the doctors to amputate my feet at the ankles in Shanghai.

I realize that my own experiences are in no way comparable to some of the miracles of plastic surgery which are being performed on war casualties, many of which I have had occasion to observe during my stay at the hospital. My own case, however, was complicated by my greatly weakened physical condition, the long-standing infection in my feet, and by the fact that I was no longer the young man who went to China a quarter of a century ago.

About five weeks after the operation I have just described, the flap which connected my heels was cut, and, as the graft gradually healed, I found myself provided with new soles covering my heels and the remnants of my feet and with new covering for my ankles. I am now gradually learning to walk once more with special shoes, which is a slow process, as the stumps of my feet are sensitive and the flesh grafted from my thighs is not yet as tough as normal soles would be. I expect soon, however, to be released from a wheel chair and to move about, if not as freely as before, at least well enough to lead a normal life.

Ever since my return to the United States I have been impressed by one thing which I had almost forgotten during my long stay in China. This is the innate sympathy and humanitarian spirit of the American people, which has been expressed to me in hundreds of letters from persons in all parts of the United States. My will to live and my fight back to normal health have been greatly aided by the financial support which I have received from all sides and the warm sympathy expressed to me for the injuries I suffered at the hands of the Japanese.

I am now beginning to think of plans for the future.

Nothing has occurred in the war to cause me to alter in any way my conviction, held long before Pearl Harbor, that America's stake in the Pacific is and will be a large one. Word of the victory to which the United States will have contributed so much in treasure and manpower will penetrate to the peoples of the remotest corners of Asia. In my opinion, millions of intelligent Asiatics, who before the war looked to European countries as the dominant powers in Asia, will now turn toward the new world of the Americas. They will want to know more about the United States and to be befriended by her. I am certain that all over Asia in the tea houses, market places and barrios native peoples are talking and thinking about America when they discuss the future of their own lands.

Having spent so much of my life in China, I find it difficult to think of my own future except in terms of hers. During the long night watches in the hospital, when sleep would not come, I have again and again gone over in my mind the experiences of those twenty-five years, many of which I have recounted in this book. I often think of the China to which I came as a young man in 1917, and I realize more and more how far she has progressed since that time and how much her two great leaders, Dr. Sun Yat-sen and Generalissimo Chiang Kai-shek, have accomplished in little more than a generation. I am convinced that after this war is over China, with the proper guidance and support, will once more forge ahead as a nation and that her future will be one of importance to all the world. I hope to have some part in that future, as I have had in her past.

Index